First World War
and Army of Occupation
War Diary
France, Belgium and Germany

35 DIVISION
106 Infantry Brigade
Highland Light Infantry
18th Battalion (4th Glasgow)
31 January 1916 - 28 February 1919

WO95/2490/2

The Naval & Military Press Ltd
www.nmarchive.com
Published in association with The National Archives

Published by

The Naval & Military Press Ltd

Unit 10 Ridgewood Industrial Park,

Uckfield, East Sussex,

TN22 5QE England

Tel: +44 (0) 1825 749494

www.naval-military-press.com

www.nmarchive.com

This diary has been reprinted in facsimile from the original. Any imperfections are inevitably reproduced and the quality may fall short of modern type and cartographic standards.

© Crown Copyright
Images reproduced by permission of The National Archives, London, England, 2015.

Contents

Document type	Place/Title	Date From	Date To
Heading	WO95/2490/2		
Heading	35th Division 106th Infy Bde 18th Bn Highland Lt Infy Jan 1916-Feb 1919		
Miscellaneous	Officer i/c Adjutant Generals Office. General Hdqrs. 3rd Echelon	27/02/1916	27/02/1916
War Diary	Perham Down	31/01/1916	31/01/1916
War Diary	Folkestone	31/01/1916	31/01/1916
War Diary	Boulogne	31/01/1916	01/02/1916
War Diary	Arques	02/02/1916	02/02/1916
War Diary	Racquinghem	03/02/1916	09/02/1916
War Diary	Thiennes	10/02/1916	18/02/1916
War Diary	Merville	19/02/1916	29/02/1916
War Diary	18th (Service) Battalion. Highland Light Infantry.		
Miscellaneous	Operation Order No. 1 Appendix II	08/02/1916	08/02/1916
Operation(al) Order(s)	Operation Order No. 1 Appendix II	17/02/1916	17/02/1916
Operation(al) Order(s)	Operation Orders No. 3 Appendix IV	27/02/1916	27/02/1916
Heading	18 Q HLI Vol 2 March 1916		
Miscellaneous	D.A.G. General Hqrs. 3rd Echelon Base	01/04/1916	01/04/1916
War Diary	Croix Barbee	01/03/1916	06/03/1916
War Diary	Riez Bailleu	07/03/1916	13/03/1916
War Diary	In Trenches	14/03/1916	15/03/1916
War Diary	La Gorgue	16/03/1916	16/03/1916
War Diary	L'Epinette	17/03/1916	19/03/1916
War Diary	Les Rues Des Vacnes	20/03/1916	26/03/1916
War Diary	Estaires	27/03/1916	27/03/1916
War Diary	Rouge De Bout	28/03/1916	31/03/1916
Operation(al) Order(s)	Operation Orders No. 4. 18th (Ser)Bn. H.L. Infantry.	06/03/1916	06/03/1916
Operation(al) Order(s)	Operation Orders No. 5. 18th (Ser)Bn. H.L. Infantry.	10/03/1916	10/03/1916
Operation(al) Order(s)	Operation Orders No. 6. 18th (Ser) Bn. H.L. Infantry	15/03/1916	15/03/1916
Operation(al) Order(s)	Operation Orders No. 7. 18th (Ser) Bn. H.L. Infantry.	18/03/1916	18/03/1916
Operation(al) Order(s)	G.O.C. 19th Division.	18/03/1916	18/03/1916
Operation(al) Order(s)	Operation Orders No. 8	25/03/1916	25/03/1916
Operation(al) Order(s)	Operation Order No. 9 18th (S) Bn. H.L. Infantry	26/03/1916	26/03/1916
Operation(al) Order(s)	Operation Order No. 10 18th (S) Bn. H.L. Infantry	30/03/1916	30/03/1916
Operation(al) Order(s)	In Trenches	01/04/1916	04/04/1916
War Diary	Sailly Sur La Lys	05/04/1916	12/04/1916
War Diary	Laventie	13/04/1916	15/04/1916
War Diary	Estaires	16/04/1916	16/04/1916
War Diary	In Trenches	17/04/1916	20/04/1916
War Diary	Croix Barbee	21/04/1916	24/04/1916
War Diary	In Trenches	25/04/1916	28/04/1916
War Diary	In Billets	29/04/1916	30/04/1916
War Diary	Operation Orders, No. 11. 18th (S) Bn. H.L. Infantry.	03/04/1916	03/04/1916
Operation(al) Order(s)	Operation Orders, No. 12. 18th (S) Bn. H.L. Infantry.	11/04/1916	11/04/1916
Operation(al) Order(s)	Operation Orders, No. 18. 18th (S) Bn. H.L. Infantry.	14/04/1916	14/04/1916
Operation(al) Order(s)	Operation Orders, No. 19. 18th (S) Bn. H.L. Infantry.	14/04/1916	14/04/1916
Operation(al) Order(s)	Operation Orders No. 11. 18th (Ser). Battn. Highland Light Infantry.	19/04/1916	19/04/1916
Operation(al) Order(s)	Operation Orders No. 16. (18th) (SER) Battn. Highland L. Infantry.	23/04/1916	23/04/1916

Operation(al) Order(s)	Operation Orders No. 17. (18th) (SE) Battn. Highland L. Infantry.	27/04/1916	27/04/1916
War Diary	Fosse	01/05/1916	05/05/1916
War Diary	In Trench	06/05/1916	14/05/1916
War Diary	La Coutre	15/05/1916	21/05/1916
War Diary	In Trenches	22/05/1916	22/05/1916
War Diary	Vieille Chappelle	23/05/1916	28/05/1916
War Diary	Festubert	29/05/1916	31/05/1916
War Diary	Festubert	01/06/1916	01/06/1916
War Diary	In Trenches	02/06/1916	05/06/1916
War Diary	Festubert	06/06/1916	11/06/1916
War Diary	Vieille Chapelle	12/06/1916	15/06/1916
War Diary	Gonnehem	16/06/1916	30/06/1916
Operation(al) Order(s)	Operation Order No. 25. 18th (Ser) Battalion Highland Light Infantry.	04/06/1916	04/06/1916
Operation(al) Order(s)	Operation Order No. 26. 18th (Ser) Battalion Highland Light Infantry	10/06/1916	10/06/1916
Operation(al) Order(s)	Operation Order No. 27. 18th (Ser) Battn. Highland Light Infantry	15/06/1916	15/06/1916
Operation(al) Order(s)	Operatipn Orders No. 27a. 18th (SER) Battn Highland Light Infantry	24/06/1916	24/06/1916
War Diary	18th (Service) Battalion Highland Light Infantry.	01/07/1916	01/07/1916
Heading	106th Bde. 35th. Div. War Diary. 18th Battalion Highland Light Infantry 1st to 31st July 1916		
Miscellaneous	D.A.G. Gn Hd. Qrs. 3rd Echelon Base	12/08/1916	12/08/1916
War Diary	Gonnehem	01/07/1916	02/07/1916
War Diary	Brevillers	03/07/1916	05/07/1916
War Diary	Bois Du Warnimont	06/07/1916	10/07/1916
War Diary	Varennes	11/07/1916	13/07/1916
War Diary	Bresle	14/07/1916	14/07/1916
War Diary	Billon Wood	15/07/1916	15/07/1916
War Diary	Talus Boise	16/07/1916	16/07/1916
War Diary	Montauban	17/07/1916	19/07/1916
War Diary	Carnoy	20/07/1916	23/07/1916
War Diary	In Trenches	24/07/1916	25/07/1916
War Diary	Carnoy	26/07/1916	26/07/1916
War Diary	In Trenches	27/07/1916	30/07/1916
War Diary	Carnoy	31/07/1916	31/07/1916
Operation(al) Order(s)	Operation Orders No. 28. 18th (Ser) Battn. Highland Light Infantry.	02/07/1916	02/07/1916
Operation(al) Order(s)	Operation Orders No. 29. 18th (Ser) Battn. Highland Light Infantry.	05/07/1916	05/07/1916
Operation(al) Order(s)	Operation Orders No. 30. 18th (Ser) Battn. Highland Light Infantry.	09/07/1916	09/07/1916
Operation(al) Order(s)	Operation Orders No. 31. 18th (Ser) Battn. Highland Light Infantry.	13/07/1916	13/07/1916
Operation(al) Order(s)	Operation Orders No. 32. 18th (Ser) Battn. Highland Light Infantry.	14/07/1916	14/07/1916
Heading	106th Brigade. 35th Division. 1/18th Battalion Highland Light Infantry August 1916		
War Diary	Meaulte	01/08/1916	01/08/1916
War Diary	Morlan Court	02/08/1916	05/08/1916
War Diary	Fourdrinoy	06/08/1916	10/08/1916
War Diary	Morlan Court	11/08/1916	16/08/1916
War Diary	Sandpit Valley	17/08/1916	19/08/1916
War Diary	Carnoy	20/08/1916	26/08/1916

Type	Description	Start	End
War Diary	Happy Valley	27/08/1916	31/08/1916
Operation(al) Order(s)	Operation Orders No. 33 18th. (S) Ben. H.L. Infantry.		
Operation(al) Order(s)	Operation Order No. 34 By Lt. Col. R.E. Lawrenson Commanding. 18th (S) Highland Light Infantry.	19/08/1916	19/08/1916
War Diary	Sus. St. Leger	01/09/1916	02/09/1916
War Diary	Agnez-Les-Duisans	03/09/1916	03/09/1916
War Diary	Roclincourt	04/09/1916	10/09/1916
War Diary	Arras	11/09/1916	15/09/1916
War Diary	Roclincourt	16/09/1916	22/09/1916
War Diary	Arras	23/09/1916	23/09/1916
War Diary	Arras & Roclincourt	24/09/1916	27/09/1916
War Diary	Roclincourt	28/09/1916	30/09/1916
Operation(al) Order(s)	Operation Orders No 35 18th (Ser) Bn. H.L.S	00/09/1916	00/09/1916
Miscellaneous	Operation Orders. 18th (S) Bn. Highland Light Infantry Reference Special Orders Issued	14/09/1916	14/09/1916
War Diary	Distribution And Equipment. Of Coy.		
Operation(al) Order(s)	Operation Order No. 36 (a) 18th (S) Battn. H.L.I	14/09/1916	14/09/1916
Operation(al) Order(s)	Operation Orders No. 37 18th (S) Bn. H.L. Infantry	17/09/1916	17/09/1916
Operation(al) Order(s)	Operation Orders No. 38 18th (S) Bn. H.L. Infantry	22/09/1916	22/09/1916
Operation(al) Order(s)	Operation Orders No. 39 18th (S) Bn. H.L. Infantry	26/09/1916	26/09/1916
Miscellaneous	18th (S) Bn Highland Light Infantry Defence Scheme.	05/09/1916	05/09/1916
Map	Roclincourt (Left Sector)		
War Diary			
Map	Roclincourt Left Sector		
War Diary	Roclincourt	01/10/1916	05/10/1916
War Diary	Duisans	06/10/1916	10/10/1916
War Diary	Arras	11/10/1916	11/10/1916
War Diary	Roclincourt	12/10/1916	16/10/1916
War Diary	Arras	17/10/1916	22/10/1916
War Diary	Arras & Roclincourt	23/10/1916	25/10/1916
War Diary	Roclincourt	26/10/1916	28/10/1916
War Diary	Arras	29/10/1916	31/10/1916
Operation(al) Order(s)	Special Operation Order No. 41 18th (S) Bn. H.L.I.	05/10/1916	05/10/1916
Operation(al) Order(s)	Operation Order No. 40. 18th. (S) Bn. High. L. Inf.	05/10/1916	05/10/1916
Operation(al) Order(s)	Operation Order No. 41. 18th. (S) Bn. High. L. Inf	10/10/1916	10/10/1916
Operation(al) Order(s)	Operation Orders No. 42. 18th. (S) Bn. High. L. Inf	16/10/1916	16/10/1916
Operation(al) Order(s)	Operation Orders No. 43. 18th. Bn. High. L. Inf	23/10/1916	23/10/1916
Operation(al) Order(s)	Operation Order No. 44. 18th Bn. High. L. Inf		
War Diary	Arras	01/11/1916	03/11/1916
War Diary	Roclincourt	04/11/1916	10/11/1916
War Diary	Brigade Reserve	11/11/1916	15/11/1916
War Diary	Roclincourt	16/11/1916	20/11/1916
War Diary	Roclincourt Arras	22/11/1916	22/11/1916
War Diary	Arras	23/11/1916	27/11/1916
War Diary	Arras & Roclincourt	28/11/1916	30/11/1916
Operation(al) Order(s)	Operation Orders No. 45. 18th., (S) Bn. High. L.I.	08/11/1916	08/11/1916
Operation(al) Order(s)	Operation Orders No. 46. 18th., (S) Bn. Highland Light Inf.	09/11/1916	09/11/1916
Operation(al) Order(s)	Operation Orders No. 47. 18th., (S) Bn. Highland. L.I.	14/11/1916	14/11/1916
Operation(al) Order(s)	Operation Orders No. 48. 18th., (S) Bn. High. Light. Inf.	21/11/1916	21/11/1916
Operation(al) Order(s)	Operation Orders No. 49. 18th., (S) Bn. High. Light. Inf.	27/11/1916	27/11/1916
War Diary	Roclincourt	01/12/1916	02/12/1916
War Diary	Wanquetin	03/12/1916	03/12/1916
War Diary	Maisnil-St-Pol	04/12/1916	29/12/1916

Type	Location/Description	Start	End
War Diary	Arras	30/12/1916	31/12/1916
War Diary	Arras	01/01/1917	03/02/1917
War Diary	Magieren	04/02/1917	06/02/1917
War Diary	Rehewes	07/02/1917	07/02/1917
War Diary	Geizencourt	08/02/1917	08/02/1917
War Diary	Vignacourt	09/02/1917	19/02/1917
War Diary	Marcel Cave	20/02/1917	22/02/1917
War Diary	C-De-Ballon	23/02/1917	28/02/1917
Operation(al) Order(s)	Operation Orders No. 50 18th., (Ser) Bn., Highland Light Inf.	01/02/1917	01/02/1917
Operation(al) Order(s)	Operation Orders No. 51 18th., (S) Bn., Highland L.I.	05/02/1917	05/02/1917
Operation(al) Order(s)	Operation Orders No. 52 18th., (S) Bn., Highland L.I.	17/02/1917	17/02/1917
Operation(al) Order(s)	Operation Orders No. 53 18th., (S) Bn., Highland L.I.	21/02/1917	21/02/1917
Operation(al) Order(s)	Operation Orders No. 54 18th., (S) Bn., Highland L.I.	25/02/1917	25/02/1917
Operation(al) Order(s)	Headquarters, 106th. Inf. Brigade.	01/04/1917	01/04/1917
War Diary	Lihons.	01/03/1917	02/03/1917
War Diary	Rosieres	03/03/1917	06/03/1917
War Diary	Lihons	07/03/1917	13/03/1917
War Diary	Decauville Camp	14/03/1917	16/03/1917
War Diary	Vrely	17/03/1917	17/03/1917
War Diary	Chilly	18/03/1917	19/03/1917
War Diary	Rosieres	20/03/1917	29/03/1917
War Diary	Marchelepot	30/03/1917	30/03/1917
Operation(al) Order(s)	Athies	31/03/1917	31/03/1917
Operation(al) Order(s)	Operation Orders No. 55. 18th (S) Bn Highland L. Inf.	09/03/1917	09/03/1917
Operation(al) Order(s)	Operation Orders No. 56. 18th (S) Bn Highland L. Inf.	13/03/1917	13/03/1917
Operation(al) Order(s)	Operation Orders No. 57. 18th (S) Bn Highland L. Inf.	20/03/1917	20/03/1917
War Diary	Athies	01/04/1917	07/04/1917
War Diary	Soyecourt	08/04/1917	08/04/1917
War Diary	Vermand	15/04/1917	15/04/1917
War Diary	Vermand	14/04/1917	14/04/1917
War Diary	Soyecourt	13/04/1917	13/04/1917
War Diary	Soyecourt	12/04/1917	12/04/1917
War Diary	Soyecourt	11/04/1917	11/04/1917
War Diary	Soyecourt	10/04/1917	10/04/1917
War Diary	Soyecourt	09/04/1917	17/04/1917
War Diary	Maissemy	16/04/1917	18/04/1917
War Diary	Maissemy	17/04/1917	20/04/1917
War Diary	Vermand	21/04/1917	23/04/1917
War Diary	Tertry	24/04/1917	30/04/1917
Operation(al) Order(s)	Operation Order No. 58. Highland Light Infantry	15/04/1917	15/04/1917
Operation(al) Order(s)	Operation Order No. 59. Highland Light Infantry	19/04/1917	19/04/1917
Operation(al) Order(s)	Operation Order No. 60. Highland Light Infantry	29/04/1917	29/04/1917
War Diary	Battalion In Line	01/05/1917	04/05/1917
War Diary	Maissemy	05/05/1917	08/05/1917
War Diary	Tertry	09/05/1917	19/05/1917
War Diary	Peronne	20/05/1917	21/05/1917
War Diary	Sorel-Le-Grand	22/05/1917	23/05/1917
War Diary	Villers-Guislan.	24/05/1917	31/05/1917
Operation(al) Order(s)	Operation Orders No. 60. Highland Light Infantry.		
Operation(al) Order(s)	Operation Orders No. 61. Highland Light Infantry.	07/05/1917	07/05/1917
Operation(al) Order(s) Miscellaneous	Operation Orders No. 62. Highland Light Infantry.	18/05/1917	18/05/1917
Operation(al) Order(s)	Operation Order No. 63. Highland Light Infantry	22/05/1917	22/05/1917
Operation(al) Order(s)	Operation Orders No. 64. Highland Light Infantry	27/05/1917	27/05/1917
Operation(al) Order(s)	Operation Orders No. 65. Highland Light Infantry	01/06/1917	01/06/1917

Type	Description	Start	End
War Diary	Vaucellette Farm	01/06/1917	02/06/1917
War Diary	Templeux-La-Fosse	03/06/1917	10/06/1917
War Diary	Gauche Wood Sector	11/06/1917	25/06/1917
War Diary	Heudicourt	26/06/1917	30/06/1917
Operation(al) Order(s)	Operation Order No. 66. Highland Light Infantry	09/06/1917	09/06/1917
Operation(al) Order(s)	Operation Orders No. 67. Highland Light Infantry	14/06/1917	14/06/1917
Operation(al) Order(s)	Operation Orders No. 68. Highland Light Infantry	17/06/1917	17/06/1917
Operation(al) Order(s)	Operation Orders No. 69. Highland Light Infantry	22/06/1917	22/06/1917
Map	Rough Copy Of R.E. Map		
Operation(al) Order(s)	Addendum To Operation Orders No. 69. (attached.)	22/06/1917	22/06/1917
Operation(al) Order(s)	Operation Orders No. 70 Highland Light Infantry.	25/06/1917	25/06/1917
Diagram etc	Standard Type Of Fire Trench Second Nights Task		
Operation(al) Order(s)	Operation Orders No. 71. Highland Light Infantry	25/06/1917	25/06/1917
Miscellaneous	204th. Field Company, Royal Engineers.		
War Diary	Heudecourt	01/07/1917	02/07/1917
War Diary	Longavesnes	03/07/1917	06/07/1917
War Diary	Lempire	07/07/1917	28/07/1917
War Diary	Aizecourt-Le-Bas	29/07/1917	31/07/1917
Operation(al) Order(s)	Operation Order No. 72. Highland Light Infantry	05/07/1917	05/07/1917
Operation(al) Order(s)	Operation Orders No. 74. Highland Light Infantry	13/07/1917	13/07/1917
Operation(al) Order(s)	Operation Orders No. 75. Highland Light Infantry	22/07/1917	22/07/1917
War Diary	Aizecourt Le Bas	01/08/1917	07/08/1917
War Diary	Longavesnes	09/08/1917	17/08/1917
War Diary	Guillemont Farm	19/08/1917	20/08/1917
War Diary	Villers Faucon	21/08/1917	25/08/1917
Operation(al) Order(s)	In The Line	26/08/1917	26/08/1917
Operation(al) Order(s)	Villers Faucon	27/08/1917	28/08/1917
War Diary	The Knoll	29/08/1917	31/08/1917
Operation(al) Order(s)	Operation Orders No. 76. Highland Light Infantry	01/08/1917	01/08/1917
Operation(al) Order(s)	Operation Orders No. 771. Highland Light Infantry		
Operation(al) Order(s)	Operation Orders No. 78. Highland Light Infantry	11/08/1917	11/08/1917
Operation(al) Order(s)	Operation Orders No. 79. Highland Light Infantry	16/08/1917	16/08/1917
Operation(al) Order(s)	Operation Orders No. 80. Highland Light Infantry.	18/08/1917	18/08/1917
Operation(al) Order(s)	Operation Orders No. 80A. Highland Light Infantry	15/08/1917	15/08/1917
Operation(al) Order(s)	Operation Orders No. 81. Highland Light Infantry.	19/08/1917	19/08/1917
Operation(al) Order(s)	Operation Orders No. 81a. Highland Light Infantry	20/08/1917	20/08/1917
War Diary	Operation Order No. 82. Highland Light Infantry	24/08/1917	24/08/1917
Operation(al) Order(s)	Operation Order No. 83. Highland Light Infantry	28/08/1917	28/08/1917
Miscellaneous	Report On Operations Carried Out On Enemy Trenches In & East of Guillemont Farm, Near Epery, On 19th, & 20th. August, 1917, By The 18th (S) Bn. Highland Light Infantry.	19/08/1917	19/08/1917
War Diary	Report On Enemy Attack On Guillemont Farm On 25th. Aug., 1917	25/08/1917	25/08/1917
War Diary	Lempire.	01/09/1917	06/09/1917
War Diary	Epehy.	07/09/1917	18/09/1917
War Diary	Aizexourt-Le-Bas	19/09/1917	26/09/1917
War Diary	Trenches	27/09/1917	30/09/1917
Operation(al) Order(s)	Operation Orders No. 73. Highland Light Infantry		
Operation(al) Order(s)	Operation Orders No. 84. Highland Light Infantry	01/09/1917	01/09/1917
War Diary	Operation Order 85 A	12/09/1917	12/09/1917
Operation(al) Order(s)	Operation Orders No. 85. Highland Light Infantry	05/09/1917	05/09/1917
Operation(al) Order(s)	Operation Order No. 86	11/09/1917	11/09/1917
Operation(al) Order(s)	Operation Orders No. 87. Highland Light Infantry	17/09/1917	17/09/1917
Operation(al) Order(s)	Operation Orders No. 88. Highland Light Infantry	25/09/1917	25/09/1917
Operation(al) Order(s)	Operation Order No. 88A. Highland Light Infantry		

Type	Description	Start	End
Miscellaneous	18th (S) Bn Highland Light Inf. Provisional Defence Scheme.	30/09/1917	30/09/1917
Miscellaneous	18th (S) Bn Highland Light Inf. Provisional Defence Scheme	10/09/1917	10/09/1917
War Diary	Guillemont Farm	02/10/1917	03/10/1917
War Diary	Peronne	04/10/1917	04/10/1917
War Diary	Agnez-Les-Duisans	06/10/1917	20/10/1917
War Diary	Houthulst Forrest (Ypres)	21/10/1917	27/10/1917
War Diary	Proven	28/10/1917	30/10/1917
War Diary	Dykes Camp	31/10/1917	31/10/1917
Miscellaneous	H & Q		
Operation(al) Order(s)	Operation Orders No. 89. Highland Light Infantry	01/10/1917	01/10/1917
Operation(al) Order(s)	Operation Orders No. 90. Highland Light Infantry	02/10/1917	02/10/1917
Operation(al) Order(s)	Operation Orders No. 91. Highland Light Infantry	02/10/1917	02/10/1917
Operation(al) Order(s)	Operation Orders No. 92. Highland Light Infantry	11/10/1917	11/10/1917
Operation(al) Order(s)	Operation Orders No. 92a. Highland Light Infantry	15/10/1917	15/10/1917
Operation(al) Order(s)	Operation Orders No. 93. Highland Light Infantry	18/10/1917	18/10/1917
Operation(al) Order(s)	Operation Orders No. 94. Highland Light Infantry	22/10/1917	22/10/1917
Operation(al) Order(s)	Operation Order No. 95. Highland Light Infantry	24/10/1917	24/10/1917
Operation(al) Order(s)	Operation Orders No. 96. Highland Light Infantry	25/10/1917	25/10/1917
Operation(al) Order(s)	Operation Orders No. 97. Highland Light Infantry	26/10/1917	26/10/1917
Operation(al) Order(s)	Operation Orders No. 98. Highland Light Infantry	31/10/1917	31/10/1917
War Diary	Dykes Camp	01/11/1917	04/11/1917
War Diary	Proven	05/11/1917	12/11/1917
War Diary	Penton Camp. Proven	13/11/1917	21/11/1917
War Diary	Elverdinghe	22/11/1917	30/11/1917
Operation(al) Order(s)	Operation Orders No. 100. Highland Light Infantry	15/11/1917	15/11/1917
Operation(al) Order(s)	Operation Order No. 100. Highland Light Infantry	16/11/1917	16/11/1917
Operation(al) Order(s)	Operation Order No. 102. Highland Light Infantry	18/11/1917	18/11/1917
Operation(al) Order(s)	Operation Orders No. 103. Highland Light Infantry	19/11/1917	19/11/1917
Operation(al) Order(s)	Operation Order No. 104. Highland Light Infantry	19/11/1917	19/11/1917
Operation(al) Order(s)	Operation Orders No. 105. Highland Light Infantry	27/11/1917	27/11/1917
Operation(al) Order(s)	Operation Order No. 106. Highland Light Infantry.	29/11/1917	29/11/1917
War Diary		01/12/1917	02/12/1917
War Diary	F.X. Camp.	03/12/1917	06/12/1917
War Diary	Dublin Camp.	07/12/1917	11/12/1917
War Diary	Road Camp.	12/12/1917	12/12/1917
War Diary	Road Camp. Watou	12/12/1917	31/12/1917
Operation(al) Order(s)	Operation Order No. 107	01/12/1917	01/12/1917
War Diary	Operation Order No. 107a Highland Light Infantry.	10/12/1917	10/12/1917
War Diary	Road Camp Watou	01/01/1918	08/01/1918
War Diary	Kempton Part Sheet 28 N.W. C.15.b.3.5	09/01/1918	12/01/1918
War Diary	Kempton Park	13/01/1918	16/01/1918
War Diary	Whitemill Camp.	17/01/1918	21/01/1918
War Diary	Burns House Sector	22/01/1918	29/01/1918
War Diary	Hilltop Farm	30/01/1918	31/01/1918
War Diary	Operation Order No. 108. Highland Light Infantry	07/01/1918	07/01/1918
Operation(al) Order(s)	Operation Order No. 109. Highland Light Infantry	15/01/1918	15/01/1918
Operation(al) Order(s)	Operation Order No. 110. Highland Light Infantry	20/01/1918	20/01/1918
Operation(al) Order(s)	Administrative Instructions accompanying Operation Orders No. 110. Highland Light Infantry	20/01/1918	20/01/1918
Operation(al) Order(s)	Operation Order No. 111. Highland Light Infantry	22/01/1918	22/01/1918
Operation(al) Order(s)	Operation Order No. 112. Highland Light Infantry	24/01/1918	24/01/1918
Operation(al) Order(s)	Operation Orders No. 113. Highland Light Infantry	28/01/1918	28/01/1918
War Diary	Burns House Sector	01/02/1918	08/02/1918
War Diary	Whitemill Camp.	09/02/1918	16/02/1918

War Diary	Staden Sector	17/02/1918	22/02/1918
War Diary	Huddleston Camp	23/02/1918	28/02/1918
Operation(al) Order(s)	Operation Orders No. 114. Highland Light Infantry	31/01/1918	31/01/1918
Operation(al) Order(s)	Operation Orders No. 114 A. Highland Light Infantry	03/02/1918	03/02/1918
Operation(al) Order(s)	Operation Orders No. 115. Highland Light Infantry	07/02/1918	07/02/1918
Miscellaneous	Addenda to Operation Orders of 7.2.18 Highland Light Infantry.	07/02/1918	07/02/1918
Operation(al) Order(s)	Operation Orders No. 116. Highland Light Infantry.	15/02/1918	15/02/1918
Operation(al) Order(s)	Operation Orders No. 117. Highland Light Infantry.	21/02/1918	21/02/1918
Miscellaneous	O.C. Coy.	15/02/1918	15/02/1918
Heading	106th. Inf. Bde. 35th Div. War Diary 18th Battn. The Highland Light Infantry. March 1918		
Heading	War Diary.		
War Diary	Whitemill Camp.	01/03/1918	09/03/1918
War Diary	H Camp.	10/03/1918	22/03/1918
Miscellaneous	18th (G.Y). Bn. Highland Light Infantry. Narrative of Operations.	31/03/1918	31/03/1918
Heading	Battalion Operation Orders.		
Operation(al) Order(s)	Operation Orders. No. 118. Highland Light Infantry.	28/02/1918	28/02/1918
Operation(al) Order(s)	Special Operation Order No. 119. 18th Highland Light Infantry.	05/03/1918	05/03/1918
Miscellaneous	Army Battle Zone.		
Operation(al) Order(s)	Operation Order No. 120. B. Bn. Highland Light Infantry.	06/03/1918	06/03/1918
Operation(al) Order(s)	Operation Orders No. 121. Highland Light Infantry.	09/03/1918	09/03/1918
Operation(al) Order(s)	Operation Orders. No. 122. Highland Light Infantry.	22/03/1918	22/03/1918
War Diary	Heilly	01/04/1918	05/04/1918
War Diary	Bazieux	06/04/1918	06/04/1918
War Diary	Aveluy Wood near Albert.	07/04/1918	11/04/1918
War Diary	Headuville	12/04/1918	14/04/1918
War Diary	Bouzincourt	15/04/1918	21/04/1918
War Diary	Hedauville	22/04/1918	23/04/1918
War Diary	Martinsart	24/04/1918	29/04/1918
War Diary	Hedauville	30/04/1918	30/04/1918
Operation(al) Order(s)	Operation Order. No. 123. Highland Light Infantry	11/04/1918	11/04/1918
Operation(al) Order(s)	Operation Order No. 124. Highland Light Infantry	14/04/1918	14/04/1918
Operation(al) Order(s)	Operation Order No. 125. Highland Light Infantry	23/04/1918	23/04/1918
War Diary		01/05/1918	01/05/1918
War Diary	Rubempre	02/05/1918	18/05/1918
War Diary	Varennes	19/05/1918	19/05/1918
War Diary	Aveluy Wood	20/05/1918	21/05/1918
War Diary	Hedauville	22/05/1918	24/05/1918
War Diary	Aveluy Wood	25/05/1918	29/05/1918
War Diary	Hedauville	30/05/1918	31/05/1918
Operation(al) Order(s)	Operation (Move) Order. No. 127 "B" Highland Light Infantry.	17/05/1918	17/05/1918
Operation(al) Order(s)	Operation (Relief) Order No. 128 "B" Highland Light Infantry.	17/05/1918	17/05/1918
Miscellaneous	Administrative Instructions issued with Operation Order No. 127 and No. 128. "B" Highland Light Infantry.	17/05/1918	17/05/1918
Operation(al) Order(s)	Operation (Relief) Order No. 129. "B" Highland Light Infantry.	21/05/1918	21/05/1918
War Diary	Martinsart	01/06/1918	16/06/1918
War Diary	Warloy-Ballion	17/06/1918	17/06/1918
War Diary	Arqueves	18/06/1918	30/06/1918
Operation(al) Order(s)	Operation Order No. 130. "B" Highland Light Infantry.	21/06/1918	21/06/1918

Type	Description	Date From	Date To
Map Miscellaneous	Addendum to Operation Orders No. 'B' Highland Light Infantry.	26/06/1918	26/06/1918
Operation(al) Order(s)	Operation Orders No. 130. 'B' Highland Light Infantry.	16/06/1918	16/06/1918
Operation(al) Order(s)	Operation Orders No. 131. 'B' Highland Light Infantry.	17/06/1918	17/06/1918
Operation(al) Order(s)	Operation Orders No. 132. 'B' Highland Light Infantry.	26/06/1918	26/06/1918
Operation(al) Order(s)	Operation Orders No. 133. 'B' Highland Light Infantry.	28/06/1918	28/06/1918
Operation(al) Order(s)	Operation Orders. 134. 'B' Highland Light Infantry.	30/06/1918	30/06/1918
Miscellaneous	Operation Orders No. 'B' Highland Light Infantry (Situation No. 5).	26/06/1918	26/06/1918
War Diary	Arques	01/07/1918	01/07/1918
War Diary	Ebblinghem	02/07/1918	02/07/1918
War Diary	Zermezeele	03/07/1918	03/07/1918
War Diary	Winnezeele	04/07/1918	04/07/1918
War Diary	Locre Sector.	05/07/1918	10/07/1918
War Diary	Godersvelde	11/07/1918	16/07/1918
War Diary	Mt. Vidagne	17/07/1918	22/07/1918
War Diary	Locre Sector	23/07/1918	26/07/1918
War Diary	Boeschepe	27/07/1918	27/07/1918
War Diary	Eecke	28/07/1918	30/07/1918
Operation(al) Order(s)	Operation Orders No. 135. 'B' Highland Light Infantry.	02/07/1918	02/07/1918
Operation(al) Order(s)	Operation Orders No. 136. 'B' Highland Light Infantry.	03/07/1918	03/07/1918
Operation(al) Order(s)	Operation Orders No. 137. 'B' Highland Light Infantry.	09/07/1918	09/07/1918
Operation(al) Order(s)	Operation Orders No. 137A. 'B' Highland Light Infantry.	14/07/1918	14/07/1918
Operation(al) Order(s)	Operation Orders No. 138. 'B' Highland Light Infantry.	15/07/1918	15/07/1918
Operation(al) Order(s)	Operation Orders No. 139. 'B' Highland Light Infantry.	25/07/1918	25/07/1918
Miscellaneous	18th. (G.Y). Bn. Highland Light Infantry.	12/07/1918	12/07/1918
Miscellaneous	Operation Orders 18th. High. L Inf.		
War Diary	Mt. Rouge.	01/08/1918	03/08/1918
War Diary	West of Boeschepe	04/08/1918	07/08/1918
War Diary	Mt. Vidagne	08/08/1918	08/08/1918
War Diary	Eecke	09/08/1918	24/08/1918
War Diary	Le Wast.	25/08/1918	28/08/1918
War Diary	Eecke	29/08/1918	31/08/1918
Operation(al) Order(s)	15th. (S) Bn. The Sherwood Foresters. Operation Order No. 54	01/08/1918	01/08/1918
Operation(al) Order(s)	Operation Orders. No. 141. 'B' Highland Light Infantry.	03/08/1918	03/08/1918
Operation(al) Order(s)	Operation Orders. No. 142. 'B' Highland Light Infantry.	04/08/1918	04/08/1918
Operation(al) Order(s)	Special Battalion Order No. 16	08/08/1918	08/08/1918
Operation(al) Order(s)	Operation Orders No. 143. 'B' Highland Light Infantry.	23/08/1918	23/08/1918
Operation(al) Order(s)	Operation Order No. 176	29/08/1918	29/08/1918
War Diary	Eecke	01/09/1918	01/09/1918
War Diary	Road Camp	02/09/1918	03/09/1918
War Diary	Canal Sector	04/09/1918	12/09/1918
War Diary	Vlamertinghe	13/09/1918	16/09/1918
War Diary	Canal Sector.	17/09/1918	22/09/1918
War Diary	Brandhoek	23/09/1918	23/09/1918
War Diary	School Camp	24/09/1918	30/09/1918
Operation(al) Order(s)	Operation Orders No. 144. "B" Highland Light Infantry.	01/09/1918	01/09/1918
Operation(al) Order(s)	Operation (March) Orders No. 145. "B" Highland Light Infantry.	03/08/1918	03/08/1918
Miscellaneous	Operation Orders No. 18th Highland Light Infantry.	04/09/1918	04/09/1918
Operation(al) Order(s)	Operation (Relief) Orders. No. 145. 'B' Highland Light Infantry.	02/09/1918	02/09/1918

Type	Description	Date From	Date To
Operation(al) Order(s)	Operation Orders No. 146. 18th. Highland Light Inf.	08/09/1918	08/09/1918
Operation(al) Order(s)	Operation Orders No. 147. 18th. Highland Light Inf.	11/09/1918	11/09/1918
Miscellaneous	Operation Orders No. 148. 'B' Highland Light Infantry.	16/09/1918	16/09/1918
Operation(al) Order(s)	Operation Orders No. 149. 'B' Highland Light Infantry.	22/09/1918	22/09/1918
Operation(al) Order(s)	Operation (Move) Order. No. 150. 'B' Highland Light Infantry.	26/09/1918	26/09/1918
Operation(al) Order(s)	Operation Order. No. 151. 'B' Highland Light Infantry.	27/09/1918	27/09/1918
Operation(al) Order(s)	Operation Order No. 152. 'B' Highland Light Infantry.	25/09/1918	25/09/1918
Miscellaneous	18th (G.Y.) Bn. Highland Light Infantry.	27/09/1918	27/09/1918
Miscellaneous	Recommendations in Order of Merit		
Miscellaneous	18th (G.Y.) Bn. Highland Light Infantry.	01/10/1918	01/10/1918
Miscellaneous	Recommendations in Order of Merit		
Operation(al) Order(s)	Operation Order No. 153 18th Highland Light Infantry.	07/10/1918	07/10/1918
Operation(al) Order(s)	Move Orders Accompanying Operation Orders No. 153	07/10/1918	07/10/1918
Operation(al) Order(s)	Operation Order. No. 154. 'B' Highland Light Infantry.	10/10/1918	10/10/1918
Operation(al) Order(s)	Operation Order. No. 155. 'B' Highland Light Infantry.	11/10/1918	11/10/1918
Operation(al) Order(s)	Operation Order. No. 156. 'B' Highland Light Infantry.	12/10/1918	12/10/1918
Operation(al) Order(s)	Move Order Issued in Conjunction With Operation Order 156 'B' Highland Light Infantry.	12/10/1918	12/10/1918
War Diary	Wervicq	01/10/1918	01/10/1918
War Diary	Kruseck	02/10/1918	02/10/1918
War Diary	Ypres	03/10/1918	12/10/1918
War Diary	Gheluvelt	13/10/1918	21/10/1918
War Diary	Courtrai	22/10/1918	26/10/1918
War Diary	Scheldt	27/10/1918	31/10/1918
Operation(al) Order(s)	Operation Order No. 153. 18th Highland Light Infantry	07/10/1918	07/10/1918
Operation(al) Order(s)	Move Orders Accompanying Operation Orders No. 153	07/10/1918	07/10/1918
Operation(al) Order(s)	Operation Order No. 154. 'B' Highland Light Infantry.	10/10/1918	10/10/1918
Operation(al) Order(s)	Operation Order No. 155. 'B' Highland Light Infantry.	11/10/1918	11/10/1918
Operation(al) Order(s)	Operation Order No. 156. 'B' Highland Light Infantry.	12/10/1918	12/10/1918
Operation(al) Order(s)	Move Order Issued in Conjunction With Operation Order 156 'B' Highland Light Infantry.	12/10/1918	12/10/1918
Operation(al) Order(s)	Operation (Move) Orders No. 157. 'B' Highland Light Infantry.	24/10/1918	24/10/1918
Operation(al) Order(s)	Operation Order No. 158. 'B' Highland Light Infantry.	26/10/1918	26/10/1918
Operation(al) Order(s)	Operation Order No. 159. 'B' Highland Light Infantry.	31/10/1918	31/10/1918
Operation(al) Order(s)	Operation (Move) Orders. No. 157. 'B' Highland Light Infantry.	24/10/1918	24/10/1918
Operation(al) Order(s)	Operation Orders. No. 158. 'B' Highland Light Infantry.	26/10/1918	26/10/1918
Operation(al) Order(s)	Operation Order No. 159. 'B' Highland Light Infantry.	31/10/1918	31/10/1918
Miscellaneous	18th (G.Y) Bn. Highland Light Infantry.	20/10/1918	20/10/1918
Miscellaneous	18th (G.Y.) Bn. Highland Light Infantry.	18/10/1918	18/10/1918
Miscellaneous	18th (G.Y.) Bn. Highland Light Infantry.	13/10/1918	13/10/1918
Miscellaneous	18th (G.Y.) Bn. Highland Light Infantry.	18/10/1918	18/10/1918
War Diary		01/11/1918	04/11/1918
War Diary	Berchem	05/11/1918	11/11/1918
War Diary	Boschstraat	12/11/1918	13/11/1918
War Diary	Dondery	14/11/1918	19/11/1918
War Diary	Courtrai	20/11/1918	30/11/1918
Operation(al) Order(s)	Operation (Warning) Order No. 160. 'B' Highland Light Infantry.	04/11/1918	04/11/1918
Miscellaneous	18th (G.Y.) Bn. Highland Light Infantry.	11/11/1918	11/11/1918
Operation(al) Order(s)	Operation Order No. 160a. 'B' Highland Light Infantry.	11/11/1918	11/11/1918
Operation(al) Order(s)	Operation (Move) Orders No. 161. 'B' Highland Light Infantry.	13/11/1918	13/11/1918
Operation(al) Order(s)	Operation Orders. No. 162	17/11/1918	17/11/1918

Operation(al) Order(s)	Operation (Move) Orders. No. 162. 'B' Highland Light Infantry.	17/11/1918	17/11/1918
Miscellaneous	Operation (Move) Orders.	18/11/1918	18/11/1918
Operation(al) Order(s)	Operation (Move) Orders No. 163. 'B' Highland Light Infantry	18/11/1918	18/11/1918
Operation(al) Order(s)	Operation (Move) Orders No. 164. 'B' Highland Light Infantry	27/11/1918	27/11/1918
Operation(al) Order(s)	Operation (Move) Orders No. 164. 'B' Highland Light Infantry		
Operation(al) Order(s)	Operation (Move) Orders No. 164. 'B' Highland Light Infantry	28/11/1918	28/11/1918
Operation(al) Order(s)	Operation (Move) Orders No. 164. 'B' Highland Light Infantry	29/11/1918	29/11/1918
War Diary	Serques	01/12/1918	06/12/1918
War Diary	Millam	07/12/1918	01/01/1919
Operation(al) Order(s)	Operation (Move) Orders. No. 165. 'B' Highland Light Infantry.	05/12/1918	05/12/1918
War Diary	Millar	01/01/1919	28/01/1919
War Diary	Calais	29/01/1919	31/01/1919
War Diary	Calais No. 6. L. Camp.	01/02/1919	02/02/1919
War Diary	Millam	03/02/1919	28/02/1919

Woosław 90/2

35TH DIVISION
106TH INFY BDE

18TH BN HIGHLAND LT INFY
JAN ~~FEB~~ 1916-FEB 1919

ORDERLY ROOM
No. H.19
Date 24/2/16
18th (S) Bn. HIGHLAND LIGHT INF.

Officer i/c.
   Adjutant General's Office.
      General Hdqrs.
         3rd Echelon
———————————————

The attached copy of War Diary, with List of Officers and copies of Operation Orders, for the month ending 28th Feb. 1916 is forwarded in accordance with F.S. Regs Part II, page 174.

                                 W.J.K.L. Lieut.
                     Adjutant. 18th H.L.I.

27/2/16

Army Form C. 2118

WAR DIARY
or
INTELLIGENCE SUMMARY
(Erase heading not required.)

Instructions regarding War Diaries and Intelligence Summaries are contained in F. S. Regs., Part II. and the Staff Manual respectively. Title Pages will be prepared in manuscript.

106/35

Place	Date	Hour	Summary of Events and Information	Remarks and references to Appendices
PERHAM DOWN	31.1.16	7.15AM	Entrained for FOLKESTONE. List of Officers with Batt.n attached	I
FOLKESTONE	31.1.16	3 PM	Embarked for BOULOGNE	
BOULOGNE	31.1.16	6 PM	Disembarked & marched to Rest Camp	
	1.2.16	11.30 PM	Left Rest Camp & marched to Pont du BRIC Station & entrained. Transport H Details about 12 noon	
ARQUES	2.2.16	8.30 AM	Detrained. 34 Off. 599 m. + marched to Billets. Area at RACQUINHEM	
RACQUINHEM	3.2.16		In Billets. Battn classes of equipment, rifles, clothing kit inspection. Bayonet uncrossed & straight wounds taken off	
"	4.2.16		" " Route march 5½ miles	
"	5.2.16		" " Route march 6 miles	
"	6.2.16		" " Battalion	
"	7.2.16		" " Route march 8 miles	
"	8.2.16		" " Inspection of habitation stoves	
"	9.2.16	12 n	marched to outskirts of Specklin. Only 6.T.wagons attached. Inspected by Sir Douglas Haig & Prince Arthur of Connaught note	II
THIENNES	10.2.16		In Billets. Accommodation limits. The Division (35th) has been allocated to 11th Corps (1st Army). Corps commander THIENNES 2.45 PM	
			Major General Haking. Army Commander Lt General Munro. The Division is at present placed in support of Bosch em & THIENNES	
			for instance. The 106 Brigade (1st and 2nd Batts in support & infilled at BOSCHEM & THIENNES	
	11.2.16	10.30 AM	Brigade inspected by Field Marshal Earl Kitchener.	
"	12.2.16		In Billets. Company & Battn work.	
"	13.2.16		In Billets. Company & Specialists training.	
"	14.2.16		" " " " Coy O/C Coys returned from tour of trenches with French Division	
"	15.2.16		In Billets " " " "	
"	16.2.16		In Billets	

Army Form C. 2118

WAR DIARY
or
INTELLIGENCE SUMMARY
(Erase heading not required.)

Instructions regarding War Diaries and Intelligence Summaries are contained in F. S. Regs., Part II. and the Staff Manual respectively. Title Pages will be prepared in manuscript.

Place	Date	Hour	Summary of Events and Information	Remarks and references to Appendices
THIENNES	17-2-16		In billets. Company & shielets training	III
"	18-2-16		Marched to new billets at MERVILLE. Construction Coaches N° 2 vehicles and attached. Stations & Arches, accommodation limited. Companies scattered over large area.	
MERVILLE	19-2-16		In billets. Party of 1 Officer and 60 men sent to LESTREM.	
"	20-2-16		" "	
"	21-2-16		" Company and shielets training. Various enemy air-craft forced on by our artillery. Prolonged and heavy bombardment on our right, in LA BASSEE direction. Our air-craft and artillery were apparently answering for in bombing the station at LA BASSEE and the town of DON.	
"	22-2-16		In Billets. Companies and shielets at training	
"	23-2-16		In Billets " "	
"	24-2-16		In Billets " "	
"	25-2-16		In Billets " "	
"	26-2-16		In Billets " "	
"	27-2-16		In Billets " "	

WAR DIARY
or
INTELLIGENCE SUMMARY
(Erase heading not required.)

Army Form C. 2118

Place	Date	Hour	Summary of Events and Information	Remarks and references to Appendices
MERVILLE	28-2-16			
	29-2-16		March to 19th Devonshire Area. Attached to 5-6th Brigades for instruction. Infantry orders N° III issued and attached. In trenches. Companies attached to other units for instruction as follows. "W" Coy att. to 1/1 R. Lanc. R. "X" Coy att. to 1/E. Lanc. R. – "Y" Coy att. to 1/5. Lanc. R. – "Z" Coy att. to 1/N. Lanc. R. Headquarters were split up and attached to the above units.	IV

Appendix V

18th (Service) Battalion., Highland Light Infantry.

Lieut-Colonel.
Lawrenson, R.R.

Majors.
Gillespie, W.

Captains.
Lumsden, C.B.
Gooderson, V.E.
Kennedy, W.
Macgowan, A.C.
Macmillan, C.
Kirk, J.
Downey, E.L.

2nd. Lieutenants.
Ferguson, J.N.
Thomson, J.K.
Barrie, J.
Bryan, W.D.
McCall, A.
Yorke, F.St.G.
Macara, W.F.M.
Gemmill, A.
Douglas, W.G.
Craig, H.J.
Stewart, D.L.
Fitzpatrick, A.
McColl, G.R.
Borland, F.H.G.

Lieutenants.
Young, W.W.
Jackson, G.
Dagger, R.
Balfour, A.C.
Maule, E.B.
Martin, H.
Steele, W.
Barr, W.S.

Adjutant:- Lieutenant, W.J. Lyle,
Quartermaster:- Lieut. R.J. Hegerty.
Medical Officer:- Lieut. C.G. McClymont.

Appendix II

OPERATION ORDERS No. 1.   8-2-16.

Reference 1/100,000, HAZEBROUCK 5A Map.

Intention.   1. The Battalion will move to-morrow into Billets in the Area at THIENNES.

Detail.   2.(a) The Battalion will follow, in order of march, the 19th Durham Light Infantry, the head of which Battn. passes starting point (Road Junction S of $\frac{7}{C}$ in RACQUINGHEM) at 12 noon, and will march via WITTES to THIENNES.

(b) Order of march as follows - "Z", "Y", "X", "W",. Each Company joining the column at its own Billeting Area.

(c) The Machine Guns will be Brigaded and follow in rear of 205th Field Coy. R. E.

(d) 1st Line Transport will be Brigaded and follow Machine Guns.

(e) The M. O. will follow in rear of Battalion.

3.   =X= Company will detail 1 N. C. O. and 4 men to proceed with Battalion 1st Line Transport.

"Y" will detail 1 N. C. O and 4 men to proceed with baggage and supply wagons, (2nd Line Transport).

4.   Reports to Head of Battalion.

(Sgd)   W. J. LYLE, Lieut. & Adjt.
18th (S) Battn. H. L. Infantry.

Issued at 5 P.M.

Dictated to O. C. Coys.
"   " O. 1/c M. Gun.
"   "   "   " Transport.
"   " Medical Officer.
Copy filed in War Diary.

Appendix III

Copy No. 1

OPERATION ORDERS, No. 2.

Reference Map 1/40000 36A.

17.2.16.

1. The Battalion will move into Reserve Divisional Billets of the XI Corps to-morrow.
   The head of the Battalion, following 19th D. L. I. will pass the Orderly Room at 9 A.M., and will march VIA CROIX MARRAISSE – LESART – Billets at LES LAURIERS & MERVILLE.

   Order of MARCH Y Coy, X Coy, Z Coy, W Coy.

   Machine Guns will be brigaded in order of march of Battalion and follow in rear of 17th W. York. Regt.

   1st Line Transport will be brigaded in order of march of Battalion and will follow 205th Field Coy. R. E.

   Divisional Train Waggons will follow 1st Line Transport

2. O. C. Z Coy. will detail 1 N. C. O. and 6 men as brakes men for Ammunition Limbers.
   O.C. W Coy. will detail 1 N.C.O. and 2 men as escort to 2nd Line Waggons.
   O.C. X Coy. will detail 2 N.C.Os to accompany Blanket Lorries.

3. The supply section of the 106th Brigade will proceed empty to LES LAURIERS, & fill up there from the Supply Column with the rations for 19th.

4. Billeting Party, Lt. Martin, the Interpreter, 1 Q.M.S. and 1 man per Coy. and Sergt. Doran for Hd. Qrs. will parade at Orderly Room at 2 A.M. and will march to Starting Point, I 29 d 4 5 and then march under senior Officer of party to take over billets.

5. Reports to head of Battalion.

(Sgd) W. J. LYLE, Lieut. & Adjt.
18th (S) Bn. H. L. Infantry.

Issued at 7.30 P.M.

Copy No. 1 Filed in War Diary.
" " 2 "W" Coy.
" " 3 "X" "
" " 4 "Y" "
" " 5 "Z" "
" " 6 O. i/c Transport.

appendix IV COPY No. 1

OPERATION ORDERS No. 3.

18th (SER) BN. H. L. INFANTRY.

Reference Maps 1/40000 BETHUNE SHEET, & 36A.

27.2.16.

1. The Battalion will move into 19th Division Area for training on 28th inst., and will be attached to 56th Brigade. W & X Coys. will move into the trenches on the 28th inst. for instruction. Y & Z Coys. will move into billets in vicinity of CROIX BARBEE on same day.

2. The head of the column will pass the starting point, CROSS ROADS, K 28 B 6 9 at 9.30 A.M. Route MERVILLE, PARADISE, EGLISE, Cross Roads Q.30 B 5 9, Cross Roads R 20 C 8 2, ZELOBES, VIELLE CHAPELLE.

3. Order of March:- Adv.Guard. - Capt. Dagger, 2 Platoons W Coy.
    W Coy. less 2 platoons.
    X "
    Y "
    Z " less 1 platoon.
    Rear Guard, 1 platoon, Z Coy.
    Machine Gunners & Bombing Section will follow Z Coy.

4. On arrival at VIELLE CHAPELLE, W & X Coys. will halt for dinners, and will move about 3.15 P.M., directed by guides of different Battalions, to their various destinations.
    The other two Coys. proceed direct to their destination.

5. 1st Line Transport, 5 Limber Waggons, 1 Maltese Cart, 4 Cookers, and 2 Water Carts, will march in rear of Battalion, 2nd Line Transport, 4 G. S. Waggons, will follow 1st Line. All 1st Line and 2nd Line Transport accompanying the Battn. will return to their respective Billets on the 28th inst. with the exception of cookers and water carts. Pack Mules will not accompany the Battn.

6. All N. C. Os and men will carry on them their tea rations for the 28th. Rations for the 29th will be issued by the various Battns. to which Companies are attached.

7. One G.S. Waggon is alloted to each Coy. for transport of blankets, Officers' Baggage, Fur Coats, Waterproofs, etc. These waggons will be sent to Companies on afternoon on 27th, & will march with Companies until they join the column.

8. The Medical Officer will march in rear of Battn.

9. The QR.MR. will accompany Baggage waggons.

10. Reports will be sent to head of Main Body.

(Sgd) W. J. LYLE, Lieut.

Adjt. 18th H. L. I.

Issued at 9.30 A.M.
Copy No. 1. Filed in War Diary. Copy No. 2, W Coy.
  "   " 3, X Coy.   "   " 4 Y "
  "   " 5, Z "   "   " 6 Med. Officer.
  "   " 7, Transport Officer.

18th HLI
Vol 2
March 1916

2. p.
14 sheets

D.A.G.
General H.Qrs.
3rd. Echelon
Base.

Herewith copy of War Diary with copies of Operation Orders attached, for the month ending 31st. March 1916, forwarded in accordance with F.S. Regs. II page 174.

W.G.Hyslop. Lieut. + Adj.
18th (S) Bn. H.L. INFANTRY.

1/4/16.

ORDERLY ROOM
No. H.248
Date 1/4/16
18th Bn. Highland Light Infy.

Army Form C. 2118

WAR DIARY
or
INTELLIGENCE SUMMARY
(Erase heading not required.)

Instructions regarding War Diaries and Intelligence Summaries are contained in F. S. Regs., Part II. and the Staff Manual respectively. Title Pages will be prepared in manuscript.

Place	Date	Hour	Summary of Events and Information	Remarks and references to Appendices
CROIX BARBÉE	1/3/16		In the trenches. Two companies W & X up for two day's instruction with units already mentioned, one man X'ly wounded.	
"	2/3/16		In the trenches. Two companies Y & Z up for two day's instruction one man killed one man wounded	
"	3/3/16		In the trenches. Two companies Y & Z " " " " one officer wounded	
"	4/3/16		" " " " W & X " " " "	
"	5/3/16		" " " " " " " "	
"	6/3/16		" " " " Y & Z " " Thirty six hours instruction	
RIEZ BAILLEU	7/3/16		" " " Battalion marched to billets at RIEZ BAILLEU. Operation orders issued and attached. Accommodation good. Major Linsden dead. Synoff buried at LAGORGUE.	V.
"	8/3/16		In billets. Battalion cleaning up of equipment rifles, checking and replenishing stores.	
"	9/3/16		In billets. Battalion resting, in Brigade Reserve. Brigade having taken over trenches in vicinity of LAVENTIE.	
"	10/3/16		In billets, still in Brigade reserve specialists in training, numerous working parties found	
"	11/3/16		Marched to trenches at LAVENTIE. Operation Orders issued and attached. Battalion took over from 12th Royal Scots. Re taking over was done in remarkably quick time and the battalion settled down to its first entire responsibility	VI
"	12/3/16		In trenches. Battalion hard at work repairing trenches, quiet day, two men killed, three wounded.	
"	13/3/16		In trenches repair work in full swing, slight activity on part of enemy's artillery, quickly silenced however by our howitzers, more or less a quiet day, five men wounded.	

WAR DIARY
or
INTELLIGENCE SUMMARY
(Erase heading not required.)

Army Form C. 2118

Instructions regarding War Diaries and Intelligence Summaries are contained in F. S. Regs., Part II. and the Staff Manual respectively. Title Pages will be prepared in manuscript.

Place	Date	Hour	Summary of Events and Information	Remarks and references to Appendices
In trenches	14/3/16		In trenches, the germans fired a mine under our trenches at Duck's Bill and followed it up with H.E. and shrapnel. Our total casualties at the mine itself was killed 33 wounded and 1 officer. At night our men occupied the crater. The germans made no attempt to advance.	
"	15/3/16		In trenches, enemy's artillery active, our trenches and posts bombarded by H.E. and shrapnel. Relieved at 8.30 p.m. marched to LA GORGUE. Operation Orders issued and attached No 6.	VII
LA GORGUE	16/3/16		In billets marched to L'EPINETTE, men tired, but in splendid spirits.	
L'EPINETTE	17/3/16		In billets cleaning and checking equipment stores etc.	
"	18/3/16		In billets cleaning and issuing equipment stores etc specialists at training.	
"	19/3/16		In billets battalion marched to LES RUES DES VACHES. Operation Orders No 7 issued and attached.	
LES RUES DES VACHES	20/3/16		In billets troops resting, cleaning and issuing of clothing, boots and equipment. Complimentary letter from G.O.C. 1st Division attached VII B, this letter was read out on parade to all the Officers & N.C.Os & men of the battalion.	VIII
"	21/3/16		In billets issuing of clothing continued, bays at training, specialists at sniping, bombing and scouting. Machine Gunners & Signallers about training.	
"	22/3/16		In billets companies at rifle exercises physical training and grenade work.	
"	23/3/16		" " " " " " " " "	
"	24/3/16		" " work physical training, route marching sniping and grenade work.	
"	25/3/16		" " " " " " " " Operation Orders No VIII. issued and attached.	

WAR DIARY
or
INTELLIGENCE SUMMARY
(Erase heading not required.)

Army Form C. 2118

Instructions regarding War Diaries and Intelligence Summaries are contained in F.S. Regs., Part II. and the Staff Manual respectively. Title Pages will be prepared in manuscript.

Place	Date	Hour	Summary of Events and Information	Remarks and references to Appendices
LES RUES DES VACHES	26/3/16		In billets. Battalion marched to ESTAIRES /operations orders No 9 issued and attached/ distance about 8 miles	IX
ESTAIRES	27/3/16		In billets. Battalion paraded at 5-20 a.m. and marched to ROUGE DE BOUT. Two battalions of Brigade in trenches (W. Yorks & 17th R. Scots) other two (18th H.L.I. & 19th D.L.I.) in Brigade Reserve. Two companies in close support to battalion in firing line and two in reserve.	
ROUGE DE BOUT	28/3/16		In billets. Brigade reserve, men at work repairing and improving strong posts.	
"	29/3/16		In billets. Companies at work repairing and improving billets and posts. 2/Lieut Y. St. J. Yorke granted Military Cross for his work in connection with the operations at Duck's Bill.	
"	30/3/16		In billets. Companies at work repairing and improving posts, speciables at motruction in trench mortar and grenade work.	
"	31/3/16		In billets. Battalion taking over trenches from 17th Royal Scots operation orders No 10 issued and attached. Relief completed in quietness. Very little Machine gun or rifle fire. no artillery firing. two men wounded in afternoon. Line held by 19th D.L.I. on left of Brigade 18th H.L.I. on right of 105th Brigade on right of 18th H.L.I.	X.

Copy No. _I_

OPERATION ORDERS No. 4.

18th (Ser) Bn. H. L. INFANTRY.

6.3.16.

1. The Battalion will assemble in billets at RIEZ BAILLEUL, M 7 d, by 9 A.M. to-morrow.

2. The Companies will march to their billets by platoons with 5 minutes interval.
   Platoons of "X" Coy. will pass CROIX BARBEE Cross Roads at 7.30, 7.35, 7.40, 7.45 A.M.
   Platoons of "W" Coy. will pass CROIX BARBEE Cross Roads at 7.50, 7.55, 8.0, & 8.5 A.M.
   "Y" & "Z" Coys. will move out of the trenches on the night of 6th & 7th inst. by sections, at ¼ hour interval, and will be at REIZ BAILLEUL before 9 A.M. on 7th inst.

3. Strong Posts will be taken over and occupied as follows:-
   ROUGE CROIX, E, (M 27 B Central) 1 Officer & 1 Platoon, W. Coy.
   "   "   W, (M 27 B 1.7.) 1 Officer, & 1 Platoon, X "
   Machine Gunners of W Coy. will go to ROUGE CROIX E.
   "   "   " X "   "   "   "   "   "   W.
   Guides will be at ROUGE CROIX at 6.30 A.M. and the relief will be completed by 7 A.M.
   N.B. Permanent Guards are _not_ to be relieved.

4. Transport for blankets & Officers Kits will be arranged and communicated later. The platoons going into the strong posts will not take their Blankets.

(Sgd)   W. J. LYLE, Lieut. & Adjt.

18th (S) Bn. H. L. INFANTRY.

Copy No. 1 & 2, War Diary.
"   "   3   O. C. "W" Coy.
"   "   4   " " "X" "
"   "   5   " " "Y" "
"   "   6   " " "Z" "
"   "   7   Transport Officer.
"   "   8   Machine Gun   "
"   "   9   Bombing   "
"   " 10   Signalling Officer.

Copy No. 1

OPERATION ORDERS. No. 5.

18th (Ser) Battn. H. L. INFANTRY.   10/3/16.

Ref. Map No. 1/40,000 and Trench Map.

1. The Battn. will take over the Right Brigade Sector of the Line to-morrow night from 17th R. Scots.

2. W Coy. will take over right of the line from Z Coy. R.S.
   X "   "   "   "   " right central " " " X " R.S.
   Y "   "   "   "   " Left   " " " W " R.S.
   Z "   "   "   "   left   " " " Y " R.S.

(b) Strong Posts occupied by the Battalion at ROUGE CROIX will be relieved by R. Scots to-morrow at 11 A.M.

(c) The Machine Gunners of each Company with one Machine Gun for each Detachment will proceed to-morrow afternoon to take over their posts, to be at ROUGE CROIX Cross Roads at 4 P.M.

(d) The Hd.Qr. Signallers and one signaller per Coy. will proceed to the trenches to-morrow afternoon at 3.30 P.M. to take over their various posts.

(e) Posts will be occupied as follows:-
    1 Off. 20 men, Y Coy. at TILLELOY SOUTH.
    2/Lt. Macara & 20 men Y Coy. at PUMP KEEP.
    1 Off. 20 men Y Coy. at LA FONE Post.

(f) The Battalion Bombers will be at LA FONE Post. These will proceed to-morrow afternoon under the Bombing Officer to take over. 4 Grenadiers per Coy. will be attached to Batt. Grenadiers.

(G) Snipers under Lt. Barr will proceed in the afternoon to take over their posts. These men will be rationed and accommodated with their Company, but will be at the disposal of Sniping Officer. They are not on any account to be used for night work.

(h) Platoons will leave their billets at intervals of 3 minutes in the following order;- W Coy. at 6.45, Z Coy, X Coy, Y Coy, and the detailed posts, HdQrs. Guides from Royal Scots will be at ROUGE CROIX at 6 P.M. for each Company and Post.

(i) The R.S.M., O.C. Coys., and C.S.Ms. will proceed to-morrow afternoon to take over the various portions of the line and also all stores.

3. 1 Limber Waggon, and 2 Pack Mules will be alloted to each Company, to convey their rations and baggage to ROUGE CROIX. From there the baggage will be taken up by trolley to a point close to Bn.Hd.Qes. Rations etc. must be carried from ROUGE CROIX by the men.

4. One guide per Coy. will be despatched to Battn. HdQes. as soon as possible after taking over. He should have his rations for the following day with him, and will remain at B.H.Q. until the Bn. is relieved.

5. A list of Trench Stores, giving those in posts and keeps seperately, will be sent to the Adjt. by 9 A.M. the day after taking over.

6. The completion of the relief of each Coy. & post will be reported to Adjt. at once.
The disposition of each Coy. will be sent in at 9 A.M. the next day.

(Sgd) W.J. LYLE, Lieut. & Adjt.
18th (S) Bn. H. L. Infantry.

Dictated at 5.30 P.M. to O.C. W,X,Y,Z, Coys Transport Off. M.G.Off. Bombing Officer, and Signalling Officer.
Copies No.1 & 2 filed in War Diary.

Copy No. 1

Operation Orders No. 6.
18th (S) BN. H. L. INFANTRY.

Reference Map 1/40000 combined sheet BETHUNE.   15.3.16.

1. The Battalion will be relieved to-night by the 8th Gloster Regt. and in being relieved from the trenches will march to LA GORGUE.

2. Machine Gunners, Signallers, will be relieved this afternoon and will march to new billets on relief.

3. Trench Stores: a list of trench stores giving those in posts and Keeps seperately, will be handed over, and receipts taken. All Officers baggage, Med. Stores, and Cooking utensils to be at rail head, South Tilleloy, by 6 P.M..

4. O.C. Coys. will have their Coys. in readiness to move at 10 A.M. to-morrow, to billets in neighbourhood of l'EPPINETTE, Q.7.&.8.

5. Reports of Coys. & Posts will be sent to Bn.Hd.Qrs. on completion.

(Sgd) W. J. LYLE, Lieut. & Adjt.
18th (S) BN. H.L. INFANTRY.

Issued at 3 P.M.
No.1-- War Diary.

Copy No. 1

OPERATION ORDERS No. 7.
18th (S) Bn. H. L. INFANTRY.

Ref. 1/40,000, Sheet 36A. 18.3.16.

1. The Battalion will move to billets at LES RUES des VACHES to--morrow.

2. The head of the column will pass the Starting Point - Cross Roads, R.13.d.4.5. at 10 A.M. Order of March :-
Signallers, W Coy. Z Coy. Y Coy. X Coy. Machine Gun Detachment.
Route- Q.24.A.4.9., Q.23.A.3.3., Q.9.b.5.1.

3. 1st & 2nd Line Transport will follow column.

4. M. O. will march in rear of Battalion.

5. Billeting parties of 1 N.C.O. per Coy. under 2/Lieut. Fitzpatrick will move at 8 A.M.

6. Reports to Head of Column.

                        (Sgd)   W. J. LYLE, Lieut. & Adjt.
                                  18th (Ser) Battn. H. L. INFANTRY.

Issued at 5 P.M.
    Copy No. 1 Filed.
    Dictated to all others.

35 D. 200 (G).

XIth Corps.
R.H.S. 783/12.

VII.B.

G.O.C. 19th Division.
Copy to G.O.C. 35th Division for his information.

    I am very pleased with the action taken by you and all ranks concerned to deal with the situation at the DUCKS BILL on the morning of 14th inst. The action of the two Officers and four men of the South Wales Borderers who retained their position in the DUCKS BILL after the explosion of the mine is highly praiseworthy and shows a fine military spirit. I am also glad to hear that there was no sign of giving way amongst the men of the 18th H. L. I. who were exposed to the full effect of the mine. This shows that although these men have only recently arrived in the country they are to be trusted to maintain their position, even in the most difficult and dangerous circumstances.

                (Sgd)   R. HAKING, Lt. General,

16.3.16.   Commanding XIth Corps.

2.

106th Bde.

    For information.

                (Sgd)   V.C. Clino,   Major,
                                          for
H.Q. 35th Div.   Lt-Col, G.S.
17.3.16.   35th Division.

                          3.

18th High. L. I.   106th Infantry Brigade.
                                     106/567.

    For information and return, please.

                (Sgd)   C. Tomes,   Capt.

18th MAR. 1916.   Brigade Major, 106th INFANTRY BRIGADE.

Copy No. 1

OPERATION ORDERS No. 9.

<u>18th (SER) BATTN. H. L. INFANTRY.</u>　　　　　　26.3.16.

Reference, Sheet 36,A 1/40,000.

1. The Battalion will move to billets at ESTAIRES to-morrow & will be billeted there on the night 26-27th.

2. The head of the column in the order of march, will pass Starting Point - Cross Roads Q.5.d.5.1., at 1.50 P.M. and march via Q.5.b.5.5., K.29.d.6.6., K.30.d.1½.2½. Signallers, W Coy. X Coy, Y Coy. Z Coy, Machine Gun Detachment, and Bombers.

3. 1st Line Transport will be Brigaded and follow in rear of Brigade.

4. Supplies for 26th will be drawn at the Refilling Point at CALONNE, and then will proceed to ESTAIRES.

5. M. O. will march in rear of Battn.

6. Reports to head of Battn.

　　　　　　　　　　　(Sgd) W. J. LYLE, Lieut. & Adj.
　　　　　　　　　　　　　18th(S) Bn. H. L. INFANTRY.

Copy No.1 Filed in War Diary.
　　　Dictated to O.C. Coys.
Copy No. 2, to QuarterMaster.
　"　 " 3, to Transport Officer.

COPY No. 1

OPERATION ORDERS No. 9.

18th (S) BN. H. L. INFANTRY.   26.3.16.

Reference Map Sheet 36 & 36A. 1/40,000.

1. The Battalion will move to billets at ROUGE DE BOUT. to-morrow, relieving 1/R. Irish Rifles, and will be in reserve for Right Sector of FLEURBAIX Sector of the line.

2. The head of the column in order of march, as below, will pass the Starting Point, Cross Roads, G.25.D.4.7. (Sheet 37) at 5.20 A.M., and will march to ROUGE DE BOUT via Cross Roads, G.22.C.1.2. Signallers W, X, Y, Z Coys. Machine Gun Det,. and Bombers.

3. 1st Line Transport and 2nd Line will follow in rear of Battalion,. The two Motor Lorries will also follow in rear of the Battalion.

4. The Machine Gun Officer will arrange for a Lewis Gun and Team to be provided for the following posts in the line. BEE & TROU. These Guns and Teams will assemble at BAR/LETTELEME at H.36.A.4.5 at 8.30 A.M. on 27th inst. Special care will be taken that the limbers carrying the guns will proceed to the point of Assembly at the distance of 800X. between each limber. The teams will be rationed for the 27th, and after that date will be rationed by the Royal Scots in the line.

5. The following will be the distribution of the Battalion while in Brigade Reserve. "X" Coy. in close support to battalion in trenches, and billeted in WEATHERCOCK HOUSE, H.31.C.9.2½. N.B. This Company will sleep with their boots on, and will stand to arms one hour before dawn daily.
"Y" Coy. quartered at WINDY POST, as Garrison of SUPPORT POST, 3 platoons will form Garrison of WINDY POST, of which 2 platoons form garrison of CHARRED POST. (to move there on alarm being given.)
"W" Coy. in billets, G.36.D.3.6. near ROUGE DE BOUT,.
"Z" Coy. between ROUGE DE BOUT and GRANNY POST, G.29&G.7.8.
2 Lewis Guns in posts in front line, 2 Lewis Guns in reserve at Battn. Hd.Qrs. The Signalling Section and Bombers at Battn.Hd.Qrs.G.36.D.8.6.

6. O.C. W & Z Coys. will supply a permanent caretaking Guard, for the following posts,.-- "W" Coy. ROUGE MAISONS, G.21. Central. - 1 N.C.O. and 3 men. "Z" Coy. GRANNY POST, G.29.D.8.9. 1 N.C.O. and 3 men. These are permanent caretaking Guards, and will not be relieved, without reference to Battn. Hd.Qrs. They are responsible for the upkeep and repair of the posts, and the stores therein. Men for these posts should be selected from those unable to stand the strain of Trench Warfare. These Posts will be relieved at 10 A.M. on the morning of the 27th.

7. Platoons and Guards taking over posts, will take over all stores, on relief, duplicate receipts being obtained, and forwarded to the Adjutant.

8. Reports to head of Battalion during march to billets, and afterwards to Bn. Hd.Qrs. at ROUGE DE BOUT.

(Sgd) W. J. LYLE, Lt. & Adj.

18th (S) BN. H. L. INFANTRY.

No. 1 Copy, filed in War Diary.
" 2 "   W Coy.
" 3 "   X "
" 4 "   Y "
" 5 "   Z "

Copy No. 1

OPERATION ORDER No. 10.
18th (S) BN. H. L. INFANTRY.   30.3.16.

Reference Map 1/40,000.

1. The Battalion will relieve 17th R. Scots in right sub-section of the line, to-morrow, 31st March, as under.

   "W" Coy. less 1 platoon relieves "W" Coy. R. Scots.
   "X"   "   "   "   "   "   "X"   "   "   "
   "Y"   "   "   "   "   "   "Y"   "   "   "
   "Z"   "   "   "   "   "   "Z"   "   "   "

2. Guides for platoons & posts will be at WEATHERCOCK CORNER (N.1.a.6.9½) at 6.45 P.M.

3. Snipers will leave Battn. Hd.Qrs. at 9.45 A.M. Lewis Gun Detachment at 10.30 A.M., Signallers at 1.45 P.M. and Bombers at 2.30 P.M., and proceed to trenches and take over their various posts.

   1 Signaller per Company, with telephone, will proceed with Battn. Signallers.

4. Billeting parties of R. Scots will take over Battn. Billets to-morrow morning.

5. One Limber Waggon per Company will convey Company Rations and baggage to TWO TREE Farm, from where they will be taken up to the trenches by each platoon.

6. Advance parties will take their dinner and tea rations with them.

7. Companies will pass WEATHERCOCK CORNER in the following order, W, Z, Y, X.. 4 minutes interval between platoons. 1st Platoon to pass at 6.45 P.M. All movement South East of this Corner to be by Platoons.

8. O.C.Coys. C.S.Ms and R.S.M. will proceed to the line before 4 P.M. to take over stores, etc.

9. All trench stores will be taken over and receipts forwarded to Orderly Room the day after relief.

                                       (Sgd) W.J. LYLE, Lt. & Adj.
Issued at 6.30 P.M.   18th (S) BN. H. L. INFANTRY.
Copy No. 1 Filed.
   "   " 2 W. Coy. Copy No. 3 . X Coy.
   "   " 4 Y "   "   " 5 . Z "
   "   " 6 War Diary.
Dictated to Signalling Off. Machine Gun Off. and Sniping Officer.

18 HLI
Army Form C. 2118
XXXV (16)
Vol 3

WAR DIARY
INTELLIGENCE SUMMARY
(Erase heading not required.)

Instructions regarding War Diaries and Intelligence Summaries are contained in F. S. Regs., Part II. and the Staff Manual respectively. Title Pages will be prepared in manuscript.

Place	Date	Hour	Summary of Events and Information	Remarks and references to Appendices
In trenches	1/4/16		In trenches, enemy's artillery shelled Battn H.Qrs from 11 am to 1 pm with H.E. No damage done, one man wounded.	
"	2/4/16		In trenches enemy very inactive, towards 3 pm shelled one of our communication trenches V.C. AVENUE two direct hits. In the evening at 6.55 pm, we co-operated with the 105th Brigade on our right in a little strafe. Artillery, machine gun and rifle fire was directed at their parapet. very little retaliation. one man killed	
"	3/4/16		In trenches enemy inactive. light shelling in afternoon. one man wounded	
"	4/4/16		In trenches. Battalion relieved by 1/4th Lancashire Regt. 104th Brigade relief completed by 9.15 pm Operation Orders No 11 issued and attached. Battalion marched to Divisional Reserve billets at SAILLY SUR LA LYS.	XI
SAILLY SUR LA LYS	5/4/16		In billets. Draft of 2 officers & 48 men posted to Battalion from the Base	
"	6/4/16		In billets, battalion resting, cleaning and checking clothing and equipment	
"	7/4/16		In billets. Companies at instruction in forenoon. Running, physical training, handling of arms, specialists at instruction in Machine Gun, signalling and bombing. In afternoon battalion paraded, short route march.	
"	8/4/16		In billets. Companies at instruction " " " " ". Specialists at instruction	
"	9/4/16		In billets. Companies at physical training, rifle drill and route marching. Specialists under instruction	
"	10/4/16		In billets " " " " " " " 2nd Lieut G. St G. Yoke presented ribbon of Military Cross by L.O.G 1st Army General C.C. Munro. Draft of 20 men posted from Base.	

WAR DIARY
INTELLIGENCE SUMMARY
(Erase heading not required.)

Army Form C. 2118

Instructions regarding War Diaries and Intelligence Summaries are contained in F.S. Regs., Part II. and the Staff Manual respectively. Title Pages will be prepared in manuscript.

Place	Date	Hour	Summary of Events and Information	Remarks and references to Appendices
SAILLY SUR LA LYS	11/4/16		In Billets, companies at physical training running, rifle drill and Route marching, Specialists under instruction.	
"	12/4/16		In Billets. Battalion marched to LAVENTIE. Operation orders No 12 issued and attached. Battalion took over from 15th Sherwood Foresters. Two battalions in first line 1st Royal Scots + 19th W. Yorks. Two battalions in Brigade Reserve 18th H.L.I. + 17th R.L.I. in LAVENTIE. One Coy in close support to Royal Scots	XII.
LAVENTIE	13/4/16		In Brigade Reserve, very quiet day, drill and specialists Training in doors enemy shelled outskirts of LAVENTIE towards 6 p.m. no damage	
"	14/4/16		Brigade Reserve quiet day specialists at training	
"	15/4/16		" Operation Orders No 13 issued and attached. Battalion relieved by 15th Welsh.	XIII.
			Regiment and marched to ESTAIRES	
ESTAIRES	16/4/16		In billets. Operation Orders No 14 issued and attached. Battalion took over trenches from Y~EAST LANC REG. Relief completed by 11 p.m.	XIV.
In trenches	17/4/16		In trenches enemy very quiet, weather dull and extremely wet. Artillery on both sides very inactive. One man killed	
"	18/4/16		In trenches, very quiet, weather disagreeable, continuous rain in afternoon and during night.	
"	19/4/16		In trenches. very quiet, weather still wet. much work being done on parapet, parados and on wire out in front.	
"	20/4/16		In trenches, weather improves slightly. Operation Orders No 15 issued and attached. Battalion relieved by 1st Royal Scots. relief completed by 11 pm. battalion marched to CROIX BARBEE and was billeted there as Brigade reserve; two men wounded.	XV.

WAR DIARY
or
INTELLIGENCE SUMMARY
(Erase heading not required.)

Army Form C. 2118

Place	Date	Hour	Summary of Events and Information	Remarks and references to Appendices
CROIX BARBEE	21/4/16		In Billets. Brigade Reserve. Companies resting. Checking and issuing new clothing equipment etc. Working parties in the evening.	
"	22/4/16		In Billets. Working parties required from 7 a.m. to 7 p.m. Weather greatly improved, slight shelling by enemy's artillery.	
"	23/4/16		In billets. Working parties required. Bathing of men. Training of specialists, slight shelling in afternoon, no damage done.	
"	24/4/16		In billets. Operation Orders No XVI issued and attached. Battalion relieved 17th Royal Scots, relief completed by 10.45 pm. Enemy machine guns extremely active on 18th Bn. Shelled BOIS DE BIEZ towards midnight.	XVI
IN TRENCHES	25/4/16		In trenches. Enemy's artillery extremely active, shelled our trenches & front & Bn H.Qrs. practically all day. In afternoon 28 shells 8" were fired. One communication trench absolutely blown in. H.E. and light shrapnel were liberally used. One man killed three wounded.	
"	26/4/16		In trenches. Enemy's artillery extremely active, reserve lines, Bn. H.Qrs. and communication trenches heavily shelled with 8" and Shrapnel some damage done to communication trenches, one man killed two wounded.	
"	27/4/16		In trenches. At 3.30 pm our combined T.M. Stokes Guns & Heavy Light Artillery opened fire for the purpose of cutting enemy's wire and making a breach in parapet. Some damage was done in two places parts of parapet blown in, wire was cut in three places. Enemy retaliated with 8" and shrapnel no damage done. 2 men killed and 2 wounded.	
"	28/4/16		In trenches. Battalion relieved by 23rd Manchester Regt., 104th Brigade. Operation Orders No 17 issued and attached. Battalion marched to FOSSE relief completed by 9.35 pm.	XVII

1875 Wt. W593/826 1,000,000 4/15 J.B.C. & A. A.D.S.S./Forms/C. 2118.

Place	Date	Hour	Summary of Events and Information	Remarks and references to Appendices
IN BILLETS	29/4/16		In Billets. Battalion resting, checking and issuing of equipment, clothing etc. Battalion in Divisional Reserve at FOSSE.	
"	30/4/16		In Billets. Battalion resting. Large fatigue parties required, specialists under instruction.	

Copy No. 18

OPERATION ORDERS, No. 11.

18th (S) BN. H. L. INFANTRY.   3.4.16.

Reference 1/40,000 Map Sheet 36.
----

1. The 20th Lancashire Fusiliers will relieve the Battalion in the right subsection of the PETILLON Section on the morning of the 4th April and night of 4th/5th, as follows :-

   "X" Coy. Lanc. Fusiliers relieves "W" Coy. H. L. I.
   "   "   "   "   "   "Y" "   " " "
   "   "   "   "   "   "X" "   " " "
   "   "   "   "   "   "Z" "   " " "

2. The relief of Lewis Guns, Signallers, Snipers, and Bombers will be carried out on the morning of the 4th, and will be completed by 7 A.M. Guides will be sent to meet these parties at the entrance to V. C. Communication Trench, in the ROUGE DU BOIS at 6 A.M.

3. 1 Officer per Coy. and 1 N. C. O. per platoon of the Lancashire Fusiliers will go into the trenches to-night for the purpose of taking over stores, etc. Guides from each platoon will be sent to meet these parties at entrance to V.C. Communication Trench.

4. The incoming Battalion will use BOND STREET and V. C. AVENUE Communication Trenches. "W" Coy. will come out by BOND STREET. "Z" Coy. by REGENT AVENUE, - "X" & "Y" Coys. by V.C. AVENUE.

   On being relieved, all parties and Companies will proceed to huts about RUE FOURNAIZE & South East, (G.22.b. to G.28.c.)

   All trench stores will be handed over, and receipts obtained and forwarded to the Adjt. on the morning after relief.

   Details of each relief to be reported to Batn. HQ. Tpn. by 'phone.

                             (Sgd).   W. E. LYLE, Lt. & Adj.
                                       18th (S) BN. H. L. INFANTRY.

   12 noon.

   Filed.
   War Diary.
   "W" Coy.
   "X" "
   "Y" "
   "Z" "
   Machine Gun Officer.

Copy No.1

OPERATION ORDERS, No. 12.

18th (S) Battn. HIGHLAND LIGHT INFANTRY.

Reference 1/40,000.   Map Sheet, 36.   11.4.16.

1. The 106th Brigade will relieve 105th Brigade on the FAUQUISSART Sect-ion on the night of 12/13th April. The Battalion will relieve 15th SHERWOOD FORESTERS at LAVENTIE in Brigade Reserve to Right Subsection.

2. Posts and Billets are alloted as follows :-
"Z" Coy - No. 1 Billets. Y Coy.- No. 2 Billets. X Coy.-No.3 Billets with 1 platoon as garrison for ESQUIN POST. "W" Coy.- 1 Officer & two platoons at WANGERIE POST, 1 platoon and 1 Lewis Gun, MASSELOT POST; 1 Officer, 1 platoon, and 1 Lewis Gun at ROAD BEND POST; 1 Section and 1 Lewis Gun at MASSELOT HOUSE; 1 section and 1 Lewis Gun at GRA POST. Headquarters, 2 Lewis Guns detachments, Signallers and Bombers at Hd.Qr. Billets, LAVENTIE.

3. Companies will pass Cross Roads at S.34.d.2.8. at 3 minutes interval as follows:- "W" Coy. and Lewis Gun detachment for posts at 8.15 P.M. X Coy. 8.18 P.M. "Y" Coy. 8.21 P.M. "Z" Coy. & Hd.Qr. units at 8.24 P.M.

4. Billeting parties of 1 Officer and 1 N.C.O. per Coy. and Hd.Qrs. will be at LAVENTIE CHURCH at 9 A.M. to take over Stores in back posts & Billets.

5. All Stores in Billets and posts will be taken over; receipts given & lists forwarded to Adjt.

6. All movements S' of BAC ST MAUR - ESTAIRES Road will be by Companies, and S' of the LAVENTIE - LA DRUMEZ Road by platoons at 2 minutes interval.

7. Quarter-Master Stores and 1st Line Transport will move to new Billets to be notified later.

8. Battalion Hd.Qrs. will close at SAILLY at 8 P.M. and will re-open at LAVENTIE at 9 P.M.

                                (Sgd) W. J. LYLE, Lieut. & Adjt.
                                18th (Ser) Battn. H. L. INFANTRY.

Issued at 9 P.M.
Copy No.1 Filed in War Diary.   Copy No.6. To O.C. "Z" Coy.
"   " 2 "   " O.O. File.   "   " 7. " M.G. Officer.
"   " 3 To"   O.C. "W" Coy.   "   " 8. " Signalling Officer.
"   " 4 "   "   "X" "   "   " 9. " Transport Off. & QrMr.
"   " 5 "   "   "Y" "   "   " 10. " 2nd in Command.

Secret. Copy No. 1

OPERATION ORDERS No. 13.

18th (S) Battn. HIGHLAND LIGHT INFANTRY.

Reference 1/40,000 Combined Sheet, BETHUNE. 14/4/16.

1. 106th Brigade will be relieved from the FAUQUISSART Section on 15th of April by the 115th Brigade. The Battalion will be relieved from Brigade Reserve by 16th WELSH REGIMENT.

2. (a) X & Z Coys. & Hd.Qrs. will be relieved at 12.20 P.M. Guides for incoming Coys. & Hd.Qrs. to be at Level Crossing, M.4.a.9½.10. at 12.15 P.M. On relief these two Coys. & Hd.Qrs. will march to billets at ESTAIRES.

   (b) W & Y Coys. will be relieved after 6.30 P.M. Guides for each post and Coy. billet to be at LAVENTIE CHURCH at 6.30 P.M. After relief these Coys. will march to billets at ESTAIRES.

   (c) Lewis Guns in posts will be relieved after 9 A.M. Guides for each Gun to be at LAVENTIE CHURCH at 9 A.M. On relief these guns & teams will join Headquarters.

3. 1 G.S. Waggon for transport of blankets and Coy. Stores will be alloted to each Company.

4. All Keeps, Supporting points and billet Stores will be handed over receipts obtained and forwarded to Adjutant.

5. All movements South of the ESTAIRES - BAC ST MAUR Road will be by Coys. at 2 minutes interval, and all movements South of the railway by Platoons at 2 minutes interval.

6. Battalion Headquarters at LAVENTIE will close at 12.30 P.M.

(Sgd) W. J. LYLE, Lieut. & Adjt.
18th (S) BN. H. L. INFANTRY.

Issued at 5 P.M.

Copies No. 1 & 2. War Diary.   Copy No. 7. M.G. Off.
Copy. " 3. O.C. W. Coy.   "   " 8. Med. Off.
  "   " 4. "   X   "   "   " 9. Sig. Offr
  "   " 5. "   Y   "   "   " 10. 2nd in Command.
  "   " 6. "   Z   "

Copy No. 1

OPERATION ORDERS No. 14.

18th (Ser) Battn. H. L. INFANTRY.   14/4/16.

Reference Map 1/40,000, Sheet 36 & 36A.

1. The 106th Brigade will relieve the 86th Brigade in the NEUVE CHAPPELLE Section on the night of the 16-17th April. The Battalion will relieve the 7th EAST LANCASHIRE REGT. in the right subsection on the night of 16-17th April.(carried out)

2. Relief will be as follows :—
   X Coy. 18th H.L.I. relieves B Coy. 7th E.LANC.Rgt. on the right of the subsection
   Y "   "   "   " A   "   "   "   "   "   " centre   do
   Z "   "   "   " C   "   "   "   "   "   " Left   do
   W "   "   "   " D   "   "   "   "   "   In Reserve at Battn. Hd.Qrs.

3. Garrisons for posts will be found as follows :—
   Z Coy. 1 N.C.O. & 20 rifles.....................HILL REDOUBT.
   W "   1 Off. & 1 Platoon (not less than 30)....PORT ARTHUR.
   W "   1 Off. & 1 Platoon (not less than 30)....LANSDOWNE POST.

(4. The relief of Machine Gunners will be carried out before 2 P.M. on 16th
    "   "   " Snipers & Signallers   " "   "   "   "   "

5. Communication Trenches will be used as follows :—
   WINDY CORNER.... X Coy.
   OXFORD STREET... Z " & HILL REDOUBT Garrison.
   HUN STREET...... Y " W Coy. Hd.Qrs. and PORT ARTHUR Garrison. (-en

6. Companies and Garrisons for Posts will leave Billets in following order
   X Coy. Y Coy. Z Coy. & HILL REDOUBT, PORT ARTHUR, W Coy. Reserve,
   LANSDOWNE POST, HEADQRS. Bombers etc. The leading platoon of X Coy.
   will not pass EUSTON POST before 8.30 P.M.

7. X Coy. will find Guard of 4 men for NOIT MAISON, N. R. 24.C.0.0.
   Y "   "   "   "   " "   "   "   FOSSE POST   R. 21.A.3.5.
   W "   " find a Guard of 1 N.C.O. & 3 men for EUSTON POST. All
   bicycles of Orderlies & Signallers will be left at the post. The
   Guard will mount at 3.30 P.M. on the 16th.

8. The Adjt. or R.S.M. will proceed to the trenches to take over
   stores, maps etc. Guides to meet them will be at EUSTON POST at 2 P.M.
   Guides for each platoon and post will be at EUSTON CORNER at 8.30 P.M.

9. 1 Officer per Coy. & 1 N.C.O. per platoon will proceed to the Trenches
   on 15th inst. to take over stores, etc. Guides to meet them will be
   at EUSTON CORNER at 6.30 P.M.

10. 1 Limber Waggon will be allotted to each Coy. for rations, company
    baggage and stores. These waggons will only be taken as far as
    EUSTON POST, and rations and baggage must be carried from there.

11. All movements N. of the LAWE RIVER will be by platoons at 2 minutes
    intervals and by sections S. of the CROIX BARBEE.

12. Relief of each Coy. & Post to be reported by telephone or wire to
    Battn. Hd. Qrs.

13. Battn. Hd.Qrs. will be at S.4.B.6.1.

                (Sgd)   W. J. LYLE, Lieut. & Adjt.
                         18th (Ser) Battn. H. L. Infantry.

Issued at 7.30 P.M.

Copy No. 1) War Diary.   Copy No. 6. to O. C. "Z" Coy.
 "   " 2)   "   " 7. " Sig. Officer.
 "   " 3 to O.C. "W" Coy.   "   " 8. " M.G.
 "   " 4 "   " "X" "   "   " 9. " 2nd in Command.
 "   " 5 "   " "Y" "   "   " 10. " O.O. File.

SECRET.   Copy No. 1

OPERATION ORDERS No. 15.
18th (SER) BATTN. HIGHLAND LIGHT INFANTRY.
                                                                          19.4.16.

Reference 1/40,000 Sheet, 36A.

1. The Battalion will be relieved by 17th Royal Scots in the Right Sub-section on the night of 20th/21st April.

2. Snipers will be relieved by 6 A.M. Lewis Gun Detachment by 10 A.M. Signallers by 12 noon on the 20th.

3. X Coy. will be relieved by W Coy. Royal Scots, in Right of Line.
    Y "   "   "   "   " X "   "   "   " Centre.
    Z "   "   "   "   " Y "   "   "   " Left.
    W "   "   "   "   " Z "   "   "   " Reserve and in
                                                        (Posts.

4. Guides for each platoon & Post, with the exception of those for Right Coy. & LANSDOWNE POST, will be at Battalion Headquarters at 6.15 P.M. The Guides for Right Company and LANSDOWNE POST will be at Cross Roads, M.32.B.6.8. at 7 P.M.

5. Relief of each Post and Company will be reported to Battn. HdQrs. by telephone or Orderly as soon as completed.

6. Each Company and Post on being relieved will march to Billets at CROIX BARBEE where C.Q.M.Sgts. will be to guide them.

7. W Coy. will relieve a Garrison of ST. VAAST POST with 1 Officer and 30 men. Guides to meet this Garrison will be at EUSTON CORNER at 2.30 P.M. This post will be relieved by 1 Off. & 30 men from Y Coy. before 6 P.M. on 21st inst.

8. Z Coy. will be the close Support Company.   Battalion Headquarters will be at PENIN MARIAGE on completion of relief.

                                    (Sgd) W.J. LYLE, Lieut. & Adjt.
                                    18th (S) BN. HIGHLAND LIGHT INFANTRY.

Issued at 6 P.M.

Copy No. 1 & 2........ War Diary.
  "   "   3........... O.C. "W" Coy.
  "   "   4........... " " "X" "
  "   "   5........... " " "Y" "
  "   "   6........... " " "Z" "
  "   "   7........... Machine Gun Officer.
  "   "   8........... Medical Officer.
  "   "   9........... Signalling Officer.
  "   " 10........... 2nd in Command.

SECRET.   Copy No. 1

OPERATION ORDERS No. 16.

18th (SER) BATTN. HIGHLAND L. INFANTRY.

Reference 1/40,000 Combined Sheet.   23.4.16.
....

1. The Battalion will relieve the 17th Royal Scots in the Right Sub-Section of NEUVE CHAPPELLE Sector on the 24th instant.

2. The relief of Machine Gunners will be completed by 10 A.M., Signallers by 12 noon, Snipers by 9 A.M.

3. "X" Coy. will hold the right of the line, "Y" Coy. the Centre, "W" Coy. the left, "Z" Coy. in Reserve.

4. Posts will be garrisoned as follows, :-

   LANSDOWNE POST,   1 Off. & not less than 50 men.   Z Coy.
   PORT ARTHUR,   1   "   "   "   "   30 "   Z "
   HILLS REDOUBT,   21 N.C.Os and men,............   W "
   EUSTON POST, Z Coy Guard of 1 N.C.O. & 4 men (to mount by 3 P.M.)

5. Companies and posts will pass EUSTON CORNER as follows :-

   "W" Coy. & HILLS REDOUBT Garrison, at 8.25 P.M.
   "Y" "   ....   " 8.35 P.M.
   PORT ARTHUR Garrison.............   " 8.45 P.M.
   Reserve Platoons, Z Coy..........   " 8.50 P.M.

   "X" Coy. and LANSDOWNE POST Garrison will pass the Shrine, (M.32.D.7.3.) at 7.45 P.M. and 7.55 P.M. respectively.

6. Guides for each platoon and post will be at EUSTON CORNER and the Shrine at hours stated above.

7. Report of Relief of each Company and Post to be reported to Battn. Hd.Qrs. EDGWARE Road.

                          (Sgd) W. J. LYLE, Lieut. & Adjt.
                      18th (SER) BN. HIGHLAND LIGHT INFANTRY.

Issued at... 5/pm ....
Copy No. 1 & 2. Filed.
  "   " 3, "W" Coy.
  "   " 4, "X" "
  "   " 5, "Y" "
  "   " 6, "Z" "
  "   " 7, M.G. Off. & Sig. Officer.
  "   " 8, 2nd in Command, & Med. Off.

N.B. The CROIX-BARBEE-ROUGE CROIX road will not be used.

SECRET.   Copy No. 1

OPERATION ORDERS No. 17.

18th (S) BN. HIGHLAND LIGHT INFANTRY.
                                                           27.4.16.

Reference 1/40,000 Combined Sheet.

1. The Battalion will be relieved by the 23rd Manchester Regt. in the Right Sub-Section on the night 28th/29th April.

2. The relief of Battalion Snipers, Signallers, and Lewis Gun Detachment will be completed by 12 noon, 28th.

3. "X" Coy. will be relieved by "W" Coy. 23rd Manch.Rgt. in Right of Line.
   "Y" "   "   "   "   " "Z" "   "   "   " " Centre " "
   "W" "   "   "   "   " "Y" "   "   "   " " Left   " "
   "Z" "   "   "   "   " "X" "   "   "   " " Reserve and
                                                                 (Posts.

4. Guides for each platoon and post, with the exception of those for Right Coy. and LANSDOWNE POST, will be at Battalion Hd.Qrs. at 6.15 P.M. The guides for Right Coy. and LANSDOWNE POST will be at Shrine, Cross Roads, M.32.B.6.8. at 7 P.M.

5. Relief of each Post and Company will be reported to Battn. Hd.Qrs. by telephone or orderly as soon as completed.

6. Each Company or Post on being relieved will march to billets at FOSSE where C.Q.M.Sgts. will be to guide them.

7. Bridge Guards at VIEILLE CHAPELLE will be relieved by 10 A.M. on 28th as follows.:-

   "W" Coy. FOSSE CHATEAU Bridge   R.15.B.1.1.   1 N.C.O. & 1 man.
   "X" "   "   "   "   R.15.D.2.4.   1   "   & 1 "
   "Y" "   FOSSE Bridge.   R.21.B.3.5.   2 men.

   These men will report at Bn.Hd.Qrs. at 6 P.M. 27th inst.

8. Battalion Headquarters will be at FOSSE on completion of relief.

                              (Sgd) W. J. LYLE, Lieut. & Adjt.
                         18th (Ser) BATTN. HIGHLAND LIGHT INFANTRY.

Issued at.. 1 P.M.

Copy No. 1 & 2. War Diary.
  "   "   3. O. C. "W" Coy.
  "   "   4.   " " "X" "
  "   "   5.   " " "Y" "
  "   "   6.   " " "Z" "
  "   "   7. Machine Gun Officer.
  "   "   8. Medical Officer.
  "   "   9. Signalling Officer.
  "   " 10. 2nd in Command.

WAR DIARY
or
INTELLIGENCE SUMMARY
(Erase heading not required.)

Army Form C. 2118

Place	Date	Hour	Summary of Events and Information	Remarks and references to Appendices
FOSSE	1/5/16		In Billets. Battalion resting, officers i/c. Machine Gunners, Signallers, bombers, Stretcher bearers, training instructors etc. at and another large fatigue parties required daily	
"	2/5/16		In billets " " " " " "	
"	3/5/16		" " " " " "	
"	4/5/16		In Billets. Battalion left fort in Brigade Concentration March. distance about 12 miles, weather very hot.	
"	5/5/16		In Billets. Battalion resting previous to taking over Brigade Reserve. Operation Orders No 18 issued and attached.	No XVIII
Sanctuary	6/5/16		In Brigade Reserve, Battalion took over from 15th Sherwood Fors.'s 105th of Brigade. Two battalions 17th R. devts and 9th W. York R. in front line.	
"	7/5/16		In Brigade Reserve. Situation quiet. Flang-fatigue parties required at night for repair of trench etc.	

2. P.
5 sheet

WAR DIARY or **INTELLIGENCE SUMMARY**
(Erase heading not required.)

Army Form C. 2118

Place	Date	Hour	Summary of Events and Information	Remarks and references to Appendices
In trenches	9/5/16		In Brigade Reserve. Very quiet day. One man wounded while on working party night 8/7/8.	
"	9/5/16		In Brigade Reserve. Very quiet day, weather disagreeable and very cold. Chinese trench No. XIX nearer and clearer.	No XIX
"	10/5/16		In trenches. Battalion took over from 17th R. Scots in right sub-section of the line. relief completed by	
"	11/5/16		In trenches. Weather bad, enemy extremely inactive, slight artillery activity on our right. Men hard at work repairing trench and building communication trenches.	
"	12/5/16		In trenches. " " very quiet day. Working parties out during day and night.	
"	13/5/16		In trenches. Slight Staff by Brigade on our left; inconsiderable retaliation by enemy, one man wounded.	
"	14/5/16		In trenches. Battalion relieved by 17th R. Scots; relief completed by 10 P.M. no casualties. Chinese trench No XX nearer and clearer.	XX
MACOQRIE	15/5/16		In Brigade Reserve. Weather stormy, rain all night.	

WAR DIARY
or
INTELLIGENCE SUMMARY
(Erase heading not required.)

Army Form C. 2118

Instructions regarding War Diaries and Intelligence Summaries are contained in F. S. Regs., Part II. and the Staff Manual respectively. Title Pages will be prepared in manuscript.

Place	Date	Hour	Summary of Events and Information	Remarks and references to Appendices
LACOUTRE	16/5/16		In Brigade Reserve. Battalion finding large fatigue parties. weather fine.	
"	17/5/16		" " " "	
"	18/5/16		In Brigade Reserve. Operation Order No. XXI issued and attack. 8/3 Reliever 17th R. Scots. relief completed by 10.35 p.m. no casualties.	No. XXI
"	19/5/16		In trenches. Weather fine. men have at work repairing trenches kits, parts and communication trenches. enemy especially quiet. 1 man killed 1 wounded.	
"	20/5/16		In trenches. " " " " " " " " " " " " " " " " enemy slightly active. two men wounded. One of our aeroplanes brought down by them. it landed in our lines. our wind motors demolished it. In trenches. usual work going on. Our artillery shelling Huns rather heavier and hills. slight retaliation by truly.	
"	21/5/16			

WAR DIARY
or
INTELLIGENCE SUMMARY
(Erase heading not required.)

Army Form C. 2118

Instructions regarding War Diaries and Intelligence Summaries are contained in F.S. Regs., Part II. and the Staff Manual respectively. Title Pages will be prepared in manuscript.

Place	Date	Hour	Summary of Events and Information	Remarks and references to Appendices
In Trenches	22/5/16		In trenches. Batt'n relieved by 23rd Manchester Regt. 104th Bde. Operation order N° 22 issued and attached. Battalion marched to Vieille Chapelle. Relief complete 10·30 p.m.	XXII
Vieille Chapelle	23/5/16		In billets. Battalion resting, bathing and viewing of equipment, clothing, etc. Battalion in Divisional Reserve at VIEILLE CHAPELLE.	
"	24/5/16		In billets in Divisional Reserve. Range working parties required at RICHEBOURG from 24th to 30th inclusive. Companies at training in wiring and offensive operation. Specialist under instruction.	
"	25/5/16		In billets. Companies at Physical Training, rifle drill and route march.	
"	26/5/16		In billets. Companies at Physical training, wiring, and practice of offensive operation.	
"	27/5/16		In billets. Companies at Physical training, rifle drill and Route Marching. Signallers, Machine Gunners, & Bombers under instruction.	
"	28/5/16		In billets. Companies at Physical Training, wiring and offensive operation.	

WAR DIARY
or
INTELLIGENCE SUMMARY
(Erase heading not required.)

Army Form C. 2118

Place	Date	Hour	Summary of Events and Information	Remarks and references to Appendices
VIEILLE CHAPPELLE	28/5/16		In billets. Operation Orders XXIII issued and attacked. Battalion marched to relieve the 1/4 Beech Hatch, 118th Brigade. Relief complete by 10:15 p.m.	XXIII
FESTUBERT	29/5/16		In Brigade Support. Battalion in close support to 17th ROYAL SCOTS & 17th WEST YORKS in the line. 19th DURHAM LIGHT INFANTRY in Reserve. Men improving trenches at Keeps & Posts. Very quiet day.	
"	30/5/16		In Brigade Support. Quiet day. Large working parties required during the day and night. In the evening considerable artillery activity on our right.	
"	31/5/16		In Brigade Support. Very quiet day. Weather fine. Large working parties in the evening. Operation Orders No XXIV issued and attacked.	XXIV

WAR DIARY
or
INTELLIGENCE SUMMARY

(Erase heading not required.)

Army Form C. 2118

18. H.L.I.
Vol 5
June

Place	Date	Hour	Summary of Events and Information	Remarks and references to Appendices
FESTUBERT	1/6/16		In Brigade Support. One Company of the 2/4th Gloster Regt attached to Battalion for instruction. Battalion relieved the 9th D.L.I. on our left & the Kings Royal Rifles on our right. Relief complete by 11 p.m. One man wounded.	XXV
IN TRENCHES	2/6/16		In Trenches enemy very quiet, men hard at work repairing & improving trenches by day and constructing islands during by night. One man wounded, one officer killed.	
"	3/6/16		In Trenches enemy very active, very little Machine Gun rifle fire at night. Large working parties at islands at night. One man killed.	
"	4/6/16		" " " "	
"	5/6/16		" " " Operation Orders No 25 issued and attached. One man killed.	
FESTUBERT	6/6/16		" " " enemy very inactive. Battalion relieved by 17th Royal Scots & marched to posts & billets in FESTUBERT. Relief completed by 10.50 p.m. No casualties.	
"	7/6/16		In Brigade Support. Very quiet day, men working repairing posts & keeps. Large working parties at night. One man of working party killed.	
"	8/6/16		In Brigade Support. Companies at Battling practice firing. Physical drill. Large working parties in the evening.	
"	9/6/16		In Brigade Support. Companies under instruction in bombing visiting. Specialists at training. Large working parties in the evening.	
"	10/6/16		In Brigade Support. Companies under instruction in bombing and wiring. Large fatigue and working parties in the evening.	
"	11/6/16		In Brigade Support. Operation Orders No 26 issued and attached. Relief completed by 11 p.m. Battalion marched to Billets at VIEILLE CHAPELLE. The Brigade was relieved by the 117th Brigade and the Battalion by the Rifle Brigade.	O. O. 8 mls XXVI

Army Form C. 2118

WAR DIARY
INTELLIGENCE SUMMARY
(Erase heading not required.)

Instructions regarding War Diaries and Intelligence Summaries are contained in F. S. Regs., Part II. and the Staff Manual respectively. Title Pages will be prepared in manuscript.

Place	Date	Hour	Summary of Events and Information	Remarks and references to Appendices
VIEILLE CHAPELLE	12/6/16		In Billets Battalion resting, bathing and refitting	XXVII.
"	13/6/16		" " " " " "	
"	14/6/16		" " " " " "	
"	15/6/16		Operation Orders No. 27 issued and attached. Battalion marched to Gonnehem, was relieved at Vieille Chapelle by the 1st Herts, 39th Division	
GONNEHEM	16/6/16		In Billets Battalion resting in Corps Reserve	
"	17/6/16		" " refitting	
"	18/6/16		Battalion training. Machine Gun and Signalling classes commenced	
"	19/6/16		In Billets Company parades Physical training, Rifle and Close order Drill Bathing & route Marching	
"	20/6/16		" " " " " " "	
"	21/6/16		Same programme	
"	22/6/16		" " " " " " "	
"	23/6/16		" " " " " " "	
"	24/6/16		Divisional Operations 2yA signalling to Aeroplanes by means of smoke candles, bombs, mirrors and flares turned all day. Operations quite successful.	XXVII A
"	25/6/16		Divine Service. In afternoon had a swimming competition with 17th Royal Scots	
"	26/6/16		Brigade Field day. Rained all day thunder and lightning, men were soaked but quite cheerful	
"	27/6/16		Battalion took part in Brigade Field day, communication with aeroplanes. In afternoon there was a Brigade Horse show. The Battalion took four 2nd and one 3rd prizes	

1875 Wt. W593/826 1,000,000 4/15 J,B.C. & A. A.D.S.S./Forms/C.2118.

Army Form C. 2118

WAR DIARY
~~INTELLIGENCE SUMMARY~~
(Erase heading not required.)

Instructions regarding War Diaries and Intelligence Summaries are contained in F. S. Regs., Part II. and the Staff Manual respectively. Title Pages will be prepared in manuscript.

Place	Date	Hour	Summary of Events and Information	Remarks and references to Appendices
GONNEHEM	28/6/16		In Billets. Specialists at instruction, companies at drill, physical training and Route marching	
	29/6/16		" " " " " "	
	30/6/16		" " " " " "	

1875 Wt. W 593/826 1,000,000 4/15 J.B.C. & A. A.D.S.S./Forms/C. 2118.

SECRET. Copy No. 2

OPERATION ORDERS, No. 25.

18th (SER) BATTALION HIGHLAND LIGHT INFANTRY.

Reference Sheet, 1/40,000, BETHUNE.   4th JUNE 1916.

1. The Battalion will be relieved by the 17th ROYAL SCOTS in the Right Subsection of the FESTUBERT SECTION on the night of the 5th-6th June.

2. Guides for each platoon will be sent to Eastern End of roads and communication trenches as follows at 8.45 P.M.
   - "W" Company .... FESTUBERT.
   - "X"   "   .... BARTON TRENCH.
   - "Y"   "   .... WILLOW ROAD.
   - "Z"   "   .... CHESHIRE ROAD.

3. Guides to conduct Island parties will be at junction of BARTON ROAD and O.B.L. at 7.30 P.M.

4. Lewis Gun Detachments in the Islands will be relieved tonight, and will return to O.B.L. Relief of Snipers, Signallers, and Lewis Gun Detachments will be completed by 12 noon to-morrow.

5. Parties for Billet Guards, Keeps, and Control Posts will be sent to take over the various duties at 2.30 P.M. to-morrow, 1 Officer from each Coy. will conduct these parties.

6. On completion of relief, Coys. will proceed to billets & posts in the VILLAGE LINE.

7. Relief of each Island & Company to be reported by signal, T.G.

         (Sgd) W. F. M. MACARA, 2/Lieut. Ac/Adjt.

         18th (Ser) BATTN. HIGHLAND LIGHT INFANTRY.

Issued at 5 P.M.

Copy No. 1 & 2. War Diary.
       3. O. O. File.
       4. "W" Coy.
       5. "X" "
       6. "Y" "
       7. "Z" "
       8. Machine Gun Officer.
       9. Medical Officer.
     10. 2nd in Command.
     11. 17th ROYAL SCOTS.

SECRET. Copy No. 2

OPERATION ORDERS No. 46.

18th (SER) BATTALION HIGHLAND LIGHT INFANTRY. 10.6.16.

Reference 1/40,000 BETHUNE Sheet.

1. The 106th Brigade will be relieved by 117th Brigade in FEST-UBERT Section on night 11/12th June. The Battalion will be relieved by the 18th Rifle Brigade in the VILLAGE LINE about 10.30 p.m.

2. All Maps, Keep & Supporting Point Stores will be handed over and Receipts obtained & forwarded to the Adjutant by 12 noon 12th.

3. Control Posts & Caretaking Guards will be relieved on afternoon of 11th.

4. On each Platoon and Post being relieved, it will march via KING'S ROAD & Road N.E. of LOISNE RIVER, to its old billets at VIEILLE CHAPELLE.

5. O. C. Coys. will report their relief either in person or by written message to Battalion Headquarters.

(Sgd) W. J. LYLE, Lieut. & Adjutant.
18th (Ser) BATTN. HIGHLAND LIGHT INFANTRY.

Issued at 11.30 a.m.

Copy No. 1 & 2... Filed in War Diary.
        3... O. C. "W" Coy.
        4... O. C. "X" "
        5... O. C. "Y" "
        6... O. C. "Z" "
        7... Machine Gun Officer.
        8... 2nd in Command.
        9... Sig. Off. & Med. Off.
       10... Oper. Order File.

SECRET.   Copy No. 2

OPERATION ORDERS, No. 27.   15th June 1916.
16th (Ser) BATTN. HIGHLAND LIGHT INFANTRY.

Reference Map 1/40,000, BETHUNE Combined Sheet.

1. The 106th (Infantry) Brigade will march to billets in the neighbourhood of GONNEHEM to-morrow. The Battalion will march to billets in GONNINGHEM.

2. The Battalion will pass Point, R.27.D.5.3. in the following Order, at 8.30 A.M. :- Signallers, "Y" Coy., "Z" Coy, Band, "X" Coy., "W" Coy., Bombers, Machine Gunners.

3. 1st Line Transport will follow in rear of Machine Gunners. 2nd Line Transport will pass X.1.d.7.8. at 10.30 A.M.

4. The Medical Officer will march in rear of the Battalion.

5. Coy. Qr.Mr. Sergts. will parade at Battn. Orderly Room, at 7.15 A.M. and proceed with 2/Lieut. Fitzpatrick to arrange billets.

6. O. C. "W" Coy. will detail a Rear Guard of 1 Officer, and 12 men to collect and bring in all stragglers.

7. Reports to Head of Battalion.

    (Sgd) W. J. LYLE, Lieut. & Adjt.
  16th (Ser) Battn. HIGHLAND LIGHT INFANTRY.

Issued at 11 P.M.

Copy No. 1 & 2. Filed in War Diary.
   3. O. C. "W" Coy.
   4. O. C. "X" "
   5. O. C. "Y" "
   6. O. C. "Z" "
   7. Medical Officer.
   8. Machine Gun Officer.
   9. Signalling Officer.
   10. QuarterMaster.
   11. Transport Officer.
   12. 2nd in Command.
   13. Operation Order File.

SECRET.   Copy No. 8

OPERATION ORDERS No. 27a.
18th (Ser) BATTN. HIGHLAND LIGHT INFANTRY.

Reference BETHUNE, 1/40,000.   24th JUNE 1916.
----

1. The 106th Brigade will attack on a two Battalion Front, H.L.I. on right, and D.L.I. on left. Rendezvous for Bn. V.27.c.4.0.

2. "W" & "Z" Coys. will be in the first line. Frontage for each Coy. 200 yards.— "W" Coy. will direct line with its right on path leading from D.2.C.2.10. to D.9.C.7.4.
   "X" & "Y" Coys. will be 300 yards in rear in support of "W" and "Z" Coys.

3. The track through Woods D.2.B.3.2. — D.3.b.2.6. (Line A) will be reached by 10 A.M. by front line.
   Track D.3.C.1.1. — D.3.5.8½.7½. (Line B) will be reached by Front Line at 11 A.M. "Y" Coy. will re-inforce front line at this point.
   Track D.9.C.6.4. — D.10.a.4.1. (Line C) will be reached at 12 noon. "X" Coy. will reinforce front line at this point.

4. When an Aeroplane approaches and fires a white Very Light, meaning "where are you", each Coy. in front line, will let off 2 Groups of 4 flares in each, and when on line A & C, a smoke candle in addition will be burnt at the same time in each group. Vigilant periscopes will be flashed by men not firing flares or smoke candles.

5. Battalion Signalling Officer will arrange a ground signalling Shelter to send messages to the aeroplanes.

6. Battalion Hd.Qrs. will be about 100 yards in rear of support line, and on the left of the line.

            (Sgd) W. J. LYLE, Lieut. & Adjutant.
               18th (Ser) Battn. Highland Light Infantry.

Issued at 8 P.M.

Copy No. 1. "W" Coy.
        2. "X" Coy.
        3. "Y" "
        4. "Z" "
        5. Sig. Officer.
        6. File.
      7 & 8. War Diary.

18th (SERVICE) BATTALION HIGHLAND LIGHT INFANTRY.

SANITARY REPORT.

Week-Ending, 1st July 1916.

GOUZEAUCOURT, 1/7/16.

Food Supply................ Good.

Water Supply............... both Quantity) Fair.
                                     and Quality.)

General Health of Troops... Good,
but there is a great deal of foot trouble, which is due to wearing badly fitting boots.

Sanitation of Billets...... Poor.
Fly-proof latrines were built in all billets.
It is extremely difficult to con--trol the depositing of fresh manure by the inhabitants. Billets at times are overcrowded.

(Sgd)   C. G. McCLYMONT, Lieut.
          R. A. M. C.
M. O. 1/c 18th (S) Bn. H. L. INFANTRY.

106th Bde.
35th Div.

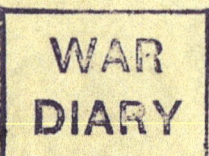

18th BATTALION

HIGHLAND LIGHT INFANTRY

1st to 31st JULY 1916.

Report on Operations 29/30th July
in G.S. War Diary.

D.Q.G.
Gn. Hd. Qrs.
3rd Echelon
~~Base~~

H 415
12.8.16.

Herewith copy of War Diary, for the month of July 1916, with copies of Operation Orders Nos 28-32 attached.

Please acknowledge receipt hereon.

W Macara
2nd Lieut
for. Lieut. Colonel.
Comdg. 18th (S)Bn. H.L.I.

12/8/16

WAR DIARY

INTELLIGENCE SUMMARY

Army Form C. 2118.

Vol 6

Place	Date	Hour	Summary of Events and Information	Remarks and references to Appendices
GONNEHEM.	1/7/16		In billets. Specialists at instruction; companies at drill, physical training and route marching.	
"	2/7/16		In billets. Operation Orders No 28 issued and attached. Instead of going by rail to GRAND RULLECOURT as per orders, the battalion went by rail to FRÉVENT. On arriving there we marched to BREVILLERS. Operation Orders amended, issued and attached. The men marched splendidly and carried an extremely heavy pack, waterproof and steel helmet. Distance about 6 miles.	XXVIII XXVIII A.
BREVILLERS.	3/7/16		In billets. Accommodation for men was, although rather crushed, ample; for officers however it was not sufficient, only 11 officers found billets, the remainder had to bivouac.	
"	4/7/16.		In billets. Checking and reissuing of kit and necessaries. Companies at Drill, wood fighting and route marching. Signalling and Machine gun classes under instruction.	
"	5/7/16.		In billets. Operation Orders No 29 issued and attached. Battalion marched as advanced guard to the Brigade. The men marched well considering that it was the first night march of any distance they had done. Distance 10 miles. No men fell out. Brigade is now in 8th Corps, 5th Army.	XXIX.

WAR DIARY
INTELLIGENCE SUMMARY.
(Erase heading not required.)

Army Form C. 2118.

Place	Date	Hour	Summary of Events and Information	Remarks and references to Appendices
BOIS DU WARNIMONT	6/7/16		In Wood. Officers and men billeted in huts in dense wood. Rain fell heavily all day, making ground, etc. in deplorable state. Transport horses had no cover of any description.	
"	7/7/16		In Wood. Instruction was carried out indoors owing to the wet weather. It rained practically all day.	
"	8/7/16		In Wood. Weather improved. Companies route marching, physical training and bayonet fighting. Machine Gun and Signalling classes under instruction. A boxing competition was held in which there were some rattling good fights.	
"	9/7/16		In Wood. Divine Service. Brigade Bombing Scheme carried out. In afternoon another boxing competition was held and at night the regimental football team played the R.A.M.C. We beat them 8 - 0.	
"	10/7/16		In Wood. Operation Orders No 30 issued and attached. Brigade split up. We are to be attached to the 29th Division for pioneer work. On reporting at H:d Q:rs 29th Division, we received orders that we were not to be attached to them. After waiting at MAILLY-MAILLET we received orders to proceed to VARENNES. On arriving there we found that the Brigade had been re-established and that the Brigade was moving South.	XXX
VARENNES.	11/7/16		In billets. Accommodation limited. All Officers in huts; half the men in ditto. This is	

Army Form C. 2118.

WAR DIARY
INTELLIGENCE SUMMARY.
(Erase heading not required.)

Instructions regarding War Diaries and Intelligence Summaries are contained in F.S. Regs., Part II. and the Staff Manual respectively. Title pages will be prepared in manuscript.

Place	Date	Hour	Summary of Events and Information	Remarks and references to Appendices
VARENNES (cont'd)	11/7/16		owing to two battalions being in one battalion area. C.O., 2nd in command and O.C. Coys away inspecting new line in view of our taking over.	
"	12/7/16		In billets. Companies at training for open warfare. Machine Gunners and Signallers at instruction.	
"	13/7/16		In billets. Operation Orders No 31 issued and attached. Brigade marched to BRESLE and arrived there at midnight. The whole battalion, with the exception of its transport, was billeted in one huge barn or store fitted with tier upon tier of shelves. The men were tired and soon fell asleep.	XXI
BRESLE	14/7/16		In billets. Operation Orders No 32 issued and attached. The Brigade marched to BOIS DU TAILLES. Accommodation bad and wood in a filthy state. After being there for about two hours orders were received that we had to move. The men had already done 10½ miles but were nevertheless in excellent spirits. Our destination was BILLON WOOD en route we marched through a big training centre. Just outside the camp there were numerous heavy guns which kept up a slow steady fire, they were 12" howitzers and 9.2". It was dark when we arrived at BILLON WOOD, and the Brigade bivouacked in the open. The night was cold and owing to the tremendous noise of the guns the men did not get much sleep.	XXII

WAR DIARY
INTELLIGENCE SUMMARY.
(Erase heading not required.)

Army Form C. 2118.

Place	Date	Hour	Summary of Events and Information	Remarks and references to Appendices
BRESLE (Cont'd)	14/7/16		We were lying about 100 yards from some 12" and 15" howitzers. There was a slight retaliation from the Hun.	
BILLON WOOD.	15/7/16		In the morning both Officers and men watched the big guns fire. At 10 a.m. orders for a move were received. At 11 a.m. the Brigade moved; the going was exceptionally bad and heavy. Mules and limbers stuck in the mud and eventually had to go by road. Our destination was TALUS BOISE. It was a re-entrant, and the wood itself but a few trees. In the valley were collected cavalry (5th D. Gds and Indian), artillery and infantry, all waiting to move. The battalion bivouacked in the open. One man wounded.	
TALUS BOISE	16/7/16		At 5 a.m. battalion marched to MONTAUBAN ALLEY TRENCH to the west of MONTAUBAN. There was a dense fog which made the move a safe one from the enemy's artillery. Tear gas in wood extremely strong. All men had to wear their tear goggles. On arriving at MONTAUBAN ALLEY we found it occupied by 10th N.W.Fs so that our men had to lie on reverse slope of parados. More or less quiet day. Towards evening an enemy observation balloon went up and within two or three minutes half-a-dozen shells landed among the men, 4 were killed and 3 wounded. They were accordingly moved into communication trenches. Only 22 Officers were with us, the remainder were left with transport. Slept there for the night.	

WAR DIARY
INTELLIGENCE SUMMARY.
(Erase heading not required.)

Army Form C. 2118.

Place	Date	Hour	Summary of Events and Information	Remarks and references to Appendices
MONTAUBAN.	17/7/16		Very heavy shelling from early morning. The Brigadier paid us a visit and the following scheme for the attack on GINCHY attached is sketch showing position and distribution previous to attack. The C.O., 2nd in command, O.C. Coys and the Signalling Officer proceeded on a reconnaissance of DELVILLE WOOD, and a most uncomfortable journey they had. It was a case of "Crump" right, left, before, behind. Shrapnel was bursting intermittently and dead bodies were in abundance. On return from the reconnaissance orders were received stating that the attack was cancelled. Later orders attached us to the 9th Division and to the 27th Brigade. The battalion accordingly moved to just in front of MONTAUBAN VILLAGE. Towards evening orders were received to send one company up to LONGUVAL VILLAGE to take over a part of the firing line. Z Coy accordingly went off and got into position without suffering casualties.	
"	18/7/16		In continuation of the previous evening's shelling the HUNS shelled DELVILLE WOOD, LONGUVAL, MONTAUBAN and all other points of importance. Towards 2 p.m. the bombardment increased in intensity, specially in direction of DELVILLE WOOD. Our artillery then opened a tremendous counter fire and placed a barrage on German front line. Towards 5 p.m. the shelling subsided and then it became known that the HUN had attacked, and at great loss captured	

WAR DIARY
INTELLIGENCE SUMMARY.
(Erase heading not required.)

Army Form C. 2118.

Place	Date	Hour	Summary of Events and Information	Remarks and references to Appendices
MONTAUBAN (Cont'd)	18/7/16		The biggest part of DELVILLE WOOD. The SOUTH AFRICAN SCOTTISH were badly cut up. Our casualties were heavy. During the first part of the bombardment "W" and "X" Coys were in support behind the wood and were in an exposed position. They were therefore ordered to retire but not until they had had 6 killed and 23 wounded. Up to 5 p.m. we had received word that Z Coy had had 2 killed and 11 wounded. Our artillery from 7 p.m. until well into the morning heavily bombarded the wood and the Hun positions.	
"	19/7/16		At 9 p.m. orders were received stating that the three remaining coys were attached to 26 Brigade and that the C.O. was required at Brigade Office. The C.O. returned about 12.15 a.m. and "Y" Coy was sent off to take over a part of firing line. Artillery activity on both sides was considerable, shells of every description were used. Many casualties in all units occupying the valley. Horses, mules and carts were virtually blown to pieces. At 1.30 p.m. a new brigade attacked DELVILLE WOOD and practically recaptured what they had lost the day before. In afternoon the Huns shelled the whole valley and orders were received that we were being relieved. The relief took place without incident so far as it concerned "W", "X" and "Z" coys. "Y" coy however were just being relieved when the HUNS counter attacked from TRONES WOOD and "Y" coy were caught by the Huns' barrage. The battalion marched	

Army Form C. 2118.

WAR DIARY
~~INTELLIGENCE SUMMARY.~~
(Erase heading not required.)

Instructions regarding War Diaries and Intelligence Summaries are contained in F. S. Regs., Part II. and the Staff Manual respectively. Title pages will be prepared in manuscript.

Place	Date	Hour	Summary of Events and Information	Remarks and references to Appendices
MONTAUBAN (contd)	19/7/16		to CARNOY and bivouacked for the night.	
CARNOY	20/7/16		In bivouac. Check roll call of men, total casualties 2 Officers wounded, 1 Officer missing, 25 men killed, 127 wounded, 13 missing, and 15 suffering from shell shock; making 183 casualties. Men resting and overhauling equipment.	
"	21/7/16		In Bivouac troops resting. enemy sent eight aeroplanes out and they passed over camp. Innumerable some twenty of our planes appeared and cleared the sky. At night the camp was shelled for half an hour. No casualties	
"	22/7/16		In Bivouac. Lovely weather companies out at drill had day's awork. Huns shelled Carnoy in forenoon and again towards 6 o'clock. We moved into trenches for safety and slept there the night.	
"	23/7/16		In Bivouac at 1:15am sudden orders were received for the battalion to move up into a position in reserve to huts at LONGUEVAL. The Battalion accordingly proceeded to place as ordered and hastily dug themselves in. They had more or less dug shelter when the Huns commenced shelling. An aeroplane one of our own, but presumably being used by the enemy dropped a Verey light over our position from then until 8am our position was under fire from every variety of shell. Men were killed others wounded while many were buried alive. Our casualties were heavy. Two Boche shells on the regiment accompanied by half a dozen smaller shells burst at Hd Qtrs. The escape was marvellous hardly half the	

WAR DIARY
INTELLIGENCE SUMMARY.
(Erase heading not required.)

Army Form C. 2118.

Instructions regarding War Diaries and Intelligence Summaries are contained in F.S. Regs., Part II. and the Staff Manual respectively. Title pages will be prepared in manuscript.

Place	Date	Hour	Summary of Events and Information	Remarks and references to Appendices
IN TRENCHES	24/7/16		dug-out fell in, but no one was hurt. During the remainder of the day we were bombarded at various hours and many men were hit.	
"			In trenches position was again bombarded. From method of shelling it was concluded that the enemy were not firing at our position, but were searching for batteries. Many of the shells came at a battery beside us missing by yards their objective, got our lines and casualties resulted. Towards evening the Hun counter attacked on Trones Wood and was repulsed with enormous loss. The artillery fire on both sides was terrific.	
"	25/7/16		In trenches positions again bombarded. Orders received that we would be relieved at 10.30 p.m. the Battalion was relieved by the Royal Fusiliers 2nd Division. Battalion marched back to old bivouacs at Carnoy. Our casualties from the 22nd were 1 Officer wounded and 75 men killed and wounded.	
CARNOY	26/7/16		In bivouacs all officers were thanked by General PINNEY for the work of the Battalion during the last 10 days. Battalion ordered to move at 9.30 P.M. to the new N of MARICOURT. The move was completed by 11 p.m. Companies moving off to their respective trenches independently. Battalion H.Qrs. was an old dug-out some twenty feet beneath the ground level. Our artillery bombarded enemy's positions especially DELVILLE WOOD from evening till dawn. An attack was in preparation for the taking of the wood and village	

WAR DIARY
or
INTELLIGENCE SUMMARY.
(Erase heading not required.)

Army Form C. 2118.

Place	Date	Hour	Summary of Events and Information	Remarks and references to Appendices
INTRENCHES	27/7/16		Artillery bombardment still continuing. Shells of every variety and size were flying through the air without a pause. The noise was deafening. Very little of the Huns retaliation troubled us in our trench. In the afternoon the enemy placed a tremendous barrage across the valley to the N.E. of our position. A few "crumps" and shrapnel landed in our vicinity. Towards evening the situation became more or less quiet again. Our attack in LONGUEVAL and DELVILLE WOOD had proved successful, both the village and wood changing hands. Some 400 prisoners were taken.	
"	28/7/16		The morning opened quietly, just a little spasmodic firing from our batteries. Towards noon fire became keener. Aerial reconnaissances frequent. No enemy planes visible. In afternoon enemy shelled ridge to N.W. of us and valley to N.E. In the evening the French opened a terrific fire with their artillery, this lasted for 15 minutes then quietened down. Our artillery then took up the gun and for some 60 minutes there was an infernal din. It gradually subsided to the usual odd shot now and again.	
"	29/7/16		Enemy sent several planes over our lines one of our airmen gallantly tackled four of them - but no casualties to either side resulted. In afternoon desultory shelling on both sides took place towards evening our fire became keener and for the remainder of the night held up fire.	
"	30/7/16		At 4.30 AM our troops, i.e. the 2nd Division from the N.W. the 90th Brigade from the west the 89th Brigade from the S.W. of Guillemont in conjunction with the French on the right attacked Guillemont and the positions. Owing to the	

WAR DIARY
INTELLIGENCE SUMMARY.
(Erase heading not required.)

Army Form C. 2118.

Instructions regarding War Diaries and Intelligence Summaries are contained in F. S. Regs., Part II. and the Staff Manual respectively. Title pages will be prepared in manuscript.

Place	Date	Hour	Summary of Events and Information	Remarks and references to Appendices
In Trenches	30/7/16		dense fog our infantry managed to get close in and surprised the Huns. Prisoners started coming in very early in the engagement some 200 passing our position within an hour. Our Battalion moved from SILESIA TRENCH to BERNAFAY TRENCH without casualties. At this point there was some horrible blocking of troops owing to two hasty orders for our advance being given. Fortunately no enemy shells landed on the road or trenches. News then came through that Guillemont had been captured but that our men had been driven out of the village again. MALTZ HORN FARM and ridge however had been taken and kept. In afternoon the adjutant proceeded to the ridge for orders but none were given. At 5.20 pm two companies were sent off to the Farm to reinforce the 90th Brigade in case of a counter-attack by the enemy. The other two marched to Carnoy and bivouaced for the night.	
CARNOY.	31/7/16		The Battalion moved at 8.30 am destination SAND PIT VALLEY. The two companies sent to 90th Brigade rejoined about 8 AM, but were too exhausted to continue the march they therefore stayed at CARNOY till 2 pm and then came on to the valley. Bivouaced there for the night.	

SECRET.   Copy No. _____

OPERATION ORDERS. No. 22.
18th (Ser) BATTN. HIGHLAND LIGHT INFANTRY.

2/7/16.

Reference 1/100000 LENS, 11.
    "   1/40000 BETHUNE Combined Sheet.
....

1. The Battalion will move on by road and rail to billets at GRAND RULLECOURT.

2. Companies will pass Starting Point, V.16.C.3.9. in following order, Hd.Qrs. & Bombers, W, Y, Z, X, the head of the column passing at 8.15 P.M. and marching to CHOCQUES station, and there entrain.

3. All Transport, Machine Gunners (22) Grooms, Medical Officer, and Medical Corporal will march in rear of Battalion and entrain in Brake Brigade Headquarters Train.

4. A loading party of 1 Officer and 25 men will be detailed by O. C. "W" Coy. to proceed to CHOCQUES Station, and report to R. T. O. three hours before departure of train.

5. Reports to Head of Column.

         (Sgd) W. J. Lyle, Lt. & Adjt.
    18th (Ser) Battn. HIGHLAND LIGHT INFANTRY.

Issued at 7 P.M.

Copy No. 1 & 2. War Diary.
         3. O. C. "W" Coy.
         4. O. C. "X" "
         5. O. C. "Y" "
         6. O. C. "Z" "
         7. Medical Off. & M. G. Officer.
         8. O. O. File.
         9. 2nd In Command.
        10. Quartermaster.

SECRET.   Copy No. 2

OPERATIONS ORDERS No. 28.

18th (SER) BATTN. HIGHLAND LIGHT INFANTRY.

Reference LENS II, 1/100,000.   5th JULY 1916.

1. The Battalion will march, to-night, to billets and bivouacs in the BOIS DU WARNIMONT.

2. Companies will pass starting point, the junction of roads ¼ mile E of the S in BREVILLERS at 8.30 P.M. in following order, and march to Brigade Starting Point, South of L in LUCHEUX.

   Headqrs., "Z" Coy., "W" Coy, "X" Coy, Machine Gunners, 1st Line Transport.

3. "Y" Coy. (Capt. Dagger) is detailed as Advanced Guard to the Brigade, and will move independently to the Brigade Starting Point, so as to be in position to move in Advance Guard Formation from there at 8.55 P.M. Lieut. Martin & Battn. Scouts will be with Adv. Guard.

   Route :- LUCHEUX, HALLOY, Road Fork ¼ mile N.E. of FAMECHON Church, AUTHIE, BOIS DU WARNIMONT.

4. First Line Transport will follow behind Battalion. 2nd Line Transport will assemble at LUCHEUX and march under Senior Transport Officer behind Brigade.

5. O. C. "Z" Coy. will detail 1 N. C. O and 7 men as brakesmen for Limber Waggons. Battn. Q.M.S. and Cpl. Smith will proceed with Baggage and Supply Waggons.

6. The Medical Officer will march in rear of Battalion.

7. Reports to head of Battalion.

                    (Sgd) W. J. LYLE, Lieut. & ADJUTANT
                    18th (SER) BATTN. HIGHLAND LIGHT INFANTRY.

Issued at 6 P.M.

Copy No. 1 & 2. War Diary.
          3.   O. C. "W" Coy.   10. QuarterMaster.
          4.   O. C. "X" "   11. 2nd in Command.
          5.   O. C. "Y" "   12. O. O. File.
          6.   O. C. "Z" "
          7.   Signalling Officer.
          8.   Machine Gun Officer.
          9.   Transport Officer.

SECRET. Copy No. ~~13~~ 2

OPERATION ORDERS No. 30.

18th (SER) BATTN. HIGHLAND LIGHT INFANTRY.

9/7/16.

Reference 1/40,000 Sheet 57 D.

1. The Battalion will march to-morrow, to MAILLY, and be at disposal of G. O. C. 29th Division.

2. Companies will pass starting point, i.84.D.10.7 at 8.15 a.m. in the following order:- Hd.Qrs. "X" Coy, "W" Coy, "Z" Coy, "Y" Coy, Machine Gunners, and Bombers.

3. 1st Line Transport will march in rear of Battalion. 2nd Line Transport and 8 Motor Lorries to convey packs of men, will follow after Battalion. O. C. "Y" Coy. will detail 1. N. C. O. and 8 men as brakesmen for limbers. The Qr.Mr. and Coy. Qr.Mr.Sgts. will accompany Baggage and Supply Waggons.

4. Reports to Head of Column.

(Sgd) W. J. LYLE, Lieut. & Adjt.

18th (SER) BATTN. HIGHLAND LIGHT INFANTRY.

Issued at _____

Copy 1 & 2. War Diary.
   3. O. C. "W" Coy.
   4.   "X" "
   5.   "Y" "
   6.   "Z" "
   7. Medical Officer.
   8. Machine Gun Officer.
   9. Signalling Officer.
  10. Transport Officer.
  11. Quartermaster.
  12. 2nd in Command.
  13. O. O. File.

SECRET.   Copy No. 2

OPERATION ORDERS. No. 31.   13th JULY 1916
18th (Ser.) BATTN. HIGHLAND LIGHT INFANTRY.

Reference Maps, 57d. S.E. and 62d. N.W.

1. The Battalion will march to billets in the neighbourhood of BRESLE, via WARLOY and BAIZIEUX.

2. Companies will leave their billets in the following order at 9 P.M. and follow in rear of the th D.L.I. Hd.Qrs, "Z", "W", "X", "Y" Coy., Machine Gunners and Bombers.

3. 1st Line Transport will be Brigaded and will follow in the order of march of units, in rear of the 104th Field Ambulance. 2nd Line Transport will follow in order of march of units, starting at 10.15. P.M.

4. O.C. "Y" Coy. will detail 1 N.C.O. and 8 men as brakesmen for Limbers, to report to Transport Officer at 8.30. P.M.

5. The M.O. will follow in rear of Battalion,. The QuarterMaster and Staff will proceed with Baggage Wagons.

6. Reports to Head of Column.

        (Sgd.) W. J. LYLE, Lieut. and ADJT.
    18th (Ser.) BATTN. HIGHLAND LIGHT INFANTRY.

Copy No. 1+2 War Diary.
       3 O.O. File.
       4 O.C. "W" Coy.
       5 " " "X" "
       6 " " "Y" "
       7 " " "Z" "
       8 Transport Officer.
       9 QuarterMaster.
      10 Machine Gun Officer.
      11 Medical Officer.
      12 Second in Command.

SECRET.   COPY No. 2

OPERATION ORDERS, No. 32.   14.4.16

18th (Ser.) HIGHLAND LIGHT INFANTRY.

Reference Sheet, 62. D. 1/40,000 and AMIENS, 14.

1. The Battalion will move to position tonight in neighbourhood of BILLON WOOD, just S of CARNOY, via route X and BRONFAY FARM Road.

2. Companies will pass Starting Point, X.14. Central, at 4.40 P.M. and march to Brigade Starting Point in the following order, "Z" Coy. Advanced Guard, "X", "Y", "W" Coys.

3. 1st Line Transport Brigaded in order of Units will march in rear of the Column, except Lewis Guns and two S.A.A. Limber Wagons per Battalion, which will accompany their own units.

4. O.C. "W" Coy. will detail 1 N.C.O. and 8 men as Brakesmen for Limber Wagons.

5. Reports to head of Column.

(Sgd.) W. J. LYLE, Lieut. and ADJT.
18th Ser. BATTN. HIGHLAND LIGHT INFANTRY.

Copy No. 1 & 2. War Diary.
         3.   O. O. File.
         4.   O.C. "W" Coy.
         5.   " " "X" "
         6.   " " "Y" "
         7.   " " "Z" "
         8.   QuarterMaster.
         9.   Transport Officer.
        10.   Machine Gun Officer.
        11.   Medical Officer.
        12.   Second in Command.

106th Brigade.
35th Division.

1/18th BATTALION

HIGHLAND LIGHT INFANTRY

AUGUST 1 9 1 6

Army Form C. 2118.

WAR DIARY
or
INTELLIGENCE SUMMARY.
(Erase heading not required.)

35 / 18 H.L.I. Vol 7   1/B   7. P. Schools

Place	Date	Hour	Summary of Events and Information	Remarks and references to Appendices
MEAULTE	1.8.16.		The Battalion somewhat exhausted in strength and depleted in numbers bivouac in this neighbourhood. Arms drill and clearing up generally, the latter by no means an unimportant item. Later marched to billets at MORLANCOURT and settled down at 8.15 p.m.	
MORLANCOURT	2.8.16.		In Billets. Refitting and reorganising. Brigade complimented by G.O.C. 35th Division.	
"	3.8.16.		In Billets. Bn. Training.	
"	4.8.16.		In Billets. Bn. Training. Transport moves to DAOURS, half-way-house for FOURDRINOY which is the next destination of the Bn. when it moves to-morrow.	
"	5.8.16.		Bn. marched to MERICOURT where it entrained for SALOX. It detrained at 8.15 p.m. and arrived at its billets at FOURDRINOY at 12.30 a.m. the Sunday morning.	
FOURDRINOY.	6.8.16.		In Billets. Bn. resting.	
"	7.8.16.		In Billets. Bn. Training.	
"	8.8.16.		In Billets. Bn. Training and what is equally important, bathing also. Small units of the Bn. in relays were motored to AILLY-SUR-SOMME in lorries. There was considerable congestion but the men greatly appreciated this much needed wash.	
"	9.8.16.		In Billets. Bn. Training & preparing to move. Transport left at 6.30 a.m. for DAOURS.	
"	10.8.16.		In Billets. In the fore noon units perform light duty. At 2.15 p.m. the Bn. set out for HENGEST	

WAR DIARY

INTELLIGENCE SUMMARY

(Erase heading not required.)

Army Form C. 2118.

Place	Date	Hour	Summary of Events and Information	Remarks and references to Appendices
FOURDRINOY	10.8.16		The afternoon was hot and oppressive and the march of 7 kilometres across country by no means easy but our way lay through the beautiful BOIS-DE-CAVILLON where for quite a long distance the men were protected from the fierce heat of the sun by an expendable canopy of green. Ample time was allowed so that the men might have a good rest before entraining. This rest was doubly useful as it enabled them to have tea. The Bn. entrained at 6 p.m., and arrived at MERICOURT at 10.10 p.m. A short cut was taken to MORLANCOURT where the Bn. arrived back in their billets at midnight.	
MORLANCOURT	11.8.16		Bn. resting and training. In Billets.	
"	12.8.16		Bn. Training and Specialists receive instruction. In Billets.	
"	13.8.16		In Billets. Church parades. Training of Specialists.	
"	14.8.16		In Billets. Training by Coys in the afternoon. Lecture to Brigade Officers in the Cinema Hall at 2 p.m. by a Staff officer. Col. 35th Divisional in the evening. Bn. practised in attack on and consolidation of a position by the Commanding Officer. Occasional bodies of Aeroplanes.	
"	15.8.16		In Billets. In the morning. Company training. From noon till 10.45 p.m. the Bn. provided a working party of 500 men which was utilized in digging a communication trench S.W. of Trones Wood. No Casualties.	
BRAY	16.8.16		Bn. moved up to Sandpit VALLEY via BRAY. Arrived 3 p.m. Bivouacs on edge of BRAY-ALBERT Road. Bright. 7 men arrived 6.0 p.m. Operation Orders No 33 issued & attached	XXIII

T2134. Wt. W708—776. 500000. 4/15. Sir J. C. & S.

WAR DIARY
or
INTELLIGENCE SUMMARY.
(Erase heading not required.)

Army Form C. 2118.

Place	Date	Hour	Summary of Events and Information	Remarks and references to Appendices
SANDPIT VALLEY	17.8.16		Bn. bivouacking. Early morning parade for Bn. by platoons. Early forenoon Draft inspected by Brigadier. Later the Bn. was paraded in "attack on a position." This operation was performed twice. Faults explained by Commanding Off. and repeated at second practice. Machine Gun Company co-operated. Bn. returned to the Bathing Parade 3.15 p.m. Draft under R.S.M. at 6 p.m. Arms Drill. A fair amount of artillery activity on Selot affords too Weather changeable. Very hot at times.	
"	18.8.16		Bn. Bivouching. Early morning parade for Bn. by platoons "attack on a position" and the customary "how-now" was followed afterwards. Afternoon Coys. available for their commanders. Specialists training. In the evening Bn. played Hqrs. 4th Hy. A Bge. High Landers at football and lost a good match by 3-1 Intense artillery activity at intervals. Rain towards evening. Bn. less than in XIV Corps but two or three Coys.	
	19.8.16		Bn. in Bivouacs. Running for platoons in the morning. Afternoon fatigue parties getting back from Bough to improve bivouacs on account of bad weather. In the evening a football match versus 10. Yorks. We won 3-2. Weather bad much rain. Artillery active during day. Annoying towards evening.	
CARNOY	20.8.16		Bn. to-day moved into bivouacs in the neighbourhood. Left Sandpit VALLEY at 9.10 a.m. and arrived at new destination at 11.30 a.m. Operation Orders attached No. 34. The rest of the day peaceful	XXXIV

Army Form C. 2118.

WAR DIARY
or
INTELLIGENCE SUMMARY.
(Erase heading not required.)

Instructions regarding War Diaries and Intelligence Summaries are contained in F. S. Regs., Part II. and the Staff Manual respectively. Title pages will be prepared in manuscript.

Place	Date	Hour	Summary of Events and Information	Remarks and references to Appendices
CARNOY	20.8.16		in arranging bivouacs as the surroundings warrants no means congenial. One only case was the abundance of thistles. The whole Brigade was close together and was holding itself in readiness to move up the line in case of eventualities. Weather cold and gloomy.	
	21.8.16		Bn. in bivouacs still. Bn. training by Companies. Specialists receive instruction. Weather fair. Artillery activity desultory & intermittent.	
	22.8.16		Bn. training in the morning, resting in the afternoon. Parade before G.O.C. 35th Div. at 5 o'clock when the 106th Brigade was informed that it was to attack a line on the SOUTH of GUILLEMONT at a date and time to be appointed later. At 6.20 p.m. Bn. fell in for assembly trenches S of BERNAFAY and TRONES Wood in the occupation of Cheshires. Relief completed 10.15 p.m. No casualties.	
	23.8.16		Bn. in support trenches. In the afternoon Officers Reconnaissance of front line trenches. Orders were received for gun attack on the SOUTH of GUILLEMONT in conjunction with 104th Brigade the following day. Three men wounded mounted on that date.	
	24.8.16		Officers Reconnaissance to ascertain exact position of assembly trenches. Bn. still in support. In the afternoon orders for attack. Bn. in support of 106th Bde. before forward. Artillery very active. Enemy shelled support trenches causing general casualties.	

T2134. Wt. W708-778. 500000. 4/15. Sir J. C. & S.

WAR DIARY or INTELLIGENCE SUMMARY.

Army Form C. 2118.
(Erase heading not required.)

Place	Date	Hour	Summary of Events and Information	Remarks and references to Appendices
CARNOY	25th		Bn. still in same trenches. "W" Coy in front the outpost line, got somewhat heavily shelled suffering quite numerous casualties. Whilst also 1st & 3rd men in front line during the night. Working parties beat occasionally gassed, suffered a few casualties.	
	26th		Bn. still in position trenches & first fatigue parties at work, clearing, renovating & on hope improving and clearing the trenches and making dug-outs. Relieved by 10th K.R.R. Relief completed at 11.30 pm. Bn. moved to tents preceded by 10th Warwicks. Rest in HAPPY VALLEY. Bn. bivouaced about 9 o'clock. There had been a shower the day of BRIQUETERIE, BERNAFAY WOOD and SUNKEN ROADS - No casualties during relief. Potential pitch at night was Bn. was fortunate in having the moderately good cover of tents, though accomodation was of course rather rough by no means luxurious.	
HAPPY VALLEY	28th		Bn. still in tents resting. Reinforcement of 2 men wanted. More fatigues came Contingent artillery activity in the evening, but more in the Northern sector of the line.	
	29th		Bn. training and resting - Critical details of recent drafts inspected by G.O.C. 35th Div. at 4 pm. Weather showery. Considerable artillery activity in the Northern sector of the line in afternoon.	
	29/30		Bn. still in tents - Coy training - Weather changable.	
	30th		Bn. marched to HEILY and after waiting several hours in the rain entrained at 12 o'clock.	

Army Form C. 2118.

WAR DIARY
INTELLIGENCE SUMMARY.
(Erase heading not required.)

Place	Date	Hour	Summary of Events and Information	Remarks and references to Appendices
HAPPY VALLEY to S.W.	31.8.16		arriving at CANDAS at 8h.n. Afterwards marching to billets at AUTHIEUX, & Bn. arriving at 9h.n. Bn. billeted by this time was partly worn out, billets about 1750 in to move to billets. SUS ST LEGER via DOULLENS and LUCHEUX. At MILLY, drafts which had arrived since 16th July, were inspected by the Adjutant General - Bn. arrived about 8h.n.	

Secret. Copy No. 1

OPERATION ORDERS No. 33.
18th.(S) Bn.-H.L. Infantry.

Ref. French Map 62 D NE.1/20,000.

1. The Battalion will march to SANDPIT VALLEY to-morrow.

2. Companies will pass starting point K8^B 9½ 5 in following order.
   HdQrs., W Coy., X Coy., Y Coy., Z COY. Lewis gunners.
   The head of the column passing at 11.40a.m.
   Route VILLIERS CHAPEL, Crossroads. K.6.D.

3. 1st. Line Transport will follow in rear of Battalion. Baggage Waggons will not start till 2p.m.

4. Reports to head of Column.

                               W.F.M.Macara. 2/Lieut. Act/Adj.
                         18th.(S) Batt. Highland Light Infantry.

Issued at 6p.m.
15-8-16

Copy No. 1 2 War Diary
         3 OO/File
         4 W Coy.
         5 X Coy.
         6 Y Coy.
         7 Z Coy.
         8 Transport Officer
         9 QrtMr.
        10 2nd. in Command.

19.8.16.

Operation Orders. No 34.
By
Lt. Col. R.R. Lawrenson Commanding
18TH (S) BN. HIGHLAND LIGHT INFANTRY.

1. The Battalion will move into bivouac SOUTH of MINDEN POST to-morrow.

2. Companies will pass starting point 'ENTRANCE TO CAMP' in the following order, head of column passing at 9.10 a.m.

   HEADQUARTERS.
   'Y' COY.
   'Z' COY.
   'X' COY.
   'W' COY.
   MACHINE GUNNERS.

3. Transport will accompany battalion to bivouacs and when unloaded, will move to Transport Lines at 'CITADEL'

4. Reports to head of Column.

   SIGNED 2ND LT. W.F. MACARA. ACT/ADT.
   18TH (S) BN HIGHLAND LIGHT INFANTRY.

COPIES   NOS 1+2 WAR DIARY.
  "   "   3 O/C 'W' COY.
  "   "   4 O/C 'X' "
  "   "   5 O/C 'Y' "
  "   "   6 O/C 'Z' "
  "   "   7 QUARTERMASTER.
  "   "   8 TRANSPORT OFFICER.
  "   "   9 MEDICAL OFFICER.
  "   "   10 SECOND IN COMMAND.

WAR DIARY
INTELLIGENCE SUMMARY.
(Erase heading not required.)

Army Form C. 2118.

Place	Date	Hour	Summary of Events and Information	Remarks and references to Appendices
SUS. ST. LEGER	1.9.16		Bn. in billets. Cleaning up and resting.	
	2.9.16		Bn. in billets. Preparation for move in forenoon. At noon Bn. moves in motor buses to AGNEZ-LES-DUISANS. Bn. rests in a field until billets are evacuated by previous units at 6½p. Appx O. drawn No. XXXV. attached	XXXV.
AGNEZ-LES-DUISANS	3.9.16		Bn. in billets cleaning up and training. Bn. billeted at 7p.m. to march to billets in ARRAS. It arrived at 9p.m. without casualties. Whole Battalion was billeted in left block of SCHRAMM barracks.	
ROCLINCOURT	4.9.16		Bn. moved off at 12.45 p.m. and proceeded to K2 sector ROCLINCOURT, relieving 9th K.O.Y.L.I. Relief completed at 4.30 p.m. No casualties.	
	5.9.16		Bn. holding trenches in K2 sector. "W""X""Z" Companies front line. "Y" Company in support in dug-outs in ROCLINCOURT. Furnishing necessary fatigue parties. No great activity. A few trench mortars on front line from immediate supports. One officer 2nd Lt. F. Taylor, slightly wounded and one man accidentally injured.	
	6.9.16		Bn. still in same trenches. Some mortaring activity to which we replied with our STOKES guns to good effect. In the evening between 5 and 6 p.m. 1 Coy. active retaliation by our artillery. Two enemy aeroplanes had keen aerial activity in the morning afternoon. A little rifle and machine gun fire by "W" Coy. at 11.15 p.m. to which the enemy made no feeble reply. One man accidentally injured.	
	7.9.16		Bn. still in same trenches. In forenoon, front line in K2 sector, visited by G.O.C. 1st Army Corps.	

8. P
15 Mar

Vol 8

18/4/1

WAR DIARY
or
INTELLIGENCE SUMMARY

(Erase heading not required.)

Army Form C. 2118.

Place	Date	Hour	Summary of Events and Information	Remarks and references to Appendices
ROCLINCOURT	7.9.16		Airmen on both sides were particularly active during the day. Night quiet in the whole of the sector. Two or three men wounded. None seriously.	
	8.9.16		Bn. still in same trenches. Usual trench mortar & grenade activity. Two or three men wounded. Weather showed some improvement.	
	9.9.16		Bn. still in same trenches. Usual activity in the forenoon. In the afternoon it became more violent and the enemy's shooting improved. Some mortars landed right in front line near head of WEDNESDAY TRENCH - we lost 2 men killed and 6 x wounded. The 6.1st Division had, during this time, been on our left and 17th Royal Scots, 35th Division, on our right.	
	10.9.16		Bn. still in same trenches - Relieved at 7 a.m. Relief completed at 9.45 a.m. the cavalries Bn. returns to billets in ARRAS. In Granary and Museum cellars.	
ARRAS	11.9.16		Bns in billets in ARRAS. Officers and refs no nearer much received attention and the men got and in the evening Bn provide a working party of 480 men divided into units of 60 men forming carrying parties. Totally not time.	
	12.9.16		Bn in billets in ARRAS. Officers and refs receive further attention and the men go by relays to the baths - In the evening Bn provide working parties similar to those of the previous evening and for the same object.	

WAR DIARY
INTELLIGENCE SUMMARY.
(Erase heading not required.)

Army Form C. 2118.

Place	Date	Hour	Summary of Events and Information	Remarks and references to Appendices
ARRAS	13.9.16		Bn in billets in ARRAS. Deficiences in fair claim further attention. Similar working parties again provided.	
	14.9.16		Bn in billets. Remainder of the Bn. Lestrelle details of an enterprise are discussed and arranged and in the evening the party in question goes up to the 3rd Sector for reconnaissance purposes. At 2.30 p.m. in the afternoon of this day at Bn.HQrs. Trooper L/Cpl O'Donnell and Pte Robertson both "Z" Coy receive the ribbon of the "Military Medal" from G.O.C. 35th Division for gallantry at LONGUEVAL. Operation Orders No. 36 and No. 36a issued & attached	XXXV & XXXVI
	15.9.16		Bn. still in billets. Enemy dropped a few shells in the Town on falling rear one of this Bn. billets wounding two men. Further discussions took place for perfecting the arrangements for the enterprise. Men receive their great-coats.	
ROCLINCOURT	16.9.16		Bn. starts at 9 am. to relieve 19th D.L.I in the same Sector which it had previously occupied. Relief completed at 11.45 a.m. Some trench mortar activity and a good deal of A.A. fire. One man in "Z" Company killed by a rifle bullet at "Stand-to". Operation Orders attached	XXXVII
	17.9.16		Bn. in trenches. Day passed fairly quietly. There were casualties- Weather fine. Theafer towards Bn. aerial activity on our side. Our airmen seemed determined to fly above as possible despite the heaviest A.A. fire.	

WAR DIARY
INTELLIGENCE SUMMARY.
(Erase heading not required.)

Army Form C. 2118.

Place	Date	Hour	Summary of Events and Information	Remarks and references to Appendices
ROCLINCOURT	18/9/16		Bn. in trenches. Weather atrocious & in consequence there was a perceptible lull in the proceedings on both sides. Nothing of importance occurred. There were no casualties. Trenches in our sector in a shocking condition. Ind. N.F. pioneers & R.E. saw subjections and do much intelligent work	
	19/9/16		Bn. in trenches. Weather fair - hostile activity normal. CAPT. KENNEDY, who was awarded the M.C. for gallantry and ability at LONGUEVAL, returned from base about five days ago. Cpl. WORKMAN received D.C.M. at the same time, first man in Bn. to be decorated with this honour. One man wounded in KING CRATER	
	20/9/16		Bn. in trenches - weather atrocious - Rain fell heavily at intervals during the day and conditions were somewhat miserable. A good deal of T.M. activity between 6 and 7 p.m. and later in the evening	
	21/9/16		Bn. in trenches. Weather showed some improvement. Usual T.M. activity between 6 and 7 p.m. during the night too many wounded.	
	22/9/16		Bn. in trenches. Weather fine. Bn. relieved by 19th R.F. Relief completed at 10.15 a.m. There were no casualties. H.Q. and W Coy. in billets in ARRAS. X & Y Coys. in billets and dug outs in ST.NICHOLAS. X & Y in support in and around ROCLIN COURT. Operation Orders 38	XXXVIII
ARRAS	23/9/16		Bn. in billets & trenches. The two Companies in billets cleaning up and training, the other two Companies in reserve in and around ROCLIN COURT.	

Army Form C. 2118.

WAR DIARY
or
INTELLIGENCE SUMMARY.
(Erase heading not required.)

Place	Date	Hour	Summary of Events and Information	Remarks and references to Appendices
ARRAS & ROCLINCOURT	24/9/16		Bn. still in same place. Arrangements are made, whereby the men can get a bath and a clean shirt. Facilities are also offered for the repair of boots, by men on semi permanent illness.	
"	25/9/16		Bn. in same locality. Bombers receive instruction while Companies provide fatigue and working parties. Weather excellent.	
"	26/9/16		Bn. in same locality. Usual fatigues and working parties. The excellent weather continues	
"	27/9/16		Bn. in same locality.	
ROCLINCOURT	28/9/16		Bn. relieves 19th B.L.I. in same Sector "K2". Relief commences 9 a.m. and is completed at 1.25 p.m. No casualties. Weather threatening at first but shows improvement later. Operation Orders 39	XXXIX
"	29/9/16		Bn. in trenches in K2 Sector. "Y" Coy on the right, "Z" Coy in the centre, "W" Coy on the left and "X" Coy in reserve. A fairly thick mist which lasted almost all day improves the activity of both sides. Two men wounded, neither serious	
"	30.9.16		Bn. in trenches. Weather shows considerable improvement. There was no trench activity whatsoever. Our airmen very busy as usual and flying very low. Huns airmen far and few between. They never seem eager to test their abilities in a fight with our men. B. now commanded by Capt. KENNEDY M.C. – Col. LAWRENSON away on leave. MAJOR GOODERSON in hospital - sick	

Operation Orders No 35.
18th (Ser) Bn H.L.I.   2/9/16.

1. The 106th Brigade will relieve the 64th Bde. during the period of the 3rd/4th Sept.

2. On 3rd Sept. the 18th H.L.I will move to Billets at ARRAS.
Coys will pass Starting point, Battn Hd. Qrs. at 6.30 P.M. in the following Order:—
Hd Qrs, Machine Gunners, Z, Y, X, & W Coy.

3. Limbers allotted to Hd Qrs & Coys. will follow their respective units.
Route:— DUISANS, HALTE east of DUISANS, by DE BAUDIMONT.

4. Transport will move to DUISANS, leaving AGNEZ at 4 P.M.

(Sgd) W.F.M. MACARA, 2/Lt & a/Adjt
18th (S) Bn. H. L. Infantry.

Issued at.
Copy No 1 & 2. War Diary   Copy No 8. Sig Off
        3. O.O. File   9. M.G.
        4. O.C. W Coy   10. 2nd in Command
        5. O.C. X "   11. O.C. H.Q.
        6. O.C. Y "   12. Transport Off.
        7. O.C. Z "

SECRET.   OPERATION ORDERS.   Copy No.
18(S) Bn. HIGHLAND LIGHT INFANTRY.
Reference Special Orders issued.   14/9/16.

(1). After the gas attack and under cover of the Artillery Bombardment the Battn. will send out two strong patrols two hours after Zero for the purpose of:
 (a) Obtaining identifications.
 (b) Inflicting damage on any enemy left in trenches.

(2) The gas discharge will take place at Zero hour and the artillery programme in conjunction is as follows:
 Zero to 8 minutes on enemy's front line system.
 8 to 15 " " " support lines.
 15 to 25 " cease fire.
 25 to 35 " On front line trenches.
 35 to 1hr 56 min. Support & reserve line & communication trenches.
 1h. 56min. to 2 hrs. Rapid fire support & communication trenches.
 2hrs to 2hrs. 20 min. Slow fire.
Heavy French Mortars and Stokes guns will fire on wire at each point of entrance to enemy's line.

(3) The patrols are detailed as follows:
 Left Patrol (Capt. A.C. Balfour) 1 Off. 2 N.C.Os + 16 men. W Coy.
 Right " (Lieut. Barrie) 1 " 2 " + 16 " Z "

(4). A covering party will be detailed by O.C. Coy as follows:
 Left Patrol. (1 N.C.O. + 10 men. 2 Stretcher Bearers + 1 Stretcher.
 Right " 1 Off. + 10 men 2 " " + 1 "
These parties will follow each patrol from point of exit & will go beyond old French Trench & take up a position there & remain till every man of the patrol has returned to our own trenches.

(5) Before Zero hour each patrol and its covering party will be in position as follows:
 Left patrol & covering party in GRAND CONDUCTEUR TRENCH, under cover.
 Right " " " " H Works under cover.
At Zero + 60 min. each patrol & covering party will move as follows:
 Left patrol via THURSDAY AVENUE to point of exit at Bay 21. Trench 123.
 Right " " FISH AVENUE to point of exit at LEWIS GUN Sap No 3

(6) Until the discharge of gas takes place the patrols will remain in ROCLINCOURT & the hour of Zero will be communicated to them through O.C. 19th D.L.I.

(7) Gas helmets will be carried in the "Gas Alert" position & when moving to the point of exit along our Front line trenches, the officers in charge of each patrol should order the helmets to be put on, should there be any trace of gas in our own trenches.

(8) Officers & N.C.O's will carry a pistol, knobkerrie & P Grenade. Bayonet men will carry a rifle, Bayonet & 50 rounds of ammunition & one P Grenade.
Throwers will carry 6 bombs each & knobkerrie.
Carriers " " 10 " " " "
Torches, axes, ropes & material necessary for crossing a trench will be carried by each party.

(9) Each patrol will take with them marking out tapes to show direction back to their own front line.

(10) All letters, identity discs, pay books, badges etc. will be left behind and also all markings on clothes which would give any indication to the enemy of the Regiment or Corps to which a man belongs, should be obliterated.

(11) The O.C. patrol, will as far as possible keep a diary showing, & will render a report to Battn. Hd Qrs as soon as possible after return.

(12) In the event of Zero hour being notified while the remainder of the Battn. is in present billets, the C.O., 2nd in Command will move to ROCLINCOURT to where all reports should be sent.

(13) All watches will be synchronized at 6.10 p.m. every night from Bde. Hd Qrs.

(Sgd) W. F. Macara,
Issued at   Lieut. A/Adj.
                              18th (S) Bn. HIGHLAND LIGHT INFANTRY.

HUN LINE

Distribution and equipment of Coy. Patrols.

1 N.C.O. 1 P. Grenade. Pistol
1 Bayonet man. 50 rounds
          1 P. Grenade.
2 Throwers. 6 bombs each
          2 Knob kerries
3 Carriers. 10 bombs each
          3 Knob kerries
1 Bayonet man. 50 rounds
          1 P. Grenade.
rope and hand axe.

Right patrol
1 N.C.O.
7 men.

× Point of Entry.
1 Officer 1 P. Grenade Pistol
1 bomber. 15 bombs. Knobkerry.
1 bayonet man.
1 line for showing way back.

Left patrol
1 Officer
1 N.C.O.
7 men.

1 Officer. 1 P. Grenade. Pistol
1 Bayonet man. 50 rounds
          1 P. Grenade.
2 Throwers. 6 bombs each
          2 Knob kerries
3 Carriers. 10 bombs each
          3 Knob kerries
1 Bayonet man. 50 rounds
          1 N.C.O. 1 P. Grenade. Pistol
Rope and hand axe.

HUN. LINE.

Total.

Personal.
2 Officers
2 N.C.O.
16 men

Equipment.
7½ P. Grenades
99 Bombs (Mills)
150 rounds S.A.A.
2 Pistols for N.C.O.
2 Ropes & axes with loops
2 Hand axes.
1 line for showing way back.

Rush bomb & plank etc. for hiding wire for trenches

Secret.   Copy No

Operation Orders No 36(a)
18th (S) Batt H. L. I.

I. A gas attack will be carried on the K 2 Sub Section from trenches 117 to 125.

II. All preparations for flotation will be completed before day light of the 4th Sept. and the gas will be discharged with unrestricted jett between the hours of 9 p.m. – 4 a.m. on the first favourable opportunity after the preparations are completed.

III. If the wind appears to be in a suitable quarter, a warning order will be issued from 35th Division two hours before the elected time for Zero.—

If after this order is issued, it becomes necessary to postpone the gas attack, the recipients of above order will be informed.

The following code will be used in sending the above message.—
"Gas to be discharged at Zero"   "DUNCAN" (hour)
"Gas discharge cancelled"   "JACK"

IV. (a) The gas operations will be in charge of Capt W. O. SALT. O/c A Coy 4th Bn Special Brigade. Address 35th Division Hd Qrs.

(b) The battle stations & code address of the officers 4th Bn. Special Brigade, superintending the flotation of the gas in K sector, are as follows:-

NAME	STATION	CODE ADDRESS
Lieut Sellars	Left Bn Hd Qrs	SELLARS
Hogg	Left Coy Hd Qrs K 2	HOGG
Jones	Centre Coy Hd Qrs	JONES

V. The gas discharge will be followed by an artillery bombardment. Details of the programme will be issued separately.

VI. The front line will be held by one double sentry post to each 100 yds of trench normally held, and all Machine & Lewis Guns in the line, & will only be entered again by the remainder when reported safe by the Officer of the Special Brigade R.E. responsible for this sector.

Dug-outs in the front line & support lines will not be occupied for at least 4 hours after Zero, even though the dug-outs have been cleared of by a Vermoral Sprayer.

All anti-gas blankets in K sector will be lowered, & as though to discharge. They must be sprayed during the day.

Continue

(Continued).

VII. All troops in 'K' Sector will wear their Gas Helmets in the 'Alert Position' on the night of the flotation. All men in front line Trenches 117-125 will have their Gas Helmets on from Zero hour till the discharge of gas is finished.

VIII. Two strong patrols, under Capt Balfour and Lieut Bonus, consisting of 1 Off. 8 N.C.O's 7 men will be sent out on the night gas is discharged, to enter enemy trenches, secure identification, and inflict damage. Special instructions will be issued.

W.J. Macara
2/Lieut a/Adjt.
18th (S) Bn. H.L. Infantry

14.9.16

SECRET.
Copy No.

Operation Orders No. 27
18th (S) Bn. H. L. Infantry
14-9-16

Reference Trench Map. ROCLINCOURT 1/10,000

1. The Battalion will relieve the 19th D.L.I. in K.2. Sub-Section on the 14th as follows:—

    W Coy relieve LEFT Company of D.L.I.
    Y   "   "   RIGHT   "   " D.L.I.
    Z   CENTRE   D.L.I.
    X   RESERVE   D.L.I.

Companies will leave billets in the above order and at intervals of 200 yards between each platoon, commencing at 1am.

2. Guides to meet each platoon will be at Battn. Headquarters at ROCLINCOURT.

3. 1 Officer and 1 N.C.O per Company for taking over stores. Snipers under Lieut. Ferguson and scouts for observation posts under Lieut. Maule will proceed to the Line at 6 a.m.

4. Reliefs will be reported to Battn. Headquarters at ROCLINCOURT by the Signal T.G.

(Signed) W. F. MAGARA 2/Lt. a/Adjt.
18th (S) Bn. H. L. INFANTRY

Issued at 12 noon

Copy No. 1 and 2. War Diary.
       3. O.C. File
       4. 19th Durh. L.I.
       5. O.C. W Coy
       6. O.C. X
       7. O.C. Y
       8. O.C. Z

No. 9. Maj. Gordenson
    10. Lieut. Ferguson
    11.   "   Maule
    12.   "   M.G. Off.
    13.   Q.M. & T. Off.

Operation Order No. 38   Copy No.
18th (S) Bn H.L.I.   22-9-16

(I) Bn. will be relieved at K.2. Sector by 19th D.L.I. on morning of 22nd inst. and will move into Brigade reserve.

II. W Coy on Left relieved by W. Coy. of D.L.I.
Z " " Centre " " Y " do
Y " " Right " " Z " do
X " in village & works " X " " do
Hdqrs do—do " " Hdqrs " do.
D.L.I. Coys will come into in above order at about 20. minutes interval, W Coy. should reach front line between 7.30 & 8. am.

III. W & X Coys will each provide 1 Guide p. platoon. to be at Bn. Hdqrs at 7am.

IV. Certificates of Trench Stores. handed over will be taken and sent to Orderly Room on day of Relief. Trenches & Dugouts will be left thoroughly clean.

V. Breakfast will be cooked and eaten as usual, but in time to allow all preparation for relief before D.L.I. reach the various trenches & works. No movement of H.L.I. in Wednesday, Fish or Bogey Avenues from 7am to 8.45 am. Coys. & Hdqrs. will carry out their cooking utensils & Cooks will join their Coys when these pass the Cook-house.

VI. Coys will move out in the following order. X. Platoons in G & H Works, W. Z. & Y. Coys. X Platoons in Roclincourt Hdqrs,. W & Z Coys will use Wednesday Avenue and Y Bogey Avenue. 6 platoons of West Yorks at present in Roclincourt will move out to Sector K.1. immediately after last of D.L.I. have passed Lawrence Avenue, and before any H.L.I. move out.

VII. Order of moving out and disposition of Bn. in Brigade Reserve X Platoons in G & H Works to start not before 9 A.M. and will proceed by Trench 30. to THELUS and OBSERVATORY Post then to take over from WEST YORKS platoons. W Coy. to go to ARRAS. Z Coy. to go to ST. NICHOLAS. Y Coy. to proceed

(Contd)

VII(Contd) to occupy ROCLINCOURT VILLAGE defence line vacated by West Yorks. X Coy Platoon in Roclincourt to proceed to occupy LAWRENCE AV. billets vacated by WEST YORKS. Hdqrs. after above to ARRAS. Machine Gun teams will go with their Coys. Raiding parties of W & X Coys. to billets with Z Coy in St NICHOLAS. and to carry unexpended rations for day.

VIII. "W" & "Z" Coy will find unexpended rations for day at New billets. X & Y. at respective Cookhouses where they draw them after whole Bn is relieved.

IX. Relief to be reported by Signals or messages to Bn Hdqrs.

X. Certificates of taking over billets & Stores to be sent to Orderly Room on day of relief.

(Sgd) W.F.M. Macan
2/Lt a/Adjt.
18th H.L.I.

21/9/16

SECRET.

Copy No.

26/9/16

Operation Orders No. 39.
18th (S) Bn. H.L.I.

Reference:- Trench Map 51 B.N.W. 1/10,000

I. The battalion will relieve the 19th D.L.I. in 'K2' sub-sector on the 28th inst.

II. 'Y' Coy. will relieve 'Right' Coy. D.L.I.
'W' " " " Left " D.L.I.
'Z' " " " Centre " D.L.I.
'X' " " " Reserve " D.L.I.

III. Companies will leave their billets in the following order & time, with 200 yards interval between platoons
'Z' Coy. leave at 9.A.M.
'W' " " 9 A.M.
'Y' " will leave 'ROCLINCOURT' at 9.45 a.m.

IV. The platoons of 'X' Coy. at present 'garrison' of 'THELUS' & 'OBSERVATORY' will, on Relief by 19th D.L.I. be in 'Reserve' at ROCLINCOURT. The 2 platoons of 'X' Coy now in Reserve at ROCLINCOURT will be detailed as permanent 'Garrison of 'G' & 'H' works. They will follow 'Y' & 'Z' Coys respectively

V. 1 Officer + 1 N.C.O. per Coy. will proceed to the line, at 8 AM to take over stores etc.

VI. 1 N.C.O. of Coys. at 'ARRAS' & 'ST. NICHOLAS' & 1 servant for each Officers' Billets will be left behind to hand over billets & rejoin their Companies on completion of Duty.

VII. Relief to be reported to Battn. Hd.Qrs by 'Code' T.G.'

Copies to 2nd in Comd. — 1
O/C 'W' Coy — 1
" 'X' " — 1
" 'Y' " — 1
" 'Z' " — 1
Bomb. & I.O. — 1
Lt Maul &
2/Lt. Gemmill } — 1
WAR DIARY — 3

(Signed) W.F. MACARA 2/Lt. Ac/adj.
18th (S) Bn H.L. Infantry.

18th (S) Bn. HIGHLAND LIGHT INFANTRY. **SECRET**

DEFENCE SCHEME. K2 SECTOR

5th Septr./16.

REFERENCE 1/10,000 Map.

1. The Battn. holds the left sub-sector of the line held by the 106th Brigade. The sub-sector is known as K2 and extends from about A.30.c.4.7. to A.23.c.9.3. The trenches are numbered 112 - 125 inclusive.

2. The Battn. is distributed as follows :- Three Coys in the front line and works line. One Coy less one platoon and Battn. Bombers in Battn. reserve.

3. **Right Coy.**

   Two platoons
   Coy Bombers } in front line 112 - 115 inclusive.
   Two platoons in 6 work.

   (a) Bombing squads are distributed as shown in attached plan. They hold the blocks in case of a rush, or help to hold the craters if a mine is sprung.

   (b) LEWIS GUN posts as per attached plan.

   (c) Consolidating party 1 N.C.O. and 10 men are left in readiness near junction of 114 - 115 in order to rush in and consolidate the crater in case the suspected mine in 116 is sprung.

   (d) Trench at junction of Right and Centre Coy has been evacuated and sentry groups posted near each end. The enemy are supposed to have a mine under this portion.

   (e) Of the two platoons in 6. work, one forms the permanent garrison of the work, the other is at the disposal of the Coy Commander for local counter attack.

4. **Centre Coy.**

   Three platoons
   Coy Bombers
   Battn. Bombers } in front line 116 - 121 inclusive.
   One platoon in I work.

   (a) Bombing squads are distributed as shown in attached plan. Right squad assists Battn. Bombers in securing the crater. Centre squad posted near abandoned sap running to the old trench line. Left squad posts guards at left flank of Coy.

   (b) LEWIS GUNS as per attached plan.

   (c) A consolidating party of 1 N.C.O. and 14 men in readiness where ever required.

   (d) The platoon in I work remains in position in case of attack.

5. **Left Coy.**

    Three platoons   } in front line 122-125 inclusive.
    Coy Bombers.
    One platoon in L work.

(a) Bombing Squads distributed as shown on attached plan. Right squad guards entrance to Short trench containing Mine shaft. Right centre squad in sap to left and in front of WEDNESDAY AVENUE. Left centre squad consists of 1 N.C.O. and 3 men in sap near head of THURSDAY AVENUE. Left squad are at left flank of coy. near block in trench on left of Sub sector K2.

(b) LEWIS GUNS as per attached plan.

(c) One platoon of Reserve Coy occupies GRAND COLLECTEUR trench by night.

6. **Reserve Coy.**

    One Coy less one platoon in LAWRENCE AVENUE.
    One platoon 1 LEWIS GUN in H work.
    1 LEWIS GUN in L work.

N.B. By night one platoon occupies GRAND COLLECTEUR trench leaving two platoons in LAWRENCE AVENUE.

IN CASE OF GENERAL ATTACK

(a) Troops in front line "Stand To" at their posts ready to open fire any moment the barrage lifts and the enemy's infantry attempt to cross NO MAN'S LAND. On the first indication of this S.O.S. signal to be sent to artillery.

(b) Works line garrison stand firm. In event of front line giving way, hold on at all costs.

(c) Coy in reserve "Stand To" in readiness to move as ordered.

LOCAL ATTACK.

The probable form is one of an enemy raid following the springing of a mine. In the event of a mine being exploded the following steps will be taken.

(a) At each end of the threatened trench there is a bombing post. These will at once rush and hold the forward lip of the crater.

(b) O/c Right and Centre Coys will at once take steps to support these bombers and to consolidate the crater with all possible speed.

(c) As a local reserve to be used in case of counter attack O/c right coy has at his disposal one platoon situated in G work (exclusive of permanent garrison of the work which consists of one platoon.

O/c centre coy has in I work one platoon which may be used for the purpose of counter attack, but as this is a permanent garrison it will only be used after the garrison of trench 117 (one platoon) has been used up. One platoon Reserve Coy situated in H work will in that case replace garrison of I work, leaving the LEWIS GUNNERS in H work until O/c Reserve

Coy has replaced the garrison by a platoon from LAWRENCE AVENUE.

Machine Guns available to bring cross fire to bear on this quarter are LEWIS GUN at Sap head at junction of 120-121. VICKERS GUN in no 117, LEWIS GUN in no 114.

Reserve Coy less 1 platoon will be used as occasion arises either for counter attack or for garrison of SPOOK TRENCH in case front line should be captured and held by the enemy.

(Sgd) V. E. Gooderson,
Major.
18th (S) Bn HIGHLAND LIGHT INF.

2 platoons of ROCLINCOURT Garrison (Batt'n Brigade reserve) are at disposal of O/C K2.

VEGooderson
Major

Scheme for

Lewis gun posts	●	Loopholed Traverses.	▭
Bombing posts.(Coy)	●	Dug outs.	▣
" " (Btn)	●	Listening post	L.P
Stokes gun posts.	✠	Disused mineshaft	Ⓜ
60ᵗʰ T.M. "	✠	night and as dugout.	
Machine gun (og)	⊙	* Russian sap to dug outs. ... to	

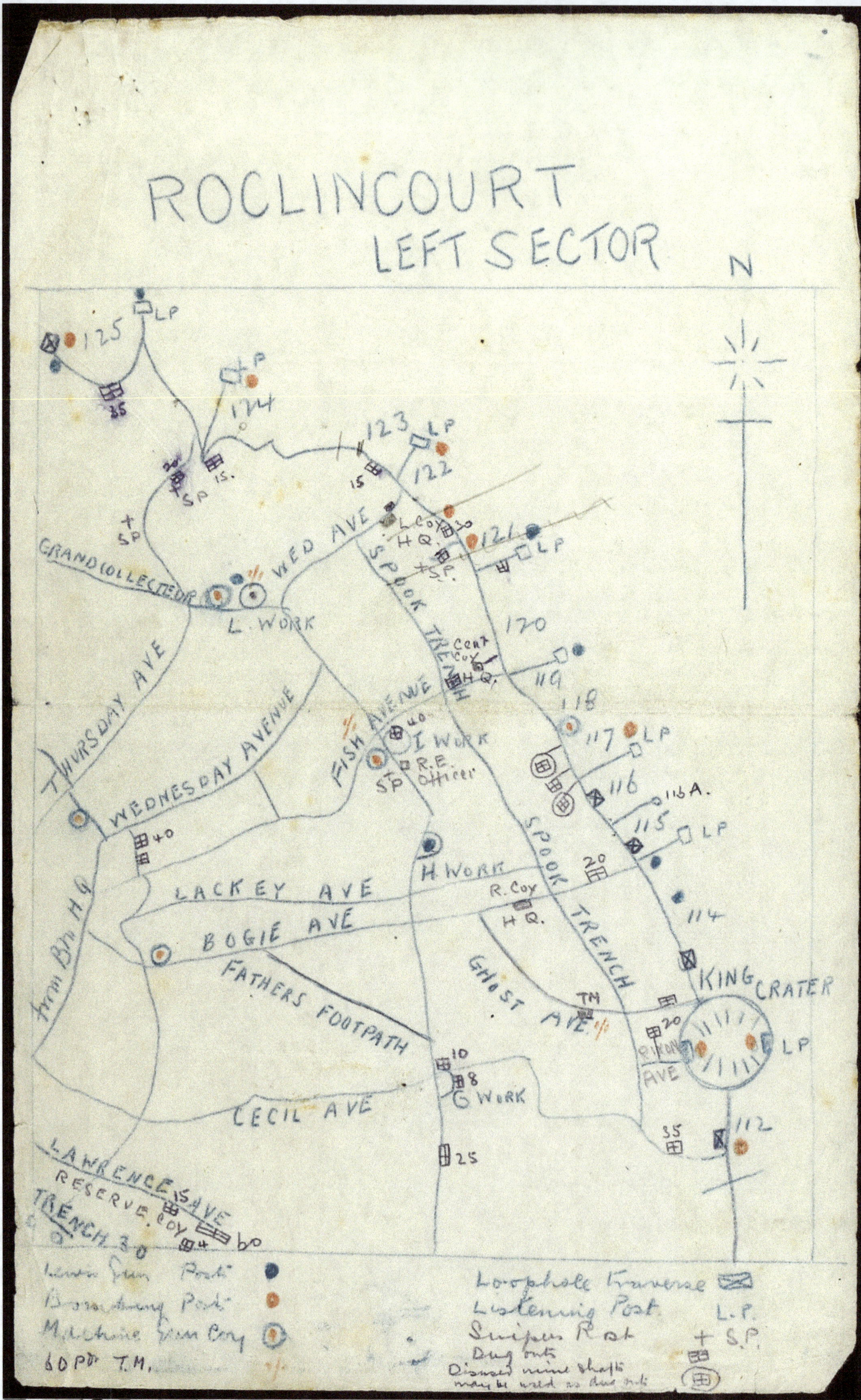

ROCLINCOURT LEFT SECTOR

N

(hand-drawn trench map with the following labels visible)

- 125, LP
- 124, LP
- 123, LP
- 122
- 121, LP
- 120
- 119
- 118
- 117, LP
- 116
- 115A
- 115, LP
- 114
- 112
- 35
- 15
- 20
- 40
- 30
- 25
- 10
- 8
- 60
- L Coy HQ
- Cent Coy HQ
- R Coy HQ
- Reserve Coy
- R.E. Officer
- SP
- GRAND COLLECTEUR
- WED AVE
- SPOOK TRENCH
- L. WORK
- I WORK
- H WORK
- G WORK
- THURSDAY AVE
- WEDNESDAY AVENUE
- FISH AVENUE
- LACKEY AVE
- BOGIE AVE
- FATHERS FOOTPATH
- CECIL AVE
- LAWRENCE AVE
- GHOST AVE
- PIKON AVE
- KING CRATER
- From Bin HQ
- TM
- TRENCH 30

Legend:
- Lewis Gun Post — ● (blue dot)
- Bombing Post — ● (orange dot)
- Machine Gun Coy — ⊙
- 60 Pdr T.M. — //
- Loophole Traverse — ⊠
- Listening Post — L.P. ▭
- Snipers Post — + S.P.
- Dug outs — ⊞
- Disused mine shafts may be used as dug outs — ⊞ (circled)

WAR DIARY
INTELLIGENCE SUMMARY

(Erase heading not required.)

Army Form C. 2118.

18 HLI Vol 9

Place	Date	Hour	Summary of Events and Information	Remarks and references to Appendices
ROCLINCOURT.	1.10.16		Bn. in trenches. Weather fine. A certain amount of T.M. activity and a few light shells exploded in and around 'ROCLINCOURT'. Companies, with the assistance of O.N.F. pioneers are busy with improvement of trenches. Our patrols encountered no hostile patrols. No Casualties.	
"	2.10.16		Bn. in trenches. Weather abominous with much rain. The enemy were again much more active than usual with their trench mortars and the sector was quite lively. Our 'Stokes Guns' effectively replied. No Casualties. Our Patrols encountered no hostile enterprise	
"	3.10.16		Bn. in trenches. This was perhaps one of the liveliest days we have had. Rain in the evening but much in the afternoon. Plenty of T.M. activity and a good deal of shrapnel. The weather was ideal in the afternoon and visibility was splendid which probably accounted for the liveliness. The enemy put some moderately heavy shells in the neighbourhood of the village as if he was searching. No casualties.	
"	4.10.16		Bn. in trenches. Weather and wind variable. Not so much activity as the previous two days, but the enemy landed a mortar in front line in the sector occupied by 'Z' Coy. killing one officer and four men and wounding one one.	
"	5.10.16		Bn. in trenches. Usual T.M. activity on both sides. Operation Order No. 40 attacked. Bn. relieved by 19th K.R.S. Relief completed at 7p.m. about 10p.m., though certain details did not arrive back until about 3.30 a.m. Bn. marched to billets at DUISANS where it arrived by Companies	XL

WAR DIARY
or
INTELLIGENCE SUMMARY.
(Erase heading not required.)

Army Form C. 2118.

Place	Date	Hour	Summary of Events and Information	Remarks and references to Appendices
DUISANS	6.10.16		Bn. in billets (huts) Cleaning up bathing and resting	
	7.10.16		Bn. in same place. At 9 p.m. Bn. inspected by G.O.C. 35th Bgde. Division, now Major General London. H.S. who appeared satisfied with the various exercises through movements with their arms but criticised the condition of their clothing and equipment. Remainder of the day spent in company training, Specialists training, and bathing at LOUEZ.	
	8.10.16		On the same place. Running parade in the early morning. Church parades and Specialists training in the afternoon. Weather wet.	
	9.10.16		a.m. in same place. Parade in the morning. Specialist training in the afternoon. Transf. of Clothing.	
	10.10.16		a.m. in same place. Parade in morning. Inspection parade by C.O. in afternoon. In the Evening Bn. left for ARRAS. Billeted in SCHRAMM Barracks. Officers on an empty house. Cold and uneventful. Operation Order No. 41 attached	X.1
ARRAS	11.10.16		Bn. commenced to relieve 19th D.L.I. in K2 sector at 10 a.m. Relief complete 1.30 p.m. No casualties. Little activity.	
ROCLINCOURT	12.10.16		a.m. in trenches. A good deal of activity. There was an artillery strafe from 2.30 to 3 p.m. The enemy replied with three Rifle Grenades. His shooting was erroneous to be pleasing. At night he obtained a direct hit with a Rifle Grenade on the right (?) Coy. front killing one	

WAR DIARY
INTELLIGENCE SUMMARY
(Erase heading not required.)

Army Form C. 2118.

Place	Date	Hour	Summary of Events and Information	Remarks and references to Appendices
ROCLINCOURT	12/10/16		Men and wounding front.	
	13/10/16		Bn. in trenches. A busy day. Trench action on both sides. Our artillery also fired more than normal. A good deal of movement in the enemy lines.	
	14/10/16		Bn. in trenches. Weather dull to cloudy but no rain. Usual Tr.M. + artillery activity during the day. Enemy's field guns fired a few shells during afternoon dropping them around ROCLINCOURT. Clear moon light - considerable M.G. + T.M. + Rifle Grenade activity at Mr. Van Bn. in trenches. Weather fine. Tr.M. + artillery activity on both sides as usual. Machine Gun very active during the night.	
	15/10/16			
	16/10/16		Bn. in trenches. Weather during day fair but cold. Very quiet day - no one permitted to "strafe" Night quiet - Some rain - Several H.E. shells fell in + around ROCLINCOURT.	
ARRAS	17/10/16		Bn. in trenches - Relieved by 19th RDF - Relief completed by 10.15am - Relief Orders No.12 attached Bn. in Brigade Reserve. W+Z Coy. paines at ROCLINCOURT etc. X + Y Coy at ST NICHOLAS + Y Coy in ARRAS.	XII
	18/10/16		Men resting + cleaning up equipment, clothing etc. also working parties. Bn in Brigade Reserve. Billets + Headquarters inspected by Commanding Officer - Boy in ROCLINCOURT allowed for bathing - Companies supply working parties.	
	19/10/16		Bn in billets - body-guard turnouts very satisfactory day - Men bathing in washing sports.	

WAR DIARY
INTELLIGENCE SUMMARY.
(Erase heading not required.)

Army Form C. 2118.

Place	Date	Hour	Summary of Events and Information	Remarks and references to Appendices
ARRAS.	20/10/16		1st Y Coy at 2.30 pm. Men bathing, also working parties carrying ammunition etc.	
	21/10/16		Bn. in billets. Clear frosty morning — Lower degree of frost at night of 20-21/10/16. Enemy fired several rounds into la Petit Place, Arras, during the morning. Men bathing. Coys supplying working parties.	
	22/10/16		Bn. in billets. Usual Church Parade in forenoon. Coys supplying working parties to front line etc. — Day bright but very cold.	
ARRAS & ROCLINCOURT.	23/10/16		Bn. in Brigade Reserve billets etc. — Commenced to relieve 9th Durh L.I. in the 2 sectors at 6 pm — Relief completed 11 am. — Y, X, & W Companies in front line, Z Coy in support at ROCLINCOURT. Quiet morning — Some heavy T.M. activity during afternoon. — 1 man wounded — Dry during day but some rain at night.	Operation Orders No 43 attached
	24/10/16		Bn. in trenches. Unusually quiet morning — Hostile T.M. fire rather heavier than usual in afternoon — Large party of front line blown in at trench 114. T.M. landed on Wednesday. Pouring in afternoon — Weather pretty miserable — rain almost all day.	
	25/10/16		Bn. in trenches. Weather showery during morning — Afternoon dry — Quiet morning — A little T.M. activity during the afternoon — Our artillery T.M. is very active between 8 & 10 pm — Hostile M.G. fire during the night.	

Army Form C. 2118.

WAR DIARY
~~INTELLIGENCE~~ SUMMARY
(Erase heading not required.)

Instructions regarding War Diaries and Intelligence Summaries are contained in F. S. Regs., Part II. and the Staff Manual respectively. Title pages will be prepared in manuscript.

Place	Date	Hour	Summary of Events and Information	Remarks and references to Appendices
ROCLINCOURT	26/10/16		Bn in trenches - Weather fine - Some T.M. Activity between the hours of 8 and 10-30 A.M. - Rest of day was exceptionally quiet.	
"	27/10/16		Bn in trenches - Weather showery - very quiet during the morning - No activity of any kind - afternoon usual T.M. fire about 4-30 P.M. two 4"2" Shells landed in ROCLIN COURT - Anxieres fire was carried on by our M.G.S. During the night.	
"	28/10/16		Bn in trenches. - Weather Dry but dull and cold - usual T.M. Activity during the day - at night one T.M. Shell landed on our parade wounding two N.C.Os.	
ARRAS	29/10/16		Bn relieved by 119th Bde. Relief completed by 12 noon Operation Order No. 44 attached. The Bn had enjoyed a tolerably quiet tour this time and returned to billets in the Granary Munition and Institute for the Deaf Dumb in ARRAS, being in Divisional Reserve.	XLV.
ARRAS	30/10/16		Bn cleaning up two recurring games of clothing etc. numerous working parties provided, about the whole of each Company being absorbed during a portion of their twenty four hours.	
"	31/10/16		Bn in billets - Men received their baths back from the Savage and water path things to was boots repaired and hair cut - Similar working parties.	

SECRET   Copy No. 2

Special Operation Order No 41
1-8th (S) Bn. H.L.I.

Ref: Bde Order regarding gas attack.

1. After the gas attack & an artillery preparatory bombardment, Bn. will send out 2 raiding patrols as under for the purpose of:—
   (a) Obtaining identifications & captures.
   (b) Inflicting damage on enemy.

2. Gas will be discharged at the "Zero" hour. From "Zero" to "Zero+30ms.", with an interval of 10ms., artillery will maintain a bombardment, and T.Ms & Stokes Guns will cut wire at the 2 points of the German line to be entered by the patrols.
   At Zero + 1hr. 5ms. artillery bombardment will recommence on the close support line. 4ms. later it will lift to lines behind and communication trenches ceasing at Zero + 2hrs. 20ms. At Zero + 1hr. 56ms. the Medium T.Ms will repeat their bombardment for 4 ms. and the Stokes Guns traverse the front line for 1 minute at Zero 1hr. 59ms. Thereafter Stokes will fire for 20ms. round points :- A.23.d.5.7 & A.30.a.25.45.

3. Gas will be discharged in I sector, and a heavy feint bombardment be carried out round about Zero + 2 hours.

(Continued.)

(Continued)

4. Patrols are detailed as follows:—
 W Coy Left patrol:- 2/Lts. Ritchie & Curle, 2 N.C.O's & 16 men
 Z Coy Right patrol:- Lt. Bryan, 2/Lt. W.A. Stewart, 2 N.C.O.s & 16 men
 A covering party for each patrol will be provided by O/C. 19th D.L.I.

5. Before Zero hour each patrol & covering party will be in position, with Gas Helmets, at the "Alert" position, as follows:—
 Left patrol in dug outs in "L" works
 Right patrol   "   "   "   "   "I" works.
 At Zero + 60 m.m. each patrol & covering party will move:—
 Left patrol via THURSDAY AV. to point of exit at Bay 19 trench 123.

 Right patrol " FISH AV. to point of exit to Bay 6 trench 118.

6. At Zero + 1hr 55m each p.tle will leave point of exit & get across old French trench into No Mans Land as far as possible under cover of bombardment. At Zero + 2hrs it will advance rapidly to points of entry namely:—
 Left point. A.23.d.5½.3
 Right   ".   A.30.a.½.7½
7. Each patrol will consist and proceed as follows:-
(a) Covering party on No Mans Land beyond old French trench for assistance of all kinds.
(Continued)

(Continued)

6. (2) Officer in charge + 2 men to remain at point of entry & give signal for return.

(3) Right party of N.C.O + 8 men to proceed right for short distance & stop near communication trench & front line, thereafter to hold this point & send surplus of men to act with next party.

(4) 1 Officer, 1 N.C.O + 8 men assisted as above to go to left as far as first communication trench and seize objects of raid.

7. At Zero + 2hr 20 m.s., at which time signals for return will be given, the patrols will come back to point of entry and return through gap in wire following white tape to be laid across "no mans land" as the parties go over.

8. Gas helmets will be worn whenever presence of gas in trenches or dug-outs makes it necessary.

9. Indication marks, as uniform, and letters, identification discs, pay-books, badges etc, will be left behind when the patrols leave the works line.

10. Officers + N.C.Os will carry revolvers & electric torches. Each patrol will have two giant wire cutters. Patrols will also carry rifles & fixed bayon-ets, knob-kerries, Mills hand grenades, & bombs

(Continued)

(Continued)

10) P'bombs, rope & long white tape. A spare duck board will be ready at point of exit for use over old 'French' trench if necessary.

11) D.L.I. will arrange for Rifle Grenading of Hun Front line & Machine Guns, if necessary, to cover retreat of patrols provided time admits, arrangements being made.

12) Officer Commanding 18th L.I. will have Hd Qrs at Telephone dugouts in the work. The Adjutant will be at signal office of D.L.I. with Sq D.L.I & Lt Sellars of the Special R.E.

W. Kennedy Cape
 OC 18th M.L.I.

5/10/16

R.J. White 2/Lt.

SECRET.   OPERATION ORDERS NO. 40.   COPY NO.----------
           18th.(S) Bn. HIGH. L. INF.,

5/10/16.

The Battalion will be relieved in K2 Sector by 10th. D.L.I. at 3p.m. on the 5th. October.

The companies will be relived in the following order: W.Y.Z.X. as follows:-

W.Coy.H.L.I. will be relieved by W.Coy.D.L.I.
Y. "   "   "   "   "   "   Z. "   "
Z. "   "   "   "   "   "   X. "   "
X. "   "   "   "   "   "   Y. "   "

Two platoons of YCoy. D."L."I. will relieve 2plattoons XCou. H.L.I. in G&H Works. Guides for these posts will be at junction of WEDNESDAY & LAWRENCE trenches at 2.15p.m. also guide for LEWIS GUN in L Work.

O.C.ZCoy. H.L.I. will send down 4guides, one per platoon to Bn. HdQrs. at 3.30p.m. to guide XCoy. D.L.I. up WEDNESDAY trench to front line. On relief, W.Y.&Z Cous. will march to billets in DUISANS via ST.NICHOLAS & BEAUDIMONT GATE. One limber per Coy. will be at ST.NICHOLAS. XCoy., on relief will proceed to billets in ARRAS. Guides to meet them will be at ST.NICHOLAS BRIDGE. On completion of relief O.C.COYs. will report to Bn. HdQrs. by the code word 'Kent'.

Issued at   (signed)   W.F.M.MACARA 2/Lt. Ac/Adj.
                          18th.(S) Bn.HIGHLAND LIGHT INFANTRY

SECRET.   OPERATION ORDERS No. 41   Copy No. _____
               18th. (S) Bn. High. L.I.

1. The battalion will move to billets in ARRAS leaving at 6p.m. to-day in following order at 20mns. interval.

   HdQrs.   6p.m.
   W Coy   6.20p.m.
   Z "   6.40p.m.
   Y "   7p.m.

2. Coys will arrange with billeting officer as to their billets.

3. Relief of K2 Sector will take place leaving ARRAS 10a.m. to-morrow. Details later. Coys. will take over the line as follows Left W.Coy., Centre X Coy., Right Y Coy., ROCLINCOURT &G&H Works Z Coy. One officer and one N.C.O will proceed to line at 8a.m. to take over stores etc.

4. Ration carts with breakfast for battalion will follow HdQrs. The ration limbers with binners and tea rations will go direct to ROCLINCOURT accompanied by a cook and one man per coy. who will remain with the rations until the battalion arrives in the line.

5. Officers walises and compamy boxes to be at QrMrs Stores at 3pm

6. Each Company will two men as a cleaning up party in DUISANS under a good N.C.O. to be detailed by Z Coy. They will come up to the line with the rations to-morrow night. Cooker dixies will be loaded on the ration limbers for ARRAS.

7. Companies will have tea at 4p.m. today, and camp thoroughly cleaned by 5.30p.m.

8. Lt. Cowan will move to ARRAS to-night. Transport and Depot party to be reduced to same number as last tour in line.

10/10/16.   (signed) W.F.M.MACARA 2/Lt. Ac/Adj.
                           18th. (S) Bn. High. L. Inf.

SECRET.   OPERATION ORDERS No.42   Copy No........
           18th (S) Bn. High. L.I.
                                     16/10/16.

Reference:- Trench Map 51B.N.W. 1/10,000

1. The battalion will be relieved by 19th D.L.I. to-morrow commencing at 7.30a.m.

2. All trench stores will be handed over to the relieving companies receipt obtained and forwarded to Adj. by 6p.m. 17th inst.

3. WEDNESDAY AVENUE will be used by W & X Coys. and BOGEY AV. by Y Coy. O/Cs. W & Y Coys. will see that there is no down traffic in these AVENUES between 7 & 8.15 a.m.

4. On relief the battalion will be in Brigade Reserve and distributed as follows:-

   W. Coy.   ROCLINCOURT & DEFENCES
   X "   Billets in ST. NICHOLAS
   Y "   do   ARRAS
   Z. "   1 platoon in garrison of THELUS, 1 platoon in garrison of OBSERVATORY, 2 platoons at ROCLINCOURT under orders of O/C 19th D.L.I.

5. One Officer and one N.C.O. for each company will proceed at 6a.m to their respective billets to take over and will give certificate as to cleanliness.

6. Relief will be reported to Bn. HdQrs. by the code word 'T.G.'

Issued at 4p.m.   (signed)   E.B. MAULE   Lt. Ac/Adj.
Copies:- 1-2 War Diary
         3   O/C W. Coy.   18th. (S) Bn. High. L.I.
         4   "   X "
         5   "   Y "
         6   "   Z "
         7   Signalling officer
         8   2nd. in Command
         9   O/O File.

SECRET.   OPERATION ORDERS no. 43   Copy No.
                    18th Bn. H.L.I.
                    ———
                     51

Reference:- Trench Map/B.N.W. 1/10,000

1. The battalion will relieve the 19th D.L.I. in K2 Sub-Sector on the morning of the 23rd as follows:-

   W.Coy. will leave ROCLINCOURT at 8a.m and relieve Left Coy. D.L.I.
   X.Coy. will leave ST.NICHOLAS at 7.30a.m. and relieve Centre Coy D.L.I.
   Y.Coy. will leave ARRAS at 7.45a.m. and relieve Right Coy. D.L.I
   Z.Coy 2 platoons at ROCLINCOURT will move after Y Coy. has pass-ed and garrison G&H Works. 2 platoons at THELUS and OBSERVATORY will, on being relieved by D.L.I. be in reserve at ROCLINCOURT
   Hd.Qrs will leave ARRAS at 8a.m.

2. One Officer and one N.C.O. per Coy. will proceed to the line one hour before their coy. to take over trench stores. Receipts to be given.

3. WEDNESDAY AVENUE WILL BE used by the Left Coy. and Centre Coy. BOGEY AV. will be used by Right Coy and garrisons of G&H Works

4. Completion of reliefs will be forwarded to the Ord. Room by the code word 'GOOD-NEWS'.

23/10/16.

                  (signed)   E.B.MAULE   Lieut. Ac/Adj.
Issued at 12noon.   18th. Bn. High. L.I.
Copy no. 1&2 W.D.
         3   W Coy.
         4   X   "
         5   Y   "
         6   Z   "
         7   2nd. in command
         8   O/O File.

SECRET.   OPERATION ORDERS No. 44   Copy No.......
           18th. (S)Bn. Highland L.I.
                                                    28/10/16

Reference:- Trench Map 51B.N.W 1/10,000

1. The Battalion will be relieved by the 19th D.L.I. on the morning of 29th as follows:-

    W Coy. will be relieved by X Coy. D.L.I.
    X   "   "   "   "   "   Y   "   "
    Y   "   "   "   "   "   Z   "   "
    Z   "   "   "   "   "   W   "   "

2. The relief will commence about 9 a.m. and Companies will be relieved in the following order:- XCOY., YCOY., WCOY., ZCOY.,

3. All trench stores, anti-gas stores, etc., in front line and work line will be handed over, receipts obtained and forwarded to the captain.

4. On relief, companies will proceed to billets at Cathedral and Museum and will be in Divisional Reserve.

5. Relief will be reported to battalion Headquarters by the code word 'GLASGOW'.

    Issued at......   (signed) E.B. MAULE Lieut. Ac/Adj.
    Copy 1-3 W.D.   18th. (S) Bn. Highland Light Infantry.
         4 WCoy.
         5 XCoy.
         6 YCoy.
         7 ZCoy.
         8 2nd. Command
         9 Signalling Officer

WAR DIARY
INTELLIGENCE SUMMARY

18th Highland L.I.
November 1916.
Vol 10

10.p
10 sheets

Place	Date	Hour	Summary of Events and Information	Remarks and references to Appendices
ARRAS	1.11.16		Bn in billets. Issue of kit etc practically completed. The place parking parties.	
	2.11.16		Bn in billets. Still more kit issues. Working parties again provided. Weather bad. H.Q.O. inspected the transport in the morning. The place was practically a sea of mud, but sundry improvements made in anticipation of winter. Work in progress. Weather improved in the course of the afternoon and there was some sunshine.	
	3.11.16		Bn in billets. The day spent tidying up. The trenches have probably been more ardous than the others in rest and many from men were provided.	
BRELINCOURT	4.11.16		Bn relieved 19th Bn in No2 Sub-Sect. Relief completed by 7 noon. Bn. relieved WEDNESDAY AVENUE with 77mm + H.	
	5.11.16		Bn in trenches. Some mortar activity but the weather stocking is not favourably accurate. Artillery is never very active on the enemy side.	Operation Orders No 45 XLV
	6.11.16		Bn in trenches. Weather slightly better with a good turn at night. One officer slightly wounded at night in King CRATER.	
	7.11.16		Bn in trenches. Weather stew. A good deal of T.M. activity in the afternoon. Heavy rain in the evening	
	8.11.16		Bn in trenches. Weather and visibility again bad - A little T.M. activity and some	

WAR DIARY
OF
INTELLIGENCE SUMMARY.
(Erase heading not required.)

Army Form C. 2118.

Place	Date	Hour	Summary of Events and Information	Remarks and references to Appendices
ROCLINCOURT	8/11/16		105 mm on left Coy (W Coy) front. One direct hit, which killed 5 men, but the shooting was indiscriminate rather than direct & one of his shells landed in his own front line. Quiet forenoon at night.	
	9/11/16		Bn. in trenches, slightly better. Enemy very inactive. Men engaged in rebuilding the trenches where they had subsided.	
	10/11/16		Bn. in trenches. Relieved by 19th D.L.I. in "K.2." Sector. Relief completed without incident by 10.30am. "Z" & Y Companies took over the WORMS line & X Company in support at ROCLINCOURT and "W" Coy in support in ST NICHOLAS. H.Qrs in ATKAS. Operation Orders No 46 attached	XLVI
BRIGADE RESERVE	11/11/16		Bn. in Brigade Reserve. Men engaged in cleaning equipment & resting. Working parties in the evening.	
	12/11/16		Bn. in Bde. Res. Day quiet. Men in WORMS line engaged in repairing superkeep of their foots. Coy in ST NICHOLAS supplied large working parties for work on the line	
	13/11/16		Bn. in Bde Res. Moved work & improving WORMS line & Reference corridor. Baths in ROCLINCOURT completed. Bathing of men started.	
	14/11/16		Bn. in Bde Res. Bathing of men and large working parties supplied	
	15/11/16		Weather fine but cold. Bathing of Bn. completed. Men engaged repairing "WORMS"	

Army Form C.2.

WAR DIARY
or
INTELLIGENCE SUMMARY.
(Erase heading not required.)

Instructions regarding War Diaries and Intelligence Summaries are contained in F. S. Regs., Part II. and the Staff Manual respectively. Title pages will be prepared in manuscript.

Place	Date	Hour	Summary of Events and Information	Remarks and references to Appendices
Brigade Res.	15/11/15		line which had been knocked in by enemy's T.M's during the day. All other available men were engaged in emptying derelict sandbags over the line.	
Roclincourt.	16/11/15		Bn. took over from 19th D.L.I in W.2. Sector. Relief completed 6.10 a.m. Enemy fairly quiet all day. In the afternoon hy. pair over 2 heavy T.M'S. Very quiet during the night then engaged rebuilding and revetting trenches. Operation Orders No.17 attached.	A.17
	17/11/15		Bn. in trenches. Weather exceptionally fair. Enemy very quiet, only of a bit of a day's over a few Rifle Grenades & heavy T.M's, near "L" Works, slightly damaging "Wednesday Avenue". Artillery carried out a small piaffe on New York behind enemy's line with good effect.	
	18/11/15		Bn. in trenches. Our artillery & T.M's active, but enemy's retaliation was very feeble. The enemy at night "hung" a great deal with rifle fire over top of his own wire. Then engaged wiring, revetting & improving trenches.	
	19/11/15		Bn. in trenches. Weather dry & bright. Very little activity on both sides. At night the enemy was very active with Machine guns & rifles. Enemy sent over several rifle grenades damaging slightly "Wednesday Avenue".	
	20/11/15		Bn. in trenches. Weather very dry with much L. mist. Day quiet. Artillery & T.M's normal. Increase of rifle & machine gunfire at night. Enemy again bombed the wire. Our patrols are active.	

WAR DIARY
INTELLIGENCE SUMMARY
(Erase heading not required.)

Army Form C. 2118.

Place	Date	Hour	Summary of Events and Information	Remarks and references to Appendices
ROCLINCOURT	21/11/15		Bn. in trenches. Weather dull but dry. Artillery & T.Ms quiet. Men were engaged in repair and strengthening trenches. Night also quiet. Rifle & Machine gun fire normal. Patrols active. Casualties 3 other ranks wounded.	
↑ AKKAS	22/11/15		Bn. in trenches. Relieved by 19th D.L.I. Relief completed by 11 A.M. Bn. to relieve normal Battalion proceeded to AKKAS & billets in Div. Reserve. Afternoon spent cleaning up. Working parties at night. Operation Order No. 118 attached	XVIII
AKKAS	23/11/15		Bn. in Div. Reserve. Weather fine. Range working parties by day & night. Raiding party of 1 Off., in training. Also specialists	
	24/11/15		Bn. in Div. Reserve. Weather fine. Working parties. Working parties training of specialists as before.	
	25/11/15		Bn. in Div. Reserve. Weather not told. Working parties training as usual. Bn. inspected by Commanding Officer. A concert was given by Officers of in evening during the evening until signal phone	
	26/11/15		Bn. in Div. Reserve. Weather showery. Working parties. Too unwell. Church parades held in the morning. Thankful for duty in trenches were inspected by Brigadier General. A band was given too men absent on working parties the previous evening.	
	27/11/15		Bn. in Div. Reserve. Weather fine but cold. Usual working parties &c. Night men were inspected by Divisional Commander at 11.30 a.m. A test alarm was carried out at 1.25 p.m. By reported nearby	

WAR DIARY

INTELLIGENCE SUMMARY.

(Erase heading not required.)

Army Form C. 2118.

Instructions regarding War Diaries and Intelligence Summaries are contained in F. S. Regs., Part II. and the Staff Manual respectively. Title pages will be prepared in manuscript.

Place	Date	Hour	Summary of Events and Information	Remarks and references to Appendices
ARRAS "Roclin Court"	28/11/16 29/11/16	to move at 1.30 pm	Bn relieved 19th D.L.I. in trenches. Relief as follows 10.30 a.m. Operation Orders No.149 attached. Weather fine but cold toward night. Morning normal. The enemy were active during the afternoon with rifle grenades & trench mortars. Our patrols were active during the night, which was very quiet. Casualties 4 W.O.R.s. On the trenches. Weather dull & misty. Morning quiet. The enemy were in action with Artillery & Trench Mortars. Enemy were also quiet during afternoon. At night our patrols were active & men were engaged in wiring & repairing trenches.	XLIX.
	30/11/16		Bn in trenches. Weather again dull & misty. Morning quiet. Men engaged in wiring, repairing & improving trenches. In the afternoon the enemy was more active with heavy trench mortars which we replied to with good effect. At night there was the usual patrolling, wiring etc.	

SECRET. OPERATION ORDERS No. 45   COPY No.
        18th., (S) Bn. High. L.I.   3/11/1

1. The Battalion will relieve the 18th., D.L.I. in the K.? Sub-sector on the 4th., November, as follows.

   'W' Company leave billet at 7.45 a.m. & relieve Left Coy. D.L.I.
   'X'   "   "   "   " 8. a.m.   "   "   Right "   "
   'Z'   "   "   "   " 8.15 a.m. "   "   Centre "   "
   'Y'   "   "   "   " 8.30 a.m. "   "   Res.   "   "
   Headquarters "   "   " 8.45 a.m. "   "   Hdqrs.

2. Snipers and Observers under Lieut. Maule, and 1 Officer and 1 N.C.O. per company, for taking over stores, will proceed to the line at 7.15 a.m.

3. All trench stores will be taken over, receipts given, and lists forwarded to the Adjutant by 6 p.m. on 4th., inst.

4. Each company in the line will have a counter attacking platoon in close support. This platoon will be available for work in the Front line.

5. Reliefs will be reported to Battalion Headquarters by the Code word 'DUNDEE'.

                                    (Signed) W.J. LYLE Lieut & Adj.
                                    18th., (Ser) Bn., Highland Light Infantry.

Issued at.........

Copy No..1 & 2 War Diary.
        3   'W' Coy.
        4   'X' "
        5   'Y' "
        6   'Z' "
        7   Transport Officer
        8   Lewis Gun Officer.
        9   Intelligence Officer.
        10   2 nd. in Command.
        11   18th., D.L.I.
        12   O.O. File.

SECRET.   Operation Orders No. 46.   Copy No..........
                 18th., (S) Bn., Highland Light Inf.,

                                                        9-11-16.

Reference trench map:- 'ROCLINCOURT' 1/10,000.

1. The Battalion will be relieved by the 19th., D.L.I. in the K.2
   Sub-sector on the 10th. inst. Relief will commence about 9 a.m.

2. All trench stores will be handed over, recipts obtained and
   forwarded to the Adjt.,

3. Companies on relief, will proceed to the following posts and
   billets in relief of 17th., W.Yorks R. and 10th., D.L.I.
   'W' Coy. less 2 Lewis Guns and Teams to ST. NICHOLAS.
   'X' "   " .... " ROCLINCOURT Defences.
   'Y' "   THELUS OBSERVATORY,'E' Work,'F' Work: One Lewis Gun &
              team near THELUS. One Lewis Gun & team in 'E' Work.
   'Z' "   'G' Work,'H' Work,'I' Work,'L' Work: One Lewis Gun &
              team in 'H' & 'I' Works. Two Lewis Guns and teams of
              'W' Coy will be in 'F' Work and 'L' Work.

4. The ammunition, stores, rations and water taken over in the
   various posts will be carefully checked and lists sent to the
   Adjt.,

5. The Battalion Bombers, snipers and Headquarters will, on relief,
   proceed to Headquarters at ARRAS.

6. Reliefs to be reported to Battalion Headquarters by the code
   word "MUD"

                              (Signed) W.J.LYLE, Lieutn& Adjt.,
                              18th., (Ser) Bn., Highland Light Infantry.

Issued at..12noon....
Copies to-War Diary Nos.1 & 2
       O.C. 'W' Coy. " 3
        "   'X' "   " 4
        "   'Y' "   " 5
        "   'Z' "   " 6
       Lewis Gun Off." 7
       O.C.17th. N.Yorks. 8
        "   19th. D.L.I. 9
        "   17th. W.Yorks. 10
            O/O File. 11.

SECRET.   Operation Orders No. 47.   COPY NO.........

18th., (S) Bn. Highland L. Inf.   14/11/16.

Reference:- 51.B.N.W. 1 & 5 1/10,000

1. The Battalion will relieve the 19th., D.L.I. in the K.2 Sub--Sector on the 15th. inst. as follows;-

   'X' Coy. will leave ROCLINCOURT at 8.45 a.m. and relieve Right Company D.L.I.
   'Y' Coy. will leave Redoubt and Works line so as to pass through ROCLINCOURT at 8.30 a.m. and relieve Left Company D.L.I.
   'Z' Coy will leave Works line at 9 a.m. and relieve Centre Coy D.L.I.
   'W' Coy. will leave billets ST.NICHOLAS at 8.45 a.m. and relieve Reserve Company D.L.I.
   Headquarters will leave billets in ARRAS at 8.45 a.m. and relieve Headquarters D.L.I.

2. All trench stores, maps etc. will be taken over, receipts given and forwarded to Adjutant.

3. 1 Officer and 1 N.C.O. per company will be sent to the line at 8 a.m. to take over stores. The Scouts and snipers, under Sgt. Kemp, will leave ARRAS at 7.30 a.m.

4. In the event of the Platoons in the Redoubt and Works lines not being relieved in time to carry out the relief as ordered above 1 N.C.O. for each work or redoubt and 1 Officer per company will be left behind to hand over, and the works and Redoubt vacated.

5. Completion of relief will be reported to Battalion Headquarters by the Code word "HOW LONG".

                                (Signed) W.J.LYLE, Lieut & Adjt
                                18th., (S) Bn. Highland Light Infantry

Issued at.......

Copies to:-
    No.1 - 3 War Diary.
        4 'W' Coy.
        5 'X' "
        6 'Y' "
        7 'Z' "
        8 D.L.I.
        9 2nd. in Command.
        10 Signalling and M.G. Officer.

SECRET.

OPERATION ORDERS No. 48   Copy No. 2
18th.(S) Bn. Highland L.I.

21/11/16

Reference:- Trench Map 51 B.N.W. 1 & S 1/10,000

1. The Battalion will be relieved by the 19th. D.L.I. in K.2
   Commencing
   Sub-Sector, on the 22nd. inst./about 9.30 a.m.

2. All trench stores will be handed over, receipts obtained and forwarded to the Adjutant.

3. Companies on relief, will proceed to their old billets in CATHEDRAL, MUSEUM, & DEAF & DUMB INSTITUTE, where the Battalion will be in Divisional Reserve.

4. One N.C.O. and 2 men per Company will be sent to ARRAS, in the evening of the 21st., to take over rations for 22nd. R.S.M. will detail 2 men for Headquarters. 2/Lieut. McColl will proceed to ARRAS in the morning of the 22nd., to take over billets from D.L.I., and give certificates.

                                            Battalion
5. Completion of relief to be reported to/Headquarters by the the code word "GLORIA"

                        (Signed) W.J. LYLE, Lieut & Adjt.,
                                 18th., (Ser) Bn., Highland Light Infantry.

Issued at 9 a.m.

Copies to:- 1 & 2 War Diary.
            3 'W' Coy.
            4 'X' "
            5 'Y' "
            6 'Z' "
            7 2nd in Command.
            8 Lewis Gun Officer.
            9 Transport Officer.
           10 19th. D.L.I.
           11 17th. R. Scots.
           12 17th. W. Yorks. R.
           13 O.C. File.

SECRET   OPERATION ORDERS No. 49   Copy No...2...
           14th.,(S) Bn., H.L.Inf.

                                                 27/11/

Reference:- Trench Map ROCLINCOURT, 1/10,000

1. The Battalion will relieve the 19th.,D.L.I. in the R.2 Sub-sector on the 28th. inst. as follows.:

    'W' Coy. will leave billets at 7.30 a.m. and relieve Left Coy. D.L.I.
    'X' "   "   "   "   " 8.00 a.m.   "   " Right   "   "
    'Y' "   "   "   "   " 8.15 a.m.   "   " Centre "   "
    'Z' "   "   "   "   " 8.30 a.m.   "   " Reserve "   "
    Headquarters "   "   " 8.45 a.m.   "   " H.Qrs. "

2. All trench stores will be taken over, receipts given, and lists forwarded to the Adjt., by O.C., 24th. Inst.

3. 1 Officer and 1 N.C.O. per Coy. to take over stores, and Snipers under 2/Lieut G.R.McColl, will leave billets at 7.30 a.m.

4. Each Company, on arriving at ROCLINCOURT, will leave the Officer and men, detailed for the Pioneers Platoon, there. Arrangements for billeting the Platoon will be made by O.C.'W' Company.

5. 1 N.C.O. and 2 men per Company and Headquarters will be sent to ROCLINCOURT in the evening of the 27th., to take over the rations for the 28th.

6. Completion of relief will be notified by the code word 'TUESDAY'.

                               (Signed) W.J.LYLE, Lieut & Adjt.,

                    14th.,(Scr) Bn., Highland Light Infantry.

Issued at ....

Copies to:- 1 & 2 War Diary
           3 1st Coy.
           4 2nd "
           5 3rd "
           6 4th "
           7 Headquarters
           8 19th.,D.L.I.
           9 17th.,F.Works, R.E.
          10 17th.,R.Scots.
          11 2nd in Command.
          12 O/C Mils.

Army Form C. 2118.

18th H.L.I

WAR DIARY
or
INTELLIGENCE SUMMARY.
(Erase heading not required.)

11. 9.
4 sheet

Vol XI

Place	Date	Hour	Summary of Events and Information	Remarks and references to Appendices
POCLINCOURT	1/12/16		Battn. in trenches. Weather fine but cold and very misty. Our artillery was active in the morning and the enemy replied briskly. The afternoon was quiet. The raid proposed for the date for which the Battn. had practised for a long time was cancelled by the Division.	
"	2/12/16		Battn. in trenches. Weather cold and dull. Relieved by 12th Royal Scots. Relief complete 11 A.M. Battn. marched to ARRAS and rested till 6 P.M. Then marched to WANQUETIN. Arrived 9 P.M. – about 6 miles.	
WANQUETIN	3/12/16		Battn. on the march. Left WANQUETIN and marched to MAISNIL-ST-POL. Distance 15 miles. No men fell out. about 6 P.M. arrived MAISNIL-ST-POL at 9 P.M. Arrived were inspected by Divisional Commander and Brigadier en route.	
MAISNIL-ST-POL	4/12/16		Battn. in billets. Billets good. Battn. engaged in cleaning and resting.	
"	5/12/16		" " Weather good with some frost. Training of men carried out under Company Officers. Specialists and training of new Specialists under respective officers.	
"	6/12/16		Battn. in billets. Some rain and mist. Training as before. Bathing of Battn. commenced at Brigade Baths, ST. MICHEL.	

Army Form C. 2118.

WAR DIARY
or
INTELLIGENCE SUMMARY.
(Erase heading not required.)

Instructions regarding War Diaries and Intelligence Summaries are contained in F. S. Regs., Part II. and the Staff Manual respectively. Title pages will be prepared in manuscript.

Place	Date	Hour	Summary of Events and Information	Remarks and references to Appendices
MAISNIL-ST-POL	7/12/16		Battn in Billets. Weather showery and cold. Training and Bathing of Battn as before in the forenoon. The Transport was inspected by the Brigadier General in the forenoon.	
Do.	8/12/16		Battn in Billets. Weather wet. Training as before. Bathing completed.	
Do.	9/12/16		Battn in Billets. Weather wet. Training as before. Unfit men were inspected by A.D.M.S.	
Do.	10/12/16		Battn in Billets. Weather wet. Church parade in morning. In afternoon held was a lecture and demonstration to all Officers and N.C.Os. on the use of Small bore repeaters.	
Do.	11/12/16		Battn in Billets. Weather bad with snow. In the morning the Battn was inspected by the Divisional Commander. In the afternoon training as before.	
Do.	12/12/16		Battn in Billets. Weather unsettled. Programme of training carried out as before. Work done improving Sanitary conditions. Work was started constructing a 25 yards rifle range.	
Do.	13/12/16		Battn in Billets. Weather showery. Training and work as before. The Divisional Commander visited the Battn in the morning.	
Do.	14/12/16		Battn in Billets. Weather wet. Training, reorganising & work as before.	
Do.	15/12/16		Battn in Billets. Weather fine. Training, reorganisation & work as before.	

WAR DIARY
or
INTELLIGENCE SUMMARY.
(Erase heading not required.)

Army Form C. 2118.

Instructions regarding War Diaries and Intelligence Summaries are contained in F. S. Regs., Part II. and the Staff Manual respectively. Title pages will be prepared in manuscript.

Place	Date	Hour	Summary of Events and Information	Remarks and references to Appendices
MAISNIL-ST. POL	16/12/16		Battn. in Billets. Weather fine. Training reorganisation work as before	
do.	17/12/16		Battn in Billets. Weather fine showery " " "	
do.	18/12/16		Battn in Billets. Weather stormy fair " " "	
do.	19/12/16		Battn. in Billets. Weather cold some snow " " "	
do.	20/12/16		Battn in Billets. Weather good hard frost. The Battn. was inspected in the morning by the Corps Commander. In the afternoon training & as before	
do.	21/12/16		Battn in Billets. Weather good. Training reorganisation work as before	
do.	22/12/16		Battn in Billets. Weather good " " "	
do.	23/12/16		Battn in Billets. Weather wet " " "	
do.	24/12/16		Battn in Billets. Weather showery. Church parade in the morning	
do.	25/12/16		Battn in Billets. Weather good. The day was spent resting	
do.	26/12/16		Battn in Billets. Weather good. Men unfit for trenches were inspected by Army Commander	
do.	27/12/16		Battn in Billets. Weather good. Training reorganisation work as before	
do.	28/12/16		Battn in Billets. Weather good " " "	
do.	29/12/16		Battn moved to forward Area (by motor buses) to relieve 19th D.L.I. Weather very wet	

Army Form C. 2118.

WAR DIARY
or
INTELLIGENCE SUMMARY.
(Erase heading not required.)

Place	Date	Hour	Summary of Events and Information	Remarks and references to Appendices
MAISNIL-ST-POL	29/12/16		Arrived ARRAS about 6 p.m. for gr working parties supplied at night 200 men 19th D.L.I. attached to bring working parties up to strength. 133 men judged unfit by A.D.M.S. left at MAISNIL-ST-POL under 2/Lt Conran to proceed to Base	
ARRAS	30/12/16		Battn in Billets. Weather good. Entire Battn engaged on working parties. Casualties.	
"	31/12/16		" " " " Battn engaged on working parties.	

Army Form C. 2118.

WAR DIARY
or
INTELLIGENCE SUMMARY.
(Erase heading not required.)

18 ¿Hugh L.I.
Vol 12

Place	Date	Hour	Summary of Events and Information	Remarks and references to Appendices
Cairo	1/1/14		Battn in Billets. Weather Good. Battn engaged on working Parties	
	2/1/14		Battn in Billets. Weather Good. Battn engaged on working Parties	
	3/1/14		Battn in Billets. Weather Good. " " " " "	
			the Camp was shelled with Gas shells for 1½ hours during the night	
	4/1/14		Battn in Billets. Weather Good. Battn engaged on working Parties	
			the Camp was again shelled with Gas Shells at night	
	5/1/14		Battn in Billets. Weather Good but Cold. Battn engaged on Working Parties	
	6/1/14		Battn in Billets. Weather very Cold. " " " "	
	7/1/14		Battn in Billets. Weather Wet. " " " "	
			Draft of 21 men arrived from Base.	
	8/1/14		Battn in Billets. Weather Wet. Battn engaged on working Parties	
			Draft of 210 men joined from Base	
	9/1/14		Battn in Billets. Weather Changeable. Battn engaged in working Parties	
			Draft left for Depot Coy for training. A Gas Shell struck the billet of "Y" Coy. Officers & wrecked two rooms, fortunately injuring no one.	

12. P.
3 sheets

WAR DIARY or INTELLIGENCE SUMMARY.
(Erase heading not required.)

Army Form C. 2118.

1⁄2 Regt L.9

Place	Date	Hour	Summary of Events and Information	Remarks and references to Appendices
Arras	10/1/14		Batn in Billets. Weather Dull. Batn engaged on working Parties	
	11/1/14		Batn in Billets. Weather Wet & cold " " " "	
	12/1/14		Batn in Billets. Weather changeable " " " "	
	13/1/14		Batn in Billets. Weather Wet " " " "	
	14/1/14		Batn in Billets. Weather Fresh " " " "	
	15/1/14		Batn in Billets. Weather Thy/Cold " " " "	
	16/1/14		Batn in Billets " " " "	
	17/1/14		Batn in Billets. Much Snow " " " "	
	18/1/14		Batn in Billets. Draft of 91 Inf men arrived	
	19/1/14		Batn in Billets. Hard frost. Batn engaged on working Parties	
			Draft of 50 men arrived	
	20/1/14		Batn in Billets. Hard frost. Unfit men inspected by Army Commander	
			Hard frost, very cold. Working Parties resumed	
			Draft of 20 men arrived	
	21/1/14		Batn in Billets. Hard frost. Working Parties. Draft of 88 men arrived	

18 Bgde ?

WAR DIARY
or
INTELLIGENCE SUMMARY.
(Erase heading not required.)

Army Form C. 2118.

Place	Date	Hour	Summary of Events and Information	Remarks and references to Appendices
Acres	22/1/17		Battn in Billets. Weather Very Cold. Working Parties provided.	
	23/1/17		Battn in Billets. Hard frost. Draft of 4 2.O.R. & 2 Officers arrived. Working Parties still small.	
	24/1/17		Battn in Billets. Hard frost. Draft of 2 O.R. arrived. Working Parties cancelled.	
	25/1/17		Battn in Billets. Hard frost. Men considered unfit by Corps & Army Commanders were sent to Divisional Base to the number of 250.	
	26/1/17		Battn in Billets. Hard frost. Working Parties resumed with all available men (80). 18th of the 2nd reg attached 19th D.L.I. left to base as unfit.	
	27/1/17		Battn in Billets. Hard frost. Very Cold. All available men on working parties.	
	28/1/17		Battn in Billets. Hard frost. Very Cold. All available men on working parties.	
	29/1/17		Battn in Billets. " " " "	
	30/1/17		Battn in Billets. " " " "	
	31/1/17		Battn in Billets. " " " "	

WAR DIARY
or
INTELLIGENCE SUMMARY
(Erase heading not required.)

Army Form C. 2118.

17481 Vol 13

13 9.
9 sheets

Place	Date	Hour	Summary of Events and Information	Remarks and references to Appendices
Arras	1/2/19		Battn. in Billets. Weather frost. Hard frost.	
"	2/2/19		Battn. on March. Weather Good. Very cold. Battalion engaged in moving to vicinity of Paris. Battalion left Arras for "NANQUÉTIN" operations Order 50. 8 miles arrived 2 p.m.	
"	3/2/19		Battalion on March. " " " Left "NANQUÉTIN" for MAZIÈRES arrived 3 P.M. 10 miles	
Mazières	4/2/19		Battalion in Billets. " " " Battn. re-engaged in Company Platoon and Section	
"	5/2/19		" " " Section parades at full strength for inspection by G.O. Remainder of troops on musque new 1 new draft arr to Base number 195.	
"	6/2/19		Battalion on March " " " Left MAZIÈRES 11 A.M. for REBREUVE arrived 2 P.M. 8 miles, operation orders 51. Draft of 146 arrived	
Rebreuve	7/2/19		" Weather Very Cold. Left Rebreuve for GEZANCOURT at 10 A.M. arrived 2.30 p.m. 11 miles	
Gezencourt	8/2/19		" Weather Good. Very Cold. Left 9.30 a.m. for VIGNACOURT arrived 3 P.M. 13 miles. Commanding Officers explained all made in their open manding and	

WAR DIARY
or
INTELLIGENCE SUMMARY.
(Erase heading not required.)

Army Form C. 2118.

Place	Date	Hour	Summary of Events and Information	Remarks and references to Appendices
Vignacourt	9/2/17			
	10/2/17		Genl. divisional G.O.C. 35th Div. inspected Batn on march and complimented transport on their turn out. Batn in Billets "B6". Weather very cold. Batn cleaning and resting after march.	
	11/2/17		Batn in Billets. Weather fine. Re-organised Batn engaged in training according to 93 Brigade circular. Batn in training as storm Appendices under Specialist officers.	
	12/2/17		" " Weather very cold. Batn engaged in training.	
	13/2/17		" " Weather milder. " " " "	
	14/2/17		" " Weather bright but very cold. " " " "	
	15/2/17		" " " " " " " " One officer and one man wounded at Bombing Practice	
	16/2/17		" " Weather cold. Batn engaged in training 22 recruits Batn for Bras.	
	17/2/17		" " Weather cold. Long rain. Final of divisional League football competition played between Batn and D.L.I. resulting	

Army Form C. 2118.

WAR DIARY
or
INTELLIGENCE SUMMARY.
(Erase heading not required.)

Instructions regarding War Diaries and Intelligence Summaries are contained in F. S. Regs., Part II. and the Staff Manual respectively. Title pages will be prepared in manuscript.

Place	Date	Hour	Summary of Events and Information	Remarks and references to Appendices
VIGNACOURT	18/2/19		Batn in Billets. Weather Wet. In a sitting for the Batn of 6 goals to 1. Football team was complimented by Divisional General and presented with a badge. 9 men recruits left for Base.	LII.
	19/2/19		Batn on the move. Batn engaged in training. Transport left to MARCELCAVE. Operation Order 52. Batn left VIGNACOURT at 10 am for MARCELCAVÉ by train, arriving 2.30 P.M.	
MARCELCAVE	20/2/19		Batn in Billets. Weather Wet. Billets good in General. Resting and cleaning up.	
	21/2/19		" " Weather mild & dull. Batn engaged in training.	
	22/2/19		Batn on the move. Weather Wet. Moved to Camp-de-BALLON. distance 6½ miles.	LIII.
	23/2/19		Batn in Billets. Weather Dull. Batn resting and cleaning.	
C-de-BALLON	24/2/19		" " " Weather Wet. Batn in training.	
	25/2/19		" "	
	26/2/19		Batn in Trenches. Batn relieved composite Batn composed of 1/1st & 2/1st Lancs Fus in the LIHON NORTH SECTOR	

Army Form C. 2118.

WAR DIARY
or
INTELLIGENCE SUMMARY.
(Erase heading not required.)

Place	Date	Hour	Summary of Events and Information	Remarks and references to Appendices
Battn in trenches Kinkin Copse	24/2/17		Relief with very well carried considering the state of the trenches. Operation Order No 54 shew how frozen quietly in the station Casualties Nil.	LIV.
"	25.2.17		Situation quiet. much work done clearing trenches which are already greatly improved. Casualties 3.	

SECRET.   OPERATION ORDERS No.50   1.2.17.
                    18th.,(Ser) Bn., Highland Light Inf.   COPY No.

Reference:- 'LENS', 1/100,000.

1. The Battalion will move to-morrow, to billets at MAZIERES, via WANQUETIN, & AVESNES, halting for the night of 2nd.-3rd., at WANQUETIN.

2. Companies will parade in their various billets at 9.15 a.m. under Capt. Barr, and will move off, via RUE D'AMIENS & DAINVILLE, as follows:-

    'W' Company.   at   9.40 a.m.
    'X'   "   "   9.45 a.m.
    'Y'   "   "   9.50 a.m.
    'Z'   "   "   10 a.m.

3. Companies will move in parties of 10 at 200 yards interval between each party until they pass DAINVILLE. From there they will move as a Battalion to WANQUETIN.

4. Transport will move independantly to MAZIERES on the 2nd. & 3rd. February. Two cookers and one water cart will be sent from GOUVES on the morning of the 2nd. to meet the Battalion at WANQUETIN.

5. Rations for the 3rd. February will be delivered at WANQUETIN in the evening of 2nd. February.

6. The Battalion will leave WANQUETIN at 9 a.m. on 3rd. under orders to be issued by Capt. Barr.

                        (Signed) W.J.LYLE, Lieut. & Adjt.,
                                 18th.,(Ser) Bn., Highland Light Inf.

Issued at:-

Copies to:- 1/3 W.D. & O.O. File.
            4 Commanding, Officer.
            5. 2nd. in Command.
            6. 'W' Company.
            7. 'X'   "
            8. 'Y'   "
            9. 'Z'   "

SECRET Operation Orders No.51 5.2.17.
18th., (S) Bn., Highland L.I. Copy No....

Reference:- 'LENS' Map. 1/100,000.

1. The 35th. Division the VI Corps Area, and march to the BOUQUEMAISON Area on the 6th., inst. The Battalion will march to billets in REBREUVE, via MAGINCOURT, HOUVIN, CANNETTEMONT, & REBREUVETTE.

2. Companies and Headquarters will parade ready to move at 10.55 a.m. on the 6th. inst., in the following order:- 'Headquarters', 'Z'Coy., 'Y'Coy., 'Band', 'X'Coy., Lewis Gun Barrows, 1st. line Transport, 2nd., line Transport. Headquarters will parade in Square, 'Z'Coy., in AMBRINES Rd., 'Y', 'X', & 'W'Coys., in MAIRIE Rd., Lewis Gun Barrows and Transport in TERNAS Rd.

3. 'Z'Company will detail 1 Platoon as 'advance guard', 'W'Coy., will detail 10 men to report to the Transport Officer as brakesmen at 10.40 a.m. and ½ Platoon as 'Rear Guard'.

4. Interpreter HYATT will report to the Staff Captain at RICAMETZ at 8.30 a.m. on the 6th., to accompany him as Battalion Billetting representative. 2/Lieut.Gemmill, and 4 Quartermaster Sergeants will be at Q.M.Stores at 8 a.m. to proceed with the lorry for billetting purposes.

5. M.O. will march in the rear of the Battalion.

6. 'Rear Guard' will collect, and bring on, any men who fall out.

7. Reports to head of column.

(Signed) W.J.LYLE, Lieut. & Ajt.,

5.2.17. 18th., (Ser) Bn., Highland Light Inf.

Issued at; 12 noon.
Copies to:- W.D. & O.O.File. 1-3
          'W' Coy.   4
          'X' "   5
          'Y' "   6
          'Z' "   7
          Q.Mr.   8
          T.O.   9
          S.O.   10
          L.G.O.   11.
          2nd. in Commd. 12.
          M.O.   13
          Interpreter.   14.

SECRET. OPERATION ORDERS No.52. 17.3.17.
15th.,(S) Bn., Highland L.I. Copy No. ...

Reference sheets, 11 & 17 1/100,000

1. The Division will move to an area south of the SOMME by Rail, and march route between the 18th., & 19th., inclusive, and will take over the front now held by the 154th French Division, with the 155th., Brigade on the right, the 166th., Brigade on the left, and the 168th., Brigade in Divisional Reserve. The 168th., Inf. Bde, less Transport, will move by rail on the 18th., inst. The Battalion will entrain at VIGNACOURT Station at 10 a.m. for MARCELCAVE.

2. Companies will pass starting point, last billet of 'Z' Company, as follows:-
Signallers, Band, 8.40 a.m., 'Z' Coy., 8.41 a.m. 'Y' Coy., 8.42 a.m. 'X' Coy., 8.43 a.m., 'W' Coy., 8.44 a.m., HdQrs., 8.45 a.m. Lewis Gun handcarts, 8.46 a.m.

3. Capt. W.Kennedy, M.C. will report to Brigade Staff Captain at Bde. HdQrs., at 9 a.m., 18th., inst, as Battalion Billeting Representative. Interpreter Hyatt and Coy., Q.M.Sgts., will report to Brigade HdQrs. at 8.45 a.m on 18th., inst. bringing two days rations. They will entrain at VIGNACOURT for MARCELCAVE at 9 a.m. and they will report to the Staff Captain at the Church at MARCELCAVE at 5 p.m.

4. 1st. & 2nd. line Transport will pass Battalion Headquarters at 7.55 a.m. on the 18th., inst., and move with the remainder of Bde. Transport via ST.VAAST, AMIENS, VECQUEMONT, to billets at AUBIGNY. On the 19th., the Transport will march via VILLERS-BRETONNEUX to billets at MARCELCAVE.

5. Two days' rations will be issued to-morrow to all ranks. One blanket and the unexpended portion of the rations for 18th., will be carried on the men. No baggage will be taken on the train. Lewis Gun handcarts will be carried in the train in a covered waggon.

6. A lorry will leave Quartermaster's Stores at 8.00 a.m. on the 18th. and the remaining blanket per men, rolled in bundles and labelled, will be carried in this. All cooking utensils will also be carried in this lorry. They will be sent to Quartermaster's Stores before 8 a.m. on the 18th., inst.

(Signed) W.J.LYLE, Lieut. & Adjt.,

Issued at .... 18th.,(Ser) Bn., Highland Light Infantry.
Copies to:- 1-3 O.C.File & War Diary.
    4 'W' Company.
    5 'X'   "
    6 'Y'   "
    7 'Z'   "
    8 2nd. in Command.
    9 Quartermaster.
   10 Transport Officer.
   11 Lewis Gun Officer.
   12 Signalling Officer.
   13 Interpreter Hyatt.
   14 R.S.M.

SECRET.
Operation Orders No. 53.
18th., (S) Bn., Highland L.I.

21.2.17.
Copy No. .....

Reference Map:- 'AMIENS' 1/100,000.

1. The 106th., Inf. Brigade will move into Divisional Reserve on the afternoon of February 22nd. The Battalion will march to hutments at 'BALLOON WOOD' tomorrow.

2. Companies will fall in on their Alarm Posts ready to move off in the following order at 12.12 p.m.,-
   'Signallers', Band, 'Y', 'W', 'X', 'Z' Coys. H.Q. Lewis Gun Barrows.

3. 1st. line Transport and 2 Baggage Waggons will march in rear of the Brigade, leaving present billets at 1.30 p.m.

4. 2nd. in Command, and Coy. Q.M.Sergeants will leave at 10.30 a.m. to arrange hutting accommodation.

5. O.C. Companies will detail 4 men each to march with Transport to assist it over any bad ground.

6. M.O. will march in rear of the Battalion.

7. Reports to Head of Battalion.

(Signed) W.J. LYLE, Lieut. & Ajt.,
18th., (Ser) Bn., Highland Light Inf.

21.2.17.
Issued at 12 noon.

Copies to:- W.D. & O.O. File, 1-3
           Dictated to O.C. Companies.

SECRET   Operation Orders No.54.   25.2.17.
                18th.,(Ser) Bn., Highland L.I.   Copy No.......

Reference Map:-'ROSIERES' 1/40,000.

1. The 106th. Inf. Brigade will relieve the 104th., Inf. Brigade. in the 'LIHONS' Sector on the night of 26-27th. February, 1917. The Battalion will relieve the 20th., Lancs. Fus, & the 17th., Lancs. Fus. in the left sub-sector on the evening of 26th. inst. The 19th., D.L.I. will be inclose support in the Old German Line The 17th., R.Scots. will be in Reserve in 'ROSIERES'.

2. Companies will leave billets as under and march, via VRELY, to ROSIERES, where they will halt for dinner.
    'Z' Coy. Cooker & 1 limber at 10.15 a.m. to relieve LEFT Coy.
    'W' "   "   "   "   "   10.30 a.m. "   "   RIGHT "
    'Y' "   "   "   "   "   10.45 a.m. "   "   CENTRE"
    'X' "   "   "   "   "   11 a.m.   "   "   RESERVE.
    Headquarters and Mess Cart" 11 a.m.
Guides will meet Battalion at ROSIERES. As soon after dinner as visibility permits, the relief will commence in above order. Movement in ROSIERES-LIHONS ROAD will be in sections at 200 yds. interval.

3. All maps, trench stores, air-photos etc., will be taken over, receipts given and lists forwarded to Battalion Headquarters by 12 noon 27th.

4. Completion of each Company Relief will be reported to Battalion Headquarters by the Code word 'LUNDI'.

                          (Signed) W.J.LYLE, Lieut. & Adjt.,
25.2.17.   18th.,(Ser) Bn., Highland Light Infantry.

Issued verbally at 7 p.m.
3 Copies to W.D. & O.O.File.

Headquarters,
    106th Inf. Brigade.

        Herewith War Diary for month ending
    31st. March, 1917, with Operation Orders attached.
        Please acknowledge.

                    [signature]   Lieut-Colonel,
    1.4.17.   Commanding, 18th (S) Bn Highland Light Inf.

WAR DIARY
or
INTELLIGENCE SUMMARY.
(Erase heading not required.)

Army Form C. 2118.

18th. #.1.9

Place	Date	Hour	Summary of Events and Information	Remarks and references to Appendices
LIHONS.	1/3/17		Bn. in trenches. Weather very good. Artillery on both sides rather active. All men engaged on improving the existing conditions. Casualties 1.O.R.	
	2/3/17	"	Weather much but fine. Men engaged on usual trench routine. Working &c. during early part of day. At night Bn. was relieved by 17th Royal Scots Relief was well & quickly carried out, being completed by 10.45 p.m. Bn. then marched to ROSIERES to billets in Bgde. Reserve. Billets good.	
ROSIERES	3/3/17	"	Bn. in Billets. Weather good. Men engaged in cleaning up & resting. At night, there were some small working parties.	
	4/3/17	"	Weather dull & cold. Battn. engaged in training. Specialists with their respective Officers. Working parties.	
	5/3/17	"	Weather cold with snow. Battn. engaged as above.	
	6/3/17	"	Weather good. In the morning men were engaged in preparations for moving. At night Bn. relieved 17th/2nd Royal Scots in front line trenches, LIHONS, N. Sector. Relief well & quickly carried out, being completed by 10 p.m. Casualties	
LIHONS	7/3/17		Bn. in trenches. Weather good. Some front line trench & Co. Company were heavily trench mortared at 9 a.m. again at 6.30 p.m. Casualties 3	

Army Form C. 2118.

WAR DIARY
or
INTELLIGENCE SUMMARY.
(Erase heading not required.)

18th High. L.I.

Instructions regarding War Diaries and Intelligence Summaries are contained in F.S. Regs., Part II. and the Staff Manual respectively. Title pages will be prepared in manuscript.

Place	Date	Hour	Summary of Events and Information	Remarks and references to Appendices
LESARS	8/3/17		Bn. in trenches. Weather good. Frost continues. Men engaged in repairing & clearing the trenches. The day & night were much more quiet.	
	9/3/17	"	Weather cold with snow. Work continues as before in the morning. Little shelling at night. Bn. relieved by 3rd WORCESTERS, of 5 Div. Relief completed by 9.30 p.m. Two platoons of Right Company went into support trenches.	L.V.
	10/3/17	"	(April) Weather dull, some rain. In accordance with Byle. move, the Bn. moved out from IRIS TRENCH to PARIS TRENCH, (still in support). The two platoons of the Right Coy., left in front line, were relieved at 12.15 a.m. Casualties 1. At night, working parties were supplied.	
	11/3/17	"	Weather good. Bn. engaged on work on trenches, cleaning, repairing. Working parties were supplied for work on communication trenches etc. Wiring parties were also supplied.	
	12/3/17	"	Weather dull. Bn. engaged as above. The support trenches were shelled during the evening without effect.	
	13/3/17	"	Weather dull, some rain. Bn. engaged on work as morning. Bn. was relieved at night by 10th CHESHIRES, 25th Div. & marched to BECOURT CAMP (so-la) (?)	L.V.

T2134. Wt. W708—776. 500000. 4/15. Sir J. C. & 8.

WAR DIARY
or
INTELLIGENCE SUMMARY.
(Erase heading not required.)

1/8th High. L.I.

Army Form C. 2118.

Place	Date	Hour	Summary of Events and Information	Remarks and references to Appendices
DECAUVILLE CAMP.	14/3/17		Bn. in Hts. Weather bad. Bn. this day employed in putting & cleaning Billets generally good.	
	15/3/17		" " Weather good. Bn. engaged in fitting, practising attack formations & musketry training in the period.	
	16/3/17		" " Weather very good. Training as above. Bn. moved to VRÉLY under O.C. orders at 10 pm. Arrived VRÉLY 1 am 17/3/17.	
VRÉLY	17/3/17		Bn. on Move. Bn. moved from VRÉLY at 9 am to CHILLY area. Working parties were detailed for work on CHILLY - HALLU Road.	
CHILLY	18/3/17		Bn. in dug-outs & shell holes. Weather cold. Work on Roads as before.	
	19/3/17		Bn. on move. Weather v. fair. Some snow. Bn. moved at 9.30 a.m. to ROSIÈRES, arriving about 2 noon. Billets very good. Afternoon putting & cleaning up.	
ROSIÈRES	20/3/17		Bn. in Billets. Weather cold & wet. Whole Bn. engaged on work repairing the LIHONS-CHAULNES R.R. vacated by picking crevices.	
	21/3/17		" " Weather colder. Same. Same work as before.	
	22/3/17		" " Weather good. Bn. engaged on work on LIHONS-CHAULNES Road	
	23/3/17		" " Weather good. Work as above	
	24/3/17		" " " " Draft of 35 O.R's & three Officers arrived. Major V.E.	

WAR DIARY or **INTELLIGENCE SUMMARY.**
(Erase heading not required.)

Army Form C. 2118.

18th. High. L.I.

Place	Date	Hour	Summary of Events and Information	Remarks and references to Appendices
ROSIERES	24/3/17		GOODERSON, DSO also arrived, reporting Bn. for duty.	
	25/3/17		Bn. in Billets. Weather good. Working parts as before. Draft of 6 I.O.R.s. arrived to join unit.	
	26/3/17		" " " " 22 O.R.s sent to Base as unfit	
	27/3/17		" " " "	
	28/3/17		Weather changeable. Much rain. Slept. Preparations for move.	
	29/3/17		Weather vile. Bn. on move to MARCHÉLEPOT via OMIÉCOURT. Bad Billets. Men drenched in rain. Trail. (9 miles) Operation Order No. 39	
MARCHÉLEPOT	30/3/17		Bn. on Move. Weather vile. Bn. left ab. 12.30 p.m. for ATHIES, arriving about 3 p.m. (marched) Thunder hail braced Somme, about 2.30 p.m. Billets fair. Working parties for filling up craters on Roads	
ATHIES	31/3/17		Bn. in Billets. Weather fair, windy, some rain. Working parties as yesterday	

18th Bn. Highland Light Infantry

SECRET.

Operation Orders No.55   9.3.17.
18th (S) Bn Highland L.Inf.

Reference map:- CHAULNES Trench.

1. Battalion, less 3 platoons will be relived by 7th WORCESTERS, 61st. Div., to-night, and on relief will take over Support lines in 'IRIS' Trench from 17th Royal Scots.

2. That portion of 'X' Occupying the trench South of LIHONS--CHAULNES Road will remain in position, until relieved by the 19th D.L.I. on the night of 10/11th. They will be under the orders of O.C.17th.W.Yorks R., for tactical purposes until relieved. O.C.'X' Coy. will arrange to establish with 7th Worcesters on left, a mixed post at the LIHONS--CHAULNES Road.

3. Guides, 1 per platoon, from Coys in the line will be at Bn. H.Q. at 6 p.m. O.C.'W' Coy. will arrange to send 9 guides to meet incoming platoons at the LIHON Ration Dump and also arrange to picket Communication Trench.

4. All trench stores will be handed over, receipt taken for same and forwarded to the Adjutant at 12 noon to-morrow.

5. O.C.Companies will report in person on completion of relief.

(Sd.) W.F.M.Macara, 2/Lt.& A/Ajt.,
9.3.17.   18th (S) Bn Highland Light Infantry.
Issued at:- 4 p.m.
Copies to O.C.Companies, (4)
          W.D.& O.O.File (3)

SECRET.
                    Operation Orders No.56.   13.3.17.
                    18th (S) Bn Highland L.Inf.

Reference map:-CHAULNES Trench.

1. The Battalion will be relieved by 16th CHESHIRES Regt. on the night of the 14/15th March.

2. Guides, 1 per platoon and 1 for H.Q. will be at Junction of Railway and PARIS Trench at 4 p.m., where an Officer of 'X' Company the party to be at Bde. H.Q. 5 p.m. These guides should reconnoitre and thoroughly know the route ROSIERES- -LIHON Road, then along the Railway to PARIS-IRIS Trench.

3. Lewis Gun Magazines and one stretcher per Company will be handed over and receipts taken from the incoming Unit.

4. All maps, air photos and trench stores will be handed over, receipts taken and handed over to the Adjutant by 12 noon, the morning after the relief.

5. On relief, the Companies will be billetted at 'A' Camp, DECAUVILLE WOOD.

6. Completion of relief will be reported to Battalion H.Q.

                            (Sd.) W.F.M.Macara, 2/Lt.& A/Ajt.,
13.3.17.   18th (S) Bn Highland Light Infantry.

Issued at 12 noon.
Copies to all Companies - 4
          W.D.& O.O.File. - 3

SECRET.   OPERATION ORDERS No. 27.   Copy No. 2
          18th (S) Bn Highland L. Inf.   28.3.17.

Reference Map:- 1/1000,000 AMIENS-ST.QUENTIN.

1.   The Division (less the 105th Brigade) will move to
        the left bank of the River SOMME on 29th. The Battalion
        will march to-morrow to billets at MARCHELEPOT.

2.   Companies will pass starting point, cross roads at
        Eastern exit of ROSIERES, in the following order;-

                Signallers, Band, & 'W' Coy. at   10.15 a.m.
                                    'Z' "   "   10.17 a.m.
                                    'Y' "   "   10.19 a.m.
                                    'X' "   "   10.21 a.m.
                                    H.Q. "   "   10.23 a.m.

        and march via LIHONS, CHAULNES Road to MARCHELEPOT.
                    & OMIECOURT

3.   East of the old German line, the Battalion will move
        by Companies at ½ mile intervals.

4.   1st. line Transport and baggage wagons will assemble
        at Q.M. Stores at 10 a.m. and pass starting point at
        10.25 a.m. and follow in rear of Battalion.

5.   O.C. 'X' Company will detail 1 N.C.O. and 6 men to
        report to Transport Officer at 10 a.m. as brakesmen.

6.   Companies will report location of their Companies,
        and Coy. H.Q. as soon as possible after arrival.

7.   Reports will be sent to head of column.

                              (Signed) R.R. LAWRENSON" Lt-Col.,
28.3.17.   Commanding, 18th (S) Bn Highland Light Infantry.

Issued at:- 7 p.m.
Copies to:- 1-3 W.D.
              4 O.C. 'W' Coy.
              5 "   'X' "
              6 "   'Y' "
              7 "   'Z' "
              8 2nd. in Command.
              9 Signalling Off.
             10 Transport Off.
             11 Quartermaster.

April 1917   Army Form C. 2118.

WAR DIARY
or
INTELLIGENCE SUMMARY.
(Erase heading not required.)

18 (S) Bn Argyle S. 9.

Vol 15

15. 9.
10 sheets

Place	Date	Hour	Summary of Events and Information	Remarks and references to Appendices
ATHIES	1/4/17		Batn in Billets. Weather fine. Some raw Batns engaged on working parties, on roads & improving communications.	
	2/4/17		Specialist training under specialist officers. Batn in Billets, Weather stormy. Work as above. Three men were injured by falling buildings	
	3/4/17		Batn in Billets. Weather Stormy. Work as above	
	4/4/17		do. Weather bad, much snow. Work as above	
	5/4/17		do. Weather good. do	
	6/4/17		do. Weather ill and cold, some snow. do	
	7/4/17		do. Weather changeable. Some snow. Work as above during forenoon. In afternoon a practice attack was carried out by Batn on a village with success.	

8/9/17 SOYECOURT Relief: both our lines from 2/6th Bucks.shire Regt. relief completed by 11-30 p.m. Weather very bad, a snow storm was on when the ground was in a muddy and foldy state.

13/4/17 VERMAND — 7th Brigade Support. Battalion resting prior to taking over line on 16/4/17 from 17th R. Scots. Weather good. Entraining of ellens etc. in town. Working parties furnished by companies from 5 A.M. till 5 P.M. Reconnaissance of line by officers.

14/4/17 VERMAND — 7th Brigade Support. Working parties employed in repairing roads and filling in craters at road junctions. One of its working parties was shelled slightly at one of the craters. Company in support at railway with drawn. Brigade support.

15/4/17 SOYÉCOURT — 7th Working parties employed in repairing roads and craters at road junctions. Company.
Brigade support.

16/4/17 SOYÉCOURT — 7th Working parties employed in repairing roads and craters at road junctions.
Brigade support.

17/4/17 SOYÉCOURT — 7th Soyécourt, 7 working parties employed in repairing roads and craters at road junction.

18/4/17 SOYÉCOURT — 7th Front line, improving our defensive trenches. Constructing shelters etc. At night a patrol went out and advanced towards ASCENTION FARM. On arriving at copse to S.E. of village they heard talking from the front, it between the turn around the copse. There was very little to be seen over the patrol returned.

19/4/17 SOYÉCOURT — 7th Front line, improving our defensive trenches. Constructing shelters etc. A patrol went out. Our advancing towards ASCENTION FARM found occupied ROUGE FARM. Finding this, also the patrol advanced towards the former farm, and also they from was occupied by the enemy and that a patrol was established between the farms and to the copse to the S.E. The patrol returned about 12 mid-night.

17/4/19. the bridges they encountered a hostile patrol which immediately went back and disappeared, owing to the darkness it was considered to ascertain where they had disappeared to & as the patrol was not strong enough for fighting the patrol moved back to our lines. It rained again during the night. On men seen from opposite during the night.

18/4/19 MAISSEMY. ✗ Inspection. Weather fine. Rain and a bit of intervals during the day. Very slight shelling on back areas. Outposts established well in front of main trench. Harassing on enemy trenches by strenuous attacks. At night three patrols were sent out. The first one moved for the S. of PONTRUET and worked at about 10 - night of 20 to S.E. On gaining all clear patrol returned. The 2nd patrol worked from S.E. of the village and reconnoitred corner of the road. On gaining all clear the patrol returned. The 3rd patrol on reaching G.E. of village from BERTHACOURT and January were harassed and held by the enemy immediately in front of the village. The advance was made by a few advanced parties, an enemy under an officer worked up to the S left about, doubles worked at the left arm of the trench and watched it the night. Our men are at 10 - to make running to running parallel to the main arm and to - to make running to BELLENGLISE. No hostile patrol was encountered and village was found to be unoccupied. All our patrols returned to our own lines just as dawn was breaking.

Battalion took over BERTHACOURT line & trenches from 17th A. Scots. Relief completed by 12 midnight. ✗

War Diary

18/4/17 MAISSEMY

At Pont-bru. Weather after unsettled, rain and slight showers snow fell in the forenoon. In afternoon enemys artillery shelling ridge behind Moor of the cemeteries, no damage was done. Between 5- and 6 an enemy shell in vicinity of ruin not what is believed 9·5- or 8-inch shells. No apparent damage done. To the enemy. W. Cy sent out a patrol to reconnoitre trenches S.E of PONTRUET, there were seen to be a number by the enemy. "Y" Coy then sent out a strong patrol of 3 offs and 60 OR's to PONTRUET. Entering the village by the BERTAMCOURT — PONTRUET road the patrol worked through the village. What is a menia state, in these trenches. The roads leading to BELLENGLISE, ERICOURT + mais. St QUENTIN rode were blocked by trails and a patrol and proceeded to bridge crossing its river to the N.N.E. of the junction of roads in village. The bridge was found to have been destroyed and was a gap of some to feet had been made. Working parties were heard at work to N and E of village, on high ground, on other roads, presumably in enemy our patrol is the village. No foe was encountered it reached the patrol then took up a position in the village and reconnoitred the gravity, in the hope of catching any hostile patrols which might enter the village. No hostile patrols appearing, our posts withdrew via BERTANCOURT at 3 A.M. Our Front line hardly shelled from 7-30 hr to 10 hr. 2 casualties, no killed and no wounded.

19/4/17 MAISSEMY

At Pont-bru, rain falling heavily practically all day. Very little shelling during forenoon. In afternoon our batteries opened a slow fire on enemys trenches. The enemy only slight retaliation. In the evening two other different patrols worked their way towards PONTRUET. One patrol entered the village and reconnoitres and worked to & of the bridge, the other was clear of the enemy, the other patrol moved towards buy- crossing the river towards STE HELENE. Just as they approached the

WAR DIARY
or
INTELLIGENCE SUMMARY.
(Erase heading not required.)

Army Form C. 2118.

Instructions regarding War Diaries and Intelligence Summaries are contained in F.S. Regs., Part II. and the Staff Manual respectively. Title pages will be prepared in manuscript.

Place	Date	Hour	Summary of Events and Information	Remarks and references to Appendices
MESSIGNY.	19/8/17		Weather bright & clear. Artillery activity medium. Some shelling of MESSIGNY in afternoon. Aerial activity	
	20/4/17		Weather —do—. Preparations for move.	
			Arra. Slight arty activity. Our own artillery concentrated their fire	
			5 minutes straffes on their batteries, ammunition dumps & storing points.	IX
VERMAND.	21/4/17		Weather Bright & fine. Bn. resting & cleaning up.	
	22/4/17		" " on working parties. Artillery & aerial activity.	
	23/4/17		" " Preparations for move to TERTRY Bn. moves about 2 pm — via	
			CAULAINCOURT.	
	24/4/17		Bn. resting, cleaning up &	
	25/4/17		" " on working parties & training	
	26/4/17		" " " " " "	
	27/4/17		" " " " " "	
	28/4/17		" " " " Taken as a Battalion both forenoon & afternoon	
TERTRY	29/4/17		" " on working parties & on much parades. O/C Coys. reconnoitre lines to be occupied by Bns. tomorrow	

Army Form C. 2118.

WAR DIARY
or
INTELLIGENCE SUMMARY.
(Erase heading not required.)

Instructions regarding War Diaries and Intelligence Summaries are contained in F. S. Regs., Part II. and the Staff Manual respectively. Title pages will be prepared in manuscript.

Place	Date	Hour	Summary of Events and Information	Remarks and references to Appendices
TERTRY.	30/4/17.		Weather exceedingly warm. Preparations for move to line. Bn. moves at 2.30 p.m. going via CAULAINCOURT and returning for tea in vicinity of GERMAND. Bn. moves up the line about 8.30 p.m. & relieves 15 L'SHIRE Reg.t in GRICOURT Area. Some patrol work during night. Casualties night 30/1st: 2 wounded & 2 missing. O.p.k.o.	

SECRET. OPERATION ORDERS No.58   15.4.17.
         HIGHLAND LIGHT INFANTRY.

Ref. sht to 52c N.E. & 62b.N.W.

1. The Battalion will relieve the 17th R.Scots on the night of the 16th/17th in the BATHACOURT District.

2. The disposition of the Battalion will be as follows:-

   'W' Coy will relieve 'A'Coy.R.Scots on Right of line.
   'Z' "   "   "   'Y' "   "   "   " Left   "
   'Y' "   "   "   'Y' "   "   "   " Support
   'X' "   "   "   'X' "   "   "   " Reserve.
   H.Qrs. will be at KRISTMY R.25.B.3.5.

   Companies will move off in above order by platoons at 200 yards interval at an hour to be notified later, not earlier than 7.15 p.m.

3. Advanced parties of 1 Officer per Company, 1 N.C.O. per platoon, Signallers, one runner per Coy, and No.1 of Lewis Gun Teams of Companies in line will proceed in advance, leaving at 5.30 p.m. and will report at Bn.H.Q. 17th.R.Scots, at KRISTMY.

4. Guides will meet Companies at R.22.S.8.5. (entrance to KRISTMY) at 6 p.m.

5. Advanced posts are being established to-night by 17th.R. Scots about M.9.c.6.0.- M.15.A.9.4.-M.15.B.5.4. These will be held by ½ platoon in each post. Owing to difficulties of communication, these ½ platoons should be rationed and have a supply of water to last them 24 hours. Posts will be found by 'W' & 'Z' Companies.

6. All S.A.A., Bombs, Flares, Shelters, Stores, etc. will be taken over and receipts handed over to the Adjutant by 12 noon day following relief.

7. Completion of relief will be notified to Adjutant, Bn. H.Q. by the code word 'BEYOND'.

                              (Signed) W.J.LYLE, Capt. & Adjt,.

Issued at:-7.30 p.m.   HIGHLAND LIGHT INFANTRY.
Copies No.1-3 to W.D.& O. File.
          4 " 'W' Coy.
          5 " 'X' "
          6 " 'Y' "
          7 " 'Z' "
          8 " 17th R.Scots.
          9 " 20th Lancs.Fus.(Bn.on Right.)
         10 " 17th.W.Yorks.
         11 " 2nd, in Command.

SECRET.

ARMOUR.   O.RATIVE ORDER. NO.59.   12.6.17.
                    HIGHLAND LIGHT INFANTRY.

Ref. Sheets 51.c.S.E. & 62.S.S.E.

1.   The Battalion will be relieved by the 17th Royal Scots
     on the night of the 30/31st. in the ROCLINCOURT Dists.

2.   The Companies will be relieved as follows:-
     'Y' Coy. R.Scots will relieve 'W' Coy on Right of line.
     'Z' "   "   "   "   'X' "   " Left   " "
     'X' "   "   "   "   'Y' "   In Support.
     'W' "   "   "   "   'Z' "   Reserve.

3.   Advance parties of the Royal Scots will be at Bn.H.Q.
     at 2 p.m. to take over stores etc., One guide per
     Company will be at Battn. H.Q. at that time.

4.   One guide per platoon from each Company and one for
     each post from 'W' & 'X' Coys. will meet their res-
     -pective parties at R.12.b.9.5.(Entrance to MOSSIARY)
     at 7.45 p.m.

5.   All S.A.A.,Bombs,Flares,Shelters,Stores, etc., will be
     handed over and receipts taken and forwarded to the
     Adjutant by 12 noon day after relief. Receipts for
     shelters handed over will be taken separately and
     forwarded to the Adjutant in duplicate.

6.   Billeting parties of 1 Officer and 1 N.C.O. per
     platoon will leave about 2 p.m. to take over the same
     billets as their Company occupied formerly at VERDREL.

7.   Completion of relief will be notified to the Adjutant
     at Battn. H.Q. by the code word "GLASGOW".

                        (Signed) W.J.LYLE, Capt. & Adjt.,

12.6.17.   HIGHLAND LIGHT INFANTRY.

Issued at:- 6 p.m.
Copies Nos. 1-3 War Diary & O.O. File.
            4 'W' Coy.
            5 'X' "
            6 'Y' "
            7 'Z' "
            8 Bn. On Right.
            9 "   " Left.
           10 17th Royal Scots.
           11 2nd. In Command.

SECRET.   OPERATION ORDERS NO.60   29.4.17.
         HIGHLAND LIGHT INFANTRY.
                                    Copy No......

Ref. 62.B.S.W. 1/20,000 & 62.c 1/40,000.

1. The Brigade will relieve the 105th.Brigade on the night 30th-1st. The Battalion will relieve the 15th.Cheshires on the left Sub-sector.

2. 'X' Coy. will relieve the coy. of 15th Cheshires holding the outpost line in M.17.w.5.0 to M.10.d.5.0 with two platoons. The remaining two platoons of 'X' Coy. will be in support in trenches on GRICOURT-PONTRUET Road about M.22.c. 'Y'Coy. will be in support on the left of the two platoons 'X' Coy on the road. 'W' & 'Z' Companies will be in reserve in the BROWN line.

3. One Officer per Company and 1 N.C.O. per platoon will proceed to the line at 1.30 p.m. to take over stores etc. One runner and two signallers per company will also proceed at that hour. 2/Lt.McColl, Sgt. Gibson, and two signallers will go with the party. All above will assemble at Battn.Hdqrs. at 1.30 p.m.

4. All trench stores, maps, shelters, accommodation etc. will be taken over, receipts given and lists forwarded to the Adjutant by 12 noon 1st.May.

5. Companies will be ready to move off at 3.30 p.m. They will take their cookers with them, and will halt for tea in the vicinity of VERMAND. One limber will be at the disposal of each Company for rations, water cans, Lewis Guns & magazines etc.

6. Movements as far as CAULAINCOURT will be by Companies at 300 yards interval, and after that by platoons at 200 yds intervals.

7. Completion of relief will be notified to Battn.Hdqrs by the code figures '601'.

                              (signed)W.P.MACARA, 2/LT.& A/Adjt,
29.4.17.   HIGHLAND LIGHT INFANTRY.

Issued at 8.30 p.m.
Copies Nos. 1-3 W.D. r O/o File.
              4 W Coy
              5 X "
              6 Y "
              7 Z "
              8 2ps in Command.
              9 Lewis Gun Officer.
             10. 15 CHESHIRE REGT

WAR DIARY
INTELLIGENCE SUMMARY.
(Erase heading not required.)

Army Form C. 2118.

Place	Date	Hour	Summary of Events and Information	Remarks and references to Appendices
Bettelidh in Line	1.5.17.	Weather Good.	The line was held by two platoons in advance posts, 6 platoons in supports to them, and two companies in support behind. Two observers went out by night from advanced posts and remained out all day. Much valuable information was obtained. At night, work was done on trenches and wire. Three strong patrols went out at night and encountered the enemy. Casualties. Wounded 2 O.Rs. Missing 2 Other Ranks.	
	2.5.17.	"	The day was quiet with little shelling. At night work was carried on as before and again, strong patrols went out. As the night was very light, these patrols were observed and fired on. Casualties, wounded 6 O.Rs.	
	3.5.17.	"	There was more artillery firing during the day. At night, work was as usual, wiring digging and improving trenches. A strong patrol with Lewis Guns & Stokes Guns went out to harass enemy working parties. Machine Gun which was turned on our patrol was fired at by our Stokes & Lewis Guns and silenced. Casualties. Killed 1 O.R. and Wounded 2 O.Rs.	
	4.5.17.	"	Enemy artillery more active. The vicinity of B.H.Q. was shelled between 4 & 6 p.m. At night the Battalion was relieved by 105th Brigade, 15th. CHESHIRE Battalion and moved back to MAISSEMY in Brigade Support.	
MAISSEMY	5.5.17.	"	Battalion Headquarters and 1 Company at MAISSEMY. 3 Companies in a Valley 300 yds. behind. No movement by day on account of enemy observation. At night, large working parties were sent to work on support trenches.	
"	6.5.17.	"	Work as above.	
"	7.5.17.	"	"	
"	8.5.17.	Wet.	MAISSEMY was shelled with 5·9's in the morning. The Battalion was relieved by 15th CHESHIRE Regt., 105th Brigade and moved to TERTRY.	
TERTRY.	9.5.17.	Good.	The day was spent in Bathing and cleaning. Inspection of clothing etc. took place.	
"	10.5.17.	"	in morning. In the evening there was rain. Training was carried out. Platoons in attack &c.	
"	11.5.17.	"	Working party of 200 men. Remainder training. Specialist training was carried out.	
"	12.5.17.	"	in morning and wet in afternoon. Training and working parties as above.	
"	13.5.17.	"	Severe storm at night. Training as usual.	
"	14.5.17.	Warm & Bright.	Training as before.	
"	15.5.17.	Wet.	"	
"	16.5.17.	"	Training carried out. Battalion practise an attack.	

Army Form C. 2118.

WAR DIARY
INTELLIGENCE SUMMARY.

(Erase heading not required.)

Place	Date	Hour	Summary of Events and Information	Remarks and references to Appendices
TERTRY.	17.5.17.		Weather dull. Training was carried out in morning. In afternoon Battalion Route March was carried out.	
"	18.5.17.	"	good. Training was carried out in morning. In afternoon Battalion made preparations for move next day.	
"	19.5.17.	"	Dull but dry. Battalion move to PERONNE. Left TERTRY. 7.30 a.m. arrived PERONNE 10.30 a.m. Distance about 8 miles. Operation Orders No. 62.	L
PERONNE	20.5.17.	"	good. Battalion rest and prepare for move next day. Brigadier-General J.H.W.POLLARD took over command of 106th Brigade vice Brigadier-General H.O'DONNELL.	
"	21.5.17.	"	" Battalion moved off at 7 a.m. for SOREL-LE-GRAND arriving about 12 noon. Distance about 12 miles. Rest during afternoon.	
SOREL-LE-GRAND.	22.5.17.	"	very wet. Preparations to proceed to line carried out. Advanced party proceeded to line at night.	
"	23.5.17.	"	good. Battalion resting during morning. Moved to line at VILLERS-GUISLAN Sector at 8 p.m. relieving 12th.SUFFOLKS,121st.Brigade, 40th Division. Relief complete without incident by 12.55 p.m. Casualties. 1 Officer 1 O.R.Wounded.Slightly.	
VILLERS-GUISLAN.	24.5.17.	"	very warm. Battalion holding Right of Division, with Cavalry on our Right, (17thLancers). on the left, 17th W.YORKS.R. of 106t Bde. Battalion engaged in working (improving trenches) and wiring. Strong patrols were sent out during the night. The front line is held by a system of posts, 18 in all. There is a continuous line, but it is in an unfinished state and lateral communication is difficult in daylight. 1 Cdy. is in Support & 1 in Reserve.	
"	25.5.17.	"	Good. Work on, & improvement of wire, of front line, special attention being paid to drainage. The attitude of the enemy in this sector is quiet with little artillery fire. At night there is considerable M.G. & Rifle fire. 1 Officer fatally wounded and 1 O.R. slightly wounded.	
"	26.5.17.	"	" Work and wiring as before. Parties of Cavalry attached to Battalion for instruction in wiring and patrolling.	
"	27.5.17.	"	" Battalion relieved by 17th R.SCOTS. Operation Orders No. 64.	LX
"	28.5.17.	"	" Battalion in Brigade Reserve. Battalion engaged on work on 'GREEN LINE' & with R.E's.	
"	29.5.17.	"	" " " " " " "	
"	30.5.17.	"	" " " " Some rain & tnight.	
"	31.5.17.	"	" " " " Much aerial activity. Hun's A.A. very active.	

SECRET.   OPERATION ORDERS No. 60.   Copy No. ____
          HIGHLAND LIGHT INFANTRY.

Reference 62.B.S.W. 1/20.000.

1. The Battalion will be relieved by 17th R.SCOTS on the night of 4/5th. as follows:-
   'X' Coy. H.L.I. by 'Z' Coy. R.Scots.
   'Y' "   "   " 'X' "   "
   'W' "   "   " 'W' "   "
   'Z' "   "   " 'Y' "   "

2. Guides 1 per platoon will be at Cross Roads M.21.c.45.2 at 8.45 p.m.

3. 1 Officer and 1 N.C.O. per Company will be sent on in advance this afternoon to take over billets from Royal Scots as follows;
   'X' Company from 'X' Company R.S. MAISSEMY
   'W'   "   "   'W'   "   " In valley R.22.D.
   'Y'   "   "   'Y'   "   "   "   "   "
   'Z'   "   "   'Z'   "   "   "   "   "
   Headquarters " Hdqrs.   MAISSEMY.

4. All trench stores, shelters, tools maps, air photographs etc. will be handed over receipts obtained & forwarded to the Adjt. by 12 noon to-morrow. Petrol tins will be taken out.

5. Companies will be careful to hand over to relieving companies exact programme of work and wiring on their Company front.

6. Relief completed will be intimated to B.H.Q. by Code word 'GIRL'.

Issued at:- 7 p.m.   (Sd.G.R.McCOLL, Ac/Adjt.,
Copies to:- 1-3 W.D.& O.O.File. HIGHLAND LIGHT INFANTRY.
            4 'W' Coy.
            5 'X' "
            6 'Y' "
            7 'Z' "
            8 2nd. in Command.
            9 17th.R.Scots.

SECRET.   OPERATION ORDERS No.61.   7.5.17.
          HIGHLAND LIGHT INFANTRY.

Reference map, sheets 62B.S.W. & 62C S.E.
----

1. The 105th Brigade will relieve the 106th Brigade in the
   FRESNOY Sector on 8th. May. The Battalion will be relieved
   by the 15th. CHESHIRE Regt. on the afternoon & evening of
   that day.

2. All trench stores, shelters etc. will be handed over, receipts
   obtained and forwarded to the Adjutant. Petrol tins and tools
   will not be handed over.

3. Billetting parties of 1 Officer & 1 N.C.O. per Company 2/Lt.
   Gemmill & Sgt. Oatts for HdQrs. will proceed to TERTRY, Arriv-
   -ing there before 1 p.m. to take over billets, tents, shelters
   and stores. Companies will occupy the same billets as before
   in TERTRY.

4. One limber will be sent to each Company on afternoon of 8th.
   to convey Lewis Guns, Magazines, 'Officers' Valises. Mess
   Cart and 1 limber will be sent for HdQrs at 6 p.m.

5. Companies will move by sections at 200 yards interval as far
   as VILLECHOLES, from there to CAULAINCOURT by platoons at
   200 yards interval, and from CAULAINCOURT movement will be by
   Companies at 200 yards interval.

6. Companies will report Completion of relief by telephone Code
   Word 'STEDINBOSH'.

                                (Signed) W.F.M. MACARA, Lt.&Ac/Ajt.

Issued at:- 9 p.m. 7th.
Copies to:- 1-3 W.D.& O.O.File.
            4 'W' Coy.
            5 'X' "
            6 'Y' "
            7 'Z' "
            8 2nd. in Command.
            9 15th. CHESHIRE Regt.
           10 Lewis Gun Officer.

SECRET.   OPERATION ORDERS No.62.   18.5.17.
                       HIGHLAND LIGHT INFANTRY.   Copy No......

Reference sheet 62 C. 1/40,000.
----

1. The Division is being relieved by the French and is marching to join the 15th. Corps. The Brigade will march to-morrow to billets in PERONNE.

2. Battalion will, pass Cross roads W.2.c.3.9. as under and march via TERTRY, DOINGT, PERONNE Road.

   Advd.Guard 'X' Coy. (H.L.I.)   at 6.25 a.m.
   Brigade HdQrs.   " 6.28 a.m.
   Battalion "   " 6.30 a.m.
   'Z' Coy.   " 6.31 a.m.
   'Y' "   " 6.32 a.m.
   'W' "   (less 1 platoon.)   " 6.33 a.m.
   Transport, 1st.& 2nd.line.   " 6.35 a.m.
   Royal Scots.   " 6.40 a.m.

3. One platoon of 'W' Coy. will march in rear of Transport for purpose of preventing straggling and assisting the Transport in difficulties. This platoon will supply necessary brakesmen for limbers.

4. One officer per Company and 1 for HdQrs. will report to Staff Captain at Town Major's Office, PERONNE at 4 p.m. to-day to arrange billets.

5. A rear party of 1 N.C.O. and 4 men will be left behind from each Company to clean up billets. This party will assemble at Cross Roads TERTRY at 10.30 a.m. and march under 2/Lt.A.McCall to new billets. 2/Lt.McCall will be responsible that all camps are left clean.

6. Transport will march in following order;- Transport, Pack animals, Lewis Gun Limbers, S.A.A. & Bomb limbers, Tools, Cookers, Water Carts, Maltese Cart, Mess Cart, Baggage wagons.

7. All tents & shelters will be handed over to representative of 105th Brigade, receipts obtained, and forwarded to Adjt., by 6 p.m. to-morrow.

8. 'Marching In' states, 'Return of men fallen out', & 'Location returns' will be sent to Orderly Room as soon as Companies are established in billets.

                              (Signed) W.J.LYLE, Capt, & Adjt.,
                                       HIGHLAND LIGHT INFANTRY.

17.5.17.
Issued at;- 11 a.m.
Copies to;- 1-3 W.D.& O.O.File.
            4 'W' Coy.
            5 'X' "
            6 'Y' "
            7 'Z' "
            8 2nd.in Command.
            9 Transport Officer.

SECRET.   OPERATION ORDER No.63.   22.5.17.
                       HIGHLAND LIGHT INFANTRY.

         Reference sheet 57c.S.E. 1/20.000.

1.   The Battalion will relieve the 12th.Suffolk Regt. in the Right
     Battalion front on the night of 23rd/24th.

2.   DISPOSITIONS.
     'W' Coy. will take over from A & D Coys. on Right of line.
     'Y' "   "   "   "   "   C Coy.& Cyclists on Left "
     'X' "   "   "   "   "   2 platoons of B Company.
     'Z' "   "   "   "   "   2 platoons of B   "
     Each front line Company will find its' own support.

3.   Companies will send Advance parties into line to-night as under.
     They will parade at 7.30 p.m., and will be met by guides at
     VAUCELLETTE FARM at 9 p.m.
          1 Officer per Company.
          1 N.C.O. per platoon.
          1 Signaller per Company.
          No.1s of Lewis Gun Teams. (Front line Coys. only).

4.   O.C.'X' Coy. will detail 2 Lewis Gun Teams to each of front
     line Companies and will arrange rations accordingly.

5.   Companies will leave present camp to-morrow night in the follow-
     -ing order:-
          'X' Company at 7.15 p.m.
          'Y'   "   " 7.25 p.m.
          'W'   "   " 7.35 p.m.
          'Z'   "   " 7.45 p.m.
          HQrs.   " 7.50 p.m.

6.   Movements by Companies as far as HEUDICOURT and then by platoons
     at suitable distances.

7.   Guides will meet Companies at VAUCELLETTE FARM at 9 p.m. Guides
     for platoons at VILLERS-GUISLAIN. No platoons to pass East of
     VAUCELLETTE FARM before 9 p.m.

8.   All sketch maps, aeroplane photographs, defence schemes, trench
     stores and tools will be taken over from Companies relieved &
     lists of articles taken over will be forwarded to the Adjutant
     by dawn 24th.

9.   Details of work on hand and proposed will be taken over by all
     Companies.

10. A sketch map showing dispositions will be forwarded to Battalion
     Headquarters as soon after relief as possible.

11. Completion of relief will be reported to Battalion Headquarters
     by the code word 'CORRECT'.

                              (Signed) W.J.LYLE, Capt. & Adjt.,
                                       HIGHLAND LIGHT INFANTRY.
H.Q.H.L.I.
Issued at:- 6.30 p.m.
Copies 1 - 2 Bat. & O.O.File.
       3   'W' Coy.
       4   'X' "
       5   'Y' "
       6   'Z' "
       7   'S' "
       8   2nd. in command.
       9   12th. SUFFOLK Regt.

SECRET.   OPERATION ORDERS No.64.   27.5.17.
                 HIGHLAND LIGHT INFANTRY.

Reference sheet 57c.S.E.   1/20,000.
----

1. The Battalion will be relieved by the 17th R.SCOTS on the
    night of 27/28th. inst as follows:-
    'Z' Coy.H.L.I. by 'W' Coy.R.SCOTS. on Right of line.
    'Y' "   "   " 'Y' "   "   " Left   "   "
    'W' "   "   " 'Z' "   "   in Support.
    'X' "   "   " 'X' "   "   " Reserve.

2. Guides, 1 per platoon, will be sent to X Tracks X.13.D.6.1.
    at 9.20 p.m.

3. Company Q.M.Ss will be sent on in advance this afternoon to
    take over billets from R.SCOTS. 2/Lt.WOODSIDE will take over
    for 'Y' Company;-

    'Y' Company ½ Coy. to HEUDICOURT & ½ Coy.to W.12.D.5.3.(App.)
    'Z'   "   to HEUDICOURT W.21.A.9.6.
    'W'   "   " Railway Embankment X.19.A.7.3.
    'X'   "   " W. of VILLERS X.2.D.2.2.
    Headquarters " Railway Embankment. X.13.c.3.2

    1 limber will be at Ration Dump for 'Y' Coy and 1 limber
    will be at X Roads for 'Z' Company.

4. All trench stores, tools, maps and air photographs, also
    food containers and details of work on hand will be handed
    over receipts obtained and forwarded to the Adjutant by 12
    noon 28th inst.

5. Completion of relief will be notified to B.H.Q. by the Code
    Word 'E.C.'

                                    (Signed) W.J.LYLE, Capt. & Adjt.,
Issued at ;- 12 noon.   HIGHLAND LIGHT INFANTRY.
Copies Nos;- 1-3 W.D.& O.O.File.
              4 'W' Coy.
              5 'X' Coy.
              6 'Y' "
              7 'Z' "
              8 2nd. in Command.
              9 17th. R.SCOTS.
             10 Transport Officer.

SECRET.   OPERATION ORDERS No.65.   **1.6.17.**
            HIGHLAND LIGHT INFANTRY.

Reference map:- Sheet 62c & 57c,   1/40,000.
----

1. The Battalion will be relieved by the 16th CHESHIRES REGT. on the night of 2nd./3rd. JUNE.

2. All trench stores, shelters, maps, aeroplane photos sketch maps etc. will be handed over, receipts obtained, and forwarded to the Adjutant by 12 noon 3rd. inst.

3. Billeting parties of 1 Officer & 1 N.C.O. per Company & 2/Lt. GEMMILL for Headquarters will proceed in advance and report to Battalion Headquarters, 15th SHERWOOD FORESTERS by 11 a.m. 3rd. inst, at D.23.B.
   The N.C.Os of the above party will be at D.23.B.4.8. at 11 p.m 3rd. inst. to guide Companies to billets. 2/Lt.GEMMILL will meet Headquarters.

4. Companies, on relief, will march by platoons to HEUDICOURT. From there, by Companies to X Roads at Point W.26.C.8.1. where the Battalion will assemble. The pipe-band will be at this point and play the Battalion in to Billets.

5. The following Transport will report at Battalion Headquarters and Companies as follows:-

        1 limber   per Company.
        1   "   for Headquarters.
        Mess Cart   "   "
        Maltese "   "   "

6. Completion of relief will be notified to this Office by the Code 'E.F'.

                            (Signed) W.J.LYLE, Capt. & Adjt.,
                                    HIGHLAND LIGHT INFANTRY.

Issued at:-   7 p.m.
Copies Nos. 1-3   W.D. & O.O.File.
            4   'W' Coy.
            5   'X' "
            6   'Y' "
            7   'Z' "
            8   2nd. in Command.
            9   16th CHESHIRES REGT.
           10   15th SHERWOOD FORESTERS.

Army Form C. 2118.

Original
16th Highland L.I.
Vol 17

17. D.
1 Sheet

WAR DIARY
INTELLIGENCE SUMMARY
(Erase heading not required.)

Instructions regarding War Diaries and Intelligence Summaries are contained in F.S. Regs., Part II. and the Staff Manual respectively. Title pages will be prepared in manuscript.

Place	Date	Hour	Summary of Events and Information	Remarks and references to Appendices
VAUCELLETTE FARM.	1.6.17.		Battalion in Brigade Reserve. Companies engaged on working parties. Very quiet day.	
"	2.6.17.		Day quiet. Battalion relieved by 16th CHESHIRES and marched to Bivouacs in TEMPLEUX-LA-FOSSE where they arrived about 4.30 a.m. on the 3rd. inst. Operation Orders No.65. Issued and attached to last month's diary.	LXV
TEMPLEUX-LA-FOSSE.	3.6.17.		Battalion in Divisional Reserve. Weather very warm. Men resting & cleaning up during the day, & bathing was also indulged in.	
	4.6.17.		Battalion Divisional Reserve. Weather exceedingly warm. Proceedure for the day was as follows:- Reveille 4.30 a.m. Battalion Parade 6 a.m. Breakfast 6.30-9 a.m. Company Parades 9-10 a.m. Company parades 10 a.m. - 1 p.m. Companies training in musketry, wiring, bayonet fighting, bombing, Lewis Guns, Signalling, Rifle Grenadiers, & Sniping. Football & Company sports in the afternoon.	
	5.6.17.		Battalion in Divisional Reserve. Fine weather still continues. Training carried out as for 4th. Brigade concert in the evening.	
	6.6.17.		Battalion in Divisional Reserve. Weather very warm. Battalion & Company training carried out during forenoon. Lewis Gunners etc. under Specialist Officers. Company sports and football in afternoon.	
	7.6.17.		Battalion in Divisional Reserve. Training carried on as usual. In afternoon companies held Coy. sports, running off preliminary heats for Battalion Sports next day.	
	8.6.17.		Battalion in Divisional Reserve. Training in forenoon. Platoon, Company and Battalion attacks were carried out. Battalion sports were carried out in afternoon. Great rivalry between Companies to carry off as many events as possible 'Z' Company leading by an easy first. The Corps Commander & Brigadier-General both attended the sports, the Brigadier presenting the winners with their prizes. A Battalion concert in the evening brought an end to a very enjoyable & successful day.	
	9.6.17.		Battalion in Divisional Reserve. Contact scheme with aeroplanes with Brigade was carried out at 6 a.m. During forenoon companies under training. C.O., 2nd. In Command, & Os.C. Companies visited new line, i.e., 'GAUCHE WOOD' Sector.	
	10.6.17.		Battalion in Divisional Reserve. Church parades during the day. Officers & N.C.Os attended lectures by C.R.E. & A.D.M.S. 35th. Division. Battalion left camp at 4.30 p.m. & marched to HEUDICOURT where men halted for tea, thereafter proceeding to 'GAUCHE WOOD' Sector & relieving 23rd. MANCHESTER REGT. Relief completed without incident. Operation Orders No. 66	LXVI

WAR DIARY

INTELLIGENCE SUMMARY.

(Erase heading not required.)

Army Form C. 2118.

Instructions regarding War Diaries and Intelligence Summaries are contained in F.S. Regs., Part II. and the Staff Manual respectively. Title pages will be prepared in manuscript.

Place	Date	Hour	Summary of Events and Information	Remarks and references to Appendices
GAUCHE WOOD SECTOR.	11.6.17.		Battalion in Front Line trenches. Weather fine till 5 p.m. after which time heavy showers fell and we had some thunder & lightening. Situation normal. Battalion engaged in Patrolling, wiring, & improving trenches. 5 men slightly wounded by H.E.Shell.	
	12.6.17.		Battalion in line. Very quiet day. Good patrolling work done. Companies engaged during night improving trenches, wiring, and building shelters. 1 man slightly wounded.	
	13.6.17.	"	Weather very warm.. Enemy still very quiet. One Officer wounded while on patrol for a sniper, in daylight. Work carried on during night. 1 Company of 17th.ROYAL SCOTS assisted in improving trenches.	
	14.6.17.	"	Quiet day & weather very warm. Inter-company relief carried/during night 14/15th. During relief, enemy fired a number of trench mortar shells into NEWTON POST (Right Company, Front) killing 2 men. Nothing further of interest to report	O.O.67.
	15.6.17.	"	Weather warm. Enemy artillery more active. usual patrols and working parties carried out at night.	
	16.6.17.	"	Weather still exceedingly warm. Work and patrols as before.	
	17.6.17.	"	" " " " " " " " " " 2 men wounded.(1 slightly gassed by gas from aerial torpedoes fired by enemy).	
	18.6.17.	"	Weather very warm, but change to dull in afternoon and at night very thundery & several heavy showers occurred. Work as usual during day. At night Battalion was relieved by 17th ROYAL SCOTS and proceeded to Brigade SUPPORT. Relief completed without incident.	Operation Orders 68
	19.6.17.		in Brigade Support. Weather warm but dull; much thunder & some rain in afternoon. Large working parties supplied for work on KITCHEN CRATER, Front Line, & BROWN LINE.	
	20.6.17.	"	Support. Weather still changeable. Work as above.	
	21.6.17.	"	" " " " " "	
	22.6.17.	"	" " " " " "	
	23.6.17.	"	" fine. At night Battalion (400 O.Rs. and some Officers.) were engaged digging a new line 200 yards in advance of present 'Front Line'. Task was completed within time without any casualties, and Brigade was complimented by Corps,&Divisional Commanders & also by Brigadier-General for their splendid work so speedily accomplished.	Operation Orders(with Addendum)No.69.
	24.6.17.	"	Support. Weather fine. Working parties on old front line & BROWN LINE as before.	
	25.6.17.	"	" Battalion engaged in completing work on new line. Task again successfully completed, without casualties.	Operation Orders. No.70.

Army Form C. 2118.

WAR DIARY
INTELLIGENCE=SUMMARY.
(Erase heading not required.)

Instructions regarding War Diaries and Intelligence Summaries are contained in F. S. Regs., Part II. and the Staff Manual respectively. Title pages will be prepared in manuscript.

Place	Date	Hour	Summary of Events and Information	Remarks and references to Appendices
HEUDICOURT.	26.6.17.		Battalion in Brigade Support. Weather fine. Battalion relieved by 15th.CHESHIRE REGT. 104th.Bde. and took over from 14th GLOSTER REGT. in Divnl.Res.billets (bivouacs) by HEUDICOURT. Accommodation was very scanty and the weather completely broke down, thereby rendering things rather uncomfortable for the men. O.O. 71	
	27.6.17.		Battalion in Divisional Reserve. Weather changeable. Two Battalions D.L.I. & H.L.I. and a half each of 106th.T.M.B. 7 M.G.Coy. were billetted near HEUDICOURT while the remainder of the Brigade were in Divisional Reserve Area at AIZECOURT-LE-BAS. Working parties of two companies supplied for work under R.Es. Battalion carried out training of specialists under Specialist Officers.	
	28.6.17.		Battalion in Divisional Reserve. Weather bad much thunder. Working parties and training as before.	
	29.6.17.		" " " " " fine. Battalion on working parties and bathing.	
	30.6.17.		" " " " " very changeable. Battalion receives orders to move, but these were eventually postponed until next day owing to the very severe weather.	

Commanding, 18th (Service) Battalion, Highland Light Infantry.

Lieut – Colonel,

SECRET.　　　　　　OPERATION ORDERS No.66.　　　9.6.17.
　　　　　　　　　HIGHLAND LIGHT INFANTRY.

Reference map. Sheets 62c & 57c.　1/40,000.
----

1. The Battalion will relieve the 23rd. Manchester Regt. on the left Battalion front on the night 10=11th inst

2. Disposition.
   'W' Company on Right of line.
   'X'   "   " Left   " "
   'Y'   "   " in Support.
   'Z'   "   " Reserve.

3. Companies will send advanced parties into line to-night 9th.inst as follows. They will parade at an hour to be notified later.

   'W' Coy.) 1 Officer, per.Company, 1 N.C.O. per Platoon, Nos.
   'X' Coy.) 1 of Lewis Gun Teams, 1 Runner,& 1 Signaller.

   'Y' Coy.) 1 Officer, 1 N.C.O. & 1 Runner per Company.
   'Z' Coy.)

4. Companies will leave camp to-morrow night at an hour to be noti--fied later.

5. Movements by companies as far as HEUDICOURT and from there by Platoons.

6. All tents, shelters, maps, etc. will be handed over to repre--sentative of 23rd. Manchester Regt to-morrow, receipts obtained and forwarded to the Adjutant by 6 p.m.

7. All sketch maps, aeroplanephotographs, defence schemes, trench stores and tools will be taken over from 23rd.Manchester Regt. in the line and lists forwarded to the Adjutant by DAWN 11th.ins

8. Details of work on hand and proposed will be carefully taken over by Companies.

9. A sketch map showing dispositions, strength etc. will be forward-ed to Battalion Headquarters as soon as possible after relief.

10. Completion of relief will be notified to B.H.Q. by code word 'H.P.'.

　　　　　　　　　　　　　　(Signed) E.J.LYLE, Capt. & Adjt.,
9.6.17.　　　　　　　18th (S) Bn. Highland Light Infantry.

Issued at:- 1 p.m.
Copies Nos.1-3 W.D.& O.C.File.
　　　　4 'W' Coy.
　　　　5 'X' Coy.
　　　　6 'Y' Coy.
　　　　7 'Z' Coy.
　　　　8 2nd. in command.
　　　　9 23rd. Manchester Regt.

SECRET? OPERATION ORDERS No.67. 14.6.17.
HIGHLAND LIGHT INFANTRY?

Reference map, 57c. S.E. 1/20,000.

1. An inter-company relief will take place to-night 14th.inst.

2. Disposition:-
   'Z' Company will relieve 'W' Coy. on Right.
   'Y'   "   "   "   'X' "   " Left.
   'W'   "   "   "   Support Company.(Right)
   'X'   "   "   "   "   "   (Left).

3. All working parties and wiring parties to go on as usual. Nothing to interfere with progress of work. Patrols will be sent out in accordance with instructions to be issued later.

4. Support Companies supplying working and wiring parties will send same in 'fighting order'. Os.C.Coys. will allocate fire-bays for above parties to leave their surplus equipment so that they will occupy that portion of trench after relief.

5. Arrangements will be made by Os.C.Coys. for advance parties to look after rations, water and allocation of dug-outs.

6. Remainder of companies not sent in advance wiring, working or patrolling will take place at 11.30 p.m.

7. 'W' & 'X' Coys. will send a guide to Battalion Headquarters for the purpose of guiding limber of 'Y' & 'Z' to new places in the line.

8. All trench stores, sketch maps, tools, petrol tins, trench shelters programmes of work in hand and contemplated etc. will be handed over receipts obtained and forwarded to the Adjutant by 12 noon to-morrow.

9. Completion of relief will be notified to Battalion Headquarters by the code word 'WORK'.

(Signed) W.J.LYLE, Capt., & Adjt.,

Issued at:- 1 p.m. Highland Light Infantry.

Copies Nos. 1-3 W.D. & O.O.File.
            4 'W' Company.
            5 'X' "
            6 'Y' "
            7 'Z' "
            8 2nd. in Command.
            9 Battalion on Right. (xxxx.W.YORKS.R.)
           10   "   "   "   (--Suffolks R.).

SECRET.   OPERATION ORDERS No.68.   17.6.17.
                            HIGHLAND LIGHT INFANTRY.

Reference sheet 57c.S.E.   1/20,000.
----

1. The Battalion will be relieved by the R.SCOTS on the night of 18/19th.inst. as follows;-
   'Z' Coy.H.L.I. by 'Z' Coy. R.SCOTS on Right of line.
   'Y' "   "   " 'X' "   "   "   " Left   "   "
   'W' "   "   " 'W' "   "   "   In Support (Right).
   'X' "   "   " 'Y' "   "   "   "   (Left).

2. Guides, 1 per platoon from companies in front line and 1 from Coys. in Support will report to the Adjutant at Battalion Headquarters at 9 p.m. 18th.inst.

3. Advance parties of R.SCOTS will report to Os.C.Companies to-night.

4. Companies will send advance parties of 1 Off., 1 N.C.O. & 1 man per Company, to-morrow afternoon, 18th. inst. to take over billets from R.SCOTS as follows. To report to the Adjutant at 3 p.m.

   'W' Coy.H.L.I. from 'X' Coy. R.SCOTS.
   'W' "   "   "   'Z' "   "   "
   'Y' "   "   "   'Y' "   "   "
   'Z' "   "   "   'W' "   "   "

5. On relief, companies will march to billets as follows;-

   Battalion Headquarters to W.16.A.5.6.
   'W' Company to (BROWN LINE)) X.11.D.
   'Y'   "   " (IRVINE LANE) W.6.D.
   'Z'   "   " (MORRIS BANK) X.7.A.3.6.

6. 1 limber per company for Lewis Guns etc. will report at each Coy. HdQrs. at 10 p.m. 18th.inst.

7. All trench stores, trench maps, aeroplane photographs, programmes of work in hand and contemplated, trench shelters, tools etc., will be handed over, receipts obtained and forwarded to the Adjutant by 12 noon 19th., inst.

8. Completion of relief will be wired to Battalion Headquarters by the Code word 'W.J.'

                              (Signed) W.J.LYLE, Capt., & Adjt.,
17.6.17.   HIGHLAND LIGHT INFANTRY.

Issued at:- 9.30 a.m. (18th.)

Copies Nos. 1-3 W.D.& O.O.File.
            4 'W' Coy.
            5 'X' "
            6 'Y' "
            7 'Z' "
            8 2nd. in Command.
            9 R.SCOTS.
           10 O.C.Right Battalion.
           11. "   Left Battalion.

SECRET.   OPERATION ORDERS No.69.   22.6.17.
                            HIGHLAND LIGHT INFANTRY.

Reference sheet 57c. S.E. 1/20,000.

1. The 106th Brigade, in conjunction with the 121st. Brigade on the
   Left, will advance the front line of the left Battalion front by
   digging a new trench about 200 yards in front of the present line
   from TURNER QUARRY to the Left Divisional Boundary about R.34.a.3.8
   This work will be commenced on night of 23rd./24th.inst.

2. Patrols will be furnished by the R.SCOTS & W.YORKS.R; wiring part-
   -ies will be furnished by the R.SCOTS, and digging parties will be
   found by the HIGH.L.I. & DURH.L.I. The HIGH.L.I. will be responsible
   for digging line B-C (see attached map) and will march to their work
   in three parties, via GAUCHE WOOD and up '22 RAVINE' to their and
   thence;-
   Right Party, 110 O.Rs.   opposite   BROADHURST AVENUE.
   Centre Party 110   "   "   R.34.a.6.3.
   Left Party 180   "   "   CHESHIRE STREET.
   Guides will meet these parties as under;-
   Right Party in BROADHURST AVENUE.
   Centre party along CHESHIRE STREET.
   Left Party at junction of present front line & CHESHIRE STREET. Offs.
   in charge of digging parties will lay tapes through gaps cut in the
   wire for the guidance of parties back to the front line. Care will be
   taken to withdraw the tapes after the parties have returned.

3. Digging will commence at 10.50 p.m. and cease at 1.30 a.m. working
   parties will be West of GAUCHE WOOD by 3 a.m. Parties will move back
   by same routes as they approached.

4. The type of trench to be dug is the ordinary pattern standard fire-
   -trench as per attached sketch.
   The task for the first night will be to dig the trench 3' X 3' the
   full length of all fire-bays and traverses. On subsequent nights, the
   sides of the traverses will be cut out and the remainder of the trench
   widened and deepened to standard pattern.
   The tapes will mark the front edge of the first night's work there-
   -fore earth must be thrown at least 2 feet forward to allow for a
   berm and subsequent sloping off of the completed trench.

5. In the event of an enemy attack, working parties will, if the attack
   is on the left Battalion Front, take an active part in the defence,
   and if on the other front, stand to in the front line and await
   orders.

                                    (Signed) W.J.LYLE, Capt., & Adjt.,

22.6.17.   HIGHLAND LIGHT INFANTRY.

Issued at;- 12 noon.

           Copies Nos. 1-3 W.D. & O.O.File.
                       4 'W' Coy.
                       5 'X' "
                       6 'Y' "
                       7 'Z' "
                       8 2nd. in Command.

Rough Copy of R.E. Map.

CIRCULAR MEMO No. 28.

O.C. 'W' COY.
 " 'Y' "
 " 'Z' "

ADDENDUM TO OPERATION ORDERS No. 69. (attached.)

1. The parties as stated in para. 2 will be found as follows:-

		Picks.	Shovels.
Right Party.. (Under Capt. Balfour.) of 110 O.Rs.	55	55
Centre Party. (Under " Barrie.) " 110 "	55	55
Left " (Under " Murray.) " 180 "	36	144

2. The strength of parties will be found by taking all N.C.Os. (who will also dig) and men in each Company. The only exceptions will be;-

   1 N.C.O. & 4 men as guard on Company shelters.
   2 Company cooks.
   1 "   HdQrs. cook.
   1 "   "   Waiter.

3. Picks and shovels will be sent to companies to-night in addition to those already in possession as follows;-

	In Possession		PLUS.		TOTAL.	
	Picks.	Shovels.	Picks.	Shovels.	Pks.	Shvls.
'W' Company.	24	177	31	NIL.	55	55
'Y' "	39	69	NIL.	75	36	144
'Z' "	52	98	3	NIL.	55	55

   If any Company should subsequently be short of either picks or shovels these can be had from Battalion Headquarters on application.

4. N.C.Os and men, to make companies up to strength will be transferred from one company to another. Headquarters will detail every available N.C.O. and man for this purpose. Details as to strength will be arranged to-morrow.

5. The water guard of 1 N.C.O. & 3 men, found by 'W' Company is to be relieved to-morrow morning by 4 men of the Pipe Band. The party of 1 N.C.O. & 10 men found by 'W' Company for salving timber in HEUDICOURT is cancelled.

6. The C.O. will see all companies at Battalion Headquarters at 11 a.m. to-morrow morning. Sketch maps, Operation Orders and Company strengths will be brought.

(Signed) W.J. LYLE, Cap. & Ajt.

22.6.17.   18th (Ser) Bn Highland Light Infantry

SECRET.   OPERATION ORDERS No.70.   25.6.17.
               HIGHLAND LIGHT INFANTRY.

Reference sheet 57c S.E. — 1/20,000.

1. Reference Operation Orders No.69 dated 22.6.17. and Addemdum to same, work will be continued on new front line to-night 25/26th. inst.

2. Companies will work on tasks as on night of 23rd/24th. as follows:-

   'Z' Coy. on Right.(Under 2/Lt.SMITH) Strength of party 108.
   'W' "   "   "   (" Capt.BARRIE)   "   "   " 108.
   'Y' "   "   "   ("   MURRAY,)   "   "   " 178.

   Companies and Headquarters will send men to complete numbers as before.

3. The R.Es will not be ablt to supply guides. Companies will therefore carry on with same tasks as on night of 23rd/24th as per sketch maps issued to-day.

4. The Centre & Left Companies,('W' & 'Y') will avail themselves of the Communication Trenchs which are being dug by the NORTHUMBERLAND FUS. (Pioneers) on night of 24th/25th.inst.

5. As the number of sides for traverses is nearly double that of the back trenches, it will be necessary for each of the working parties to close their traverse digging parties on the centre so as to ensure that each party will construct a continuous section, the remaining portion to be completed on subsequent occasions.

6. Digging will cease not later than 2 a.m. Working parties will be West of CHAPEL CROSSING by 3.30 a.m.

7. Medical arrangements will be as on night 23rd/24th. inst.

                          (Signed) W.J.LYLE,Captn & Adjt.
25.6.17.   HIGHLAND LIGHT INFANTRY.
Issued at:- 1.30 p.m.
         Copies Nos.1-3 W.D.& O.O.File.
                     4 'W' Company.
                     5 'X'   "
                     6 'Y'   "
                     7 'Z'   "
                     8 2nd. in Command.

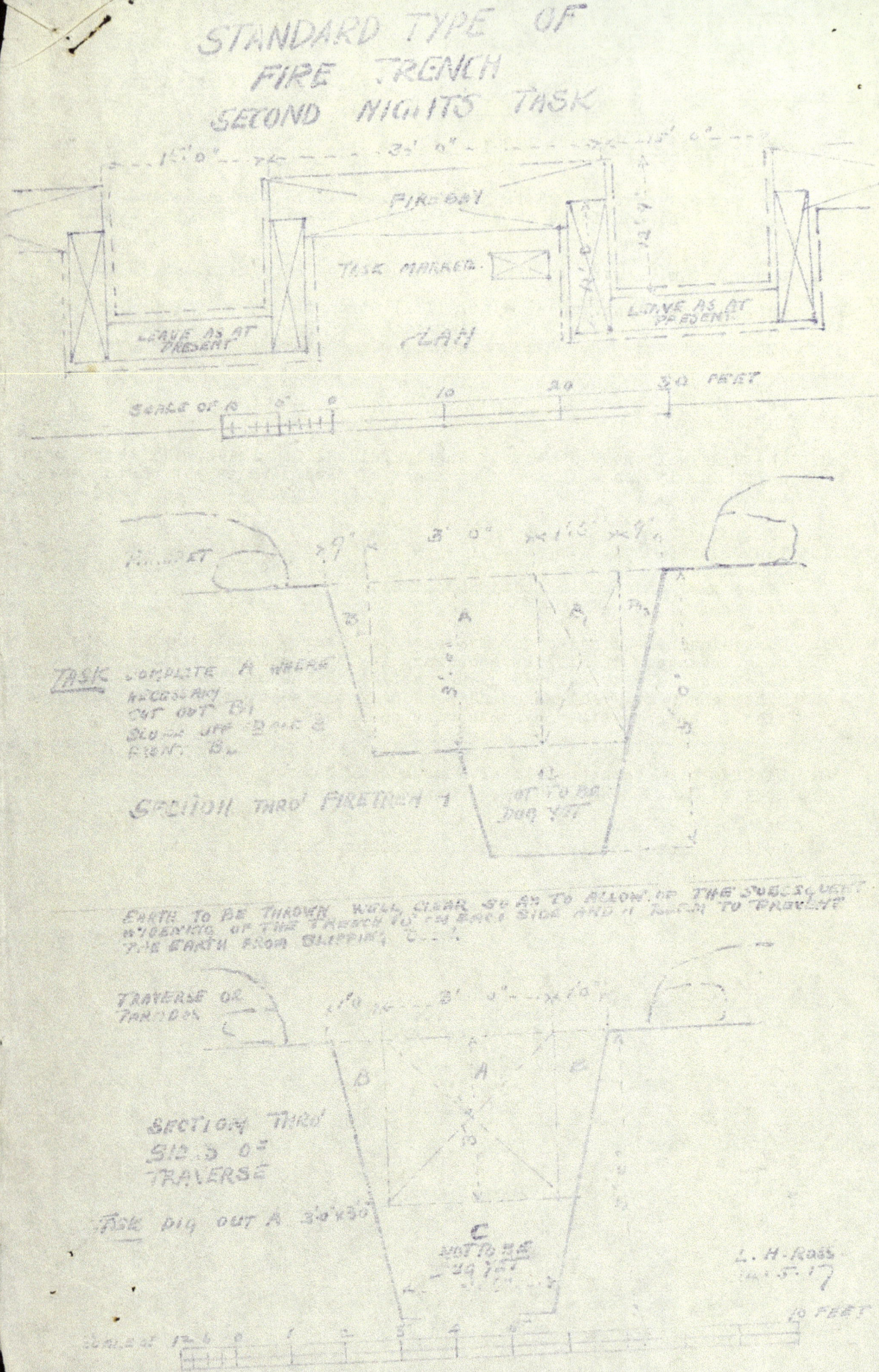

SECRET.   OPERATION ORDERS No. 71.   25.6.17.
                       HIGHLAND LIGHT INFANTRY.   Copy No. 3.

Reference sheet 57c. S.E. 1/20,000.
----

1. The Battalion will be relieved by the --- CHESHIRE REGT. on the night 26/27th.

2. Guides, 1 per platoon and 1 for Headquarters, will report at Battalion Headquarters at 9.15a.m. to conduct advanced parties of --- CHESHIRE REGT. to positions of companies.

3. Guides 1 per platoon and 1 for Headquarters will report at Battalion Headquarters at 7 p.m. to guide relieving companies to respective positions.

4. Two Companies of the CHESHIRE REGT. will take over from 'W' Coy. in BROWN LINE.

5. O.C. Companies will send advanced parties of 1 Officer & 1 N.C.O. to Battalion Headquarters at 4.30 p.m. Guides of GLOSTER REGT. will meet same at Railway W.15.B.2.4. at 5 p.m.

6. 2 limbers per Company will report at Company Headquarters at 10 p.m. 26th. inst.

7. Companies on relief will march to camp evacuated by GLOSTER REGT. at W.15.A. The N.C.O. of advanced party will meet companies at railway as in 5, and guide companies to Company lines.

8. 'X' Company will not be relieved and will remain in present position.

9. All trench stores, maps, sketches, aeroplane photographs, details of work in hand and contemplated, shelters & tools will be handed over, receipts obtained and forwarded to the Adjutant by 12 noon 27th. inst.

10. Completion of relief will be reported to Battalion Headquarters by Code word 'E.F.'

                                      (Signed.) W.J.LYLE, Capt.& Adjt.,
25.6.17.   HIGHLAND   LIGHT   INFANTRY.
   Issued at 6.30 p.m.
   Copies Nos. 1-3 W.D. & O.O. File.
             4 'W' Company.
             5 'X'   "
             6 'Y'   "
             7 'Z'   "
             8 2nd. in Command.
             9 GLOSTER REGT.

204th. Field Company,   Royal Engineers.

NEWTON POST to TURNER QUARRY.

CHORD.

WIRING.
----

1. Reference attached plan, this shows the line of obstacle proposed. The work to be done on the night 23rd/24th JUNE, as per Infantry Brigade Order No.111 is shown xxx. Work shown xxx will be carried out at a later date.

2. Material for the work has been dumped at the points marked on the ground by boards painted with luminous paint 'X' & 'Y'.

3. Infantry Wiring Parties (in two equal parties of 100 O.Rs.) will meet R.E. at CHESHIRE QUARRY 9.30 p.m. and TURNER QUARRY at 10 p.m. whence they will be guided by R.E.

4. Wiring will be commenced at points 'X' & 'Y', two parties of 50 at each, working in opposite directions.

5. Type of obstacle and method of construction as per attached scheme. This is the same wiring drill as that recently done on the Reserve line. Obstacle North of the road running East and West through NEWTON POST will be doubled.

6. As the Infantry are not available to practice a new drill building the obstacle from front to rear, the old method as used on back lines has been adopted, although this necessitates working in front of the obstacle.
Gaps will be made at intervals of 200 yards, and gap notice boards fixed. A piece of white rag will be fixed at all gaps during this operation.

7. Lieut.McPhail R.E. will be in charge of the work from TURNER QUARRY to B, and 2/Lt.Gayford, R.E. from B to NEWTON POST.

18th B. High L.I.
(July 1917)
M.U. 18

Army Form C. 2118.

WAR DIARY
INTELLIGENCE SUMMARY
(Erase heading not required.)

Instructions regarding War Diaries and Intelligence Summaries are contained in F. S. Regs., Part II. and the Staff Manual respectively. Title pages will be prepared in manuscript.

Place	Date	Hour	Summary of Events and Information	Remarks and references to Appendices
HEUDECOURT.	1.7.17.		Battalion on the move. Weather dull. Marched to AIZECOURT-LE-BAS (about 2 miles). Under canvas.	
-Do-	2.7.17.		" " " " LONGAVESNES Area. (about three miles) and encamped there. Weather good. Situation of camp good.	
LONGAVESNES.	3.7.17.		" in Reserve. Weather good. A brigade attack was practised. The village of LONGAVESNES being attacked and laison with aeroplanes practised.	
-Do-	4.7.17.		" " " Weather good. A Brigade practise attack carried out, with Battalion on the left, also contact with aeroplanes practised during attack.	
-Do-	5.7.17.		" " " Weather changeable. Training was carried out. specialists being under specialist Officers. In the afternoon, preparations were made for move into the line next day.	
-Do-	6.7.17.		" moves into line. Weather very warm. Battalion left camp at 4 p.m. and halted at ST.EMILIE for tea, thereafter proceeding to the line and relieving 3rd. HUSSARS & OX. & BUCKS. HUSSARS of 4th. Cavalry BRIGADE. Battalion on left of Bde. Sector 'C' Sector. with 17th.W.YORKS. R on right and 15th. SHERWOOD FORESTERS on left.	LXII. Operations Orders No.72.
LEMPIRE.	7.7.17.		Battalion in the line. Weather very warm. The line consists of a line of Posts which are not connected up. GUILLEMONT FARM, the chief point, is within 15 yards of the enemy line. The rest of the Posts are some 500 yds. from the enemy line.	
-Do-	8.7.17.		" " " Weather very warm, afterwards changing to rain & thunder. GUILLEMONT FARM bombarded with Gas shells and T.M's. Casualties, 1 Off. & 11 O.Rs gassed.	
-Do-	9.7.17.		" " " line. Weather very warm. Situation normal.	
-Do-	10.7.17.		" " " " " " " Much work was done wiring and improving trenches. Inter-Company relief was carried out. Operation Orders No.72.	
-Do-	11.7.17.		" " " line. Weather fine. Enemy artillery very active on all Posts apparently registering. Much work was carried out on Posts and wire, and joining up F & E Posts.	LXXIII
-Do-	12.7.17.		" " " the line. Weather good. Enemy artillery active. At 12 midnight, he heavily bombarded all Posts and afterwards attempted to raid the FARM. This was beaten off. At 1 p.m. he attempted to capture the garrison of 'F.1' Post (a subsidiary post to 'F' Post). The garrison (1 N.C.O. & 8 men) fought the enemy off, and made good their retiral carrying their wounded (4 men) with them. At dawn an Officers' patrol went out to retake M.1 Post, but found it unoccupied. It was so badly blown in, that it could not be occupied that day. Casualties Killed 1 O.R. wounded 1 Off. 7 O.Rs. All ranks showed great steadiness and were commended on their devotion to duty.	

T2134. Wt. W708—776. 500000. 4/15. Sir J. C. & S.

Army Form C. 2118.

WAR DIARY
or
INTELLIGENCE=SUMMARY.
(Erase heading not required.)

Instructions regarding War Diaries and Intelligence Summaries are contained in F. S. Regs., Part II. and the Staff Manual respectively. Title pages will be prepared in manuscript.

Place	Date	Hour	Summary of Events and Information	Remarks and references to Appendices
LEMPIRE.	13.7.17.		Battalion in the line. Weather very warm. Our artillery very active. Usual work was carried out wiring and improving the trenches. The following Officers and O.Rs were especially mentioned for good work and conspicuous gallantry on the occasion of the attempted enemy raid last night. Lieut. HAMILTON. In command at FARM. Lt. JURLE. C.S.M. Smith. C.S.M. McQUILLAN. Cpl. Brown. L/Cpl. LEGG.	
-Do.-	14.7.17.		Battalion in the line. Weather very warm. Situation normal. Battalion working as usual. Heavy enemy artillery bombardment in the morning. Casualties 9 O.Rs wounded. 1 enemy prisoner was captured belonging to 49th.P.I.R. Battalion was relieved by 17th. ROYAL SCOTS and proceeded to Support. Relief complete about 12 midnight. O.O.74.	
-Do.-	15.7.17.		Battalion in Bde. Support. Weather dull. Battalion was engaged almost entirely on working parties in and near GUILLEMONT FARM wiring and digging a new trench on either side of it.	
-Do.-	16.7.17.		Battalion in Bde. Support. Weather good. Usual working parties at night, digging and wiring. Work as before. Casualties. Wounded 1 O.R.	
-Do.-	17.7.17.		" " " " " " " NIL.	
-Do.-	18.7.17.		" " " " " " " Killed. 1 O.R.	
-Do.-	19.7.17.		" " " " " " " Killed 1 O.R. Wounded 1 O.R.	
-Do.-	20.7.17.		" " " " " " " Killed 1 O.R.	
-Do.-	21.7.17.		" " " " " " " L/Cpl. Legg, & Cpl. Brown awarded the MILITARY MEDAL for good work on night of 12th. 13th.	
-Do.-	22.7.17.		Battalion in Bde. Support. Weather warm. 14 Officers & 300 O.Rs. proceed to the Depot to training Area for training for a raid on enemy trenches at GUILLEMONT FARM. Battalion complimented by Corps & Divisional Commanders & by Brigadier for good work on occasion of the attempted enemy raid 12/13th.	
-Do.-	23.7.17.		Battalion in Bde. Support. Weather warm. Enemy artillery was active on our Battery positions close to billets. Battalion relieved by 15th. SHERWOOD FORESTERS (105th Inf. Bde) Relief completed about 12 midnight. Battalion then marched to billets at AIZECOURT-LE-BAS a distance of about 7 miles. Operation Orders 75.	
-Do.-	24.7.17.		Battalion in Bde. Reserve. Weather good. Special Raiding Party preparing for raid receive special training. Remainder of Battalion resting and cleaning up.	
-Do.-	25.7.17.		Battalion in Div. Reserve. Weather good. training of special raiding party carried on. Remainder of Battalion get normal training.	
-Do.-	26.7.17.		Battalion in Div. Reserve. Weather good. Training as before.	
-Do.-	27.7.17.		" " " " " " "	
-Do.-	28.7.17.		" " " " " " "	

WAR DIARY
INTELLIGENCE=SUMMARY.
(Erase heading not required.)

Army Form C. 2118.

Place	Date	Hour	Summary of Events and Information	Remarks and references to Appendices
AIRECOURT-LE-BAS	29.7.17.		Battalion in Div. Reserve. Weather bad. Much rain and thunder. Church parades were held in the morning and afterwards Officers & men recommended for bravery on the night 12/13th. were personally congratulated by the Divisional Commander. There was no training carried out during the day.	
-Do.-	30.7.17.		Battalion in Div. Reserve. Weather still very bad. Continuous rains and strong wind impeded training a good deal. Preparations for possible move to-morrow were carried out.	
-Do.-	31.7.17.		Battalion in Div. Reserve. Weather continues to be bad. Battalion was fully prepared to move, the Special party, Quartermaster's Stores & Transport having already moved to new area, when orders were received to return to old billets as relief had been postponed for another day.	

SECRET. OPERATION ORDERS No.72.   Copy No. 2
        HIGHLAND LIGHT INFANTRY.   5.7.17.

Reference 62 c & 57 c   1/40,000

1. 106th Inf. Brigade will relieve the 4th Cavalry Brigade on the night of 6/7th. JULY. 1917. The Battalion will relieve the 3rd. HUSSARS & OX & BUCKS HUSSARS. in the '6.2' Sub-sector.

2. 'X' Company will take over GUILLEMONT FARM, D.1 Post, Road Post & BANK Post.
   'W' "   "   "   "   'D', 'E', & 'F' Posts.
   'Y' Company will be in Support to 'X' Company in Sunken Road at F.17.c
   'Z' "   "   " "   "   " 'W'   "   "   "   "   " F.11.c
   Battalion Headquarters will be at F.16.a.8.6.

3. Guides, 1 per Company and 1 for Headquarters will be at Cross roads at F.21.c.3.9. at 10 p.m. Guides for Posts for 'X' Company will be at Road junction at D.15.d.8.6. Guides for Posts for 'W' Company will be at Battalion Headquarters.

4. The following advance parties will leave camp at 9 a.m. to-morrow:-

   'X' Company) 1 Off., & 1 N.C.O. per platoon, 2 signallers,
   'W'   "   ) 2 Runners & Nos.1's of Lewis Gun Teams.

   'Y'   "   )
   'Z'   "   ) 1 Officer 1 N.C.O. 1 Runner & 1 signaller.
   Guides for advance parties will be at F.21.c.3.9. at 10.30 a.m.

5. All trench stores maps, tools aeroplane photographs, details of work etc will be taken over and receipts given, copies of which will be forwarded to the Adjutant by 12 noon next day.

6. Companies will leave Camp in following order:-
       'X' Company at 4.15 p.m.   'W' Company at 4.25 p.m.
       'Y'   "   " 4.35 p.m.   'Z'   "   " 4.45 p.m.
       Headquarters 4.50 p.m.
   Movement will be by Companies as far as VILLERS-FAUCON and from thence by platoons at 200 yds. interval. A long halt will be made at ST.EMILIE for tea.

7. Transport & Q.M.Stores will move to new billets early to-morrow. T.O. will detail transport as follows:-

            1 limber per company.
            1   "   for headquarters.

8. Completion of relief will be wired to Bn. HdQrs. by the code word 'E.F'.

                           (Signed) W.J.LYLE, Capt.& Ajt.,
                                   HIGHLAND LIGHT INFANTRY.
5.7.17.
Issued at:-12 noon.
   Copies Nos.1-3 W.D.& O.O.File.
            4 'W' Company.
            5 'X'   "
            6 'Y'   "
            7 'Z'   "
            8 2nd. in Command.
            9 3rd. HUSSARS.   )
           10 OX & BUCKS HUSSARS.   ) 4th. CAVALRY BRIGADE.

SECRET.   OPERATION ORDERS No.74   Copy No. 2
          HIGHLAND LIGHT INFANTRY.   13.7.17.

Reference 62c N.E.2 1/10,000.

1. The Battalion will be relieved by the R.SCOTS in the C2 Sub-Sector on the night 14/15th. as follows:-

   'Y' Coy.H.L.I. by 'W' Coy.R.SCOTS in GUILLEMONT & Posts.
   'X'   "   "   " 'Z'   "   "   " Right Support.
   'Z'   "   "   " 'Y'   "   "   " F.E.D Posts & Observation Posts
   'W'   "   "   " 'X'   "   "   " Left Support.

2. Guides will be found as follows:-

   'Y' Coy. will send 3 guides for GUILLEMONT Farm & 1 from D 1. to 'X' Coy.HdQrs at 9.30 p.m. Guides for BANK & ROAD Posts will be sent to D 1.
   'Z' Coy. will send 1 guide for each Posts to be on road at EMPIRE EAST Post at 9.30 p.m.
   'W' Coy. will send 2 guides from SUNKEN Road at SART FARM to Battalion Headquarters at 9.30 p.m. No guides are required for other 2 platoons.
   'X' Coy. will not send guides but will have an N.C.O. at junction of track at their Headquarters.

3. Advanced parties of 1 Officer and 2 N.C.Os per Company will report to the Adjutant at Battalion Headquarters at 3 p.m. 14th. inst.

4. All trench stores, maps, sketch maps, aeroplane photographs, and programmes of work in hand and contemplated will be handed over on relief and receipts obtained. These will be forwarded to the Adjutant by 12 noon 15th. inst.

5. Companies on relief will move to posts and billets as per attached sketch.

6. Completion of relief will be wired to Battalion Headquarters by the Code Word 'SUMMER'.

                                (Signed) W.J.LYLE, Capt., & Adjt.,
                                         HIGHLAND LIGHT INFANTRY.

Issued at:- 10.30 p.m.
Copies Nos. 1-3 W.D. & O.O.File.
          4 'W' Company.
          5 'X'   "
          6 'Y'   "
          7 'Z'   "
          8 2nd. in Command.
          9 R.SCOTS.
         10 W.YORKS.R.
         11. Bn. On Left.

SECRET. OPERATION ORDERS No.75.   22.7.17.
HIGHLAND LIGHT INFANTRY.
Copy No. 2

Reference sheet 62c N.E.

1. The Battalion will be relieved by the SHERWOOD FORRESTERS on night 23rd/24th. inst. as follows:-

   'W' Coy.H.L.I. will be relieved by 'Z' Coy.SHERWOODS in billets
   'X'   "   "   "   "   "   " 'X'   "   "   "   "
   'Y'   "   "   "   "   "   " 105th.T.M.Btty.   "   "
   'Z'   "   "   "   "   "   " 'W' Coy.SHERWOODS in Posts.

2. Guides, 1 per platoon from 'W' 'X' & 'Y' Coy.s & 1 per Post from 'Z' Coy. will report to the Adjutant at Battn. HdQrs. at 10 p.m. 23rd. inst.
   The Adjutant will detail 2 guides from Battn. HdQrs. to be at E.24.A.9½.3 (ST.EMILIE) to guide Advanced parties of SHERWOOD FORRESTERS to LEMPIRE. Guides to be in position by 11 a.m. 23rd
   The Adjutant will detail 5 guides from Battn. HdQrs. to be at same point as above at 9 p.m. 23rd. inst. to guide HdQrs. & Coys. of SHERWOOD FORRESTERS to LEMPIRE.

3. Companies will send advanced parties of 1 N.C.O. per Company to take over Camp at D.18.c.5.5 near AIZECOURT-LE-BAS. They will report at Battn.HdQrs. at 8 a.m. 23rd. inst. Lt.GEMMILL will be in charge of this party.

4. Companies, on relief, will march to Camp at D.18.c.555 as follows.

   Track through F.14.Central.
      "   Branch at F.19.B.3½.9½
   ST.EMILIE-VILLERS FAUCON-LONGAVESNES-AIZECOURT LE BAS Rd.

   Movement will be by platoons to W. of ST.EMILIE and thence by Coys.

5. 1 limber per Coy. will report at Coy.H.Q. for transport of L.Guns, valises etc.

6. All trench stores, trench shelters, sketch maps, aeroplane photo--graphs, programmes of work in hand and contemplated, tools etc. will be handed over, receipts obtained and forwarded to the Adjt. by 12 noon 24th. inst.

7. Completion of relief will be wired to Battn. H.Q. by the Code Word '8090'.

(Sd.) G.R.McCOLL, Lieut. & A/Adjt.,
HIGHLAND LIGHT INFANTRY.

22.7.17.
Issued at:- 11 p.m.
Copies to:- 1-3 W.D. & O.O.File.
            4 'W' Coy.
            5 'X' "
            6 'Y' "
            7 'Z' "
            8 2nd. in Command.
            9 Q.Mr. & T.O.
           10 SHERWOOD FORRESTERS.

WAR DIARY or INTELLIGENCE SUMMARY

Army Form C. 2118.

(Erase heading not required.)

Place	Date	Hour	Summary of Events and Information	Remarks and references to Appendices
AIZECOURT LE BAS.	1.8.17.		Weather dry. Preparations for move to line during the day. In the evening Battalion (less special party) moved to front line taking over the three left posts of LEMPIRE Sector (D,E,&F) Relief completed about midnight. Numbers of battalion. Battn.HdQrs. plus 8 officers and 250 O.Rs. On our right the ROYAL SCOTS held GUILLEMONT FARM. On our left were the W.YORKS. We relieved the 15th.SHERWOODS. 105th.Brigade. O.O.76. The special party remained at LONGAVESNES for special training. There were attached to the Battn in the line 2 companies of the 19th.NORTHUMBERLAND FUS.(Pioneers).	8/0.76(a)
-do-	2.8.17.		Weather changeable. Garrisons of posts were engaged in maintaining and improving trenches, patrolling etc. During the period the battalion was in the line special party carried on with special training.	
-do-	3.8.17.		Weather bad. Work and training as above.	
-do-	4.8.17.		Weather changeable. Some rain. Training as before. C.S.Ms SMITH & McQUILLAN awarded the D.C.M. for gallant conduct on nights of 12th. JULY, & 8/9th.JULY.	
-do-	5.8.17.		Weather bad. Workmand training as before. Casualties 1 O.R. wounded.	
-do-	6.8.17.		Weather good. " " " " 2 platoons of Cycle Corps were sent to Battalion to assist in holding posts.	
-do-	7.8.17.		Weather dull. Work as usual during the day. At night Battalion relieved by 17th.W.YORKS. Relief complete about 11 p.m. Battn. marched to LONGAVESNES to join special party.	9/0.77.
LONGAVESNES	8.8.17.		Weather good. Rain at night. Battalion resting reorganizing and cleaning up. Bathing also.	
-do-	9.8.17.		Weather fair. Entire battalion take part in special training for attack. Bathing completed.	
-do-	10.8.17.		" good. Training as before.	
-do-	11.8.17.		" fair, some rain. Battalion inspected in attack by Divnl.Staff & Brigadier. at night 5 officers, and 200 O.Rs reported to O.C.17th.R.SCOTS for duty in front line, at GUILLEMONT FARM.	8/0/8.
-do-	12.8.17.		" fair. Training as before with practices.	
-do-	13.8.17.		" changeable. " " " "	
-do-	14.8.17.		" fair, some rain. " " " "	
-do-	15.8.17.		" good. Battalion inspected in attack by Army, Corps, & Divisional staffs and Brigadier. Final practice attack was carried out at night.	
-do-	16.8.17.		" " Battalion engaged in further training and preparations for move to the line.	
-do-	17.8.17.		" " Bn. cleaning up, taking in identifications etc.& general preparations for attack. Bn. moved into line leaving camp about 7 p.m. They relieved 19th.D.L.I.relief completed about midnight. Casualties NIL. Operations Orders 77.	

WAR DIARY

~~INTELLIGENCE~~ SUMMARY

(Erase heading not required.)

Army Form C. 2118.

Instructions regarding War Diaries and Intelligence Summaries are contained in F.S. Regs, Part II. and the Staff Manual respectively. Title pages will be prepared in manuscript.

Place	Date	Hour	Summary of Events and Information	Remarks and references to Appendices
GUILLEMONT FARM.	18.8.17.		Battalion in FARM with special attacking & carrying parties in BASSE BOULOGNE & ROHSSOY. D Post & D1 Post.	
-do-	19.8.17.		Weather good. Attacking & carrying parties moved into position in GUILLEMONT FARM. ZERO Hour at 2 a.m. Particulars of attack on attached notes on operations at 4 a.m.	96 80 4/0 81 & 81a
-do-	20.8.17.	"	Battalion was relieved by 19th.D.L.I. in GUILLEMONT FARM. Relief complete 12.30 p.m. Battalion marched to camp at VILLERS FAUCON arriving about 4 a.m.	9/0 81 & 81a
VILLERS FAUCON.	21.8.17.	dull.	Battalion resting, cleaning reorganising etc. At 6 p.m. the Brigadier thanked the Battalion personally for their good work.	
-do-	22.8.17.	good.	Battalion bathing reorganising etc.	
-do-	23.8.17.	"	" Battalion inspected by Divisional General and complimented on their good work on the attack at GUILLEMONT FARM. General preparations for move to front line. Battalion relieved 19th.D.L.I. in GUILLEMONT FARM.	
-do-	24.8.17.	"	"	
THE KNOLL	25.8.17.	"	Battalion in the line. Enemy carried out heavy counter-attack at 4 a.m. See attached report on operations.	9/0 82.
In the Line.	26.8.17.	"	Battalion was relieved in the early morning by 19th.D.L.I. and marched back to VILLERS FAUCON to reorganise and rest the much worn men.	
VILLERS FAUCON.	27.8.17.	"	Battalion resting. Some training & general reorganising was carried out.	
"	28.8.17.	Weather stormy. much rain.	Battalion employed as on 27th. inst.	
THE KNOLL	29.8.17.	Changeable.	Bn. moved up to the line and relieved the 15th.CHESHIRE, Regt.; in The KNOLL Sector in Bde. Support. Digging & wiring parties carried out at night.	9/0 83
"	30.8.17.	Fair.	Bn. carry on work as before, at night and rest during day.	
"	31.8.17.	"	Enemy heavily counter-attacked on the KNOLL and 2 companies were engaged in carrying material and supporting front line battalion (W.YORKS.R.) 'Z' Coys. moved to and took over CAT POST from R.SCOTS. while 'X' Coy. moved to KEN LANE, also R.SCOTS. casualties 3 men wounded.	

SECRET. OPERATION ORDERS No.76(a) Copy No. 2
HIGHLAND LIGHT INFANTRY. 1.8.17.

Reference sheet 62c.N.E. 1/20,000

1. The Battalion, less Special Party, will relieve the SHERWOOD FORRESTERS in D, E, & F Posts as follows;-

   'W' Company will take over F (1, 2 & 3) Posts
   'X' & 'Z'   "   "   "   " E & E1 Posts.
   'Y' Company   "   "   " D Post.

2. Guides for these Posts will be at Battalion Headquarters at 9.30 p.m. at LEMPIRE (F.16.a.8.6)

3. Two Companies of Pioneers (NORTHUMBERLAND FUS.) will be attached to the Battalion from night 1st./2nd. AUGUST. O.C.Detachment Pioneers will arrange to take over billets & shelters in Hollow Road N. of SART FARM and S.of TOMBOIS FARM from SHERWOOD'S. All details of the relief will be arranged between O.C. Detachment Pioneers & SHERWOODS. This company will act as Support to D, E, & F Posts. One Company of Pioneers will remain in present billets & shelters in Quarry by arrangements with 101 st. Brigade.

4. All trench stores, aeroplane photographs, details of work in hand and contemplated, etc., will be taken over and lists forwarded ro the Adjutant by 12 noon day after relief.

5. Advance party of 1 Off, 1 N.C.O., 1 Signaller, & 1 Runner per Post will proceed to the line after dinner to take over Posts. They will report at Battalion Headquarters, SHERWOOD's.

6. Transport will move to VILLERS-FAUCON, O.C.Transport will arrange for 1 limber per Company, 1 limber, Mess-cart, & Maltese-cart for Headquarters to carry up rations, water etc.

7. Companies will be ready to move off at 4 p.m. and arrange to have tea behind Railway Embankment at (F.23.d)

8. Battalion Headquarters will close at 4 p.m. at AIZECOURT-LE-BAS and reopen at LEMPIRE, (F.16.a.8.6) on completion of relief.

9. Completion of relief will be wired to Battalion Headquarters by the Code Word 'RAIN'.

(Signed) W.F.M.MACARA, Lt.& A/Ajt.,

HIGHLAND LIGHT INFANTRY.

1.8.17.

Issued at :- 10 a.m.
Copies Nos 1-3 W.D. & O.O.File.
         4 'W' Company.
         5 'X' "
         6 'Y' "
         7 'Z' "
         8 N.F's (Pioneers)
         9 ~~SHERWOOD's~~ Pioneers (Detachment)
        10 SHERWOOD FORRESTERS.

SECRET.   OPERATION ORDERS No. 771   Copy NO. 2
          HIGHLAND LIGHT INFANTRY.

Reference map 62 c Edn. 3 A 1/20,000.
----

1. The Battalion & 2 companies Pioneers will be relieved by W.YORKS.R. in Centre Battalion Front on night 7/8th. as follows:-

   'W' Coy. will be relieved by ½ 'Y' Coy.W.YORKS. in F,F2,F3 & Barrier Post
   'X'&'Z'   "   "   "   "   " 'W'   "   "   "   " E, & F1 Posts.
   'Y' Coy. "   "   "   "   " 'Z'   "   "   "   " D Post.
   Platoon of Pioneers will be relieved by ½ 'Y' Coy.W.YORKS. in SUNKEN Rd.
   S. of TOMBOIS FARM. Coy. of Pioneers will be relieved by 'X' Coy.W.YORKS
   in Sunken Road & SART FARM. No.1 & 2 platoons of cyclists presently
   attached, will remain in E & F Posts and will come under command of C.O.
   W.YORKS.R.

2. Guides, 1 per Posts & 1 per platoon for Pioneers will be at Battalion Headquarters at 8 p.m. in LEMPIRE, (F.16.a.8.6)

3. All trench stores, aeroplane photographs, details of work on hand and contemplated etc. will be handed over, receipts obtained and forwarded to teh Adjutant by 12 noon day after relief.

4. On relief, companies will march back to join special party at LONGAVESNES. 2 Companies pioneers, on relief, will come into Brigade Reserve in LEMPIRE and take over billets of W.YORKS.Regt.

5. Transport Officer will detail 1 limber per company and 1 limber, MALTESE Cart and MESS Cart for Headquarters to Carry Lewis Guns, petrol tins etc.

6. Completiong of relief will be notified to Battalion Headquarters by the code word 'RATS'.

                              (Sd.) W.F.MACARA, Lieut.& A/Adjt.,
                                    HIGHLAND LIGHT INFANTRY.

7.8.17.

Issued at:- 2 p.m.
Copies to:- 1-3 W.D.& O.O.File.
            4 'W' Coy.
            5 'X' "
            6 'Y' "
            7 'Z' "
            8 W.YORKS.R.

SECRET.   OPERATION ORDERS No. 79.   11.8.19.
             HIGHLAND LIGHT INFANTRY.

Reference map 62C. 1/20,000

1. A composite company composed as follows:- 'W' Coy. 1 Off. 45 O.Rs. with 1 Lewis Gun, 'X' Coy. 1 Off. 25 O.Rs & 1 L.G., 'Y' Coy. 2 Offs. 25 O.Rs. & 1 L.G., 'Z' Coy. 1 Off. 45 O.Rs. & 1 L.G., in all 5 Officers, 140 O.Rs and 5 Lewis Guns, will relieve one company Royal Scots in GUILLEMONT FARM trenches on night 11/12th as follows:-

    'X' & 'Y' Coys. in GUILLEMONT FARM.
    'W' Coy. in GUILLEMONT-CAT Trench.
    'Z'   "   "   D.1 Post.

2. 2/Lt. J.W. BOW will be in command of above composite company and will, on relief, come under the command of the C.O. Royal Scots for tactical & working purposes.

3. Guides, one per company, will be at Battalion Headquarters, Royal Scots at 9.30 p.m. (LEMPIRE).

4. Advance party composed of 2/Lt. WOODSIDE, 'Y' Coy, 1 N.C.O. per Company, & 1 Signaller from 'X' & 'Z' will proceed to the line after lunch to take over trench stores, aeroplane photographs etc. They will report at Battalion Headquarters, ROYAL SCOTS.

5. All trench stores, aeroplane photographs, details of work on hand and contemplated etc. will be taken over, and lists forwarded to the Adjt. Royal Scots on morning after relief.

6. Transport Officer will detail 1 limber for rations and 1 limber for water, Lewis Guns etc. to be at Battalion Headquarters at 4 p.m. The companies will take up the following tins of water and will return a corresponding number of empty ones each night with empty ration limbers

   'W' Coy. 8 tins, 'X' Coy. 5 tins, 'Y' Coy. 5 tins, 'Z' Coy. 8 tins.

7. The companies will be ready to move off at   p.m. and arrange to have Tea behind the Railway Embankment at F.23.d.

8. Completion of relief will be notified to Battalion Headquarters, ROYAL SCOTS, by the code word, 'DOG'.

                        (Sd.) W.P.M. MACARA, Lt.& A/Ajt.,
11.8.17.   HIGHLAND LIGHT INFANTRY.
Issued at:- 2 p.m.
Copy Nos. 1-3 W.D. & O.O. File.
         4 'W' Coy.
         5 'X' "
         6 'Y' "
         7 'Z' "
         8 2/Lt. J.W. BOW.
         9 ROYAL SCOTS.

SECRET.　　　　　　OPERATION ORDERS No.79.　　　Copy No. 3
　　　　　　　　　　HIGHLAND LIGHT INFANTRY.　　　　16.8.17.

Reference 62c N.E. 1/10,000
----

1. The H.L.I. will relieve the W.YORKS.R. in KEN LANE, GUILLEMONT FARM, DOG Trench, and D Post. D.1 Post, BASSE BOULOGNE on night of 17th./18th. as follows:-

   'W' Coy.　　1 platoon (1 Off. & 7 men) DOG Trench.
   　　　　　　3 platoons (less 1 N.C.O. & 20 men) KEN LANE.
   　　　　　　1 N.C.O. & 20 men. BASSE BOULOGNE.

   'X' Coy.　　2 Offs. & 36 men (1 platoon) GUILLEMONT FARM.
   　　　　　　4 Offs. & 100 men in billets in RONSSOY.

   'Y' Coy.　　1 Off. & 45 men in GUILLEMONT FARM.
   　　　　　　4 Offs. & 100 men in billets in RONSSOY.

   'Z' Coy.　　1 Off. & 40 men in D.1 Post.
   　　　　　　3 platoons (less 1 N.C.O. & 20 men) DOLEFUL Post.
   　　　　　　1 N.C.O. & 20 men in BASSE BOULOGNE.

2. Guides for GUILLEMONT FARM, D.1 Post, DOLEFUL Post, & KEN LANE will be at Cross Roads at F.15.d.6.8. at 9 p.m.

3. Advance parties of 1 Off., 1 N.C.O., 1 Signaller, & 1 runner per Coy. & Lt.GEMMILL and signallers will go on in advance, to take over stores and arrange for billets, at 3 p.m.

4. All trench stores, aeroplane photographs, maps, sketch maps etc. will be taken over and lists forwarded to the Adjutant at 12 noon day after relief.

5. Companies will leave camp as under:-

   Garrisons of GUILLEMONT FARM, DOG Trench, & BASSE BOULOGNE at 5 p.m.
   　'Z' Company.　at 6.30 p.m.
   　'W'　"　　　　"　7 p.m.
   　'Y'　"　　　　"　7.15 p.m.
   　'X'　"　　　　"　7.30 p.m.
   Garrisons of FARM & posts will halt for tea at ST.EMILIE and move on again about 8.15 p.m.

6. Transport Officer will arrange to take back to Quartermaster's Stores all Officers' Valises & packs during the morning. He will have 1 G.S. wagon per company at camp at 4 p.m. to carry stores.
   2 limbers will be placed at the disposal of the Garrisons, and 2 limbers and Mess Cart for Headquarters.

7. Completion of relief will be notified to Bn. HdQrs by the code word. 'BRIGGS'.

　　　　　　　　　　　　　　　　(Sd.) W.F.M.MACARA, Lieut.& A/Adjt.,

　　　　　　　　　　　　　　　　　　HIGHLAND LIGHT INFANTRY.

16.8.17.

Issued at:- 6 p.m.
Copies to:-　1-3　W.D. & O.O.File.
　　　　　　　4　'W' Coy.
　　　　　　　5　'X'　"
　　　　　　　6　'Y'　"
　　　　　　　7　'Z'　"
　　　　　　　8　W.YORKS.R.
　　　　　　　9　2nd. in command.
　　　　　　　10. Transport Officer.

SECRET.   OPERATION ORDERS No.80.   Copy No.
                 HIGHLAND LIGHT INFANTRY.   18.8.17.

Reference special map. 'GUILLEMONT FARM'.
----

1. As soon as artillery bombardment has ceased, garrisons of posts of FARM & DOG Trench will be reoccupied.

2. By 12.30 a.m. gaps in wire to be cut, tapes laid for jumping off places and ladders placed in position. This is to be started as soon as it is dark enough.

3. Covering parties will be in position by 12.30 a.m. as follows;-

   'Z' Coy. covering assembly of troops on N.of FARM in BLUNT NOSE Trench.
   'W' "   "   "   "   " " between N.of FARM & GUILLEMONT ROAD
                                         about 100 Yds. in front of DOG Trench.
   Coy. W.YORKS.R. covering assembly of troops in DOG Trench to the S. of
                                         the GUILLEMONT ROAD.
   These covering parties will remain in position until 10 minutes before ZERO hour. They will then withdraw back to their original positions taking care **not** to go into trenches occupied by the attacking troops.

4. O.i/c garrison will arrange to provide a working party as soon after dark as possible to complete clearing and cleaning of jumping off trench of platoon of 'X' Coy. in the FARM.

5. Garrisons of advanced Posts in GUILLEMONT will be withdrawn 10 minutes before ZERO hour.

6. Companies will move to their assembly positions passing D.1 Post as follows;-
                 'W' Coy.   12.45 a.m.
                 'Y' "   1.5 a.m.
                 'X' "   1.25 a.m.
                 'Z' "   1.45 a.m.

7. Lewis Guns in Left & Right of FARM will fire frequent bursts from 11 p.m onwards to cover the noise of the troops moving into their assembly places

8. Battle police will be posted at D.1 Post and also where communication trench divides Coy.HdQrs. These will be in position at 12.30 a.m. and will be responsible that no traffic is going up and down communication trench between the hours of 12.30 a.m. & 2 p.m.

9. ZERO Hour will be at 4 a.m.

                              (Sd.) W.F.M.MACARA, Lieut. & A/Adjt.,
18.8.17.   HIGHLAND LIGHT INFANTRY.
Copies to;- 1-3 W.D.& O.O.File.
             4 'W' Coy.
             5 'X' "
             6 'Y' "
             7 'Z' "
             8 Capt.MURRAY, W.A.
             9 O.C.W.YORKS. CAT POST.
            10 O.C.GUILLEMONT FARM GARRISON.

SECRET.   HIGHLAND LIGHT INFANTRY.   COPY No._____
                       OPERATION ORDERS No.59.   80A

Reference Special GUILLEMONT Map.
----

1. The Highland Light Infantry will attack the enemy's Saps & Front Line
   Trench from A.13.b.56.75 to A.13.d.35.95 (L-A). The 105th.Inf.Bde.
   will carry out an attack on the KNOLL at the same time.

2. OBJECT. To capture enemy's Front Line Trench on above frontage and to
           kill or capture the garrison.

3. TIME & DATE. Time & date will be notified later. (19/8/17)

4. COMPOSITION & STRENGTH. The attack will be carried out by two compan-
   -ies. 'X' Coy. (Capt.W.D.BRYAN) on the right, 'Y' Coy.(Lt.HAMIL-
   -TON) on the left. 2 platoons of 'W' Coy. will be in Support to
   right of attack and will act as carrying parties. 2 platoons
   'Z' Coys. will be in Support to left of attack and act as carry
   -ing parties. 2 platoons of 'W' & 2 platoons of 'Z' Coys. will
   be in Reserve in GUILLEMONT & D.1 Posts respectively.

5. PLACES OF ASSEMBLY. 'W' & 'X' Coys. will assemble in DOW Trench. 'X'
   Coy. to the North & 'W' Coy. to the South, both companies on the
   North side of GUILLEMONT ROAD. 'X' Coy. will have one platoon
   in Trench T-T'. 'Y' Coy. will assemble in new trench to North
   of FARM (S-U). 'Z' Coy. will assemble in Communication Trench
   from S running Westwards to O.

6. ACTION. At ZERO Hour assaulting companies will leave their assembly
   trenches and form up for attack on a taped line about 30 Yds.
   in front. At ZERO & 3 minutes, these companies will advance to
   attack.
   Objectives.-'X' Coy.- Saps A-B, D-E, & Front Line Trench from
   A-F. Special party will be detailed to mop up FARM buildings.
   As soon as Front Line is captured, Posts will be consolidated.
   at A, C, & F.
   Objectives.- 'Y' Coy.- Saps K-H, I-G, & Front Line Trench from
   L-F. As soon as objectives have been captured, Posts will be
   established at L, K', & G.
   At ZERO plus 8 minutes, 'W' & 'Z' Coys. will advance with their
   loads to Support attack. As soon as loads are dumped at various
   Posts, special parties will be detailed to be in readiness to
   raid the enemy Support Line at ZERO plus 30 minutes should opp-
   -ortunity offer. At ZERO plus 75 minutes, all men not required
   for the various Posts will be withdrawn to GUILLEMONT Trenches.
   'W' & 'Z' Coys. will move to KEN & D Posts respectively.

7. TIME TABLE OF ARTILLERY & INFANTRY.

   ZERO - 2 Hours. Attacking & Supporting Coys. to be in assembly positns.
   Z to & 3'. Intense bombardment of Front Line, Saps & FARM buildings.
   Z & 3'. Artillery & STOKES' lift to 100 Yds. in Front of Support line
           'X' & 'Y' Coys. advance to attack.
   Z & 5'. Artillery lift to Support line.
   Z & 8'. Support companies, ('W' & 'Z') move forward from assembly
           trenches.
   Z & 30'. Artillery lift to 150 Yds. beyond Support line. STOKES'
            cease fire. Raiding parties advance to Support line if oppor-
            -tunity offers.
   Z & 42'. Raiding parties leave Support line and return through Front
            Line to GUILLEMONT Trenches.
   Z & 45'. Artillery lift to Support line.(& STOKES').
   Z & 75'. Posts formed & Garrisons established.
   Z & 90'. Artillery cease fire & 'stand by'.

8. TIME TABLE OF MACHINE GUNS.
   ZERO to & 5'. Creeping barrage from enemy Front line to enemy Support
                 line.
   Z & 5' to & 20'. Standing barrage on enemy Support line.
   Z & 20' to & 45'. Cease fire except blocks on each flank of attack.

8. (Continued).

    Z ₊ 45'. to ₊ 90'. Standing barrage on enemy Support Line with blocks on each flank of frontage of attack.

    Z ₊ 90'. Cease fire and 'stand by' ready for emergencies.

9. **STOKES MORTARS.**

    ZERO to ₊ 3'. Intense barrage on enemy Front Line A,C,F,G,K,L.
    Z ₊ 3' to ₊ 30'. Standing barrage on enemy Support Line X,Y,Q.
    Z ₊ 30' to ₊ 45'. Cease fire.
    Z ₊ 45' to ₊ 90'. Standing barrage on enemy Support Line.
    Z ₊ 90'. Cease fire and 'stand by' ready for emergencies.

10. **DISPOSITION OF BATTALION AFTER ATTACK.** As soon as Posts have been consolidated and thinned out, the Battalion will be disposed as follows:-

    'X' Coy. Holding Posts at A,C,& F with Coy. H.Q. at B. (2½ platoons) 1½ platoons in Support in GUILLEMONT.
    'Y' Coy. Holding Posts at L,K,& G with Coy. H.Q. at I. (2½ platoons) 1½ platoons in Support in GUILLEMONT.
    'W' Coy. One platoon in DOG Trench. H.Q. & 3 platoons in KEN.
    'Z' Coy. " " " D.1 Post. H.Q. & 3 platoons in DOLEFUL Post.

11. **PRISONERS & BOOTY.** All prisoners captured by 'X' Coy. will be collected at B. Those captured by 'Y' Coy. will be collected at I. They will be taken by the carrying parties when they are moving back, and will be brought to attack H.Q. at GUILLEMONT.

    All material captured will be sent back to Attack H.Q. with men withdrawn from Posts. Special men in each party will be detailed to collect letters or correspondence. These will be sent back to Attack H.Q. by runner.

12. **WOUNDED.** All wounded will be taken by stretcher-bearers to attack H.Q. A relay post will be established there to carry them on to Aid Post at D.1 Post.

13. **COMMUNICATION.** Battalion Signalling Officer will arrange for telephone communication from Attack H.Q. in GUILLEMONT to places of assembly of each Company. He will also arrange for lines to be run out from T & S" to B & I respectively to connect up attack H.Q. with Coy. H.Q. of 'X' & 'Y' Coys. A special line will connect Attack H.Q. with Battalion H.Q. at KEN.

14. **RUNNER POST.** Each company will detail 2 runners to be attached to Battn. H.Q. A relay runner post of 1 runner per coy. will be established at Attack H.Q. at GUILLEMONT.

15. **DRESS & EQUIPMENT.** Officers will wear the same dress & equipment as the N.C.Os and men except that they will carry revolvers instead of rifles. N.C.Os & men:- 'fighting order', fixed bayonets, 120 rounds S.A.A. in pouches, Magazines charged, one bandolier slung over left shoulder. Gas helmet will be worn at 'Alert' position.

    Each N.C.O. & man will carry 2 sandbags, 4 MILLS' No.5 bombs 1 pick or shovel (proportion of 1 pick to 10 shovels). N.C.Os i/c sections or parties will carry a giant wire-cutter. Bombing parties of assaulting companies will carry buckets with 12 bombs (MILLS' No.23). One bucket to have rods detached. They will also carry, distributed between them, 4 'P' Bombs and 2 M.S.K.

    Lewis Gun sections of assaulting companies will carry in addition to their guns, 1 bag spare parts and 32 magazines per gun.

    Supporting Coys. ('W' & 'Z') will each arrange to carry 18 boxes MILLS' No.23, 6 cases HALES' No.20, 3 boxes S.A.A., 600 sandbags, 24 gallons water, 9 picks, & 15 shovels, 36 Iron-screw-pickets, 9 coils concertina wire, and 48 Lewis Gun magazines.

-2-

16. **IDENTIFICATIONS.** Os.C.Companies will arrange to carefully inspect their men before leaving camp to see that all identifications such as shoulder titles, letters, pay-books, etc. are left behind, and they will arrange for their safe custody.

17. **RATIONS.** All Officers and men will carry a day's rations in addit--ion to their Iron Rations.

18. **SYNCHRONIZATION OF WATCHES.** The Adjutant will arrange to synchronize watches of all Officers & N.C.Os at 12 noon, 6 p.m. and 12 mid-night on B Day.

19. **MEDICAL OFFICER.** The Medical Officer will be at D.1 Post where an Advanced Dressing Station will be established.

20. **HEADQUARTERS.** Battalion Headquarters will be in K&N. Headquarters of O. i/c attacking Force will be in Company Headquarters at GUILLEMONT FARM.

(Signed) W.F.M.MACARA, Lieut. & A/Ajt.

15.3.17.

HIGHLAND LIGHT INFANTRY.

Issued at:-

Copies to:- 1-3 W.D. & O.O.File.
4-5 106th.Inf.Brigade.(2 copies).
6 O.C.'W' Coy.
7 " 'X' "
8 " 'Y' "
9 " 'Z' "
10 Capt.W.A.MURRAY.(O.i/c.Attacking Force).
11.Capt.A.C.BALFOUR. (2nd.In Command. Battn).
12.Commanding Officer Battn.
13.106th.T.M.Battery.
14.106th.M.G.Company.
15.203rd. Coy. R.E's.
16.Group Commander. Right Group R.A.
17.M.O.
18.Sigs. Officer.

SECRET. OPERATION ORDERS No.81. Copy No.
         HIGHLAND LIGHT INFANTRY.   19.8.17.

Reference Special map.'GUILLEMONT FARM'.
----

1. 'W' Coy. will relieve 'X' Coy. in Posts A, C, & F.
   'Z' "   "   " 'Y' " "   " L, K, & G.
   These reliefs will take place to-night at dusk. 'W' & 'Z' Coys. should
   leave their present stations as soon after 8.15 p.m. as possible, so as
   to carry out the relief before working & wiring parties come up.
   They will carry in a supply of bombs, rifle grenades, & S.A.A. to
   increase the reserve in each post. 'X' & 'Y' Coys. on relief will be
   in Support in GUILLEMONT FARM. O.C.GUILLEMONT FARM will arrange acc-
   -ommodation for these companies until after dawn when they will move back
   into Reserve at DOLEFUL Post & KEN LANE.

2. Covering parties and flank guards will be found as follows to-night.
   Platoon of 'W' Coy. in FARM with 1 Lewis Gun, under 2/Lt.SMITH, will take
   up a position S.O. of Post A to cover the flank A.R.
   Platoon & 1 Lewis Gun of 'Z' Coy. from D.1 Post under 2/Lt.FLEMING will
   take up a position WEST of post L to cover the flank L.U. These flank
   defence positions platoons will be in position by 9.15 p.m.
   2/Lt.SMITH's platoon will also act as covering party to NORTHUMBERLAND
   FUSILIERS digging a communication trench from A.to R1.

3. Carrying parties for each Post will be detailed by O.C.FARM. These carry
   -ing parties under 2/Lt.SUMMERS & 2/LT.McINTYRE will carry up a supply of
   bombs, S.A.A. & Rifle Grenades to each Post. These parties should move
   as much as possible over the open and so keep the communication trenches
   clear.

4. 203rd. Field Coy.R.E. with carrying party of 2 Offs.& 100 men R.SCOTS to
   construct a continuous belt of wire round captured Posts. 2 platoons of
   R.SCOTS will act as covering party to these parties. Wiring party will
   commence work at 10 p.m. The O.i/c R.E.Party will report completion of
   work, to O.C.'W' Coy. at Coy.HdQrs at B before withdrawing his party.
   O.C.'W' Coy. will then notify covering parties.

5. (a) 19th.N.F's will dig 2 communication trenches as follows. Hedge to
   point I and thence along old GERMAN C.T.
   (b) A Communication Trench will be cut from the most Easterly corner of
   the present front line S.of FARM Buildings (point T) North of the hedge
   to point B and thence to New Front line between points A & C.
   (c) A Communication Trench, traversed for 60 Yds. at the Eastern end,
   will be cut from point A towards new trench recently dug forward from
   DOG Trench (R.R.)

6. ACTION IN CASE OF ATTACK.
   The wiring party will man the captured trench A,C,E,F,G,K,L. The 2 platoon
   17th.R.SCOTS covering the wiring party will also fall back and man this
   trench when the wirers are all safely back in it. The party working on
   C.T. (A.R.) will man DOG Trench, N. of GUILLEMONT-BASSE BOULOGNE Rd.
   The platoon 18th.H.L.I. forming the covering party on this flank will
   hold on where it is as long as possible, but if forced to withdraw will
   man DOG Trench, S. of GUILLEMONT-BASSE BOULOGNE Rd. The 2 parties work-
   -ing on C.Ts. T.B.C, S.I.G, will fall back into trenches W. of GUILLEMONT
   FARM. The platoon 18th.H.L.I. forming covering party on the left flank
   will hold on where it is as long as possible, but if forced to withdraw
   will man the captured trench L,K,G, or BLUNT NOSE Trench U.S. according
   to direction of attack.

                          (Sd.). W.F.M.MACARA, Lieut. & A/Adjt.,
                                          HIGHLAND LIGHT INF.
19.8.17.
Copies to:- 1-3 W.D.& O.O.File.
            4-8 Os.C. 'W', 'X', 'Y', 'Z' Coys.
            8 Capt.MURRAY, 9 Capt. BALFOUR, 10 O.C CAT POST,
            11.2/Lt.SMITH.   12.2/LT.HUNTER.

SECRET.   OPERATION ORDERS No. 82a.   20.8.17.
HIGHLAND LIGHT INFANTRY.

Reference 62c N.E. 1/20,000.

1. The Battalion will be relieved by D.L.I. on night 20/21st. as follows

              (A Post) by 1 Lewis Gun and 20 men for each Post from
   'Z' Coy.H.L.I.(C ")
              (F ") right half Battalion, D.L.I.
   Remainder of right half batt. D.L.I. will relieve platoon of 'W'Coy.
   in DOG Trench and platoon of 'X' Coy. in GUILLEMONT.
              (G Post)
   'W' Coy.H.L.I.(K' ") by 1 Lewis Gun & 20 men for each post from
              (K   ") left half battalion D.L.I.
   'Z' Coy.D.1 Post by 1 Lewis Gun & 20 Men D.L.I.
          (DOLEFUL Post by 2 L.Guns & 50 men D.L.I.
   'Y' Coy.(GUILLEMONT " " remainder of left half batt. D.L.I.
   'X' " in KEN by 1 Company ROYAL SCOTS.

2. Guides for A,C,F,G,K' & K Posts, D1 Post, DOLEFUL, DOG Trench, GUILLE
   -MONT FARM ('X' Coy) GUILLEMONT FARM ('Y' Coy.) will be at Cross Roads
   BASSE BOULOGNE (F.16.c.8.1) at 9 p.m. They will report to Battalion
   Headquarters at 8.30 p.m.
   Guides for A.C.F. Posts will use right communication trench GUILLE-
   -MONT. Guides for G.K' & K Posts will use left communication trench
   GUILLEMONT.
   Guide for DOLEFUL will bring his relief in via KEN & SART FARM.
   Guide for DOG Trench will bring his relief in by communication trench
   to Coy. HdQrs. GUILLEMONT.

3. The Battalion on relief will march to VILLERS FAUCON. C.QM.Sergts.
   will arrange tents etc.

4. Trench stores, maps, aeroplane photographs etc. will behanded over
   receipts obtained and forwarded to the Adjutant on the morning after
   relief.

5. One limber for 'W','X','Y',& 'Z' Coys. will be at Cross Roads BASSE
   BOULOGNE to take Lewis Guns Stores etc.
   3 limbers and mess cart for Headquarters.

6. Completion of relief will be notified by the code word 'WELL DONE'.

                              (Sd.)W.F.MACARA, Lieut. & A/Adjt.,
20.8.17.   HIGHLAND LIGHT INFANTRY.
Copies to:- 1-3 W.D.&.O.O.File.
            4 'W' Company.
            5 'X' "
            6 'Y' "
            7 'Z' "
            8 Transport Officer.
            9 D.L.I.

SECRET.　　　　　OPERATION ORDERS no.82.　　　24.8.17.
　　　　　　　　　HIGHLAND LIGHT INFANTRY.
　　　　　　　　　　　　　　　　　　　　　　　Copy No.

Reference Special 'GUILLEMONT' map.

1. Battalion will relieve D.L.I. in GUILLEMONT FARM trenches, D.1 Post, DOLEFUL Post, and KEN LANE on the night 24th/25th. inst. as follows:-
    'X' Coy. will take over A, C, F Posts. Remainder of Coy. will be in Support in DOG Trench.
    'Y' Coy. will take over G, K', & F Posts. Remainder of company will be in Support in dug-outs in GUILLEMONT FARM.
    'Z' Coy. will take over D.1 Post and DOLEFUL, finding garrison for BANK Post from D.1
    'W' Coy. will relieve ROYAL SCOTS in KEN.

2. Front line companies will each be responsible for the safety of their own flanks. 'X' & 'Y' Coys. will each detail a platoon nightly for counter-attacking purposes. They will be stationed in DOG & C.S.M's dug-out respectively during the night and will return to their own companies at 5 a.m.

3. One officer per company, one N.C.O. per Post, company signallers, runners, Lt.GEMMILL & signallers for Bn. H.Q., will leave in advance for the line at 5 p.m. to take over stores etc.

4. Headquarters of front line companies will be in Company Headquarters in GUILLEMONT. Headquarters of 'Z' Coy. will be in DOLEFUL, and Hdqrs. of 'W' Coy. and Battn. Hdqrs will be in KEN LANE.

5. Battalion will parade at　　　 p.m. and coys. will move in following order:-
　　　　　　　　'Z' Company at
　　　　　　　　'Y'　 " 　 "
　　　　　　　　'X'　 " 　 "
　　　　　　　　'W'　 " 　 "

6. All trench stores, aeroplane photographs, sketch maps, etc. will be taken over, receipts given and lists forwarded to the Adjutant by 12 noon day after relief.

7. Transport Officer will detail the following limbers:-
　　　2 limbers for 'X' Company.　　2 limbers for 'Y' Company.
　　　1　 "　　 " 'W'　 "　　　　1　 "　　 " 'Z'　 "
　　　1 limber, MALTESE Cart, & MESS Cart for Bn. Headquarters.

8. Completion of relief will be notified to Bn. Headquarters by the code word 'O.K.'

　　　　　　　　　　　　　　(Signed) C.F.M.MACARA, Lieut.& A/Adjt.,
24.8.17.　　　　　　　　　　　　　　　　　　HIGHLAND LIGHT INFANTRY.
Issued at:- 10 a.m.
Copies to:- 1-2 W.D. & O.C.File.
　　　　　　4 O.C.'W' Coy.
　　　　　　5　 "　'X'　 "
　　　　　　6　 "　'Y'　 "
　　　　　　7　 "　'Z'　 "
　　　　　　8　 "　D.L.I.
　　　　　　9 Transport Officer.

SECRET.   OPERATION ORDERS No.83.   28.8.17.
HIGHLAND LIGHT INFANTRY.

Reference maps 57c S.E. & 62c N.E.   1/20,000.

1. The Battalion will relieve the 15th. CHESHIRE Regt. in shelters in IEMPIRE Rd. and billets in IEMPIRE on the night 29th./30th. as follows

    'W' Coy.)
    'Z' "   ) shelters in IEMPIRE Rd.
    'X' "   )

    'Y' Coy. Billets in IEMPIRE.
    Battn. HdQrs. at F.16.a.8.6.(IEMPIRE).

2. Guides, one per company will be at Cross Roads at 9 p.m.

3. Advance parties of one Officer and 1 N.C.O. per Coy. Lt.GEMMILL and signallers from HdQrs. will proceed to the line at 5 p.m. to take over billets and any stores.

4. All trench stores, aeroplane photos, and sketch maps also details of work in hand and proposed will be taken over on relief, receipts given and lists forwarded to the Adjutant on morning after relief.

5. The Battalion will be ready to move at 7 p.m. Battalion Headquarters at VILLERS FAUCON will close at   and reopen in IEMPIRE (F.16. a.8.6) immediately after relief.

6. The Transport Officer will detail one limber per company and one limber & Mess cart for HdQrs. to carry up Lewis Guns, Trench stores rations etc.

7. Completion of relief will be wired to Battn. HdQrs by the Code word 'SKIPPER'.

8. Special wiring & carrying parties (' ')wiring 1 N.C.O. & 10 O.Rs., 60 O.Rs carrying, and 'Z' Coy. 1 N.C.O. &13 O.R. wiring, & 60 O.Rs carrying) will move up to Road junction R.17.d.8. route
F.8.a.55.a.(Just South

28.8.17.

Issued at:- 7.30 p.m.
Copies to:- 1-3 W.D.
             4 'W'
             5 'X'
             6 'Y'
             7 'Z'
             8 15

SECRET.

REPORT ON OPERATIONS CARRIED OUT
on enemy trenches in &
EAST of GUILLEMONT FARM, near EPEHY, on 19th.,
& 20th. August, 1917, by the
18th.(S) Bn. Highland Light Infantry.

Reference special map:- 'GUILLEMONT FARM'.

The attack was timed to take place at 4 a.m. on the morning of the 19th. August, 1917.

The dispositions of attack were as follows:-

The attack was to be carried out by 'X' & 'Y' Coys. with 'W' & 'Z' coys. carrying material for consolidation and supporting the attack. 'X' Company.(Capt.W.D.BRYAN Commanding) was responsible for the enemy front from points A-F inclusive with 'W' Company (Capt.J.BARRIE) in support. On the left, 'Y' Company (Lieut.J.B.HAMILTON Commanding) was responsible for the enemy line from F (exclusive) - K inclusive with 'Z' Coy. (Lieut.R.J.W. RITCHIE) Commanding in Support.

The attack was under the command of Capt.W.A.MURRAY.

At 2 a.m. on the morning of 19th., August, the various companies were in their assembly positions and all preparations were ready.

Between 2 a.m. and 4 a.m. the attacking company on the left was subjected to a severe trench mortar bombardment and a number of casualties were caused. There was grave danger of the company being disorganised particularly as the centre party had lost its' officers and a large number of men. Steps were therefore taken to reorganized the party and it was decided to have the company attack in its' depleted state with an officer of the carrying party to replace the officer lost. As an additional precaution 'Z' Company, which was in support to the left, and was to advance at 4.8 a.m. was ordered to advance in close support at 4.5 a.m. and co-operate in clearing and consolidating the positions when captured.

Promptly at 4 a.m. the bombardment opened. It was exceedingly well carried out and excited the admiration of the attacking parties. At 4.3 a.m both attacking companies moved forward in the assault followed by their carrying and supporting parties at 4.8 a.m. on the right and 4.5 a.m. on the left.

The enemy trenches were found to be heavily garrisoned and hand to hand fighting ensued along the front. So great was the dash and determination of the attacking forces, that the enemy was swept aside and all objectives were at once reached, taken and consolidation commenced.
It is worthy of note that, in the course of the hand to hand fighting, not one single officer or man of our attack was wounded or killed by the german garrison.

Communication was early established by telephone on the right and the taking of all objectives was reported at 4.37 a.m. On the left flank communication was broken, but thr report was received at 4.52 a.m. that all the objectives on the left had been taken. In both cases consolidation was proceeding. About this stage the enemy started to develope a bombing attack on the right flank, but Lewis Gun fire was brought to bear on them and the attack ceased.

The casualties sustained by the left company, both before and after the assault were fairly severe and they were reinforced by the troops left in reserve. The carrying and support companies were withdrawn after assisting in the consolidation.

The day on the whole was quiet except for desultory shelling and trench mortaring at intervals during the day.

According to arrangements, the two attacking companies were relieved in the evening of the 19th. by 'W' & 'Z' Companies who had been withdrawn after supporting the attack.

Nothing of importance happened during the night 19th-20th, and further consolidation was effected. The front was also wired by 203rd., Field Company R.E. during the night assisted by carrying parties of the Royal Scots. Two Communications trenches were dug by the 19th.NORTHUMBERLAND FUS.

At about 4.20 a.m. on the 20th. the enemy commenced to shell and trench mortar our positions, increasing the intensity until 4.40 a.m. when, under cover of a smoke barrage and a ground mist, the enemy advanced to

to/
counter-attack. This was developed along the whole of the captured front. The S.O.S. was called for and came down immediately behind the first enemy wave completely demoralising and destroying them. The first wave came on apparently unaware of our wire and was caught by our Lewis Gun and rifle fire on the wire. Those succeeded in penetrating the wire (which happened on the right) were killed before reaching our trenches. An attempted bombing attack up the right communication trench was frustrated by our bombers.

There is not much to report during the rest of the day. The enemy bombarded our trenches heavily at intervals and kept up a fairly heavy fire with shells and trenchmortars. About 6.30 p.m. counter preparation was called for and the enemy was effectively silenced.

As further arranged, relief of the positions was carried out during the night 20th/21st. August, 1917.

The following number of prisoners were captured during these operations

        2 Officers (1 wounded)
      18 Other ranks (4 wounded)

The following materials was also captured.

    3 Ammunition belts in boxes.
    3 maching guns.
    1 spare parts bag.
    1 ammunition belt & container. 1 M.G. Body shield.
    & other miscellaneous correspondence etc.

Casualties during the period 17th-20th. inst. have been heavy viz;-

    2 Officers wounded.
    2 "   shell-shock
  22 N.C.Os and men killed.
    4 " " " Missing. (believed killed).
  86 " " " wounded.

Most of the casualties occurred while the companies were in their assembly positions and after the enemy positions had been captured.

The behaviour of all ranks was beyond all praise, not only are they to be specially commended for the dash and energy with which they carried the positions, but in addition for their untiring efforts and devotion to duty in holding the line.

Where all have done so well it is difficult and invidious to mention individuals, but I have forwarded, under separate cover, the names of Offs N.C.Os and men for immediate award for gallantry and able leadership.

I cannot conclude without mentioning the following;-

<u>Right Group Artillery.</u> for the most effective barrage which immediately preceeded the assault.

<u>106th.M.G.Coy.</u>- for their splendid work during the assault and the effective manner in which they covered the front afterwards and the help which Capt., MERISON gave me throughout.

<u>106th. & 103rd. T.M.Batteries.</u> for their intense and accurate barrage prior to the assault.

<u>19th.NORTHUMBERLAND FUSILIERS.(Pioneers).</u> For the excellent model of GUILLEMONT FARM which they dug and which enabled the Battalion to be thoroughly trained for the attck.

<u>My Medical Officer.(Capt.SCADE)</u> Who worked most indefatigably throughout in attending to and evacuating wounded.

                                        (Sd.) R.R.LAWRENSON, Lt.- Col.,

<u>23.8.17.</u>   <u>Commanding, 18th(S) Bn. Highland Light Infantry.</u>

SECRET.   Report on enemy attack on
                    GUILLEMONT FARM on 25th. Aug., 1917.

   The Battalion relieved the 19th.D.L.I. in GUILLEMONT FARM on night
24th/25th, 1917 about midnight. The night was quiet and the only
sounds heard were of the enemy wiring his line.
   About 4 a.m. the enemy commenced shelling in the rear of the FARM,
and this shell fire gradually increased in intensity until 4.15 a.m.
when a very intense shell and trench mortar bombardment was opened on
the posts. So intense and accurate was the shooting that within a few
minutes, practically the whole line was laid flat, a great number of
the garrison being buried or killed, bombs & rifles buried, and most
of the Lewis Guns being put out of action.
   After about 15 minutes of this intense bombardment, the enemy attack
-ed the line in strong force. Owing to the smoke and dust it was diff-
-icult to see where the attack was developing, but it appears to have
been carried out as follows.
   On each flank an attack was carried out along the trench to each
flank block. In addition, an attack was made up the two communication
trenches leading to C and G Posts respectively. The right flank
held alright and beat of the enemy, but the left flank was not faring
so well meantime. On this flank the casualties were very heavy and out
of the 70 men in Posts only some 14-20 survived. There were no bombs
left and those rifles which were still in action jammed after a few
rounds had been fired. The only Lewis Gun in action when the attack
developed was smashed after firing half a magazine. Of the three
officers on this flank, one was wounded, a second buried and badly
shocked and the third slightly wounded and buried but still remaining
at duty. The enemy attacked in strength estimated at 1 company on K
Post. Of this Post only 1 man survived and despite the efforts of the
remainder of the posts, the enemy succeeded in affecting an entrance
by bombing and siezed the trench junction at K. He thereupon entered
the Northern C.T. through the FARM and bombed down to cut off the
garrison at K8 & G Posts of which only a few survived and they retired
fighting to F Post. This post was still holding out and continued to
hold until the enemy commenced to bomb across towards the Southern
C.T. in the FARM, when they were forced to withdraw to avoid being
surrounded. The enemy meantimed forced an entrance at A Post all the
garrison being killed or wounded, and had attacked frontally with 2
companies between G & K'. The remnants of C & F posts, having no bombs
and very few rifles working, were drawn back down GLASGOW Trench and
joined forces with that garrison establishing a block in the trench.
   The counter-attack platoon on the right held this block and co-
-operated in holding the block at hedge on S. side of FARM and junction
of that trench with DOG Trench. On the left a block was made at trench
junction W. of BLUNT NOSE and a clearing party moved up trench behind
CRATER to Garrison it.   Reinforcements were hurried up from DOLEFUL
and KEN, and these having got up through a heavy barrage, a counter-
-attack on STOKES Trench was led by Captain G.JACKSON who was command-
-ing the left company. This attack was caught by the enemy barrage and
two attempts to advance were forced back, Captain G.JACKSON being killed
and another officer wounded in this attempt. The left flank support
platoon was meantime supporting the counter-attack and holding the
approach by MACQUINCOURT VALLEY, the Vickers' Gun in BLUNT NOSE having
been smashed by shell fire.
   After the attack across the open was tried in vain, the block
parties were strengthened and an attempt was made to advance up the
various C.T's. These however were heald by fairly strong parties of the
enemy supported by heavy knife rests, and it was found that the enemy
had a range of about 20 yards more than our parties with his bombs and
were able to keep our parties back. An attampt to get at the enemy's
positions over the top was frustrated by his maching gun fire and sniping
It appeared now that nothing but an organised attack with artillery
preparation would be effective, so the blocks were strengthened and held
against the enemy in the positions abovementioned. These blocks were
moved forward where possible, and close touch with the enemy maintained
all day.
   The enemy barrage was particularlu intense and most effective. The
enemy appeared to have a system of cummunication by GREEN lights and on
several occasions brought down a barrage in response to that signal, on

on/
    our counter-attacking parties. The approaches to the forward positions were absolutely shut in by enemy shell fire.

    Our own fire was unfortunately not strong and was very tardy. Not for some time after our S.O.S. was sent up did our barrage come down and that only weakly. The result was that the enemy was able to develope his attack without interuption from anything except our rifle fire. Had artillery been effective and our Lewis Guns & bombs not been destroyed, I am confident that the enemy would not have succeeded in his attack.

    Our casualties were heavy, amounting to some 160 in all. Of the 5 officers in the posts at the time of attack, 2 were wounded, 2 shell-shocked and 1 wounded & missing. Of the counter-attacking Officers, 1 was killed and 1 wounded.

    The casualties inflicted by our garrison on the enemy are calculated to have been heavy. The few survivors of thr front line posts held out as long as they could with what rifles and bombs were left, and from statements taken from these, it appears that the enemy at one time had been driven back, but came on again when reinforced and when most of the garrison had ceased to exist.

    I very much regret that the Battalion should have lost a position so recently taken by them, but they did not do so without having put up a splendid fight and having accounted for very many of the enemy.

                                        (Sd.) R.R.LAWRENSON, Lt-Col.,

27.8.17.   Commanding, 18th.(S) Bn. Highland Light Infantry.

WAR DIARY
INTELLIGENCE SUMMARY
(Erase heading not required.)

Army Form C. 2118.

18 H L I
106/35

Place	Date	Hour	Summary of Events and Information	Remarks and references to Appendices
LEMPIRE.	1.9.17.		Batt. disposed as follows. H.Q., 'W' & 'Y' Coys. in billets in LEMPIRE, 'X' Coy. in KEN LANE & 'Z' Coy. 11 CAT POST. Day quiet. Weather fine relieved at night by 15th.CHESHIRE R. on relief, Battalion marched back to camp at AIZECOURT-LE-BAS.	
"	2.9.17.		Bn. in camp at AIZECOURT-LE-BAS. Day spent in cleaning up clothing, equipment etc. & in resting. Weather bright and warm.	
"	3.9.17.		Bn still in camp. Weather perfect. Battalion engaged in bathing cleaning up etc.	
"	4.9.17.		" " " " " Training of Specialists etc. Also specialist training.	
"	5.9.17.		" " " " " Training of Bn. in Musketry.	
"	6.9.17.		Weather fine. Preparations for move to line. Cleaning up lines, camp etc. Bn. left camp at 4.30 p.m. and marched to EPEHY where tea was served. At dusk they marched to trenches and relieved the 20th.Lancs.Fus. Very quiet night. 'W' & 'X' Coys. in front line, 'Z' Coy. in Support and 'Y' in Reserve.	
EPEHY.	7.9.17.		Bn. in Line. Weather fine. Enemy very quiet, Usual work carried out.	
"	8.9.17.		" " " " Very little activity by the enemy. A few bursts of M.G.fire during night.	
"	9.9.17.		" " " " Usual trench routine carried out. M.G.activity at night.	
"	10.9.17.		" " " " Weather as before. Misty morning. No activity by enemy during day. Usual M.G.fire at night.	
"	11.9.17.		" " " " Day warm and clear. Usual M.G.activity at night.	
"	12.9.17.		" " " " Weather fine. Very little enemy activity. Inter-company relief took place after tea 'Z' Coy. relieved 'W' Coy. on Right Coy. front. 'Y' relieved 'X' on left Coy. front 'W' Coy. came into Support in SHERWOOD LANE and 'X' Coy. came into Reserve in GLOSTER ROAD. O.O.85 A attached	
"	13.9.17.		" " " " Situation normal. Weather as usual. The usual work on trenches carried on. Capt. W.A.MURRAY & 2/Lt.J.M.SUMMERS awarded the MILITARY CROSS for gallantry and good work on 19th. & 25th. AUGUST.	
"	14.9.17.		" " " " Weather good. Enemy inactive. Usual routine. Bathing of Coys. at H.Q.(Battn.)	
"	15.9.17.		" " " " Morning misty. Slight M.G.fire during night. Bathing carried on.	
"	16.9.17.		" " " " A raid was carried out by 17th.R.SCOTS at night and the enemy's attention was diverted by a sheet in which our Battn. assisted as per O.O.88 attached.1 O.R.wounded for last night's raid.	
"	17.9.17.		" " " " Weather dull but dry. Considerable damage done in CORD LINE during enemy retaliation for last night's raid.	
"	18.9.17.		" " " " Relieved by GLOSTER REGT. as per O.O.87 attached. Relief carried out without incident and Battalion marched back to AIZECOURT-LE-BAS.	

WAR DIARY
or
INTELLIGENCE SUMMARY

(Erase heading not required.)

Army Form C. 2118.

Instructions regarding War Diaries and Intelligence Summaries are contained in F. S. Regs., Part II. and the Staff Manual respectively. Title pages will be prepared in manuscript.

Place	Date	Hour	Summary of Events and Information	Remarks and references to Appendices
AIZECOURT-LE-	Bas.19.9.17.		Bn. in Camp. Men resting and cleaning clothing and equipment.	
"	20.9.17.		Bn. still in camp. Weather fine. Bathing, cleaning of equipment, organisation of Coys. and specialists.	
"	21.9.17.	"	still in camp. Bn. parade in morning. forenoon devoted to Coy. drill and instruction of specialists. afternoon to sports etc. Working parties found for 35th. Div. Pioneers at LONGAVESNES. and 203rd. Field Coy. R.E. at VILLERS-FAUCON. Draft of 11 Off. & 50 N Other ranks from Base.	
"	22.9.17.		Bn. still in camp. Coys. on parade for Musketry. Physical training. and Bayonet fighting. working parties as yesterday.	
"	23.9.17.		Bn. in camp. Company & platoon drill. Organisation of new drafts into platoons and companies. training of specialists etc. Draft of 4 Off. & 146 O.Rs. from GLASGOW YEOMANRY. The Corps Commander presented ribbons to Officers & men who had gained some, viz:- 5 M.C's. 2 D.C.M's. & 14 M.M's.	
"	24.9.17.	"	Men passed Unfit by A.D.M.S. Class for training L.Gunners formed.	
"	25.9.17.	"	A second draft of 4 Off. & 84 O.Rs. arrived i1 GLASGOW YEOMANRY. Parades and train- -ing as before.	
"	26.9.17.	"	Cleaning lines, and storing blankets, valises boxes etc. in Quartermaster's Stores preparatory to moving into the line. The Bn talion marched from camp at 3 p.m. and proceeded to ST.EMILIE where a halt was made for tea. Thereafter the Battalion marched to the line and relieved the 23rd. MANCHESTER REGT. & LANCS. FUS. in the LEMPIRE Sector as per O.O.88 attached.	
Trenches	27.9.17.	Bn. in the line.	Day warm & dry. Bn. H.Q. in LEMPIRE very congested. Enemy lightly shelled vicinity of our lines with light & heavy T.M8s. A party of about 6 Germans entered our trenches at about A.13.a.0.15. and inflicted casualties 3 being wounded. The enemy left 2 caps and 1 pair of wire-cutters. He also approached our trenches at another point, but was driven off by Rifle fire. Enemy merry. Bombing his own wire. line. Weather good. Our artillery active shelling enemy back areas. Bn. H.Q. removed to KEN LANE on arrival of Transport. at night.	
"	28.9.17. "	"	line. Weather warm & dry. Situation normal. Usual trench work carried on. 1 O.R. kill -ed.	
"	29.9.17. "	"	line. Weather bright & clear. Enemy unusually alert at night. M.G. fire on our wiring parties. Strong moonlight in his favour. Later-Coy. relief carried out as per O.O.89	
"	30.9.17. "	"		

V.E. [signature]
Commanding. 18th.(S) Bn. Highland Light Infantry.

SECRET.　　　　　　　　OPERATION ORDERS No. 73.　　Copy No. 2
　　　　　　　　　　　　HIGHLAND LIGHT INFANTRY

1. Inter-Company relief will be carried out to-morrow as follows;-

　　'Y' Company will relieve 'X' Company and take over GUILLIMONT
　　　　FARM, 'D 1' Post, Road Post, and Bank Post.
　　'Z' Company will relieve 'W' Company and take over D.E.& F Posts.

2. Relief will be carried out as early as possible. All details to be
arranged between O.C.Companies concerned.

3. All trench stores, petrol cans, tools, Aeroplane photographs, and
sketch maps will be handed over on relief, lists of articles being
forwarded to the Adjutant by 9 a.m. on day after relief.

4. Completion of relief will be wired to Battalion Headquarters the
Code word 'E.F.'

　　　　　　　　　　　　　　　　(Signed) W.F.M.MACARA, Lieut.& A/Adjt.,
　　　　　　　　　　　　　　　　　　　　　Highland Light Infantry.

Issued at 8 a.m. 10th.ins.
Copies Nos. 1-3 W.D. & O.O.File.
　　　　　　4 'W' Company.
　　　　　　5 'X'　"
　　　　　　6 'Y'　"
　　　　　　7 'Z'　"
　　　　　　8 2nd. in Command.

SECRET. OPERATION ORDRS No.84. 1.9.17.
         HIGHLAND LIGHT INFANTRY.   COPY NO.

Reference map. 62c. N.E. 1/20,000.

The Battalion will be relieved in the LEMPIRE Sector by the night 1/2nd. inst, as follows.

    'W' Coy.)
    'Y' "   ) by 15th.CHESHIRE REGT.
    HdQrs.   )

    'X' Coy.) by 14th.GLOSTER REGT.
    'Z' "   )

2. Advance parties as follows will proceed to AIZECOURT-LE-BAS at 3 p.m. to take over billets.

   'W' & 'Z' Coys. 1 Off. & 1 N.C.O. per Company.
   'X' & 'Y' Coys. 2/Lt.WOODSIDE & 1 N.C.O. per Company.

3. All trench stores, aeroplane photographs, sketch maps, etc. will be handed over, receipts obtained and forwarded to the Adjutant the morning after relief. Details of work on hand and proposed will also be handed over.

4. Companies, on relief, will march to camp at AIZECOURT-LE-BAS. On the road, cookers will be met and tea given to the men at Ordnance stores. beyond Divisional Headquarters at VILLERS-FAUCON.

5. Limbers, 1 per Coy. for 'X' & 'Z' Coys. will be at Cross roads GUILLEMONT-BASSE BOULOGNE.
'W' & 'Y' Coys. will report at Company Headquarters. All petrol tins will be sent from 'W' & 'Y' Coys. to Battn. HdQrs. at 8 p.m.
2 limbers, Mess Cart & M.O's Cart will report at Battn. HdQrs.

6. Completion of relief will be notified to Battalion Headquarters by the code words 'DONE AGAIN'.

        (Sd.) W.F.M.MACARA, Lt. & Adjutant.

1.9.17.   HIGHLAND LIGHT INFANTRY.

Issued at:- 11.30 a.m.

Copies to:- 1-3 W.D.&.O.O.File.
    4 O.C.'W' Coy.
    5 " 'X' "
    6 " 'Y' "
    7 " 'Z' "
    8 15th.CHESHIRE REGT.
    9 14th.GLOSTER REGT.

SECRET.   COPY No 1.
                    OPERATION ORDERS 85.A

I. INTERCOMPANY RELIEF will take place on the night 12th/13th SEPTR.
   as follows:-
            Z Coy will relieve W Coy on RIGHT Coy Front.
            Y "   "   "   X "   " Left   "   "
            W " on relief will come into Support in SHERWOOD LANE
            X "   "   "   "   " Reserve – GLOSTER ROAD.

II. The RELIEF will be arranged between O.C. Coys direct and will take
    place during daylight immediately after tea about 6 p.m.

III. ALL TRENCH STORES, maps, aeroplane photos, sketches, and all
     details of work in hand and contemplated will be handed over,
     and receipts taken and forwarded to the ADJUTANT on the
     morning after relief.

IV. ADVANCE PARTIES of 1 officer and 1 N.C.O. per coy should be sent
    on in advance to take over stores and billets.

V. COMPLETION OF RELIEF will be wired to BATTN H.Q. by code word
   "FLYING CORPS."

        Issued at 11 a.m.
    Nos. 1, 2 + 3   War diary + File.   (Sgd) W.F. Macara Lt. & Adjt.
    No   4   O.C. W. Coy.
     "   5   " X "   18th (S) Bn HIGHLAND LIGHT INFY
     "   6   " Y "
     "   7   " Z "
     "   8   2/m Command.
     "   9   20th MIDDLESEX REGT.
     "   10   17th ROYAL SCOTS.
     "   11   Quartermaster.

        12/9/17.

SECRET.   BATTALION ORDER No.99   B.2317.
                           ABCDE HIGHLAND LIGHT INFANTRY

Reference 57c S.E. Edn.4a 1/20,000.
_____

1. The Battalion will relieve the 20th LANCS. FUS. in the EBENY Sector
    on the night 6/7th. Sept., 1917 as follows:-

         "A" Coy.H.L.I. will relieve "E" Coy.L.F's. (Right Front Coy.)
         "B" "   "   "   "   "   "B" "   "   (Left   "   ")
         "C" "   "   "   "   "   "C" "   "   (Support Line   )
         "D" "   "   "   "   "   "D" "   "   (Reserve "   )
         Hdrs. "   "   "   "   Hdrs. "   GLOUCESTER HD. about
                                                    (K.15.d.9.8.)

2. Guides for companies and platoons will meet Battalion at Cross roads
    X.13.d.6.1

3. Advance parties 1 Off., 1 N.C.O., 1 runner, 1 signaller, Lt.GEMMILL
    Signallers & Batt.Sergt.Major will parade at Battalion Orderly Room
    at 8 p.m. to-morrow to proceed to the line to take over stores etc.
    They will report at Battalion Headquarters L.F's before proceeding to
    the line.

4. All trench stores, aeroplane photographs, sketches, maps, details of
    work on hand and contemplated will be taken over, receipts given and
    lists forwarded to the Adjutant on returning after relief.

5. Battalion will parade on Battalion Parade Ground at 4.15 p.m. and
    will move off at 4.30 p.m. and march as a Battalion to roads junction
    at E.14.B.9.4 and thence by companies with markers to about 300 yds
    West of BIRR CROSS where the men will have tea, resuming the march by
    platoons when it is dusk.

6. Transport. O.C.Transport will detail 1 limber per company to carry
    Lewis Guns, magazines, rations and 15 tins of water. Also 1 limber,
    mess cart and Maltese cart for Hdrs.

7. Completion of relief will be notified to Battalion Headquarters by
    the Code Word 'AMIENS'.

                                        (Sd.) W.F.M.MOORE, Lt-C.A/A.A.,
                                              HIGHLAND LIGHT INFANTRY.
5.9.17.
Issued at:- 6 p.m.
Copies to:- 1-3 B.A.B.O.O.File.
            4 "A" Coy.
            5 "B" "
            6 "C" "
            7 "D" "
            8 Transport Officer.
            9 20th. LANCASHIRE FUSIL. BDE.
           10 2nd. in command.
           11 M.O.

SECRET.   OPERATION ORDERS No 86.   Copy No 2.

REF. MAP - NAUROY Edn 2B. - 1/20.000.

1. On the night 16/17 SEPT. a small raid will be carried out by selected party of 17th Royal Scots on the enemy trenches immediately South of CANAL WOOD (from X. 24. a. 20. 87 Southwards to X. 24. a. 20. 30)

2. Zero hour ~~to be intimated later~~ will be 9.5 p.m.

3. To distract enemy's attention a demonstration will be carried out on HONNECOURT WOOD by 2 batteries 18 prs (40th Division) 4 M.Gs (40th Division) 4 M.Gs (106 M.G.C.) and 5 L.Gs 18th HIGH. L.I. from ZERO - 5 mins. to ZERO + 10 mins. The action of the other arms will correspond as regards time to that of the Coy L.Gs undernoted.

4. Three L.Gs of Y Coy will fire from selected post on left flank of Coy front and 2 L.Gs of Z Coy will fire from selected position in Coy front. Y Coy will arrange to leave 1 L.G. covering approach by HONNECOURT VALLEY and Z Coy to leave 2 L.Gs to hold road approaches on right flank.

5. The action of the 3 L.Gs of Y Coy and 2 L.Gs of Z Coy will be as follows :-

   ZERO -5 — ZERO   Barrage WESTERN END OF HONNECOURT WOOD.
   ZERO   — ZERO +10   Raise to line EAST of X.11.6.70.00. to X.11.6.80.50.
   ZERO +10   Cease fire.

   The remaining L.Gs of the Coy will only fire for defensive purposes.

6. O.C. front line Coys will arrange to skeletonise the line 15 minutes before ZERO leaving L.G. teams and a double sentry at each post. The deep dugouts at left Coy H.Q, STORAR AVENUE and right Coy H.Q. will be used for sheltering garrison who will stand to in readiness for any emergency.

7. Normal conditions will be resumed when artillery fire quietens down. No listening or protective patrols will be out before ZERO but will be sent out when normal conditions are resumed.

8. The night working party of X Coy will report to R.Es at SAPPER QUARRY at 10 p.m. Any other working or wiring parties that may be arranged will not proceed to or commence work until after 10 p.m.

9. Watches will be synchronised by TURNER.

Issued at 5 p.m.
Copies 1.2.+3 WAR DIARY + FILE.
Copy   4   O.C. W Coy
  "   5   "   X "
  "   6   "   Y "
  "   7   "   Z "
  "   8   Commdg. Officer.
16.9.17.

(Sgd) G.T. Macara Lt. t/Adjt.
18 (S) Bn HIGH. L.I.

SECRET.   OPERATION ORDERS No 8Y   COPY No 2
          HIGHLAND LIGHT INFANTRY.   14-9-17.

I. The battalion will be relieved in the EPEHY sector on the night of 18th/19th Septr. by the GLOSTER REGT. as follows:
   Y Coy HIGH. L.I. will be relieved by X Coy GLOSTER REGT. Left Coy front.
   Z   "   "   "   "   "   " W "   "   "   Right   "   "
   W   "   "   "   "   "   " Y "   "   " Support Coy SHERWOOD LANE.
   X   "   "   "   "   "   " Z "   "   " Reserve " GLOSTER LANE.
   Bn H.Q. "   "   "   "   "   " H.Q.   "   " GLOSTER ROAD.

II. Guides. 1 per platoon, will meet companies at Cross Roads X.13.d.6.1. at 7.30 p.m. These guides will report at Battn H.Q. at 6.30 p.m.

III. All trench stores, aeroplane photographs & sketch maps, also details of work on hand & proposed will be handed over, receipts obtained & forwarded to the ADJUTANT by 12 noon on the day after relief.

IV. Advance parties consisting of 1 off. & 1 N.C.O. per coy will parade at Bn Orderly Room at 2 p.m. for the purpose of proceeding to AIZECOURT LE BAS to take over tents etc.

V. Coys on relief will march to same camp as last occupied in AIZECOURT LE BAS. On the road, cookers will be met and tea given to the men at Fork road between HEUDICOURT & LIERAMONT W.26.8.9.6.
Route on relief will be as follows: VAUCELOTTE FARM, RAILTON, HEUDICOURT, LIERAMONT, AIZECOURT LE BAS.

VI. Limbers. 1 per coy will be sent up as follows:
       Z. Coy's to Coy H.Q.
       Y + W Coy's to SHERWOOD LANE.
       X Coy's to GLOSTER ROAD.
1 Limber, Mess Cart + M.O's cart will be sent to Bn H.Q.
Petrol tins taken into the line will be brought out on relief.

VII. Completion of relief will be wired to Bn H.Q. by the code word "REPEAT."

       Issued at 9 p.m.
       Copies 1.2 + 3 War Diary, File.   Copy 11 2nd in + T.O.
       Copy   4   O.C. W Coy.   "   12 2/in Command
        "   5   " X "
        "   6   " Y "
        "   7   " Z "   (Sgd) W.F. Manara Lt. + Adj.
        "   8   GLOSTER REGT.   HIGHLAND LIGHT INFANTRY.
        "   9   MIDDLESEX REGT.
        "   10   ROYAL SCOTS.

SECRET.   OPERATION ORDERS. No. 88 Copy No..... 2

HIGHLAND LIGHT INFANTRY. 25. 9. 17

Reference Map 62. C. N.E.   1/20,000

I. The Batt. will relieve - Manchester Regt. and Lancs. Fus. in the Lempire Sector on the night of the 26/27 September as follows:
W. Coy. H.L.I. will relieve W.Coy. Man. Regt in Cat Post.
X. Coy. H.L.I.   "   " Y & Z Coy. Man.Regt. in Gilliment Farm
Y. Coy. H.L.I.   "   "part X Coy Man.Regt in Ken Lane
Z. Coy. H.L.I   "   "(part X Coy. Man Regt in Doleful Post
                        (and I Coy. L.F. in Ege Post

Batt. Headquarters will be in Batt. Headquarters in Lempire.

II. GUIDES. 1 per Platoon will be supplied as follows:-

Guides for Ege and Doleful Posts will be at Batt. Headquarters L.F. about (F I5a 80, 65) at 7-45 p.m.

Guides for Cat. Gilliment and Ken will be at X roads. Basse a Bumlenge and D I roads.

III. ADVANCE PARTIES. as follows will leave Camp tomorrow at 2 p.m. to proceed up the line to take over all stores &c.   I Officer and I N.C.O. I runner and I signaller per Coy. and signallers for ~~Headquarters~~ ~~will~~ ~~report~~ ~~at~~ ~~their~~ ~~respective~~ ~~Batt~~ Headquarters. They should report at their respective Batt. Headquarters namely L.F. Headquarters for "Z" Coy. and the remainder at Batt. Headquarters Man. Regt. in Ken Lane.

IV. All trench maps, stores, petrol tins, tools, aeroplane photographs, sketch maps, programmes of work in hand and contemplated &c. will be taken over and receipts given, copies of which will be forwarded to the Adjutant by 12 noon on the day after relief.

V. Companies will Parade on Batt. Parade Ground ready to move at 3p.m to-morrow. Movement will be made by Coys. 200 Yds interval. A long halt will be made at St. Emilie for tea.

VI. The Transport Officer will detail the following Limbers to take up stores, Lewis Guns, &c.   ONE limber per Coy. One limber, Mess cart and Maltese Cart for Headquarters.

VII. Completion of relief will be wired to Batt Headquarters by the code word "LAST"

Issued at 8-30 p.m.
Copies Nos. I - 3 W.D. & Q.C.   FILE.   8 Transport Officer
            4 - W   9 Manchester Regt.
            5 - X   10 Lancs. Fus.
            6 - Y   11 Quartermaster
            7 - Z   12 2nd. in Command.

25. 9. 17.

(Sgd) W. F. MACARA. Lieut. & A/Adjt.
HIGHLAND LIGHT INFANTRY.

SECRET.   OPERATION ORDERS No. 88.   Copy No.
                       HIGHLAND LIGHT INFANTRY.

1.   Inter-company relief will take place on the night 29/30th. as
     follows:-

              'Y' Coy. will relieve 'X' in GUILLEMONT FARM & D.1 Post.

2.   The relief will be arranged between O.C.Companies direct and will
     take place at dusk.

3.   All trench stores, maps, aeroplane photographs, sketches and all
     details of work on hand and contemplated will be handed over and
     receipts taken and forwarded to the Adjutant on the morning after
     relief.

4.   'Y' Coy. will hand over to 'X' Coy. all details of work and wiring
     on hand. Immediately after relief 'X' Coy. will carry out work and
     wiring and on completion of same, will return to billets in KEN LANE
     and LEMPIRE.

5.   Advance parties of 1 Officer and 1 N.C.O. per company should be sent
     on in advance to take over stores and billets.

6.   Completion of relief will be wired to Battalion Headquarters by the
     code word 'RIGG'.

Issued at:- 1 p.m. 29.9.17.
                                (Sd.) W.F.M.MACARA, Lieut. & Adjutant.
                                (GLASGOW YEOMANRY) HIGHLAND LIGHT INFANTRY.
Nos. 1-3 W.D. & O.O.File.
     4 'W' Coy.
     5 'X' "
     6 'Y' "
     7 'Z' "

SECRET.   -18th.(S) Bn Highland Light Inf. -   Copy No.____

PROVISIONAL DEFENCE SCHEME.

Right Sector GUILLEMONT FARM. - Ref. NAUROY MAP Edn. 2 B.

The Battalion front extends from F.24.a.35.50 (NEW POST) to F.12.a.10.45 and includes the following posts;-

        NEW POST
        CAT POST
        GUILLEMONT FARM.
        DUNCAN POST.
        DOLEFUL POST.
        EGO POST.

2. DISPOSITIONS. Three companies in front line and posts and 1 company in Reserve. The companies are disposed as follows;-

   Right Coy.;- NEW POST & CAT POST including DOG TRENCH to F.18.c.95.60
             Coy. H.Q. in CAT POST.

   Centre Coy.;- DOG TRENCH from F.18.c.95.60 including GUILLEMONT FARM to
             DANIEL TRENCH at F.12.c.80.00 with 1 platoon less 1 L.G.
             in DUNCAN POST in Support.
             Coy. H.Q. in ~~EGO POST~~. A.13.a.10.30.

   Left Coy.;- DANIEL TRENCH from F.12.c.80.00 including EGO POST to
            F.12.a.10.45 with 1 platoon less 1 L.G. in Support in
            SART LANE (F.11.c.50.00).
            Coy. H.Q. in EGO POST.

Reserve Coy. & Battalion Headquarters in KEN LANE. (F.17.c.20.80).

3. ACTION. The front line must be held at all costs and if any part of it is occupied by the enemy, immediate steps must be taken to counter-attack, all possible support being provided by troops on both flanks.

WORKING PARTIES. In the event of alarm all working parties in the front line will occupy the nearest defendable trench and report for orders to O.C.Coy. whose front they are in. They will not vacate the trench without his orders.
      Working parties in rear of front line will at once return to their companies and there await orders.
(a) GENERAL ATTACK. The front line and all the posts are the main line of defence. None of the garrisons of these posts will be available for counter-attack unless relief garrisons are provided.
      O.C.Companies will use their own discretions in withdrawing to a flank or moving in front of or behind the front line during bombard-ment but will immediately reoccupy the threatened portion on the barrage lifting. Flank troops will co-operate with fire and counter-attacking as above detailed.
(b) LOCAL COUNTER-ATTACK. As in (a). Action will be taken by flank troops to bomb enemy out to prevent his retiral to his own trenches by Lewis Gun fire and flank patrols.
(c) RAID. As in (a). Urgent steps will be taken to exploit success after the enemy is driven out.

      In all cases of alarm all troops of the Battalion 'Stand to' All except the Posts'garrisons and the Reserve Coy. will take immediate steps to co-operate in its' own part of the line in counter-attacking.
      The Reserve Company will be available for counter-attack on any portion of the front.

-2-

4. FLANKS.   Patrols will be sent out at frequent intervals to keep touch with companies on either flanks, and with flank battalions.

5. MEDICAL.   The Regimental Aid Post is at DUNCAN POST (F.17.d.80.70).

                                                    Captain,

30.9.177   Acting C.O. 18th.(S) Bn. Highland Light Infantry.

Copy No.1   File.
        2   O.C. 'W' Coy.
        3   " 'X' "
        4   " 'Y' "
        5   " 'Z' "
        6   H.Q. 106th. Inf. Brigade.
        7   2nd. in command.

SECRET   COPY No. 1

18th (S) Bn. HIGHLAND LIGHT INFy.
PROVISIONAL DEFENCE SCHEME.

LEFT SUBSECTOR
HONNECOURT SECTOR.   REF. TRENCH MAP 1/10.000.

1. **DISPOSITIONS:-**
   (a) **Front Line:-** From CANNONGATE (inclusive) to X.11.a.20.65. Line is held by 2 Coys.
   Right Coy:- From CANNONGATE (inclusive) to X.11.c.40.30. The Coy has 3 platoons plus 1 Lewis Gun section in the front line and 1 platoon less 1 Lewis Gun team in close support in COTTON TRENCH. Coy. H.Q. at X.17.a.90.50.
   Left Coy:- From X.11.c.40.30. to X.11.a.20.65. - The Coy has 3 platoons plus 1 Lewis Gun section in the front line and 1 platoon less 1 Lewis Gun section in close support in COTTON TRENCH. Coy. H.Q. at X.10.d.40.60.
   (b) **Support:-** One Coy less 1 platoon and 1 Lewis Gun section in SHERWOOD LANE. One platoon in FAWCUS STRONG POINT. One L.G. section at X.16.b.10.05. Coy. H.Q. in SHERWOOD LANE.
   (c) **Reserve:-** Bn H.Q. and 1 Coy in GLOSTER ROAD.

2. **DEFENCE LINE.**
   The front line is the line of resistance. The intermediate posts at FAWCUS STRONG POINT and X.16.b.10.05. will also be held and in neither case will the garrison be used for counterattack.

3. **DEFENSIVE ACTION.**
   (a) **Raid:-** The O.C. Coy concerned will use his discretion in vacating the area under bombardment by moving forward, back, or to a flank, the trench line to be at once re-occupied and held when the bombardment lifts. If an entry into the trench is effected clearing operations from both flanks will be commenced and the position re-established. The counterattacking force (i.e. 2 platoons Support Coy and Reserve Coy) will 'stand to' and await orders from O.C. Battalion.
   (b) **Local Counter-attack:-** Action will be the same as in the case of a raid.
   (c) **General Attack:-** The front line will be held at all costs. The Support Coy will occupy and hold SILK TRENCH and the two STRONG POINTS. The Reserve Coy will occupy and hold the GREEN LINE. Both the Support and Reserve Coys (less the STRONG POINT garrisons) will be available for counter attack.

4. **WORKING PARTIES.**
   On the alarm being given all front line working parties will occupy and defend the nearest tenable trench, and come under orders of O.C. Coy in whose front they are. They will report to O.C. Coy for orders and will not vacate the position without his instructions. Working parties in rear of front line will at once return to alarm posts.

5. O.C. SUPPORT and RESERVE Coys will ensure that all officers know the routes by trench and across the open to any part of the front line.

Copy No 1   O.O. & File.   (SIGNED) W.A. Murray. CAPT.
"   "   2   O.C. W. Coy   Acting/C.O. 18th (S) Bn HIGH. L.I.
"   "   3   "   X   "
"   "   4   "   Y   "
"   "   5   "   Z   "
"   "   6   106th INF. BDE.
"   "   7   2/in COMMAND.

10.9.17.

Army Form C. 2118.

18th (99) Bn 10/6/35
Highland Light Infantry
October 1917

21. p
13 cols

WAR DIARY
or
INTELLIGENCE SUMMARY

(Erase heading not required.)

Place	Date	Hour	Summary of Events and Information	Remarks and references to Appendices
GUILLEMONT FARM.	1.10.17.	Bn. in line.	Weather warm and dry. Preparations for move to-morrow. Work etc. carried on.	
"	2.10.17.	Bn. in line.	Weather warm. Some rain at night. Bn. relieved by 5th. & 6th. KING'S LIVERPOOL RIFLES and marched to LONGAVESNES.	
PERONNE.	4.10.17.	Div. on the move.	Bn. conveyed by 'bus to PERONNE arrived about 4 p.m. Rested for a day.	
"	5.10.17.	"	Bn. entrained for ARRAS at 1 p.m. and arrived there about 6.30 p.m. then marched to AGNEZ-LES-DUISANS arriving in billets at CALVARY CAMP about 9 p.m.	
AGNEZ-LES-DUISANS	5.10.17.	Bn. in billets.	Weather showery. Cleaning up and training.	
"	6.10.17.	Bn. in billets.	Weather showery. Bn. training in attack. Musketry etc. & Specialists training.	
"	7.10.17.	"	" bad. Training as usual. Divnl. Comdr. lectured all Officers & N.C.Os.	
"	8.10.17.	"	" " Training carried out with special attention being paid to the attack.	
"	9.10.17.	"	Special training carried on. Weather very bad. Training much hindered by the inclemency of the weather.	
"	10.10.17.	"	Specialists training carried out indoors.	
"	11.10.17.	"	Weather fair. Some sunshine. Training carried out as usual.	
"	12.10.17.	"	" " Some training carried out. Specialists also receive instruction.	
"	13.10.17.	"	One company moved up to ARRAS Station to act as leading party. Weather fine. Some training carried out. Preparations for move. Stores etc. being packed.	
"	14.10.17.	on move.	Weather warm & dry. Bn. marched to ARRAS at 1 p.m. and entrained there at 4.30 p. Arrived at CASSEL at 11.50 p.m. and marched to billets at DOORNAERT near ROEBRUICK arriving in billets at 4.30 a.m.	
"	15.10.17.	in billets.	Weather good. Resting for a day in preparation for move into forward Area.	
"	16.10.17.	on move.	Left ROEBRUICK at 8.0 a.m. and marched to ARHEEM Station where we entrained for PROVEN arriving there at 1 p.m. & marched to camp near PROVEN. Weather fair.	
"	17.10.17.	"	Weather fair. Left PROVEN and marched to DUBLIN CAMP near WORSTEN arriving there about mid-day.	
"	18.10.17.	"	O's.C.Companies reconnoitred the line and preparing for move into the line. at 11 a.m. to the line relieving 13th.Lancs. Fus. on Left Batt. Front.(HOUTHULST FOREST. Bn. H.Q. a 'Pill-box' at LOUVOIS FARM. Weather fine. Men cleaning up and preparing for move into the line. Bn. moved off at	
"	19.10.17.	in line.	(HOUTHULST FOREST) Weather showery. Conditions fearful. Mud indescribable and shell-holes everywhere. No trenches, but a mere line of organised shell-holes	
"	20.10.17.	"	Weather changeable. Bn. relieved by 15th.GLOSTER REGT. and marched back to DUBLIN CAMP arriving there about 3 a.m. 21st. Men tired out & weary.	

Army Form C. 2118.

WAR DIARY
or
INTELLIGENCE SUMMARY.
(Erase heading not required.)

Place	Date	Hour	Summary of Events and Information	Remarks and references to Appendices
HOUTHULST FOREST (YPRES)	21.10.17.		Bn. in billets at DUBLIN CAMP. Weather very showery. General cleaning up and resting. Camp bombed at night by 'Hun' planes.	
"	22.10.17.	"	Camp. Weather still showery. Clear night. Enemy planes still active in bombing at nights; be be seems to do very little material damage and few casualties. No casualties in this Unit.	
"	23.10.17.	"	moved into Bde. Support (1 Coy. at KOEKUIT, 2 Coys. & Bn. H.Q. at WIDJERDRIFT, and 1 Coy. at 15 WOOD. Weather dull.	
"	24.10.17.	"	in Bde. Support. Bn. relieved 15th. CHESHIRES at night in front line. Wet & disagreeable and an conditions are very bad. Enemy artillery very active during relief.	
"	25.10.17.	"	line. Weather bad. Right Battalion Sector. Weather very wet and disagreeable. Enemy aeroplanes very active. Also artillery.	
"	26.10.17.	"	Usual artillery activity by the enemy and greater aeroplane activity. These fly pretty low and fire M.Gs on troops not in cover. Weather showery.	
"	27.10.17.	"	Bn. Artillery very active on both sides. Aeroplanes active as usual. Bn. relieved at night by 7th. BORDER REGT. & marched to BOESINGHE where they entrained for PROVEN arriving about 6 a.m. A most pitiful sight to see the Bn. marching in after its' four strenuous days in the front line under such conditions as prevail here.	
PROVEN.	28.10.17.	"	in Camp. Resting all day. Weather good.	
"	29.10.17.	"	" Cleaning up and still resting. & = Weather dry but very dull.	
"	30.10.17.	"	Bn move. Weather fine and bright. Bn. left camp at PROVEN and marched to Station, entrain -ing there at 11 a.m. and proceeded to OUDANK, afterwards marching to DYKES CAMP. Men pretty badly crowded in huts. Afternoon spent in resting.	
DYKES CAMP.	31.10.17.	"	In camp. Weather fine. Bathing and musketing up drill occupied the whole day.	

Operation Orders attached.

M Munro Lieut-Col.,
Commanding 1/8th (G.H.) Bn. Highland L. Infy.

SECRET.　　　　　　　OPERATION ORDERS No. 89　　　　　Copy No. 4
　　　　　　　　　　　HIGHLAND LIGHT INFANTRY.　　　　　　1.10.17.

1. The 106th. Inf. Brigade will be relieved by the 165th. Inf. Brigade in the EMPIRE Sector on the night 2nd./3rd. inst. The Battalion will be relieved by the 5th. & 6th. Batts. KING'S LIVERPOOL REGT. as follows:-

            GUILLEMONT FARM   )
            DUNCAN POST.   )
            DOLEFUL POST.   ) by 5th. Bn. KING'S LIVERPOOL REGT.
            GAP POST.   )
            KEN LANE.   )
            BATTN. HDQRS.'KEN')

            EGO POST.   )
            FAG TRENCH.   ) by 6th. Bn. KING'S LIVERPOOL REGT.
            Platoon in SANT LANE).

2. Guides 1 per platoon will report at Battn. HdQrs. at 4 p.m. to guide in the relieving platoons.

3. All trench stores, aeroplane photographs, sketch maps, etc. also details of work on hand and proposed will be handed over, receipts obtained and forwarded to the Adjutant by 12 noon day after relief.

4. Advance parties consisting of 1 Off. & 1 N.C.O. per Coy. also Capt. BALFOUR, will parade at Battn. HdQrs at 2 p.m. for the purpose of proceeding to LONGAVESNES to take over tents etc.

5. Companies on relief will march to camp at LONGAVESNES and the limbers 1 per company will be sent up to report at place where rations are dumped. Also 1 limber, Mess cart & Maltese Cart will be sent to Battn HdQrs in KEN LANE.

6. Completion of relief will be notified by the code word 'ROUKEN GLEN' to Battn Headquarters.

　　　　　　　　　　　　　　　　　(Sd.) W.F.M.MACARA, Lieut. & Adjt.,

Issued at:-　　　　　　　　　　　　HIGHLAND LIGHT INFANTRY.

Copies to:- 1-3 W.D. & O.O.File.
            4 O.C.'W' Coy.
            5 " 'X' "
            6 " 'Y' "
            7 " 'Z' "
            8 O.C.5th.KING'S LIVERPOOL Regt.
            9 " 6th.   "   "   "
           10.Q.MT. & T.O.
           11.2nd. In Command.

SECRET.	OPERATION ORDERS No.90.	Copy No. ____
HIGHLAND LIGHT INFANTRY.	2.10.17.

1. The 106th.Inf.Brigade will move to PERONNE on the 3rd. inst. and to the XVII Corps Area, West of ARRAS on the 4th. October, 1917. The battalion going into billets at AGNEZ LES DUISANS.

2. The Battalion, less Transport going by road, will proceed to PERONNE by bus on 3rd. inst. Busses will be drawn up along SAULCOURT-LONGAVES-NES Road - head of column at cross roads at E.19.c.9.1. Parties of 25 will be detailed off for each 'bus.
Buses will report at above rendezvous at 1.30 p.m. and move off at 2 p.m.

3. Advance billeting parties as under for PERONNE Area will report to Capt.EDGAR, 17th.ROYAL SCOTS at Town Major's Office, PERONNE at 9 a.m. on 3rd. October.

   2/Lieut.A.P.CURRIE and 1 N.C.O. per company and 1 for H.Q. will parade at QrMr.STORES at 6 p.m. to-night to proceed to PERONNE by the DECAUVILLE Railway from No.6 Siding.

   If extra billets are required, the Officer should make application to the Town Major's Office direct.

   Guides from billeting parties will meet buses at the GRANDE PLACE, PERONNE to conduct companies to their billets about 3 p.m.

4. Transport, including baggage wagons, and less limbers required to draw supplies will march to PERONNE, brigaded under Lt.HARDACRE, West. YORKS REGT. Starting point, - Road junction J.4.d.6.6 and will pass starting point at following times;-

   ROYAL SCOTS.   1.25 p.m.
   106th.M.G.Coy.   1.30 p.m.
   Bde.HdQrs.   1.35 p.m.
   D.L.I.   1.38 p.m.
   H.L.I.   1.43 p.m.
   W.YORKS.R.   1.48 p.m.
   D.A.C.   1.53 p.m.
   241st.M.G.Coy.   1.58 p.m.

   Route;- via BUSSU to PERONNE.
   All cyclists will march 100 yards in front of the column.

5. Companies will notify Battalion Headquarters when their companies are settled in new billets, and give map reference of Coy.HdQrs'. Battalion Headquarters will close at LONGAVESNES at 1.30 p.m. on the 3rd. inst. and reopen at PERONNE on completion of move.

(Sd.).W.F.M.MACARA, Lieut. & Adjutant.
HIGHLAND LIGHT INFANTRY.

2.10.17.
Issued at;- ____

Copies to;- 1-3 W.D.&.O.O.File.
            4 O.C.'W' Coy.
            5 "   'X' "
            6 "   'Y' "
            7 "   'Z' "
            8 2nd. in Command.
            9 QrMr. & T.O.
           10 M.O.

SECRET.   OPERATION ORDERS No. 91.   Copy No.
           HIGHLAND LIGHT INFANTRY.   2.10.17.

1. The Brigade will continue the move to XVII Corps Area. The Battalion going into billets at AGNES LES DUISANS.

2. The Battalion, less certain personnel proceeding in Omnibus Train, will proceed by the first train leaving PERONNE at 9 a.m. and arriving at ARRAS at 2.10 p.m. along with the undermentioned troops:-

    106th. Inf. Brigade Headquarters.
    17th. W.YORKS. REGT.
    18th. H.L.I.
    106th. M.G. Coy.
    106th. T.M. Battery.

Troops will be drawn up in above order at PERONNE-FLAMICOURT Stn. 1 hour before departure of train.

3. Billeting parties as under will accompany the Staff Captain to the new area and will report at Brigade HdQrs. at 8.30 p.m. on 3rd. inst.

    Lieut. R. KEAN.
    Interpreter HYATT. F.
    4 Sergts. (1 per Coy.)

4. 1st. line Transport will move by road under Lt. ROBINSON, No.4 Coy. X.X.R.Train to BAPAUME on October, 4th. and from BAPAUME to new Area on October 5th.

    Starting point. - I.21.Central. Map 62c.
    Time.   - 6 a.m.
    Order of march. - No.4 Coy.Train.- Bde.HdQrs.- 106th.M.G. Coy.- D.L.I.- H.L.I.- 241st.M.G.Coy.- Rest.D.A.C.- 107th.F.A.

5. The undermentioned will proceed by second train leaving PERONNE - -FLAMICOURT Station at 12 noon arriving at ARRAS at 5.02 p.m. Personnel for the train will be drawn up 2½ hours before time of departure.

    Medical Officer.
    Capt. J. SPEIRS.
    4 cookers. 4 drivers & 4 cooks (1 per coy.)
    2 water carts & drivers.
    1 Mess cart & driver.
    1 Maltese cart driver & 1 Car.
    11 chargers & grooms.
    7 pack mules & drivers.
    1 tool cart, Driver & brakesman.
    Transport Sergeant.
    R.QM.S. HENDRY.

6. On arrival at ARRAS Station, Units will march by road to billets at AGNES LES DUISANS, having first loaded packs and blankets on to lorries provided. Packs & blankets will be removed from the rest of the equipment & equipment made up into fighting order during train journey. Battn. HdQrs. will be notified immediately coys. arrive in new billets.

7. Battn. HdQrs. will close at PERONNE at 8.30 a.m. 4th.inst. & reopen at AGNES LES DUISANS on arrival.

                (Sd.) W.F.M.MACARA, Lieut. & Adjutant.
                      HIGHLAND LIGHT INFANTRY.
2.10.17.
Issued at:-
Copies to:- 1-3 W.D.A.C.O. FILE. 4-7 O.C. 'W','X','Y', & 'Z' Coys.
           8 2nd. in Command. 9 M.O. 10. QMR. 11. T.O.

SECRET. OPERATION ORDERS No.92. Copy No. 2
HIGHLAND LIGHT INFANTRY. 11.10.17.

1. The 106th. Inf.Brigade will move into the GASPAR BAGGERS CAPPER Area.
   The Battalion will move into same Area as follows on the 14th. inst:

   (a) 'Y' Company, cookers and teams will leave present billets so as to
       arrive at ARRAS Station at 7.30 a.m. on the morning of the 14th.
       They will entrain in Train No.22 which is timed to leave ARRAS
       Station at 8.54 a.m.

   (b) 'X' Company will leave present billets at 10 a.m. on the 12th. inst
       and march to ARRAS Station for duty as loading party. They will work
       throughout the entrainment there and will entrain with remainder of
       Battalion on Train No.26 leaving ARRAS Station at 4.54 p.m. on 14th.
       O.C.'X' Company will report his Company ready for duty. to the R.T.O
       at 1.15 p.m. Cooker and Tomm and Lewis Gunn limber will go with the
       Company. Horses for these will be returned when finished at ARRAS
       Station on 12th. 2 G.S.wagons will report at 'X' Company HdQrs. at
       9.30 a.m. to carry packs, valises etc.

   (c) 'W' & 'Z' Companies and Battalion Headquarters will leave present
       billets at 1.15p.m. and march to ARRAS Station. They will travel by
       Train No.26 leaving ARRAS at 4.54 p.m.

   (d) Transport. will leave billets at such time to be at ARRAS Station
       at 2 p.m. and travel with train No.26 leaving at 4.54 p.m.

2. Billeting parties. Capt. MURRAY, Interpreter HAYETT and 1 N.C.O. per
   Company will parade at Battalion HdQrs. at 8.45 a.m. on 12th. & proceed
   to the Staff Captain. They will arrange to take bicycles.

3. Men will travel on the train in fighting order with greatcoats neatly
   rolled underneath the haversacks. The blankets will be placed in packs
   instead of greatcoats and will be carried by motor lorries to ARRAS Stn.
   All Officers' Mess stores will be carried on Coy. Lewis Gun limbers.

4.

4. Rations. Quartermaster's will arrange to issue all companies with
   rations for the 13th. & 14th. O.C.Companies will keep back such rations
   so as to provide breakfast on the morning of the 15th.

5. Billets. All billets will be left in a thoroughly clean condition and
   in the case of Officers'& men in billets owned by inhabitants, certifi-
   -cates will be obtained that the owner has no claim for damage done.

                                              (Sd.).N.F.M.MACARA, Capt. & Adjt.

                                              HIGHLAND LIGHT INFANTRY.
11.10.17.

Issued at:- 8.30 p.m.
Copies to:- 1-3 W.D.& O.O.File.
             4 O.C 'W' Coy.
             5 " 'X' "
             6 " 'Y' "
             7 " 'Z' "
             8 Q.M. & T.O.
             9 2nd. in Command.
            10 Capt. MURRAY.

SECRET.   OPERATION ORDERS No.92a.   Copy No.
                HIGHLAND LIGHT INFANTRY.   15.10.17.

Ref. Map Sheet HAZEBROUCK 1/10,000.

1. The 106th.Bde. Group will move to the PROVEN NORTH Area by Road and Rail to-morrow preparatory to relieving a Brigade of the GUARDS Division in Left CENTRE XIV Corps. The Battalion will move to Camp P.4. Personnel going by rail and Transport going by road.

2. Companies will parade at company billets ready to move by march to ARNEKE Station at 8.45 a.m.

3. Brigade Transport will move by Road via WORMHOUDT & HOUTKERQUE under Lt.ROBINSON A.S.C., Battalion Transport will pass Cross roads B.6.c.2. at 9.20 a.m.

4. Advance parties of 1 Officer per company and Lt.BOW for Headquarters and 'Y' Coy. will report at Bde. H.Q. at 7 a.m. to-morrow. Cycles not to be taken. They will be responsible for meeting the Battalion and guiding them to their camp.

5. Packs and blankets will be carried on the men to the entraining station.

6. One lorry will be available to carry Officers' valises etc. to the new Area. These will be stacked at Q.M.Stores at 8.15 a.m.

7. Breakfast will be at 7.45 a.m. and arrangements will be made for each N.C.O. and man to carry a haversack ration. Water-bottles to be filled. Dinners will be eaten on arrival in new billets.

                         (Sd.)W.F.M.MACARA, Capt., & Adjutant.
                              HIGHLAND LIGHT INFANTRY.

15.10.17.
Issued at :- 9 p.m.
Copies to Coys. M.D. & File.

SECRET.   OPERATION ORDERS No.93.   Copy No.
                       HIGHLAND LIGHT INFANTRY.   18.10.17.

1. The Battalion will relieve L.Fus. Battalion in Left Sector of Corps to-
   -night as follows:-
        'W' Coy. relieve 'W' Coy.L.F. in Right.
        'X' "   "   'X' "   "   " Centre.
        'Z' "   "   'X' "   "   " Left.
        'Y' "   "   'Z' "   "   " Support.

2. Companies will leave the position where they bivouaced for dinner and
   march by platoons at 200 Yds. interval to WIDJENDRIFT. From there move-
   -ment will be by sections at suitable intervals.
   Order of march will be:- Bn. HdQrs. 'W' Coy. 'X' Coy. 'Z' Coy. & 'Y' Coy.
   Hour of leaving dinner bivouacs will be 3 p.m.
   "   "   "   WIDJENDRIFT will be according to light, but probably at
   4.30 p.m.

3. Lewis Gun Limbers will be sent on ahead to meet companies at WIDJENDRIFT
   Water, Guns, and ammunition will be carried from there. If possible each
   man should be supplied with 3 sandbags at WIDJENDRIFT.

4. Guides for each platoon, Coy.HdQrs & Bn. HdQrs will be at WIDJENDRIFT
   at 6 p.m. Route to be followed is Duck-board track (GLASGOW STREET).

5. Completion of relief will be notified by the Code word 'MUD' to Bn.H.Q.

                                (Sd.) W.F.M.MACARA, Capt., & Adjt.,

                                        Highland Light Infantry.

Sent by Orderly to 2nd. in Command for communication to all.

SECRET. OPERATION ORDERS No. 94   Copy No. 2
HIGHLAND LIGHT INFANTRY.   22.10.17.

Reference Map SCHAAP-BALIE 1/10,000
----

1. 106th.Inf.Bde. will relieve the 105th.Inf.Bde. on the left Divnl.
   Sector on the night 23rd/24th.
   The H.L.I. will relieve the Left Battalion of the 105th.Bde.
   The D.L.I. will be on the right of the H.L.I.

2. The front line will be held as follows:-
   'W' Coy. on the right from Junction of D.L.I. at U.6.a.7.9. to junction
   of roads at U.5.b.95.8
   'X' Coy. from this point to approximately U.5.b.4.7.
   'Y' Coy. from this point to junction with French at U.5.b.0.6.
   'Z' Coy. will be in Reserve on approximate line along road from U.B.Cen
   -tral to U.6.a.7.3.
   Hdqrs. at left Bn. Hdqrs as at present (probably LOUVOIS FARM).
   The front line will be held lightly, and each company will be disposed
   in depth as far as possible, with 2 platoons in front line & 2 platoons
   in Support, so as to admit of carrying out their own local counter-
   -attacks if necessary.

3. Garrisons of strong points will be found as follows, with on complete
   platoon;-

   'Y' Coy. FARM at U.5.b.0.5.   'Z' Company PANAMA HOUSE at U.5.b.1.1.

4. Guides, if available, will be at BOESINGHE Cross Roads at 2.30 p.m. to
   meet companies.

5. All stores etc. will be taken over, receipts given, and lists forwarded
   to the Adjutant by 12 noon on day after relief.

6. The Battalion will move by train to BOESINGHE, leaving Camp about 1.15 p.m
   to-morrow. They will move up the line by platoons at suitable intervals
   (via CLARGHES STREET).

7. The 17th.W.YORKS R. will be in close support in our Old Front Line and
   the ROYAL SCOTS will be in Reserve in '15 WOOD FARM' Camp about
   B.6.b.1.1.

8. Completion of relief will be notified to Battalion Headquarters by
   runner or 'phone by the code word 'SMILE'.

                                        (Sd.) E.F.M.MACARA, Capt.& Ajt.,
22.10.17.   HIGHLAND LIGHT INFANTRY.

Issued at:- 11 p.m.
Copies to:- 1-3 W.D.& O.C.File.
             4 O.C.'W' Coy.
             5 " 'X' "
             6 " 'Y' "
             7 " 'Z' "
             8 2nd. in command.
             9 T.O.
            10 Quartermaster.

SECRET.   OPERATION ORDERS No.95.   Copy No.
                       HIGHLAND LIGHT INFANTRY.   24.10.17.

Ref.Map. BROEMBEEK.

1. The Battalion will relieve part of the 15th.CHESHIRES & 17th.R.SCOTS in the Right Brigade Sub-Sector to-night as follows:-
   'Y' Coy. will relieve R.SCOTS from PANAMA HOUSE (exclusive) to U.c.b.9.4 junction with 50th.Divn.
   'W' Coy. will relieve Right Coy. of 15th.CHESHIRES from PANAMA Ho. (Inclusive) to junction with Centre Coy. of 15th.CHESHIRES.
   'X' Coy. will relieve Left Coy. 15th.CHESHIRES to junction with D.L.I.
   'Z' Coy. will be in Reserve about LES 5 CHEMINS.

2. Front line companies will have three platoons in Front line and one in Close Support for counter-attacking purposes. The Reserve Coy. will be held ready for immediate counter-attacking if necessary.

3. OC.'Y' Coy. will arrange relief of R.SCOTS direct with O.C.Batt. at EGYPT HOUSE. Guides for 'W' & 'X' Coys. will be at end of CLARGES STREET where duck-boards end. 'Z' Coy. will arrange their own dispositions as they will not be relieving anyone.

4. Companies will be prepared to move at 5.30 p.m. 'W', 'X', & 'Z' Coys. moving via CLARGES STREET and 'Y' Coy. going via HUNTER STREET.

5. Companies will take all available rations & water in with them, as they will probably not get any until they are relieved about the 27th.inst. They will also take all their bombs, ammunition and Rifle grenades, also tools.

6. Battalion Headquarters will be at EGYPT HOUSE. Completion of relief to be notified by code word 'HOME' to be sent by runner.

7. 'W' & 'X' Coys. will arrange for a patrol to ascertain if the road in front of their Coy. fronts from COLOMBO HOUSE to PANAMA HOUSE is held by the enemy and if not to hold it with small advanced posts.

                           (Sd.) W.F.M.MAGARA, Capt., & Adjt.,
                                 Highland Light Infantry.

24.10.17.

Issued at 10 p.m.
Copies to all Coys. & W.D. & File.

SECRET.   OPERATION ORDERS No.96.   Copy No.
           HIGHLAND LIGHT INFANTRY.   25.10.17.

1. 'Z' Coy. will relieve 'Y' Coy. on the right of the Brigade Sector to-night after dark.

2. All details of the relief will be arranged between Os.C Companies concerned.

3. 'Y' Coy. after relief will come into Battalion Reserve about U.6.c.7.5.

4. Reserve Coy. will be in readiness to reinforce any part of the Battalion front threatened. They will also take up a position in the neighbourhood of LES 5 CHEMINS and hold it to the last.

5. Os.C. 'X' & 'W' Coys. will arrange to push forward posts after reconnaissances so as to straighten out the line. Approximate position of these post will be on a line from 'W' Coy. Lewis Gun Post at U.6.b.2.5 to U.6.a.8.8 (about 100 yards inside HOUTHULST FOREST).
O.C.'X' Coy. will be careful to notify O.C.D.L.I. as to location of these posts when established.

6. O.C.'X' Coy. will be careful to keep touch with Coy.N.Fs.(50th Div.)on his right and to keep touch with 50th.Div. in advance forward to-morrow.

7. O.C.'Y' Coy. will report completion of relief when his company is in new position direct to Bn. Headquarters.

8. Battalion Aid Post at EGYPT HOUSE U.12.b.2.98.

                                    (Sd.) W.F.M.MACARA, Capt., & Adjt.,
                                          HIGHLAND LIGHT INFANTRY.

Copies to O.C.Coys. & File.

SECRET.   OPERATION ORDERS No.97.   Copy No.
                 HIGHLAND LIGHT INFANTRY.   26.10.17.

1. The Battalion will be relieved to-morrow night by the 7th. LINCOLNS.

2. Battalion Headquarters will supply 1 Guide per company and 1 for HdQrs. to guide in incoming troops to Bn. HdQrs. Immediately after dark, Coys. will send to Bn. HdQrs. 1 guide per platoon and 1 guide for Coy.H.Q.

3. Each shell-hole post will form a dump of S.A.A., bombs, rifle grenades and shovels which will be handed over to incoming Units.

4. Battalion Headquarters and Companies will hand over any aeroplane photographs and maps.

5. Companies will see that all L.G.Magazines and spare parts and empty petrol tins are taken out with them.

6. On completion of relief companies will move independantly via CLARGES STREET to railhead at BORSINGHE. From there they will be taken by train to PROVEN Area.

7. Completion of relief will be reported by companies direct to Bn.HdQrs.

                              (Sd.) W.F.M.MACARA, Capt. & Adjutant.
                              HIGHLAND LIGHT INFANTRY.

Copies to all companies & File.

SECRET.   OPERATION ORDERS No.90.   31.10.17.
                           HIGHLAND LIGHT INFANTRY.

Ref. Sheet 20, 27, 28, 1/40,000 & HOUTHULST FOREST 1/10,000.
----

1. The 106th.Inf.Bde. will relieve the 105th.Inf.Bde. in the PANAMA HOUSE - COLOMBO HOUSE line on night 1st./2nd. ~~Nov.~~ The Battalion will relieve the 15th.SHERWOOD FORRESTERS in the Right Sector, the R.SCOTS relieving GLOUCESTER Battalion in Left Sector. D.L.I. in support at WIDJENDRIFT & KEY WOOD.

2. The dispositions taken over will be the same as the battalion being relieved. If three companies are up 'Z' will be on the Right, 'W' in the centre, 'X' on Left and 'Y' Coy. in Support. If two companies are up, 'X' Coy. will drop back into Support.

3. Guides will meet Battalion at WIDJENDRIFT at 8 p.m. The relief will be carried out via CLARGHES STREET.

4. All maps, photos, details of work in hand and proposed, tools, flares, ammunition, bombs, etc. will be taken over, receipts given and lists forwarded to the Adjutant at dawn next day.

5. O.C.Transport will arrange to convey Lewis Guns & Magazines, water etc. to WIDJENDRIFT, where companies will pick them up on arrival, and also arrange to have cookers sent to BOESINGHE with men's tea.

6. Companies will leave camp in following order:- Z Coy, W, X, Y, & H.Q. at 2.30 p.m., march to ONDANK station and entrain there for BOESINGHE at 3.30 p.m. Tea at BOESINGHE at 4.30 p.m. and move up the line in same order at 5.45 p.m.

7. All T.P.Rs will be sent to B.H.Q. as soon after dawn as possible. Each Coy. will arrange every night to send out fighting patrols to harass the enemy and secure prisoners. Reports as to these patrols will be sent in with T.P.Reports.

8. Completion of relief will be reported to Battalion Headquarters by runner the code word 'STICK IT' being used.

                           (SD.)J.W.BOW, Lieut. & A/Adjt.,

31.10.17.   HIGHLAND LIGHT INFANTRY.

Issued at:- 4.15 p.m.

Copies to:- 1.-3. W.D. & O.O.File.
            4 O.C. 'W' Coy.
            5   "   'X' "
            6   "   'Y' "
            7   "   'Z' "
            8 2nd. in command.
            9 Transport Officer.
           10 Signalling Officer.

WAR DIARY

~~INTELLIGENCE SUMMARY~~

(Erase heading not required.)

Army Form C. 2118.

Instructions regarding War Diaries and Intelligence Summaries are contained in F.S. Regs, Part II and the Staff Manual respectively. Title pages will be prepared in manuscript.

Place	Date	Hour	Summary of Events and Information	Remarks and references to Appendices
DYKES CAMP.	1.11.17.		Battalion in camp. Preparing to go to the line. Divnl. General visited the camp and complimented the Battalion on their good work during the previous tour. Battalion marched to ONDANK SIDING and entrained for BOESINGHE where they halted for tea. At 5.30 p.m. they marched for line relieving 15th. SHERWOOD FORRESTERS. Relief completed without incident at 10.15 p.m. Operation Orders attached. Weather good but cold.	
HOUTHULST FORREST.	2.11.17.		Bn. in the line. Right Battalion Front opposite HOUTHULST FORREST. Usual artillery activity during the day. Enemy's aeroplanes very active during the day flying very low and firing M.G's at troops in the line. M.G's rather active during the night. Weather wet and stormy. Conditions very bad.	
	3.11.17.		Battalion in the line. Usual artillery activity during the morning, increasing in intensity about 4 p.m. No infantry action on either side however. Enemy's aeroplanes were active as usual. Weather dull but dry.	
	4.11.17.		Battalion in the line. Artillery on both sides active, also M.G's during the night. Battalion relieved by 5th. ROYAL BERKS Regt. at night. Relief completed without casualties. at 7.45 p.m. when Battalion marched to BOESINGHE Station and entrained for PROVEN. at 1 a.m. arriving there at 2.15 a.m. and marched to PLUMSTEAD Camp. Weather good. Operation Orders attached.	
PROVEN.	5.11.17.		Battalion in camp. Men resting and cleaning up. Weather fine.	
	6.11.17.		" " Brigade inspected by Divisional Commander, the Battalion taking part. All Units complimented on the part taken during recent operations. Remainder of day spent in cleaning up. Recreation during afternoon. Morning very wet. Afternoon dry.	
	7.11.17.		Battalion still in camp. Weather very wet and camp muddy. Engaged in training of specialists during the morning. Usual recreation in the afternoon and preparations for move to another camp.	
	8.11.17.		Battalion moves to PETWORTH Camp. Weather dull and showery. New camp quite commodious and comfortable, men resting during the afternoon.	
	9.11.17.		Battalion in camp. Weather changeable. Usual Battalion training in the morning and recreation in the afternoon.	
	10.11.17.		Battalion moved to PENTON Camp. Rather a bad change. Camp muddy and not too much room. Very heavy rain. Day spent in improving the camp.	
	11.11.17.		Battalion in camp. Weather showery. Very little training, owing to lack of space. Most of the time spent in improving the camp.	
	12.11.17.		Battalion in camp Usual improvements carried out, laying duck-boards etc. Weather fine. Afternoon spent in preparing to move.	

WAR DIARY
INTELLIGENCE-SUMMARY.
(Erase heading not required.)

Army Form C. 2118.

Instructions regarding War Diaries and Intelligence Summaries are contained in F. S. Regs., Part II and the Staff Manual respectively. Title pages will be prepared in manuscript.

Place	Date	Hour	Summary of Events and Information	Remarks and references to Appendices
PENTON CAMP. PROVEN.	13.11.17.		Battalion in camp. Morning spent in cleaning up and preparing to move. Weather fine.	
"	14.11.17.		Battalion in PENTON Camp and moved at 9 a.m. to PROVEN Station. Entrained there at 10 a.m. and marshed for ELVERDINGHE and on arrival there marched to No.4 SIEGE Camp. Morning dull & afternoon wet.	
	15.11.17.		Battalion at ELVERDINGHE. Moved at 2 p.m. to CANAL BANK at ESSEX FARM East of BRIELEN. Men billeted in shelters along Western bank of Canal. Weather fine. Electric light in billets. 3 Officers wounded by long-range shell which pierced dug-out.	
	16.11.17.		Battalion in SUPPORT. Orders received to take over from 2nd. WELSH Regt. on right of POELCAPPEL Sector. Preparations made for relief following night.	
	17.11.17.		Battalion relieving the xxxxxxx 2nd. WELSH REGT. 1st. Division. Relief completed without incident at 7.45 p.m.	
	18.11.17.		Battalion in line. POELCAPPEL. Our artillery very active especially about 6 a.m. when they carried out a practice barrage. The enemy retaliated with an equally heavy barrage on our lines Our Lewis Gunners brought an enemy aeroplane. down.	
	19.11.17.		Battalion in line. Inter-company relief carried out. During the day artillery on both sides very active. Operations Orders attached.	
	20.11.17.		Battalion in line. Preparations made for relief by 23rd. Manchester Regt. Day in the line was moderately quiet. Relief completed by 7.30 p.m. 3 men killed and 2 wounded early in the day by shell fire.	
	21.11.17.		Battalion under canvas in Divisional Reserve at SIEGE Camp. Men resting and cleaning equipments clothing etc. Weather showery.	
ELVERDINGHE.	22.11.17.		Battalion in same place. Weather fine. Men cleaning up and improving the camp. Specialists training being carried out.	
	23.11.17.		Battalion in camp. Companies in training. Specialists also receive usual instruction. Weather fine.	
	24.11.17.		Battalion in camp. Training carried on as usual. Weather still good.	
	25.11.17.		" " Church parades held in forenoon. Weather cold and dull. Recreation etc. in the afternoon.	
	26.11.17.		Battalion in camp. Training again carried out. Weather wet and showery in afternoon.	
	27.11.17.		Battalion in camp. Training as usual, with more improvements on the camp being done.	
	28.11.17.		" " Marched off at mid-day for the line. Tea at ADMIRAL ROAD. Left there at 3 p.m. and relieved 1/5th. & CHESHIRE REGT. in the line. Relief completed at 6.25 p.m. without.	

Army Form C. 2118.

WAR DIARY
or
INTELLIGENCE=SUMMARY.
(Erase heading not required.)

Instructions regarding War Diaries and Intelligence Summaries are contained in F. S. Regs., Part II. and the Staff Manual respectively. Title pages will be prepared in manuscript.

Place	Date	Hour	Summary of Events and Information	Remarks and references to Appendices
	28.11.17.		Battalion moving into line. (without) incident. Battalion Headquarters at ALBERTA HOUSE. Weather fine. Two companies in the line.	
	29.11.17.		Battalion in the line at POELCAPPEL.- PASSCHAENDAIE Sector. Artillery fire normal on both sides Pretty quiet day and night, Weather dull, but dry.	
	30.11.17.		Battalion in the line. Artilleryfire quite normal. Day and night pretty quiet. Weather dull but dry. Inter-company relief carried out without incident Weather fine. Day and night quiet.	
	3.12.17.			

_____ Lieut - Colonel,

Commanding, 18th.(G.Y.) Bn. Highland Light Infantry.

SECRET. OPERATION ORDER No. 100   15.11.17.
HIGHLAND LIGHT INFANTRY.

1. The Battalion will take over in the forward Area the "POELCAPPELE" Sector on the 15th. & 16th. as follows:-

   15th. Novr. - The Battalion will relieve the 2/8th. POST OFFICE RIFLES in Reserve CANAL Bank.

2. Companies will move as follows:-

   1.45 p.m.   'Y' Coy.
   1.50 p.m.   'X' "
   1.55 p.m.   'W' Coy.
   2 p.m.   'Z' " & Headquarters.

   Route:- is via BRIELEN (B.29.a.) X Roads (B.29.d.8.5) to ESSEX FARM (C.25.a.2.9)

3. Guides from Advance parties will meet companies at ESSEX FARM (C.25.a.2.9) on arrival there.

   16th. NOVR.

4. The Battalion will relieve the Royal SCOTS in Support as follows:- (Time will be notified later, but will probably in the afternoon.)

   HdQrs., 'W', 'X', & 'Z' Coys. will relieve Headquarters & 3 Companies of ROYAL SCOTS at KEMPTON PARK (C.15.b.)
   'Y' Company will relieve 1 company ROYAL SCOTS at PHEASANT Trench (   )

5. Guides for this day will be notified later.

6. All trench stores, airphotos, sketch maps, defence schemes, details of work on hand and contemplated will be taken over, receipts given and lists forwarded to the Adjutant at Bn. HdQrs. as soon after completion of relief as possible. Care should be taken that stores are carefully checked.

7. Completion of relief on each day will be notified to Battn. HdQrs by the quickest means available; the Code Word to be used will be 'AGAIN".

(Sd.) W.F.M. MACARA, Capt., & Adjt.,
HIGHLAND LIGHT INFANTRY.

15.11.17.
Issued at:- 1 p.m.

Copies to:- W, X, Y, & Z Coys.
2nd. in command.
T.O.
Q.M.
2 W.D. & 1 O.O. File.
2/8th. P.O.R.
17th. R. SCOTS.

SECRET.　　　　　　　OPERATION ORDERS No.101.　　　16.11.17.
　　　　　　　　　　　HIGHLAND LIGHT INFANTRY.

1. The Battalion, less 2 companies will relieve 2nd. WELSH Regt. in part
   of the 1st. Divnl. Front on the night of 17th./18th. Novr. as follows:-

   　　　'W' Company will relieve D Coy. WELSH REGT. on left.
   　　　'Y'　　" 　　　" 　　" A "　　" 　　" 　　" right.
   　　　HdQrs are at BURNS HOUSE V.25.d.(Cenxtral.)

2. Guides, 1 per platoon, will be met at junction of the duckboard track.
   (ALBERTA) and ADMIRAL ROAD.

3. Companies will mofe off in the followijg order at 1.45 p.m.;-

   　　　Headquarters, 'Y' Company, 'W' Company.
   Movement will be by platoons at 200 Yds. intervla.

4. The remaining 2 xompanies('X' & 'Z') will stay in dug-outs in CANAL
   BANK and will be ready to move at a moments notice. They will be under
   the charge of Capt. Balfour.

5. These companies will relieve 'W' & 'Y' Coys. on the night of 19th/20th.
   Novr. (Further particulars will be issued later.)

6. All trench stores, air photos, defence schemes, skecth maps, details of
   of work on hand and contemplated will be taken over, receipts given and
   lists forwarded to the Adjutant at dawn following morning.

7. Lewis Gun limbers will accompany the companies as far as ADMIRAL ROAD
   where they will be unloaded. Lewis Gunsxrx etc. being from there to the
   line.

8. Medical Aid Post is about 200 Yds. in front of Battn. HdQrs and is near
   OXFORD HOUSE. All cases will be vacated there by company stretcher-
   -bearers.

9. Completion of relief will be notified to Battalion Headquarters by the
   quickest means available, the code word 'RABBIE' being used.

　　　　　　　　　　　　　　　(Sd.).W.F.M.MACARA, Capt., & Adjt.,

16.11.17.　　　　　　　　　　　　　　HIGHLAND LIGHT INFANTRY.

Issued at 7.30 p.m. to All coys. 2nd. in command. and Transport Offr.
　　　2 W.D. & 1 O.O.File.

SECRET. OPERATION ORDERS No 1102. 18.11.17.
HIGHLAND LIGHT INFANTRY.

1. On the night of the 18th/19th. the 1st1 BLACK WATCH will capture VOX FARM (V.30.a.0.8) VIRILE FARM (V.29.b.8.5) and establish a line of and establish a line of posts as far as V.29.b.2.4. connecting with 10th.GLOSTER REGT on the left. The 10th. GLOSTER REGT. will capture the German strong points at V.29.a.25.35 and V.28.b.5.4 and will obtain touch with the 18th.H.L.I. on the left bank of PADDEBEEK at V.28.a.5.3.

2. 'Y' Company will send out a patrol to get touch with the 10th.GLOSTER Regt. at V.28.a.5.3.

3. The advance will be made without a barrage at at night at ZERO Hour which will be communicated later.

4. The S.O.S. signal will not be sent up unless the enemy counter--attacks.

5. A contact aeroplane will fly over in the morning of the 19th. and will call for flares at 7 a.m.

6. 'W' Company will send out patrols to get in touch with 'Y' Coy. on right & ROYAL SCOTS on left.

(Sd.).R.R.LAWRENSON, Lieut- Colonel,
18.11.17. Commanding, 18th.Highland Light Infantry.
Issued at 2 p.m.

Copie to 'W' & 'Y' Coys1 and W.D. & O.O.File.

SECRET. OPERATION ORDERS No.103.   19.11.17.
         HIGHLAND LIGHT INFANTRY.

1. 'Z' Coy. and 2 Lewis Guns of 'X' Coy. will relieve 'W' & 'Y' Coys. in the front line to-dat as follows;-

   2 Platoons 'Z' Coy. and 1 L.G.Section 'X' Coyl will relieve 'Y' company in the SOURD FARM Sector.
   2 Platoons 'Z' and 1 L.G.Section 'X' Coy. will relieve 'W' Coy. in the BERKS HOUSE Sector.

   Company Headquarters will be at Shaft, but O.C.'Z' Coy. will place his senior Platoon Commander in command of the SOURD FARM Sector This Officer's Headquarters will be at SOURD FARM.
   'X' Company will move into support and will be accommodated as follows
      1 Platoon and 3 sections will relieve platoon of 'Y' Coy. at WINCHESTER FARM. Extra accommodation will be made by men themselves by digging in shell-holes.
      O.C.'X' Company will leave an officer in charge.
      Remainder of 'X' Coy. will remain in neighbourhood of Battalion Headquarters about V.26.d.r3.2. and will require to dig themselves in there as there is no accommodation.

2. Platoon of 'W' & 'Y' Coys. in HUBNER FARM will not be relieved, but will march back to CANAL BABK as soon as IX' Coy. have all passed up the duck-boards.

3. <u>Guides.</u> 1 guide for each ½ Coy. of 'Z' Coy. will be met at junction of ALBERTA Track and ADMIRAL Road. These guides will conduct as far as Battalion Headquarters, where 1 guide per platoon from 'W' & 'Y' Coys. will be met at 4.30 p.m. Lt.LINDSAY 'Y' Coy. will arrange to send back guides for platoon and 3 sections of 'X' Coy. going to WINCHESTER FARM to junction of ADMIRAL ROAD & ALBERTA Track to be there at 2.30 p.m. Guide from Battalion Headquarters will meet remainder of 'X' Coy.

4. 'W' & 'Y' Coys. on relief will carry out all empty petrol tins, but will leave in all their Lewis Gun Magazines and telephones. Platoon of 'X' Coy. accommodated near Battalion HdQrs. will bring in their Lewis Gun and Magazines. 'Z' Coy. assisted by 'X' Coy. will have to furnish signallers to man 3 telephones stations in the front line in addition to station at WINCHESTER FARM.

5. Capt. Balfour will arrange to start moving from ADMIRAL Road not later than 3 p.m. O.C.'W' & 'Y' Coys. will report relief complete personally at Battn. HdQrs.

6. All trench stores, air photos, defence schemes, sketch maps, details of work on hand and contemplated etc. will be handed over and receipts obtained handed to the Adjutaht on morning after relief.

7. Completion of relief will be notifed to Bn. HdQrs by the code word 'PILL'

                    (Sd.).W.F.M.MACARA, Capt & Adjt.,

19.11.17.   HIGHLAND LIGHT INFANTRY.

Issued at 4 a.m. to All Coys. 2nd. in command. W.D. & O.O.File.

SECRET.   OPERATION ORDERS No.104.   19.11.17.
            HIGHLAND LIGHT INFANTRY.

1. The Battalion will be relieved by the 23rd. MANCHESTER Regt. on the night of 20th./21st. as follows;-

   'X' Coy. Manchesters will relieve 2 platoons 'Z' Coy. in SOURD FARM.
   'Z' "   "   "   " 2   "   'Z' " Shaft Sctn.
   ½ 'W' Coy. Manch.   "   "   'X' Coy in vicinity of BN.H.Q. (BURNS HOUSE).
   ½ 'W' "   "   "   "   'X' " at WINCHESTER FARM.
   'Y' Coy.   "   "   'W' & 'Y' at CANAL Bank.

2. Guides, 1 per coy. for front line coys. 1 guide for 'X' Coy. at WINCH-ESTER FARM. 1 guide for remainder of 'X' Coy. in vicinity of B.H.Q. Capt. Balfour and O.i/c. of 2 platoons at AOURD FARM will each detail 2 runners to guide in platoons from Battn. HdQrs. They will report at Battn. HdQrs by 4.30 p.m.
   Runners from Bn. HdQrs will guide all Companies as far as Bn. H.Q. and will meet relieving battalion at 3.30 p.m. at TRIANGLE Cross Roads. O.C. 'X' Coy. will detail guides to be at duck-board track opposite to where platoons are situated.

3. Companies on relief will march back to No.4 SIEGE Camp. where billets will be allotted to them.

4. All trench stores, air photos, defence schemes, sketch maps, details of work on hand and contemplated will be handed over, receipts obtained and forwarded to the Adjutant on the morning after the relief.

5. The completion of relief will be notified to Battalion Headquarters by the code word 'T.G.'

6. Limbers for carrying Lewis Gun Magazines, spare parts, empty petrol tins etc. will be met at junction of ADMIRAL Road and ALBERTA Track.

                              (Sd.) W.B.M.MACARA, Capt & Adjt.,

20.11.17"   HIGHLAND LIGHT INFANTRY.

Issued at;- 8 p.m.
Copies to ;- O.C. 'W' Coy.
        "   " 'X' "
        "   " 'Y' "
        "   " 'Z' "
        2nd. in command.
        T.O.
        W.D. & O.O. File.
        23rd. Manchester Regt.

SECRET. OPERATION ORDERS No.105.   27.11.17.
         HIGHLAND LIGHT INFANTRY.

1. The battalion will relieve the 15th. CHESHIRE Regt. in the Right Battalion front to-morrow night 28th/29th. Novr.

2. The Battalion will be distributed as follows;-

   'X' Company will be on left as folows;-

   2 Platoons and 1 L.G.Section at Shaft.
   2   "   less L.G.Sction. at WINCHESTER FARM.

   'Y' Company will be on right as follows;-

   2 Platoons and 1 L.G.Section at SOURD FARM.
   2   "   less 1 L.G.Team near Battalion Headquarters.

   'W' Company 2 Platoons at ALBERTA.
               2 Platoons at Coy. HdQrs at CANAL BANK.

   'Z' Coy. 4 Platoons at CANAL Bank.

3. Guides will be supplied as follows;-

   2 Battalion guides each for 'X' & 'Y' Platoons going into the line will be met at HUBNER FARM to guide them to Battn. HdQrs. at BURN's HOUSE where other 2 guides per coy. will be met.
   1 for Platoons going into Battalion Headquarters.
   1 for WINCHESTER FARM will also be met at HUBNER FARM.
   O.C. 'W' & 'Z' Coys will arrange to guide in their own companies.

4. Companies will move in following order;- 'Y', 'X', 'W', & 'Z' starting at 12 noon. Companies will move in file at 200 Yds. interval between each company.

5. All trench stores, air photos, trench maps, defence schemes, details of work on hand and contemplated will be taken over, receipts given and lists for-warded to B.H.Q. by dawn the next morning.

6. Completion of relief will be notified to Battalion Headquarters by the quickest means available, the code word 'SKIPPER' being used.

                        (Sd.).W.F.M.MACARA, Capt. & Adjt.
                                   HIGHLAND LIGHT INFANTRY.

27.11.17.
Issued at:- 10 p.m.
Copies to:- O.C. 'W' Coy.
              "   'X' "
              "   'Y' "
              "   'Z' "
             2nd. in command.
             W.D. & O.O.File.

SECRET.   OPERATION ORDERS No.1061   29.11.17.
                HIGHLAND LIGHT INFANTRY.

1. 'W' & 'Z' Coys. will relieve 'X' & 'Y' Coys. in the front line on the night of 30.11.17. as follows;-

    2 platoons and 1 L.G. of 'Z' Coy. will relieve similar party of 'Y' at SOURD FARM Sector.
    2 platoons less 1 L.G. and Coy. H.Q. of 'Z' Coy. will relieve similar party of 'Y' around BURNS HOUSE.
    2 platoons of 'W' Coy. plus 1 L.G. will relieve similar party of 'X' Coy. in SHAFT Section.
    2 platoons (less 1 L.G.) of 'W' Coy. will relieve similar party of 'X' Coy. at WINCHESTER FARM.
   Joint Company H.Qs. of 'W' & 'Z' Coys. will be at BURNS HOUSE.

2. On relief, 'Y' & 'X' Coys. (less 2 platoons) will proceed to billets at CANAL Bank. The remaining 2 platoons of 'X' Coy. (with an officer) will move back to occupy positions held by 2 platoons of 'W' Coy. in and around Bn. H.Q.

3. <u>Guides.</u> 1 Guide for each platoon of 'Z' Coy. going to SOURD FARM will be sent by O.C.'Y'Coy. at HUBNER FARM. 1 guide of 'Y' Coy. will also meet 2 platoons of 'Z' Coy. going to BURNS HOUSE at HUBNER FARM O.C.'X' Coy. will send 2 guides to HUBNER FARM for platoons of 'W' Coy going to Shaft. He will also send to HUBNER 1 guide for 2 platoons of 'W' Company going to WINCHESTER FARM.
   All guides will be at HUBNER FARM by 4.30 p.m.

4. 'X' & 'Y' Coys. on relief will carry out all petrol tins (empty) but will leave Lewis Guns, Magazines and Telephones.
   The 2 platoons of 'X' Coy. coming to Bn. H.Q. will take over the L.G.s. if left there by 2 platoons of 'W' Coy.

5. O.C.'W' & 'Z' Coys. will arrange to leave ADMIRAL'S ROAD not later than 3 p.m. Relief of Right Front will precede left.

6. All trench stores, air photos, sketch maps, defence schemes, details of work on hand and contemplated will be handed over, receipts obtained and forwarded to the Adjutant on the morning after relief.

7. Completion of relief will be notified to Battalion Headquarters by the code word. 'RYAN'.

                         (SD.).   W.B.M.MACARA, Capt. & Adjt.,
29.11.17.   HIGHLAND LIGHT INFANTRY.

<u>Issued at 10 p.m.</u>
Copies to All Coys. 2nd. in command. & W.D. & O.O. File.

Instructions regarding War Diaries and Intelligence Summaries are contained in F.S. Regs., Part II and the Staff Manual respectively. Title pages will be prepared in manuscript.

Army Form C. 2118.

WAR DIARY From 1st to 31st December 1917, inclusive

INTELLIGENCE-SUMMARY 18th (G.Y.) Bn. HIGHLAND LIGHT INFANTRY.

(Erase heading not required.)

Index No.28.

Place	Date	Hour	Summary of Events and Information	Remarks and references to Appendices
	1.12.17.		Battalion in the line in POMLCAPPEL - PASSCHAENDAELE Sector. Everything quite normal on Battalion front. Artillery of enemy pretty quiet except on back areas. Ours rather more active than usual.	
	2.12.17.		Battalion in line. Attack carried out successfully by Division on our immediate right. Co-operation by Coy. on right Coy. front. Weather fine but cold. Battalion relieved at night by 17th LAN. FUS. Relief completed without incident at 7.30 p.m. when Battalion came back to camp by light railway, arriving at 2 a.m. Very cold travelling in open trucks. Operation Orders attached.	107
F.X.Camp.	3.12.17.		Battalion in hutment camp (F.X.)close to the POPERINGHE - WOESTEN ROAD. Quarters very comfortable indeed. The day was spent in resting, and cleaning up. Weather clear and cold. Brigade in Divisional Reserve.	
	4.12.17.		Battalion in same place. Morning spent in cleaning of equipment and clothing etc. Recreational training during the afternoon. Weather still clear and frosty.	
	5.12.17.		Battalion in same camp. Weather dry but dull. Coy. training and training of specialists carried out during the morning. In the afternoon Battalion was on parade at the distribution of medal ribbons to Officers, N.C.O's and Men of the Division by the Corps Commander.	
	6.12.17.		Battalion in same camp. Morning spent in packing up preparatory to moving. At 1 p.m. Battalion marched from F.X. Camp about a mile up the road to DUBLIN CAMP. During the afternoon the men were allowed to rest and settle down. Weather fine.	
DUBLIN CAMP.	7.12.17.		Battalion in DUBLIN CAMP. Weather good. Battalion parade from 9.15 a.m. till 10 a.m. when Coys carried out training in Musketry, Bayonet Fighting etc. until 12.30 p.m. Specialist training from 10 a.m. after Battalion Parade. Recreational training in afternoon.	
	8.12.17.		Battalion in same place. Weather fine. Battalion parade in the morning and usual training carried on afterwards. Recreational training in afternoon.	
	9.12.17		Battalion in same place. Wet and disagreeable day. Church Parades held at 10 a.m., and remainder of day men were allowed to rest.	
	10.12.17		Battalion in same place. Weather very wet. Battalion parade as usual in the morning and remainder of the day spent in packing up and making preparations for move.	
	11.12.17.		Battalion in same camp. Moved from DUBLIN CAMP at 8 a.m. and marched to ROAD CAMP on the POPERINGHE - WATOU ROAD about 2 kilos from WATOU. Very good camp indeed and men very comfortable. Weather fine. Operation Orders attached.	107s
ROAD CAMP.	12.12.17.			

Army Form C. 2118.

WAR DIARY Continued.

INTELLIGENCE SUMMARY. 18th (G.Y.) Bn. HIGHLAND LIGHT INFANTRY.

(Erase heading not required.)

Instructions regarding War Diaries and Intelligence Summaries are contained in F.S. Regs., Part II and the Staff Manual respectively. Title pages will be prepared in manuscript.

Place	Date	Hour	Summary of Events and Information	Remarks and references to Appendices
ROAD CAMP, WATOU.	12.12.17.		Battalion in ROAD CAMP. Men cleaning up and training. Coy. on duty carrying out work on improve--ment of camp. Recreational training as usual in afternoon. Weather bright and cold.	
	13.12.17.		Battalion in same place. Weather good. Usual daily programme of training carried out.	
	14.12.17.		Battalion in same place. Weather very cold, but dry. Battalion parade in morning, and Coys. carried out training in Bayonet Fighting, Musketry, Handling of Arms, and Gas Drill for the remainder of the time. Football and Brigade Boxing Competitions carried on during the afternoon.	
	15.12.17.		Battalion parade and Coy. training as usual. Weather fine with hard frost. Recreational training in afternoon.	
	16.12.17.		Battalion in camp. Weather good - frosty. Church Parades held for all denominations at 10 a.m. No training carried out.	
	17.12.17.		Battalion in camp. Weather bright and frosty. Battalion parade and usual training of Coys and specialists during morning. Recreational training in afternoon.	
	18.12.17.		Battalion in camp. Weather good. Usual daily programme of work and Recreation carried opt.	
	19.12.17.		Battalion in camp. Weather fine. Usual training carried out combined with practice for Guard Mounting Competition. Final of Brigade Boxing Tournament in afternoon.	
	20.12.17.		Battalion in camp. Weather good. Training as usual. Brigade Guard Mounting Competition and Best Cycle Orderly held at 11 a.m. Usual recreational training in afternoon.	
	21.12.17.		Battalion in camp. Weather fine. Training of Coys in Bayonet Fighting, Drill, Musketry, etc. Recreational training in afternoon.	
	22.12.17.		Battalion in camp. Usual training of Battalion during morning. Judging of best turned out cooker limber and water cart in the Brigade was held in the afternoon. Weather cold; very keen frost. Snow fell during the night.	
	23.12.17.		Battalion in camp. Church Parades for all denominations at 10 a.m. Recreational training took the form of an Inter-company Cross-country run in order to decide the team to run in Brigade Competition. Weather clear and frosty.	
	24.12.17.		Battalion in camp. Training programme was carried out during the morning, and the Brigade "Wrestling on Mules" Competition and football in the afternoon. Weather fine. Snow fell during the night.	
	25.12.17.		Christmas Day. Battalion in camp. Church Parades were held in the morning after which a Battalion Parade was held for the purpose of distributing "Jocks' Boxes" (gift of the Glasgow Evening News) cigarettes, etc. At 5 p.m. the men had Christmas dinner. Weather clear and cold. Ground covered with snow to a depth of three inches.	

Army Form C. 2118.

WAR DIARY Continued.

~INTELLIGENCE~ SUMMARY. 18th (G.Y.) Bn. HIGHLAND LIGHT INFANTRY.

(Erase heading not required.)

Place	Date	Hour	Summary of Events and Information	Remarks and references to Appendices
ROAD CAMP, WARCU.	26.12.17.		Battalion in camp. Usual training programme carried out during the day. Snow fell heavily during the afternoon.	
	27.12.17.		Battalion in camp. Weather fine. Training during the morning. Brigade Cross-country run held in afternoon.	
	28.12.17.		Battalion in camp. Training as usual during the morning. Brigade Lewis Gun "stripping and Assembling" Competition held in afternoon. Weather good.	
	29.12.17.		Battalion in camp. Men bathing during morning. All men in the Battalion were bathed and given clean changes of clothing. Recreational Training if afternoon.	
	30.12.17.		Battalion in camp. Church Parades held at 10 a.m. Recreational training in afternoon. Final of Brigade Football Cup played. Weather dry but dull.	
	31.12.17.		Battalion in camp. Usual training and recreational training carried out. Weather showery. New Year dinner held at 4 p.m. Concert at 5.30 p.m.	

Alx Gemmill, Lieut. Intelligence Officer.
for Lieut.- Colonel.
Commanding 18th (G.Y.) Bn. HIGHLAND LIGHT INFANTRY.

SECRET.   OPERATION ORDER No.107.   Copy No.1.

                                                     1.12.17.

I. The Battalion will be relieved in the SOURD FARM - SHAFT
    Sector by the 17th L. Fusiliers on the night 2/3 December 1917.

II. Relief will be as follows:-

    X Coy. 17th L. Fusiliers will relieve 2 Platoons of Z Coy.
                                          H. L. I. at SOURD FARM.
    W "   "   "   "   "   2 Platoons of W Coy.
                                          H. L. I. at SHAFT.
    Y "   "   "   "   "   2 Platoons W Coy. H. L. I.
                                          at WINCHESTER FARM.
    Z "   "   "   "   "   Y Coy. and 2 Platoons of
                                          X Coy. H. L. I. at CANAL
                                          BANK.

III. The 2 Platoons of Z Coy. at BURNS HOUSE and 2 Platoons of X Coy.
     at ALBERTA will not be relieved. O.C. Z Coy. will arrange for
     the 2 Platoons at BURNS HOUSE to march out in time for rendezvous
     as in para VI. Marching out time of 2 Platoons at ALBERTA will
     be arranged by Battalion Headquarters.

IV. On relief, O.C. Coys. will hand over all trench stores, maps,
     air photos and schemes of defence and programmes of work on hand.
     Receipts for same to be sent to Battalion Orderly Room by 12
     noon, 3rd December.

V.   Guides will be provided as under:-
     Front Line Platoons:- 2 guides per Platoon = 8.
     WINCHESTER FARM   :- 2   "   "   " = 4.
     These guides will report at ALBERTA (Battalion Headquarters) any
     time before 3 p.m., 2nd December, and conduct relieving Platoons
     to their various posts.

VI. On relief, W and Z Coys. will proceed to HIBOU, near TRIANGLE
     and entrain there at C.6C.1.3.. Train will be ready to move at
     7.30 p.m. and O.C. Coys. should have route reconnoitred by day-
     -light and be at entraining point with Coys. as near 7.30 p.m.
     as possible. Detraining point A.15.d. (near "P" Camp) from
     which Coys. will march to billets at F.X. Camp (A.16.C.4.3.)
     Y Coy and ½X Coy at CANAL BANK will on relief march back to
     F.X. Camp.

VII. Completion of relief will be notified by quickest means to
     Battalion Headquarters by code word "Saint Andrew".

                                    (Sgd) W.A. Murray Capt.
                                          for Adjt.
                                          18th H. L. I.

    Copy No.1. O.O. File.
      "   2 War Diary.
      "   3 Do.
      "   4 O.C. W Coy.
      "   5   " X "
      "   6   " Y "
      "   7   " Z "

SECRET.

OPERATION ORDERS No.107a.   10.12.17
HIGHLAND LIGHT INFANTRY.   Copy No. 10

1. The Brigade will move to ROAD CAMP F.25. C and D by march route tomorrow. The H.L.I. will follow the Royal Scots and will pass the starting point, Cornish Corner Cross Roads, A.16.A.31. at 8.30 a.m. The Battalion will, therefore, move off from Battalion Parade Ground at 8.10 a.m.

2. The route will be WOESTON-POPERINGHE road, - NORTH SWITCH ROAD - POPERINGHE-WATOU to ROAD CAMP, at F.25 C and D.

3. The usual clock hour halts will be observed.
The following distances will be kept on the march:- 500 yds between units, and 200 yds between Coys. The 1st Line Transport will march 200 yds behind the last Coy of the Battalion.

4. A loading party as under will be left to load the G.S. wagons, etc., and will come on with the G.S. wagons when loaded.
1 officer to be detailed by Z Coy, and 1 N.C.O. and 10 men per Coy., to report to the Quartermaster at 7 a.m.

10.12.17   (Sgd) W.F.M.MACARA. CAPT. & ADJT.
Issued at 9 p.m.   HIGHLAND LIGHT INFANTRY.
Copies to- O.C. W Coy.No.1 O.C. X Coy. No.2 O.C. Y Coy. No.3
    O.C. Z Coy. No.4 2nd in Comm. No.5. T. O. No.6.
    Q.M. No. 7. War Diary Nos. 8/9. O/O File No.10.

Army Form C. 2118.

WAR DIARY From 1st to 31st January 1918 inclusive.

~~INTELLIGENCE SUMMARY.~~ 18th (G.Y.) Bn. HIGHLAND LIGHT INFANTRY.

Index No. 24.

(Erase heading not required.)

Instructions regarding War Diaries and Intelligence Summaries are contained in F. S. Regs., Part II. and the Staff Manual respectively. Title pages will be prepared in manuscript.

Place	Date	Hour	Summary of Events and Information	Remarks and references to Appendices
ROAD CAMP, WATOU.	1.1.18.		Battalion in camp. Weather bright and clear. Men were given a holiday and the afternoon was spent in football and recreation.	
	2.1.18.		Battalion in camp. Weather cold, with keen frost. During the morning training in bayonet fighting, musketry, Lewis Gunnery, and Signalling was carried out. The afternoon was spent in recreational training.	
	3.1.18.		Battalion in same place. Weather fine. Training was carried out by Companies till 11 a.m. when the 35th Divisional Assault-at-Arms commenced. Boxing took place at ROAD CAMP, while the Marching and Shooting Competition was held in another part of the Divisional Area.	
	4.1.18.		Battalion in camp. Weather dry but dull. Second day of Assault-at-Arms. Finals of Boxing, Tug-of-War, and Guard Mounting were held, and at the end prizes were presented by the Corps Commander. Training in Musketry, Signalling and Lewis Gunnery was carried out until 11 a.m.	
	5.1.18.		Battalion in camp. Weather fine. Usual training took place during the morning, and the afternoon was spent in recreation.	
	6.1.18.		Battalion in camp. Weather good. Church Parades were held for all at 10 a.m. Recreational training in the afternoon. Rain fell during the night.	
	7.1.18.		Battalion in camp. Weather fine, but roads and camp in a very muddy condition. Advance parties left at 9 a.m. to take over billets at KEMPTON PARK (Sheet 28 N.W.1/20000.C.15.b.3.5.) afternoon was spent in loading and packing up preparatory to moving.	
	8.1.18.		Battalion left ROAD CAMP and marched to PROVEN STATION at 10.30 a.m. There they entrained and arrived at BOESINGHE at 1.30 p.m., marching from there to camp at KEMPTON PARK (map ref. above) The move was carried out in a very heavy snowstorm. Battalion employed on working parties. Operation Orders attached.	
KEMPTON PARK. Sheet 28 N.W. C.15.b.3.5.	9.1.18.		Battalion in camp. Working parties of 200 O.R. supplied at night to carry wiring material to Battalion in line. Snow fell heavily during the afternoon. Casualties 1 man killed, 1 missing and 4 wounded.	108
	10.1.18.		Battalion in camp. Weather fine. Men resting and improving camp.	
	11.1.18.	"	Weather changeable. Some working parties supplied. No Casualties.	
	12.1.18.	"	Some rain in forenoon, with a change to snow and frost at night. Men resting and making several camp improvements.	

Army Form C. 2118.

WAR DIARY Continued. 2.

INTELLIGENCE SUMMARY. 18th (G.Y.) Bn. HIGHLAND LIGHT INFANTRY.

(Erase heading not required.)

Instructions regarding War Diaries and Intelligence Summaries are contained in F.S. Regs., Part II and the Staff Manual respectively. Title pages will be prepared in manuscript.

Place	Date	Hour	Summary of Events and Information	Remarks and references to Appendices
KEMPTON PARK	13.1.18.		Battalion in camp. Weather bad. Much rain and some snow. Some carrying and working parties supplied. 1 O.R. wounded.	
	14.1.18.		Battalion in camp. Weather slightly improved. Some work carried on.	
	15.1.18.		Battalion in camp. Weather changeable. Men resting and carrying out improvements.	
	16.1.18.		Battalion in camp. Weather dull. Some rain. Very cold. Some working and carrying parties supplied. Battalion moved to WHITEMILL CAMP near ELVERDINGHE, arriving there about 2 p.m. Operation Order attached. 1 O.R. wounded.	109
WHITEMILL CAMP.	17.1.18.		Battalion in camp. Weather fair. Battalion resting and cleaning up.	
	18.1.18.		Battalion in camp. Weather fair. Refitting and bathing carried out. Training also carried on.	
	19.1.18.		Battalion in camp. Weather good. Battalion in training. Specialists under instruction.	
	20.1.18.		Do. Do.	
	21.1.18.		Do. Do. Preparations for move to take over the line at BURNS HOUSE.	
BURNS HOUSE SECTOR.	22.1.18.		Battalion moved to line about 2 p.m. One party moved off about noon. Operation Order attached. Enemy fairly active during the day, his fire being directed on back areas. Battalion engaged in improving posts etc. The ground was rapidly drying owing to the dry weather.	110
	23.1.18.		Battalion in line. Weather good. Enemy very quiet, with exception of M.G. firing at intervals during the night. Operation Orders issued for inter-company Relief for that night. Operation Orders attached.	111
	24.1.18.		Battalion in line. Weather good. Inter-company relief carried out without incident. Practically no activity all day, with exception that our artillery kept up continuous fire most of the time. Men engaged on improving posts etc., and wiring.	
	25.1.18.		Battalion in the line. Enemy's Artillery practically Nil. Aircraft on both sides was fairly active, but no fights ensued. Battalion relieved by the 17thROYAL SCOTS. Relief was carried out without incident. Battalion on relief went into support CORPS LINE in HUGEL HALLES. Operation Orders attaches.	112
	26.1.18.		Battalion in Support. Very quiet. Battalion engaged on Working Parties and Carrying Parties.	
	27.1.18.		Do. Do.	
	28.1.18.		Do. Do.	

Army Form C. 2118.

WAR DIARY Continued. 3.
INTELLIGENCE SUMMARY 18th (G.Y.) Bn. HIGHLAND LIGHT INFANTRY.

(Erase heading not required.)

Instructions regarding War Diaries and Intelligence Summaries are contained in F. S. Regs., Part II and the Staff Manual respectively. Title pages will be prepared in manuscript.

Place	Date	Hour	Summary of Events and Information	Remarks and references to Appendices
	29.1.18.		Battalion in Support. Very quiet. Battalion engaged on Working Parties and Carrying Parties. Battalion relieved by 4th NORTH STAFFS. On the relief, Battalion came into Reserve and were billeted at HILLTOP FARM. Operation Orders attached.	113
HILLTOP FARM.	30.1.18.		Battalion engaged on Working Parties, Feet Rebbing etc. Weather good. Hard frost during night. Do.	
	31.1.18.		Do.	

[signature]
Capt. and Adjt.
18th (G.Y.) Bn. HIGHLAND LIGHT INFANTRY.

SECRET. OPERATION ORDERS. No. 108. 711.18.
          HIGHLAND LIGHT INFANTRY.   Copy No.

1. The Battalion will move up to KEMPTON PARK tomorrow and will take over from the 5th LONDON REGIMENT.

2. Whilst the Battalion is in support the following Working Party will be supplied:- 1 Officer and 250 men to be permanently attached to, and rationed by, 183rd TUNNELLING Coy. R.E. at HULL'S FARM, for work on Dug-outs. This party will be supplied as follows:-
   1 Officer Z Coy.
   63 men W "   63 men Y Coy.
   62 men X "   62 men Z "
   This party will parade on Battalion Parade Ground tomorrow morning at 7.15 a.m. and will proceed by train leaving PROVEN for BOESINGHE at 9 a.m., arriving at PROVEN half an hour before train goes. They will be met at BOESINGHE by a guide who will guide the Working Party to their destination. Dress for the above party will be full marching order with one blanket rolled on top of pack and rations for the day.

3. The second blankets of this party will be rolled in bundles of 10 and stacked, by Companies, at the Quartermaster's stores by 6.30 a.m.

4. The remainder of the Battalion will parade on Battalion Parade Ground at 10 a.m. and will proceed by train leaving PROVEN at 12 noon. Dress:- Full marching order, with one blanket rolled on top of pack.

5. Blankets of the remainder of the Battalion will be stacked in the Quartermaster's stores by 7 a.m.
   Officers' Valises will be stacked in the Quartermaster's stores by 7.30.

6. Rations for the remainder of the Battalion will be carried on the cookers, and dinners will be cooked on the way. Cookers and Lewis Gun Limbers will meet Companies at BOESINGHE, and proceed with them to KEMPTON PARK. All Mess Stores will be packed in the Companies' Lewis Gun Limbers by 8 a.m.

7. Transport Officer will detail 1 Limber and the Mess Cart for the Headquarters' Mess and a Limber for the Orderly Room, and will make arrangements for collecting all vehicles ready to move off at 8.30 a.m.

8. The Quartermaster will arrange to send up to KEMPTON PARK the rations for the next day. Rations for the working party for the next day will be sent up to the 183rd TUNNELLING Coy. Headquarters, HULL'S FARM on the CANAL BANK (B.18.c.8.3.)

9. O.C. Companies will render to the Adjutant on the Battalion Parade Ground a correct entraining State.

10. The number of details to be left behind will be notified later.

7.1.18.   (Sgd.) W. F. M. MACARA. Capt. & Adjt.
Issued at 9 p.m.   HIGHLAND LIGHT INFANTRY.

Copy No. 1 O.O. File.
  "   " 2 War Diary.
  "   " 3   Do.
  "   " 4 O.C. W Coy.
  "   " 5 O.C. X "
  "   " 6 O.C. Y "
  "   " 7 O.C. Z "
  "   " 8 2nd in Command.
  "   " 9 T.O.
  "   " 10 Q.M.

SECRET.   OPERATION ORDERS No. 109.   Copy No.
           HIGHLAND LIGHT INFANTRY.   15th Jan. 1918.

Ref. Map. BELGIUM.
      Sheet 25 N.W. 1.20000

1. The 106 Inf. Brigade will move to WHITEMILL area on the 16/1/18 in relief of the 105 Inf. Brigade. The 104 Inf. Brigade will take over the accommodation now occupied by the 106 Inf. Brigade.

2. The H.L.I. will move to WHITEMILL CAMP (B.14.d.) and take over from the SHERWOODS.
   Transport lines and details will remain as at present.

3. March. Starting point: Junction of BARD CAUSEWAY and BOESINGHE-
          -YPRES ROAD (B.18d.6.2.)   Time 12 noon.
          Route:- Road junction B.12d.3.4, MAGENTA X. ROADS. DAWSON'S CORNER. ELVERDINGHE.
          Assembly. Battalion will assemble on road outside X Coy. huts at 10.30 a.m. (H.Q. X. Y. Z. W Coys. Transport.)
          Dress: Full marching order, blankets rolled on packs.

4. Working Parties. Working Parties will be provided by the 106 Brigade on the 16th, Night parties being left behind in present camps and rejoining in new positions on completion of work. Details of working parties will be issued later. Permanent parties with Tunnellers will not be relieved until the 18th and will continue work till 12 NOON on that day. On relief they will rejoin their Battalions.

5. Transport. - Separate Orders.-

6. Baggage. Officers' Valises, spare blankets, and packs of men on night working parties will be stacked outside Batt. H.Q. by 9.30 a.m. Pioneers and police will form loading parties for G.S. Wagons, and will move off with them.
   O.C. COYs will each detail 1 man to take charge of all Company packs and blankets on G.S. Wagons.

7. Brigade H.Q. will close at CANAL BANK at 3 p.m. 16/1/18 and will re-open at WHITEMILL at the same hour.

8. Defence Schemes, Maps, and details as to action of working parties in case of attack will be handed over to relieving unit of 104 Brigade.

                              (SGD.) V. E. GOODERSON,
                                        Major,
Issued at 2.30 p.m.   Comdg. 18th (G.Y.) Bn. Highland Light Inf.

       Copies. 1 O.C. W Coy.   5. T.O. & Q.M.
               2 O.C. X "   6. M.O.
               3 O.C. Y "   7. Office.
               4 O.C. Z "   8 War Diary.
                                 9   Do.

SECRET.   OPERATION ORDERS. No.110.   20.1.18.
           HIGHLAND LIGHT INFANTRY.   Copy No. 1

1. The 106th Brigade will relieve the 116th Infantry Brigade in the BURNS HOUSE Sector.
   The Battalion will relieve the 14th HAMPSHIRE REGT. as follows:-
       X Coy. on the left. Z Coy. on the right. Y Coy. in support in and around BURNS HOUSE. W Coy. in reserve at WINCHESTER FARM.
   Battalion Headquarters are at HUBNER FARM (D.1.c.40.65.)

2. Coys. will proceed by train (narrow guage) from READING(B.22.d.1.5.) to BOGSIDE (C.23.a.8.9.), thence by road to CORNER COT, as follows:-
       The two front line Coys.(X and Z Coys.) at 1.30 p.m. tomorrow Y and W Coys. and Headquarters at 3.30 p.m.

3. GUIDES. Guides as follows will be supplied:-
       1 Guide per front line Company will be met at CORNER COT (C.17.b.6.4.) at 3.30 p.m.
       1 Guide per Support and Reserve Coys. and Battalion Headquarte will be at the smae place at 5 p.m. Relay Guides will be picked up at Battalion Headquarters, and Post Guides at either Battalion Headquarters or Coy. Headquarters.
   O.C. X and Z Coys. should make arrangements that they do not pass Battalion Headquarters, HUBNER FARM, before 5 p.m. They will proceed by road as far as Battalion Headquarters, and then by ALBERTA track to front line.

4. All trench stores, including tools, Aeroplane photographs, Defence Schemes, also details of work in hand and proposed, will be carefully checked and taken over, and list of stores taken over will be forwarded to the Adjutant as soon as possible after completion of Relief.

5. Completion of Relief will be notified to Battalion Headquarters by the quickest method, the code word "CLICK" being used.

    Issued at 6.30 p.m.   (Sgd.) W.F. MACARA. Capt. & Adjt.
                                          HIGHLAND LIGHT INFANTRY.

Copy No. 1. War Diary.
       2. Do.
       3. O. O. File.
       4. O.C., W Coy.
       5. O. C. X "
       6. O.C., Y "
       7. O.C., Z "
       8. Second in Command.
       9. Transport Officer.
      10. Quartermaster.

ADMINISTRATIVE INSTRUCTIONS
accompanying
OPERATION ORDERS. No. 110.   20.1.18.
HIGHLAND LIGHT INFANTRY.

1. Transport Lines and Quartermaster's Stores will remain as at present. Details Camp will be notified later.

2. RATIONS. Coys. will take into the line 2 days' rations, and 10 petrol tins of water per Coy. The remaining 2 days' rations will be taken up by Limbers to Ration Dump at CORPS ROAD, near HUBNER FARM on the night of the 22nd/23rd. From there the rations will be carried up by W. Coy., taking their own and X Coy's to WINCHESTER FARM, and Y and Z Coys' to BURNS HOUSE.

3. GUARDS. O.C. W Coy. will detail 1 N.C.O. and 4 men to report to the Adjutant at 9 a.m. tomorrow, with fighting order and 2 days' rations. This party should be taken from the details and will be attached to Headquarters, as a Ration Dump Guard. O.C. Y Coy. will detail 1 N.C.O. and 3 men to report to the R.S.M. tomorrow at 2 p.m. with fighting order and rations. This Guard should be chosen from the details and will be attached to the Headquarters for Guard.

4. SOUP KITCHENS. It is hoped to be able to run a soup kitchen to supply hot food to the front lines. O.C. Coys. will detail 1 cook per Coy for the purpose of running this. Two Camp kettles will be supplied by each Coy. The Cooks, with kettles, will report to the R.S.M. at 2 p.m. tomorrow.

5. The Transport Officer will detail 1 Limber per Coy. and 1 Limber for Headquarters for the purpose of carrying up Lewis Guns, Trench stores, etc. Coys will have the loads ready by 12.30 p.m. Transport Officer will be responsible to see that they get to CORNER COT, X and Z Coys. at 3.30 p.m. and W and Y at 4.30 p.m. Each Coy. will detail 1 man to go with the Limbers and sit on the Lewis Guns etc. at CORNER COT, where they are being dumped. Coys. will pick up their guns etc. when passing CORNER COT. The Limber for Headquarters will be taken right up to HUBNER FARM, where the load will be dumped.

Issued at 6.30 p.m.   (Sgd.) W.F. MACARA. Capt. & Adjt.
                                    HIGHLAND LIGHT INFANTRY.

Copy No. 1 War Diary.
     2   Do.
     3 O.O. File.
     4 O.C. W Coy.
     5 O.C. X "
     6 O.C. Y "
     7 O.C. Z "
     8 Second in Command.
     9 Transport Officer.
    10 Quartermaster.

SECRET.

OPERATION ORDERS. No. 111.   22.1.18.
HIGHLAND LIGHT INFANTRY.   Copy No.1

I. The following Reliefs will take place tomorrow
   Y Coy. will relieve Z Coy. on the right.
   W "   "   "   X "   "   " left.
   Z Coy. on relief will come into Support at BURNS HOUSE.
   X Coy. on relief will come into Reserve at WINCHESTER FARM.

II. Guides. 1 per post from X and Z Coys. will be sent out at dawn tomorrow, and will report as follows:-
   X Coy. Guides to WINCHESTER FARM, and
   Z Coy. Guides to BURNS HOUSE.
   O.C. Z Coy. will arrange that N.C.Os from his Platoon presently at BURNS HOUSE will act as Guide for his Coy. coming out to VACHER AND BURNS.
   X Coy. will also arrange to send out N.C.Os as an Advance party to WINCHESTER FARM.

III. All Trench Stores, Aeroplane Photos, Maps, Defence Schemes, Work on hand and proposed, will be handed over, receipts taken, and forwarded to the Adjutant on morning after Relief.

IV. Coys. will not move off from their respective posts, namely BURNS and WINCHESTER until 5.30 p.m.

V. Coys. in the line will bring out with them all empty Petrol tins and food containers.

VI. Completion of Relief will be notified to Battn. Hd.Qrs. by code word "Pip".

Issued at 10 p.m.   (Sgd.) W. F. MACARA.
                                            Capt. & Adjt.
                                            18th H. L. I.

Copy No.1 War Diary.
     2   Do.
     3 O.O. File.
     4 O.C. W Coy.
     5 O.C. X "
     6 O.C. Y "
     7 O.C. Z "
     8 Second in Command.

SECRET. OPERATION ORDERS. No.112. 24.1.18.
HIGHLAND LIGHT INFANTRY. Copy No. 1.

I. The Battalion will be relieved by the ROYAL SCOTS on the night of the 25/26th Jany.

II. Guides will be supplied as follows:-
   1 per Post for Front Line Coys.
   1 "   "   " Support Coy.
   1 per Platoon for Reserve Coy.
   These Guides will be sent down at dawn tomorrow, bringing rations for the day, and report at Battn. Hd.Qrs.

III. Battalion on relief will come into Support and the Disposition will be as follows:-
   W, Y and Z Coys. in Corps Line near HUBNER FARM.
   X and Batt.Hd.Qrs. on the banks of the STEENBEEK by HUGELHHALLES
   Advance Parties will be sent down at dawn as follows:-
   1 N.C.O. and 4 men per Coy. and 1 Signaller per Coy.
   X Coy. will also send an officer.
   These Advance Parties will bring all their kit and rations for the day. They will report to Battn. Hd.Qrs. HUBNER FARM.
   These Advance Parties will take over trenches etc. as follows:-
   CORPS LINE. Z Coy. on right. W Coy. Centre. Y Coy. Left.
   HUGEL HALLES   X Coy.
   These Advance Parties will also act as Guides to Coys. coming out, and they will meet them at junction of CORPS LINE and wooden CORPS ROAD and guide platoons to their posts.

IV. All Trench Stores, Trench Photographs, Defence Schemes, information about the front and particulars of work in hand and proposed will be carefully handed over to relieving Coys. Lists to be forwarded to the Adjutant next day.

V. Completion of Relief will be wired to Batt. Hd.Qrs., the code word "Hot" being used.
   Coys. will also wire when they are settled in Support Trenches, the code word "Home" being used.

VI. All empty Petrol Tins, exclusive of those taken over will be brought out and dumped at ration dump on CORPS ROAD.

   Issued at 7 p.m.   (Sgd.) W.F. MACARA.
                                    Capt. & Adjt.
                                    18th H. L. I.

Copy No.1 War Diary.
     2 Do.
     3 O.O. File.
     4 O.C. W Coy.
     5 O.C. X "
     6 O.C. Y "
     7 O.C. Z "
     8 Second in Command.

SECRET. OPERATION ORDERS. No.113. 28.1.18.
HIGHLAND LIGHT INFANTRY. Copy No.1.

I. The Battalion will be relieved by the NORTH STAFFS. in Support in CORPS LINE on the night of 29/30th.

II. Coys. will not be actually relieved Company per Company, but as soon as the first Company of the NORTH STAFFS. arrives for the CORPS LINE O.C. X Coy. will notify Hd.Qrs., also O.C. W Coy. and O.C. Y Coy. As soon as this has been done the Companies will move out as follows, the recognised intervals being kept.
Z, W, Y.
X Coy will await orders from Batt. Hd.Qrs.

III. On Relief Coys. will proceed by ALBERTA Duckboard track to HILLTOP FARM. An Officer, who will act as Guide at night, will reconnoitre this track by day.

IV. All Trench Stores, (including tools and gum boots) Air Photos, Defence Schemes, work in hand and proposed, will be handed over and receipts taken and forwarded to the Adjutant early next morning.

V. One Limber per Coy. will be at Ration Dump tomorrow night to take down Lewis Guns, Magazines, and Empty Petrol Tins. As soon as Coys have been relieved, O.C. Coys. will send their Limbers by road to HILLTOP CAMP.

VI. Completion of Relief will be notified to Batt. Hd.Qrs., the code word "Rest" being used.

VII. Transport Officer and C.Q.M.Ss will arrange all accommodation etc. at the camp.

(Sgd.) W. F. MACARA. Capt. & Adjt.
18th H. L. I.

Issued at 10 p.m.

Copy No.1 War Diary.
    2   Do.
    3 O.O.File.
    4 O.C. W Coy.
    5 O.C. X "
    6 O.C. Y "
    7 O.C. Z "
    8 Second in Command.
    9 Transport Officer.

WAR DIARY From 1st to 28th February 1918 inclusive. Army Form C. 2118.

INTELLIGENCE SUMMARY 18th (G.Y.) Bn. HIGHLAND LIGHT INFANTRY.

Index No. 25.

Place	Date	Hour	Summary of Events and Information	Remarks and references to Appendices
BURNS HOUSE SECTOR.	1.2.18.		Battalion in the Line. Weather dry and cold. Battalion relieved 19th D.L.I. in the Line. No Casualties. Relief completed about 10 p.m. Operation Orders attached.	114
	2.2.18.		Battalion in the Line. Weather still cold, but dry. Artillery and Aircraft were rather below normal, nothing of note taking place.	
	3.2.18.		Battalion in the line. No Change. Weather same.	
	4.2.18.		Battalion in Support. Weather very good. Battalion moved to Support. Operation Orders attached. 105th Brigade raided an enemy post at GRAVEL FARM, taking 1 wounded prisoner, and killing the rest of the garrison. Casualties caused by retaliatory barrage on our Support Lines were 1 O.R. killed and 2 O.R. wounded.	114
	5.2.18.		Battalion in Reserve. Weather still very good. Situation normal.	
	6.2.18.		Do. Do. The Battalion front was visited by War Correspondents from the 'Glasgow Herald' and the 'Scotsman', interviewing several of the men. Nothing of note.	
	7.2.18.		Battalion in Reserve. Weather still good. No change.	
	8.2.18.		Do. Do. Battalion was relieved by 2nd Battalion R. SUSSEX REGT. (1st Div.) marching to WHITEMILL CAMP on relief. Operation Orders attached.	115
WHITE-MILL CAMP.	9.2.18.		Battalion in camp. Day spent resting, cleaning and refitting. Weather good.	
	10.2.18.		Do. New formations of Brigades cause 19th D.L.I. and 4/N. STAFFS R. to be transferred to another Brigade of the same Division, and the 12th H.L.I. taking their place in 106th Brigade. This now forms a Scottish Brigade, (17th R. SCOTS. 12th H.L.I. and 18th H.L.I.)	
	11.2.18.		Battalion in camp. Weather still good. Battalion in training and cleaning up. Some bathing carried out.	
	12.2.18.		Do. Weather dull but dry. Training carried out as usual.	
	13.2.18.		Do. Do. Do.	
	14.2.18.		Do. Weather very stormy. Some rain. Do.	
	15.2.18.		Do. Weather good. Some training carried out. Afternoon spent in preparations for move to line tomorrow.	
	16.2.18.		Battalion in camp. Weather good. Battalion moved to line at STADEN SECTOR, relieving 18th LANCS. FUSILIERS -(104th Brigade.) Relief completed about 9.30 p.m. No Casualties. Operation Orders attached.	
STADEN SECTOR.	17.2.18.		Battalion in the line. Enemy activity normal. Artillery and aircraft normal. Nothing of note. Weather dull and dry. 1 O.R. wounded.	116

Army Form C. 2118.

WAR DIARY Continued. 2.
or
INTELLIGENCE SUMMARY.
18th (G.Y.) Bn. HIGHLAND LIGHT INFANTRY.

(Erase heading not required.)

Instructions regarding War Diaries and Intelligence Summaries are contained in F.S. Regs., Part II and the Staff Manual respectively. Title pages will be prepared in manuscript.

Place	Date	Hour	Summary of Events and Information	Remarks and references to Appendices
STADEN SECTOR.	18.2.18.		Battalion in the line. Weather good. No Casualties. Situation normal. Battalion relieved by 17th R. SCOTS. and moved to RESERVE, Battalion H.Q. being at Pill-box PIG & WHISTLE, near LANGEMARCK.	
	19.2.18.		Battalion in Reserve. Several working and carrying parties. No Casualties. Weather dry but dull.	
	20.2.18.		Do. Working Parties as before. Weather dull; heavy rain at night.	
	21.2.18.		Do. Weather cold, but dry and bright. Battalion moved to take up line again, relieving 12th H.L.I. Relief completed about 9.30 p.m. 3 O.R. wounded. Battalion H.Q. at SOUVENIR HOUSE.	
	22.2.18.		Battalion in the line. Weather good. Situation normal. No Casualties. The Brigade was relieved by 15th SHERWOOD FORESTERS. Relief completed about 9 p.m. Operation Orders attached.	117
HUDDLESTON CAMP.	23.2.18.		Battalion in Divisional Reserve at HUDDLESTON CAMP. Day spent in cleaning up and inspecting of equipments etc. Weather dull.	
	24.2.18.		Battalion in Divisional Reserve. Weather dull and cloudy. Battalion engaged in Bathing and cleaning up. Divine Services attended.	
	25.2.18.		Battalion in Divisional Reserve. Weather very dull. Some rain. Battalion engaged on working parties and improvement of billets in vicinity of camp.	
	26.2.18.		Battalion in Divisional Reserve. Weather cloudy and stormy. Work as before.	
	27.2.18.		Do.	
	28.2.18.		Do.	

[signature]
Lt.-Col.
Commanding 18th (G.Y.) Bn. HIGHLAND LIGHT INFANTRY.

SECRET. OPERATION ORDERS. No. 114.   31.1.18.
HIGHLAND LIGHT INFANTRY.

1. The Battalion will relieve the 19th D.L.I. in the BURNS HOUSE SECTOR tomorrow night as follows:-
   Z Coy. on the right. X Coy. in the Centre, and W Coy. on the left.
   Y Coy. will be in Reserve at WINCHESTER FARM.
   Battalion Headquarters are at HUBNER FARM (D.1.c.40.65.)
   Companies will proceed by the ALBERTA Track, and will move off in the following order at 4.30 p.m.
        Z,   X,   W,   Y.
   No Company will pass HUBNER FARM BEFORE 6 p.m.

2. GUIDES. Guides as follows will be supplied:-
   1 Guide per Post will be met at BURNS HOUSE at 6 p.m.
   1 Guide for TERRIER FARM, this Post being supplied by Y Coy. will be met at junction of ALBERTA Track and WINCHESTER Track.

3. Lewis Guns and Petrol tins will proceed in Limbers as far as junction of ALBERTA Track and POELCAPPEL-St.JULIEN Road, where they will be unloaded, and Companies will pick up same when passing.

4. All trench stores, including tools, Aeroplane photographs, Defence Schemes, also details of work in hand and proposed, will be carefully checked and taken over, and list of stores taken over will be forwarded to the Adjutant as soon as possible after completion of Relief.

5. Completion of Relief will be notified to Battalion Headquarters by the quickest method, the code word "RUNNER" being used.

Issued at 7 p.m.   (Sgd.) W. F. MACARA. Capt. & Adjt.
                                       HIGHLAND LIGHT INFANTRY.

Copy No. 1. War Diary.
        2.   Do.
        3. O.O. File.
        4. O.C. W Coy.
        5. O.C. X "
        6. O.C. Y "
        7. O.C. Z "
        8. Second in Command.

SECRET. OPERATION ORDERS. No.114. (A) 3.2.18.
HIGHLAND LIGHT INFANTRY. Copy No.

I. The Battalion will be relieved by the 17th ROYAL SCOTS on the night of the 4/5th inst.

II. **GUIDES.** One Guide per post from each Company will be sent down to BURNS HOUSE at dawn, and will be ready to receive incoming Battalion at 5.45 p.m.
O.C. Z Coy will arrange that their guides are well under cover during the day.
One Guide from Y Coy will be at junction of ALBERTA and WINCHESTER TRACKS at 5.45 p.m. to guide in garrison for TERRIER FARM.
O.C. Y Coy. will detail an Officer to superintend distribution of guides at BURNS HOUSE.
ADVANCE PARTIES. Advance parties of 1 N.C.O. and 3 O.R. and 1 Signaller per Coy. will also move out at dawn and report at Battalion Headquarters.

III. The Battalion, on relief, will occupy position in Support. W, Y, and Z Coys. in CORPS LINE. X Coy. and Headquarters at HUGEL HOLLOW (Steenbeek).
Coys. in CORPS LINE will occupy same position as formerly.

IV. All trench stores, photos, maps and details of defence, work in hand and proposed will be handed over on relief. Receipts for stores will be forwarded to Adjutant at HUGEL HOLLOW by 10 a.m. 5th February.
All empty petrol tins will be brought out of the line and taken to position occupied in support.

V. Completion of relief will be sent by wire, Code word "QUICK" being used.

VI. Arrival CORPS LINE will be sent by code word "MARCH".

(Sgd.) J.W. BOW. Lieut. & A/Adjt.
for Major,
Issued at noon. Comdg. 18th (G.Y.) Bn. HIGHLAND LIGHT INFANTRY.

Copy No.1 War Diary.
  2   Do.
  3 O.O. File.
  4 O. C. W Coy.
  5 O. C. X "
  6 O. C. Y "
  7 O. C. Z "
  8 Second in Command.

SECRET.   OPERATION ORDERS. No.115.   7.2.18.
                       HIGHLAND LIGHT INFANTRY.   Copy No.

I. The Battalion will be relieved on the night 8/9th February by the Headquarters and two Coys. of the 2nd R. SUSSEX REGT.

II. C Coy. R. SUSSEX will relieve Z and W Coy. H.L.I. D Coy. R. SUSSEX will relieve Y Coy. H.L.I.

III. The following guides will report to Battalion Headquarters at 4.15 p.m. 8th February.
    W Coy.   1 guide for Coy. Headquarters.
              2 guides for 2 platoons C Coy. R. SUSSEX.
    Z "   2 guides for 2 platoons C Coy. R. SUSSEX.
    Y "   1 guide for Coy. Headquarters.
              4 guides for 4 platoons of D Coy. R. SUSSEX.
Headquarters. 1 guide.
Guides will conduct relief from REGINA X ROADS to CORPS LINE on duck walk via ALBERTA - HUGEL HOLLOW.

IV. The R. SUSSEX will send advance parties tomorrow. O.C. Coys. are to hand over all accommodation clean.

V. Coys. on relief will move to CHEDDAR VILLA to entrain at 7.30 p.m. for WHITEMILL CAMP.
    X Coy. will move out as soon as the last Coy. of the R. SUSSEX passes the STEENBEEK.
    W, Y, and Z Coys. will remain in CORPS LINE until relieved.

VI. TRANSPORT. 1 Limber per Coy (W, Y, and Z) to convey L.G.s, petrol tins and Mess stores, will be at the junction of ALBERTA TRACK and St. JULIEN ROAD (by the 2 TANKS) at 4.30 p.m.
    1 Limber for Headquarters, and 1 for X Coy. will be at REGINA X ROADS at 4.30 p.m.
    Lewis Guns will not be moved from CORPS LINE until relieved.

VII. Coy. Q.M.S. will be at RED CHATEAU (ELVERDINGHE-BRIELEN ROAD) ready to meet their Companies as they pass, and to conduct them to their billets.

VIII. All trench stores, photos, defence schemes, etc. will be carefully handed over on relief, and receipts obtained and forwarded to the Adjutant by 10 a.m. 9th Feby.
    A.A. positions and mountings will be carefully handed over, being actually pointed out on the ground.
    Receipts will be obtained and forwarded with receipts for trench stores etc. by 10 a.m. 9th Feby.

IX. Coys. will notify relief to Battalion Headquarters by code word "CANTEEN".

Issued at 10 p.m.   (Sgd.) J. W. BOW. Lieut. & A/Adjt.
                                     HIGHLAND LIGHT INFANTRY.

Copies as usual.

SECRET.   ADDENDA to OPERATION ORDERS of 7.2.18.
                HIGHLAND LIGHT INFANTRY.

I. Guides as arranged will report to Adjutant at Battalion Headquarters
    at 6 p.m. 8.2.18.
        X Coy. will detail 1 Officer to take charge of guides. The
    Officer will report to Adjutant at 6 p.m.

II. Limbers for Companies and Headquarters will be at point arranged
    at 6.15 p.m.

III. The train from BOGSIDE is cancelled. Companies march to WHITEMILL
     CAMP on relief.

IV. Coys. will report arrival to Battalion Headquarters at WHITEMILL.

                            (Sgd.) J. W. BOW. Lieut. & A/Adjt.
    8.2.18.   HIGHLAND LIGHT INFANTRY.
    Issued at noon.
    Copy No.1 War Diary.   Copy No.6 O. C. Y Coy.
         2   Do.   7 O. C. Z "
         3 O.O. File.   8 Second in Command.
         4 O. C. W Coy.   9 Transport Officer.
         5 O. C. X "

SECRET.   OPERATION ORDERS. No.116.   15.2.18.
                       HIGHLAND LIGHT INFANTRY.

         Ref. Maps. BIXCHUTE 1/10000.
                    SCHAAP-BALIE 1/10000.

1. The 105th Infantry Brigade will relieve the 104th Infantry Brigade in the STADEN Sector on the night of the 16/17 Feby. The Battn will relieve 18th L. FUSILIERS in the left Sub-sector, the 12th H.L.I. taking over the Right Sub-sector, and the ROYAL SCOTS being in Support.

2. W Coy. will relieve Right Coy. L.F.   H.Q. at V.12.d.6.8.
   Z "   "   " Left   "   "   H.Q. " V.6.c.9.1.
   Y "   "   " Support "   "   H.Q.   EGYPT HOUSE.
   X "   "   " Reserve "   "   H.Q.   "   "   "
   AID POST.   "   "   "
   Battn. Headquarters   " PASCAL FARM.

3. Y Coy. will detail one platoon to be stationed at MEY CROSS ROADS to act as a carrying platoon to the front line Coys. O.C.Y Coy. will arrange to send on an officer in advance to arrange accommo--dation of the platoon.

4. All trench stores, maps, photographs, details of work in hand and contemplated, will be taken over, receipts given and lists forwarded to the Adjutant the day after Relief.

5. The Battn. will probably be moved by train from ELVERDINGHE to the east side of the CANAL. From there the routes to be followed will be as follows:-
   W Coy, X Coy. and Battn. HdQrs. via RAILWAY DUCKBOARD Track.
   Z "   Y "   " HUNTER STREET.

6. One guide per platoon from the LANC. FUSILIERS and one guide for Battn. HdQrs. will be at junction of RAILWAY STREET and HUNTER STREET with the LANGERMARK-KOEKUIT Road at 5.30 p.m. Companies will not arrive at these junctions before that hour. The two Reserve platoons of X Coy. for VEE BEND will move by the above Road to VEE BEND after meeting their guides.

7. All ranks will take in rations and water for 48 hours.

8. Transport Officer will arrange for 1 Limber per Coy. and 1 for Battn. HdQrs. to carry Lewis Guns, Magazines, Water etc. to the junction of the LANGERMARK-KOEKUIT Road with HUNTER and RAILWAY Streets.

9. On the night of the 28th February, the Battn. will be relieved by the ROYAL SCOTS, and will be in Reserve as follows:-
            X and Y Coys. at LANGERMARK.
            Z and Half W Coy. at GROYTERAZALE FARM.
             "   "   "   at BEAR Support.
            Battn. H.Q. at PIG & WHISTLE.
   Coys./

Coys. will arrange to send platoon guides to these places at dawn on the 18th, who will act as guides to the ROYAL SCOTS coming in, and also guide Coys. after Relief.

10. The completion of these reliefs will be wired to Battn. HdQrs. by the code word "MANGLE".

15.2.18. (Sgd.) J. W. BOW. Lieut. & A/Adjt.
Issued at 4 p.m. HIGHLAND LIGHT INFANTRY.

Copy No. 1 War Diary.
" 2 O.O. File.
" 3 " Do.
" 4 O.C. W Coy.
" 5 O.C. X "
" 6 O.C. Y "
" 7 O.C. Z "
" 8 Second in Command.
" 9 Transport Officer.
" 10 Quartermaster.
" 11 Lanc. Fusiliers.
" 12 Royal Scots.

SECRET.   OPERATION ORDERS. No.117.   21.2.18.
                       HIGHLAND LIGHT INFANTRY.   Copy No.

Reference Map (Special) B.2. 1/10,000

I. The 105th Inf. Brigade will relieve the 106th Inf. Brigade in the STADEN Sector on the night of the 22/23rd and 23/24th. The 106th Inf. Brigade on relief will move into Divisional Support on CANAL BANK.

II. The Battalion will be relieved by the NOTTS & DERBY (Sherwood Foresters) on the night of the 23/24th as follows:-
X Front Line Coy. will be relieved by Y Coy.
Y   "   "   "   "   "   " Z "
½ W Support Coy.   "   "   ½ X Coy.
½ W and Z Reserve by"   "   W and ½X Coy.

III. Platoon Guides for the Left and Support Coys. of the incoming Battn. will be at EAGLE DUMP at 6 p.m.
Guides for the Right Coy. will be at junction of LANGEMARCK road (U.23.c.9.4.) at 6 p.m.
No Guides required for Reserve Coy.
O.C. Front Line Coys. and Support Coy. will arrange to send out these guides at dawn to EAGLE DUMP and report to O.C. Z Coy. who will see guides are in their proper places at 6 p.m.

IV. All trench stores, maps, photographs, details of work in hand and contemplated, will be handed over, receipts taken and lists forwarded to the Adjutant the day after Relief.

V. Coys., on relief, will proceed to billets as follows:-
W, X, Y, & B.H.Q. to HUDDLESTON CAMP.
Z Coy. to CANAL BANK.
All Coys. will proceed on relief by track A and will be met by their Q.M.S. to guide them to their new billets at junction of track A with PILKEM-ESSEX FARM Road. (C.8.a.8.1.)

VI. Q.M. will arrange to have all blankets, Packs and Valises in various billets. T.O. will arrange the necessary transport accordingly.

VII. Completion of Relief will be sent by wire to B.H.Q. by code word "T.G."

21.2.18.   (Sgd.) J. W. BOW. Lieut. & A/Adjt.
Issued at 4 a.m.   18th HIGHLAND LIGHT INFANTRY.

Copy No.1. File.   Copy No.7. O.C. Z Coy.
       2. War Diary.   8 Second in Command.
       3. File.   9 Transport Officer.
       4. O.C. W Coy.   10 Quartermaster.
       5. O.C. X "   11 Notts & Derbys.
       6. O.C. Y "

SECRET.

O.C.' ' COY.
----

1. During the tour in the line each company will thoroughly reconnoitre their front and locate the posts definitely held by the enemy, with a view to carrying out a small enterprise with or without the assistance of artillery to capture or destroy the post. A report on the post eslected for this enterprise will be sent in to Battn. HdQrs. as soon as possible.

2. Each company front will be patrolled during the night and early morning. Roads and tracks leading to our posts will be very carefully watched, and ambush patrols will be placed on these if it is suspected that they are used by the enemy.

3. Instances have occurred lately of some of our posts having disappeared without leaving any trace. This indicates slackness in patrolling, want of vigilance and lack of supervision. No post should be left unvisited longer than an hour.

4. Offensive action is to be developed by all our patrols, and consequently patrols should be of sufficient strength to seize any opportunity of offence offered to them.

(Sd.) R.R.LAWRENSON, Lieut. - Col.,

15.2.18.   Commanding, 18th. (G.Y.) Bn. Highland Light Inf.

106th Inf.Bde.
35th Div.

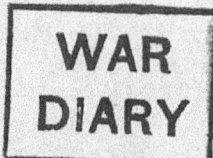

18th BATTN. THE HIGHLAND LIGHT INFANTRY.

M A R C H

1 9 1 8

Attached:-

Narrative of Operations
23rd to 31st March.

Battn. Operation Orders.

WAR DIARY

Army Form C. 2118.

WAR DIARY

INTELLIGENCE=SUMMARY

From 1st to 31st March 1918 inclusive.

18th (G.Y.) Bn. HIGHLAND LIGHT INFANTRY.

Index No. 26.

(Erase heading not required.)

Place	Date	Hour	Summary of Events and Information	Remarks and references to Appendices
WHITEMILL CAMP.	1.3.18.		Battalion in Training in Whitemill Camp. Weather good.	
	2.3.18.		Do.	
	3.3.18.		Battalion attend Divine Services. Weather fine and warm.	
	4.3.18.		Battalion in Training. Weather continues to be extra good. Concerts were given at night by the Brigade Troupe, and were largely attended.	
	5.3.18.		One half Battalion in training, while other half attended the Delousing station near POPERINGHE. Owing to the time taken to delouse the one half Battalion second half were unable to go through the process. Weather fairly good; some rain in latter part of the day.	
	6.3.18.		Battalion in training. Weather changeable.	
	7.3.18.		Battalion moved to take up the line, relieving the 19th D.L.I. of the 104th Brigade. Relief completed without casualties.	120 Operation Order attached
	8.3.18.		Battalion in the line. Enemy activity on left Divisional front where he gained a small success but was almost immediately repulsed. No activity on our front. Weather good.	
	9.3.18.		Battalion was relieved from the line, our Division(35th) being placed in G.H.Q. Reserve. Battalion moved to H. Camp that day.	121 Operation Order attached
H CAMP.	10.3.18.		Battalion in H Camp, near INTERNATIONAL CORNER. Some training carried out, also general preparations for a possible sudden move. Battalion under 12 hours' notice. Weather good.	
	11.3.18.		Do. Weather good. Training carried out as per programme.	
	12.3.18.		Do. Weather dull and sharp, but no rain. Do. General practice for various competitions, within the Division.	
	13.3.18.		Do. Weather wet; some heavy rain fell during the night 12/13th, but towards the afternoon of the 13th the atmosphere cleared a good deal. Some training carried out.	
	14.3.18.		Battalion engaged on working parties in Army Battle Zone. Weather very good. No Casualties.	
	15.3.18.		Do. Do.	
	16.3.18.		Do. Do.	
	17.3.18.		Do. Do.	
	18.3.18.		Do. Some rain.	
	19.3.18.		Do. Weather good.	
	20.3.18.		Do. Casualties 1 O.R. killed and 2 O.R. wounded.	

Army Form C. 2118.

WAR DIARY Continued.

INTELLIGENCE SUMMARY 18th (G.Y.) Bn. HIGHLAND LIGHT INFANTRY.

(Erase heading not required.)

Instructions regarding War Diaries and Intelligence Summaries are contained in F. S. Regs., Part II and the Staff Manual respectively. Title pages will be prepared in manuscript.

Place	Date	Hour	Summary of Events and Information	Remarks and references to Appendices
H CAMP.	21.3.18.		Battalion make preparations for move tomorrow. Weather very good.	
	22.3.18.		Battalion moved to PROVEN station entraining there about 6.45 p.m. and after travelling all night arrived at HEILLY sur SOMME some 8 miles west of BRAY. Operation Order attached.	122
			For period from 23rd March to 31st March 1918 see special report.	

Signature

Lt.-Col.
Commanding 18th (G.Y.) Bn. HIGHLAND LIGHT INFANTRY.

18th (G.Y.) Bn. HIGHLAND LIGHT INFANTRY.

Narrative of Operations.

23rd March to 31st March, 1918.

23.3.18. Battalion entrained at PROVEN at 6.45 p.m.

24.3.18. Battalion detrained at MAILLY at 12.45 p.m. All packs and blankets were dumped and at 3.30 p.m. Battalion marched to J.22.b., and were conveyed in lorries from there to BRAY. Debussed at BRAY 7 p.m. and marched to CARNOY VALLEY arriving there at 9 p.m. At 11 p.m. orders were received for the Battalion to move up and take up a support position in BRIQUETERIE-MARICOURT Road.

25.3.18. Battalion marched off from CARNOY VALLEY at 12 midnight, and took up position at 1.30 a.m. from BRIQUATERIE inclusive southwards along MARICOURT Road for about 1000 yards. On northern flank touch was effected with Composite Battalion, as also on southern flank. The outposts in front were formed by Composite Battalion from southern edge of BERNAFAY wood A.4.b.6.9. to A.4.d.9.7. Patrols were sent out in front and to the flanks but no signs of enemy could be found. The remainder of the night was quiet.
At 7.45 a.m. a heavy barrage of H.E. was put down by the enemy and when this lifted further back the enemy were seen advancing in several waves from the eastwards, preceded by a heavy machine gun barrage. The outpost line of the Composite Battalion immediately broke and rushed through my lines in the BRIQUETERIE-MARICOURT Road. I only succeeded, with the assistance of my 2nd in Command, in stopping them and eventually got them into position on my left flank. I ordered my left flank Company to counter attack and restore the outpost line. This they most gallantly did, ably led by Capt. Mawer. Many of the enemy were killed and the remainder fell hurriedly back and took up a position 300 yards away where they kept up a harassing fire with their machine guns and snipers.
At 11 a.m. the enemy again advanced to the attack but were driven back by Lewis gun and rifle fire. At 11.30 a.m. position round BRIQUETERIE was heavily shelled and just then I received a report from the Cavalry Brigade whom I was in touch with on the left at A.4.b.4.9. that the enemy were pressing him hard from the northern corner of BERNAFAY wood and that considerable bodies of the enemy were seen moving westwards along the valley north of MONTAUBAN. I sent half of my reserve Company to help the Cavalry with orders to hold on to the last to prevent enemy breaking through along the LONGUEVAL-MARICOURT Road. Ammunition was very short and the only means of replenishing it was from Casualties.
At 2.30 p.m. the enemy were seen massing for attack again and commenced to advance, but were again driven back. At 4.45 p.m. the enemy again advanced, their objective being my left flank between BRIQUETERIE and where my left joined the Cavalry Brigade. For a short time the line gave but I organised a counter attack and restored the line, the enemy hastily retiring.
At 7 p.m. the enemy were again seen to be assembling as reinforcements had arrived, and about 7 p.m. attacked again. For a time the position was critical, as ammunition was exhausted, and the left of the line was driven back, but with the able assistance of my 2nd in Command we re-organised and advanced to our original position. The enemy then commenced to work away to both our flanks and heavy firing would be heard from these places. No farther attacks were made after 7.45 p.m. and the firing on our front gradually died away. Casualties were necessarily heavy owing to the heavy fighting throughout the day which commenced at 8 a.m. and died away at 8 p.m. The stretcher bearers and runners worked continuously during this period and did magnificent work.

26.3.18. At 2 a.m. reports came in saying that the Cavalry on the left and the Composite Battalion on my right had retired. As no orders to this effect had reached me I gave orders to left and right Coys. to bend back and make definite flanks and tohold on. Ammunition had arrived about 11.30 p.m.
At 3.30 a.m. orders were received to evacuate the line and to assemble in CARNOY VALLEY. The Battalion left their position which they had held for 24 hours, brought all wounded with them and assembled at CARNOY VALLEY at 5 a.m. The evacuation of the position with both flanks in the air was most ably carried out by my 2nd in Command, and unmolested by the enemy.
5.30 a.m. the Battalion was ordered to march backwards via CARNOY and FRICOURT.
7.30 a.m. Arrived at MEAULTE and orders were received to march southwards to BRAY. Battalion bivouacked at F.25.b.central at 8 a.m. Cookers arrived and men had a hot meal, the first they had since they entrained at PROVEN.
9.30 a.m. Owing to the weakness of the 9th Division the Battalion was ordered to fill in the gap on the BRAY-MEAULTE Road, between the 9th Division and the 105th Brigade. The 105th Brigade, less the 18th H.L.I. were ordered to proceed to MORLANCOURT.
The Battalion took up position, 2 Coys on the road, and 2 Coys. in support in a trench about 300 yards behind. About 1 p.m. enemy were seen advancing in extended order over ridge S.E. from MARI-COURT. About 2.30 p.m. received information that 105th Brigade on my right had retired. I immediately moved back my right and formed a definite flank, still keeping in touch with the 9th Division on my left on the MEAULTE-BRAY Road. I ordered one Coy. to take up position in strong points situated about K.5.a.& c. Liason was at once established between the Coy. and a Coy. of 12th H.L.I. situated near wood about K.12. I then sent in new Disposition report to Brigade H.Q.
2 p.m. Received information that enemy cavalry were seen approaching on my left. Gave orders to keep sharp look out.
At 4 p.m. orders were received from 106th Brigade that in the event of the 105th Brigade retiring on my right I was to conform to this movement, but remain outside MORLANCOURT and take up position in old G.H.Q. line. About this time I received information that troops of the 9th Division on my left were retiring. I gave orders for the leading Companies to withdraw towards MORLANCOURT, keeping one Company in strong points acting as rearguard until all companies had passed on their way to take up position in G.H.Q. line outside MORLANCOURT. The retirement was carried out in a fine orderly manner without haste, each Company going to its appointed place in G.H.Q. line and along railway embankment, the 12th H.L.I. being in defensive position on right about MORLANCOURT.
By 6 p.m. most of the 105th and 104th Brigades had passed the G.H.Q. line on their way to MORLANCOURT. The enemy who were now approaching in considerable force opened rifle and M.G. fire and a rearguard action was fought across high ground from G.H.Q. line towards MORLANCOURT. I gave orders that Companies were not to retire through the village but were to move across country to MORLANCOURT-VILLE sur ANCRE Road. This was carried out splendidly, the men withdrawing steadily and orderly by alternate companies maintaining a steady rifle and L.G. fire all the time. On arriving at the MORLANCOURT-VILLE sur ANCRE Road about 7.30 p.m. the Battalion proceeded to BUIRE and waited on the BUIRE-LAVIEVILLE Road for orders.

27.3.18. About 12.30 a.m. orders were recieved for Battalion to march to LAVIEVILLE and bivouac there. Arrived in billets about 1.30 a.m. Battalion had tea and settled down for well earned rest.
At 11 a.m. Battalion was ordered to move from LAVIEVILLE to valley in D.18.central and be in support to the rest of the Brigade who were relieving the 105th Brigade in the DERNACOURT-BUIRE line. Battalion moved off in artillery formation in good order and immediately came under shell fire, but the new position was reached with few casualties and the men lay sheltered in the bank and remained there for the rest of the day.

28.3.18.   ...m. orders were received to despatch two ... to reinforce
             the 17th M.... who were being attacked by the e... at D......
             Sent off at 9.30 p.m. W and X Coys under Major G......son. Had to
             Coys. had to go over the high ground in full observation of the
             enemy and immediately were met by an intense artillery barrage.
             Casualties were many but not a man hesitated but moved forward as
             on parade. Going down forward slopes near DERNACOURT these also
             came under Machine Gun fire. On reaching new position they were
             ordered to man the line at once which they did, W Coy. on the left
             of the Railway Bridge, and X Coy. on left. W Coy. became engaged
             with some of the enemy on the Railway bank. These they quickly
             disposed of, capturing a Machine Gun and killing all the team. The
             remainder of the Battalion was sent up at 7 p.m. to further reinforce
             the DERNACOURT line. The rest of the night was quiet.

29.3.18.   Quiet day. Enemy moving about in small parties on the southern
             side of the river. Our Lewis Guns and snipers caused many casualties
             Relieved by the 17th L.F. at 9.30 p.m. and marched back to Reserve
             position in D.18.central.

30.3.18.   Quiet and uneventful day. Battalion ordered to move to HEILLY at
             8.15 p.m. Arrived HEILLY at 10.45 p.m. and Battalion billeted in
             comfortable billets by 11 p.m.

General Remarks.

I cannot speak too highly of the conduct of all officers, N.C.O's
and men of the Battalion throughout the above operations. Without
water for long periods, no hot meals, very weary and footsore, there
was not a single grumble. Whether called upon to counter attack,
to hold on, to advance over the open, there was never any hesitation
and the manner in which they held on to the BRIQUATERIE position
although seriously short of ammunition deserves the highest praise.
They have come out of the battle with the spirit embued in them
that they are better than the enemy, notwithstanding the fact that
they were fighting a rearguard action most of the time, which tends
to lower the "morale" of all ranks.
I am indeed proud to command such a Battalion.

Our casualties have been heavy - 6 officers and 320 other ranks, but
I am confident that the enemy have suffered far heavier.
Every officer and N.C.O. and man has done well but I would specially
like to bring to the notice of the Brigadier-General Commanding
the following:-
          Major Gooderson, 2nd in Command,
          Capt. Macara,   Adjutant.
          Capt. Mawer,   O.C. Y Coy.
          2/Lt. Smith   O.C. W Coy.
          C.S.M. Turner. (Killed.)
          C.S.M. McQuillan.
          C.S.M. Bolton.
          Sgt. Armstrong.
          Sgt. Thomson.
          L/Cpl. Taylor.
          All Runners.
          All Stretcher Bearers.

31.3.18

BATTALION OPERATION ORDERS.

SECRET.   OPERATION ORDERS. No.118.   28.2.18.
                       HIGHLAND LIGHT INFANTRY.   Copy No.

1. The Battalion will move to WHITEMILL CAMP (B.14.d.) and take over from the LANCS. FUSILIERS.

2. Companies, on reaching WHITEMILL CAMP, will take over same lines as on previous occupation of said CAMP.

3. March. Order of march will be Headquarters, W, X, Y, and Z, and 300 yards interval will be allowed between Companies. Time of Parade and moving off will be notified later.

4. Brigade Working Party. O.C. Coys. will arrange for the men of the Brigade Working Party to have their packs ready, blankets rolled on packs, before parties move off for work tomorrow morning. O.C., W Coy. will arrange to have a hut cleared, and all Coys. will stack their packs, by Companies (distinctly separate) in said hut. Arrangements have been made for these packs to be taken by transport to WHITEMILL CAMP.

5. Baggage. Officers' Valises will be stacked on road opposite Z Coy's Cooker by 11 a.m. O.C. Coys. will detail 3 men, who will take full marching order, and proceed with G.S. wagon to WHITEMILL CAMP and there act as an unloading party for all transport coming down.

6. One half Limber per Coy. will report at Bn. H.Q. at 2 p.m. tomorrow to take down Lewis Guns, Magazines, and Coy. Mess Stores, which should all be ready for loading by 1.45 p.m.
1 Limber for H.Q. will report at 2 p.m. to convey stores.
1 Limber will report at 2 p.m. to convey Orderly Room and Sergeants' Mess Stores.

7. Defence Schemes, Maps, A.A. Mountings (the positions of the latter being pointed out on the ground) will be handed over, and receipts obtained and forwarded to the Orderly Room by 9 a.m. on 2nd March.

28.2.18.   (Sgd.) J.W. BOW. Lieut. & A/Adjt.
Issued at 9 p.m.   HIGHLAND LIGHT INFANTRY.

Copy No.1. War Diary.
      2. O. O. File.
      3.   Do.
      4. O.C. W Coy.
      5. O.C. X "
      6. O.C. Y "
      7. O.C. Z "
      8. Second in Command.
      9. Transport Officer.
     10. Quartermaster.

SECRET.

SPECIAL OPERATION ORDER No.119.
18th HIGHLAND LIGHT INFANTRY.

Copy No.
5.3.18.

Ref. Map. Map A.1/10000
            and Appendix D.

1. **INTENTION.** The Battalion will man the ARMY BATTLE ZONE on the night 4/5 March, and will take up position allotted to D Batt.

2. **INSTRUCTIONS.** (a). "Stand by". On receipt of orders to "STAND BY" Coys. will fall in on Parade Ground. O.C. Coys. will report to Adjutant when ready to move off.
   (b) Move. On receipt of orders to "MOVE" Coys. will move off in the following order. W, X, Y, Z, H.Q. Usual intervals and march discipline will be observed.
   (c) Disposition.
   No.1 Coy.(Outpost Coy.) W Coy. H.Q. at COMEDY FARM
                                                    (C.4.b.1.5.)
   No.2 Coy. X Coys H.Q. at KLEIST FARM (C.9.b.9.9.)
   No.3 Coy. Y Coy. H.Q. at MACDONALD FARM (C.9.d.8.5.)
   No.4 Coy.(Reserve Coy.) Z Coy. H.Q. at CANE TRENCH.
                                                    (C.9.b.2.1.)
   (d) Route. ELVERDINGHE. DAWSON'S CORNER. MAJENTA X ROADS. BOESINGHE-YPRES ROAD. TRACK B across CANAL. 5 CHEMINS ESTAMINET. UNNAMED TRACK to CANE POST. CORPS ROAD. N.E. of GOUNIER FARM. GROUSE AVENUE.
   (e) Dress: Fighting Order. (Haversack rations in haversack.)
   (f) Carrying party. O.C. Reserve Coy (Z Coy.) will detail three carrying parties of 1 N.C.O. and 4 men each to carry S.A.A. from Batt. H.Q.(GOUNIER FARM) to W, X, and Y Coys., and one additional party of 1 N.C.O. and 4 men to carry grenades to W Coy. Parties to report to Batt. H.Q. as soon as possible after the occupation of CANE TRENCH.

3. **AMMUNITION.** Transport Officer will arrange to send the following to FIVE CHEMINS ESTAMINET:-
   (a) One Limber S.A.A.
       One Limber Grenades No.23.
   (b) Two boxes S.A.A. per Coy., four boxes S.A.A. Batt.reserve
       (by mules.)

4. **MEDICAL.** Aid Post at GOUNIER FARM.

5. **REPORTS.** Coys. will report occupation of their areas by runner to Batt. H.Q. Code word "HERE".
   Batt. H.Q. GOUNIER FARM.
   Bde. H.Q. FUSILIER FARM.

Issued at 6.30 p.m.

(Sgd.) J. W. BOW. Lieut. & A/Adjt.
HIGHLAND LIGHT INFANTRY.

Copy No. 1. File.War Diary.
        2. O.O. File.
        3. Do.
        4. O.C. W Coy.
        5. O.C. X "
        6. O.C. Y "
        7. O.C. Z "
        8. Second in Command.
        9 Transport Officer.

SECRET.

ARMY BATTLE ZONE.

1. In order to test the accuracy of the dispositions of companies as shown on Map "A", O.C. Companies will forward to Batt. H.Q. a report under the following headings:-

   a. Any difficulty experienced by officers of units in finding their way by the map issued.
   b. Sufficiency of accommodation provided for Companies by appendix D, and accuracy of Appendix D. State accommodation of each post, pill box etc.
   c. Any improvements recommended in the distribution of platoons as shown on map A.
   d. Selection, if not already done, of actual fire position to be manned in case of attack. These to be in close proximity to accommodation provided in pill boxes.

2. All maps A and Appendix D to be returned to Orderly Room by noon 6.3.18. Reports as about para.1.a,b,c,d, to be rendered to Orderly Room by NOON 6.3.18.

SECRET.

OPERATION ORDERS. No. 120.
B.Bn. HIGHLAND LIGHT INFANTRY.

6.3.18.
Copy No.

Ref. Map. Sheet 20. S.W.4., and
Sheet 28. N.W.2. 1/10000.

1. The 106th Inf. Brigade will relieve the 104th Inf. Brigade in the line on the night of the 7/8 March.

2. The Batt. will relieve the 19th D.L.I. in support at LANGEMARK.
W Coy. H.L.I. will relieve Y Coy. 19th D.L.I.
X   "   "   "   "   Z "   "   "
Y   "   "   "   "   X "   "   "
Z   "   "   "   "   W "   "   "

3. INSTRUCTIONS.
a. Disposition.
W Coy. 2 platoons near KOEKUIT.
       2 platoons near CORPS LINE.
X Coy. at LANGEMARK.
Y Coy. at LANGEMARK.
Z Coy. at KOEKUIT.
Special Party at CANDLE TRENCH.

b. Guides. Guides to conduct Companies will be at PIG and WHISTLE at 5.30 p.m.

c. March. Coys. will move off from WHITEMILL CAMP in the following order:- W. Z. X. Y. H.Q. Special Party.

d. Time. 3 p.m. No Coy. to pass IRON CROSS before 5.30.p.m.

e. Route. ELVERDINGHE. DAWSON'S CORNER. CACTUS PONTOON. HUDDLESTON X ROADS. BIG CLUMP. IRON CROSS. CHIEN FARM. PIG and WHISTLE. Special Party will branch from Batt. at HUDDLESTON X ROADS, and will proceed via 5 CHEMINS ESTAMINET. DUCKWALK. via CANE POST to GOUNIER FARM ROAD. CANDLE TRENCH.

4. TRANSPORT. All vehicles to convey Lewis Guns, Baggage etc., to be ready to move off by 3 p.m. Vehicles will be offloaded as under:-
W Coy.(½ Limber at junction of RAILWAY TRACK and LANGEMARK-
                                                        -KOEKUIT ROAD.
      (½ Limber at NEY X ROADS.
X Coy. LANGEMARK STATION.
Y Coy. LANGEMARK STATION.
Z Coy. Junction of HUNTER STREET and LANGEMARK-KOEKUIT ROAD.
H.Q.   PIG and WHISTLE.
Special Party. Junction of CANE POST DUCKWALK and GOUNIER-VARNA
                        FARM ROAD.

5. BRIGADE WORKING PARTY. O.C. W Coy. will detail a Working Party of 1 Off. and 50 O.R. to be accommodated at BEAR TRENCH. On the morning of the 8th inst. the officer i/c of this Party will meet an R.E. officer at 7 a.m. at YORK HOUSE U.17.c.8.2.

6. PATROLS. Special Parties will patrol "NO MAN'S LAND" every night, commencing on 7th inst. Officers in charge of these parties will report at Bn. H.Q. on going to and returning from Patrol.

7. All Anti-Aircraft positions, trench stores, S.O.S. signals, maps, etc. will be taken over and report rendered with lists of stores taken over, to Batt. H.Q. by NOON 8.3.18.

8. MEDICAL. Aid Post at PIG and WHISTLE.

9. REPORTS. Completion of Relief will be notified to Batt. H.Q. by code word "SLICK".

Batt. H.Q.   PIG and WHISTLE.
Bde. H.Q.   VARNA FARM.

Issued at 9.30 p.m.   (Sgd.) J. W. BOW. Lieut. & A/Adjt.
                                    HIGHLAND LIGHT INFANTRY.

Copy No. 1 War Diary.
        2 O.O. File.
        3   Do.
        4 O.C. W Coy.
        5 O.C. X "
        6 O.C. Y "
        7 O.C. Z "
        8 Second in Command.
        9 Transport Officer.
       10 Quartermaster.
       11 2nd/Lt. H. Smith.
       12. "   T. Johnstone.

SECRET.

OPERATION ORDERS. No.121.
HIGHLAND LIGHT INFANTRY.

9.3.18.
Copy No.

Map. Sheet 28. 1/40000.

1. 35th Division to be withdrawn from the line of Reserve, and front alrea[dy] held will be taken over by 1st and 32nd Divisions.

2. On the night 9/10th March the 106th Brigade will be relieved in the line by the 1st and 97th Brigades. It is not certain whether the Battalion will be relieved by any other Battalion, but in the event of their being so, subsequent instructions will be issued.

3. If relieved, all maps, trench stores, A.A. positions will be handed over and receipts obtained and forwarded to Adjutant by noon tomorrow. If no Unit relieves, all maps will be taken out.

4. If it is not intended to relieve the Battalion, Coys. will march out from their present positions as soon as the two Battalions relieving the front line Battalions have passed up, but no Coy. will move without first notifying Bn. H.Q.

5. On being relieved, or vacating their present positions, Coys. will proceed to BOESINGHE and entrain there at midnight, (Summer time) for International Corner, Z and half W proceeding via HUNTER STREET, the other half W Coy. by RAILWAY STREET.
X and Y via LANGEMARK - PILKEM ROAD.

6. Battalion will be accommodated in H Camp A.9.d.9.9. and will be ready to move at short notice anywhere.
If relieved, completion of relief will be telephoned by Code Word "LUCK"

9.3.18.

(Sgd.) J. W. BOW. Lieut. & A/Adjt.
HIGHLAND LIGHT INFANTRY.

Copy No.1. War Diary.
     2. O.O. File.
     3.   Do.
     4. O.C. W Coy.
     5. O.C. X "
     6. O.C. Y "
     7. O.C. Z "
     8. Second in Command.
     9. Transport Officer.
    10. Quartermaster.

SECRET.   OPERATION ORDERS. No.122.   22.3.18.
                       HIGHLAND LIGHT INFANTRY.   Copy No. 1

1. The 35th Division is under orders to be prepared to entrain tonight.
   The 106th Infantry Brigade will entrain at PROVEN STATION.
   Train No.1 leaving at ZERO hour 12 o'clock, midnight.

2. the Battalion less 1 Coy. will entrain at PROVEN at ZERO hour plus
   21 hours and travel in No.7 train.

3. Z Coy. and Cooker team will entrain at ZERO hour plus 18 hours and
   travel in No.6 train.

4. Y Coy. with its cooker and Lewis Gun Limber will proceed to PROVEN
   STATION for the purpose of entraining the Brigade and will report
   there at ZERO minus four hours. This Coy. will travel on No.7 train
   with the rest of the Battalion.

5. Transport 1st and 2nd line will entrain with the Battalion and will
   arrive at the entraining station three hours before the departure of
   the train. Coys. will arrive 1½ hours before the departure of the
   train.

6. All trains consist of 1 Officer carriage, 17 flat trucks and 30 covered
   trucks. Each flat truck will take an average of four axles. Each
   covered truck will take 6 H.D. horses or 8 L.D. horses or mules or
   40 men.

7. Coys. will entrain with the following rations:- (1) Iron rations.
   (2) Unexpended portion of day's rations. (3) Next day's rations. The
   second day's ration will be carried on the supply wagon which will
   entrain with the Battalion.

8. Three lorries have been allotted to the Battalion to carry blankets
   and surplus stores. Coy. Mess Stores will be carried on their L.G.
   Limbers.

9. Transport Officer will allot 1 limber for four L.G's of Headquarters
   and Orderly Room Boxes.

10. Blankets will be rolled by sections and securely tied also well labelled
    Officers' valises and deed boxes and all blankets will be stacked at
    the entrance to the camp for loading on lorries and G.S. Wagons.

11. All Limbers will be loaded this afternoon.

    Issued at 12 noon.   (Sgd.)W.F.M. MAGARA. Capt. & Adjt.
                                               HIGHLAND LIGHT INFANTRY.

    Copy No.1. War Diary.
         2. O.O.File.
         3.   Do.
         4. O.C. W Coy.
         5. O.C. X "
         6. O.C. Y "
         7. O.C. Z "
         8. Second in Command.
         9. Transport Officer.
        10. Quartermaster.
        11. Medical Officer.

Instructions regarding War Diaries and Intelligence Summaries are contained in F.S. Regs, Part II and the Staff Manual respectively. Title pages will be prepared in manuscript.

WAR DIARY From 1st to 30th April 1918 inclusive
INTELLIGENCE=SUMMARY.
18th (G.Y.) Bn. HIGHLAND LIGHT INFANTRY.
Index No.27.

Army Form C. 2118.

(Erase heading not required.)

Place	Date	Hour	Summary of Events and Information	Remarks and references to Appendices
HEILLY.	1.4.18.		Battalion in rest in billets at HEILLY. Day spent in cleaning up and re-organising Companies. Weather good.	
	2.4.18.		Battalion still resting, cleaning and re-organising at HEILLY. Weather changeable: some heavy rain fell in the afternoon.	
	3.4.18.		Battalion still in HEILLY. No training other than specialists could be carried out, so men were allowed further rest, which was really much needed. Weather changeable.	
	4.4.18.		Battalion still in HEILLY, but under 30 minutes' orders to move. No training. Weather very wet.	
	5.4.18.		Battalion at HEILLY and "under orders" "Stand to" orders at dawn. (5 a.m.) Battalion ordered up to support Australian Division at BAZIEUX.	
BAZIEUX.	6.4.18.		Battalion in support to Australians at BAZIEUX. Notified at 12 noon to evacuate position and after marching some ten miles we took over from 19/20th LONDON REGT. (47th Division) South of AVELUY WOOD. After wandering about in a downpour of rain the Guides meeting us lost their way. We eventually got our position about dawn.	
AVELUY WOOD.	7.4.18.		Battalion in the line at AVELUY WOOD. Situation normal. Artillery fairly quiet. Weather very cold with some showers.	
near ALBERT.	8.4.18.		Battalion in the line. Situation very quiet. Weather cold but dry.	
	9.4.18.		Do. Do.	
	10.4.18.		Do. Weather very fine. Several aerial combats were witnessed during the day. Two enemy planes were brought down.	
	11.4.18.		Battalion in the line. Weather good. Battalion was relieved by 19th D.L.I. (104th Inf. Brigade. Operation Order attached.	123
HEDAUVILLE.	12.4.18.		Battalion moved to Brigade Reserve at HEDAUVILLE. Day quiet generally. "Stand to" observed at dawn. (4 a.m.)	
	13.4.18.		Battalion in Brigade Reserve. Our Artillery 'opened up' and were very active, during the night. Bathing carried out during the day.	
	14.4.18.		Battalion in Brigade Reserve. Weather very dull. Battalion preparing to move into the line. Battalion relieved the SHERWOOD FORESTERS. Relief completed 11 p.m. 1 man killed and 1 wounded. Artillery on both sides was comparatively quiet. Operation Order attached.	
BOUZINCOURT.	15.4.18.		Battalion in the line at BOUZINCOURT (near ALBERT.) Fairly quiet day. Enemy artillery sent 50 4.2s and 5.9s into village about 12 - 12.30 p.m. Night quiet.	124
	16.4.18.		Battalion in the line. Observation very bad. Our Artillery very active throughout the night. Inter-Company relief carried out without incident.	

WAR DIARY
INTELLIGENCE SUMMARY

(Erase heading not required.)

Army Form C. 2118.

Place	Date	Hour	Summary of Events and Information	Remarks and references to Appendices
BOUZINCOURT	17.4.18.		Battalion in the line. Light shelling of front line at "stand to". 150 m.m. shells on village. No action followed. Weather dull.	
	18.4.18.		Battalion in the line. Machine guns fairly active. Weather changeable: some rain in afternoon. Line quiet. Battalion relieved by 17th Royal SCOTS, and went into Support.	
	19.4.18.		Battalion in Support in BOUZINCOURT: 2 Companies at disposal of the Officers Commanding Left and Right Battalions in the line. Remainder of Battalion engaged on working parties. Some artillery activity on both sides. 1 Officer and 3 O.R. wounded.	
	20.4.18.		Battalion in Support. Word arrived that Battalion would be relieved, but this was cancelled. Day very quiet, but enemy 'opened up' with Gas shells at night. Our artillery gave him a good return and silenced him.	
	21.4.18.		Battalion still in Support to 104th Brigade. Enemy shelled Battalion Headquarters for 2 hours and one direct hit landed on Headquarters cellar, but it was a 'dud'. Battalion relieved at 9.20 p.m. and marched through gas barrage to HEDAUVILLE.	
HEDAUVILLE	22.4.18.		Battalion in Divisional Reserve in tents and shelters outside village. Enemy shelled adjacent valley, but did no damage. Weather good. Our Division (35th) and 38th Division 'go over' tonight, but our Brigade (105th) are not 'in'.	125
	23.4.18.		Battalion in Divisional Reserve. Weather good. Battalion proceeded to line in Left Brigade Sector. Night quiet. No Casualties. Operation Order attached.	
MARTINSART	24.4.18.		Battalion in line opposite AVELUY WOOD. Visibility very low. No activity on either side. Men engaged on improvement of line. 1 man wounded.	
	25.4.18.		Battalion in line. Very misty morning. Very slight enemy activity. Thundery, and some showers during the day. 2 men wounded.	
	26.4.18.		Battalion in line. Another misty day. Our Commanding Officer (Lieut. Colonel R.R. LAWRENSON, D.S.O.) was wounded seriously about 12 noon while on tour round the line.	
	27.4.18.		Battalion in line. Very clear day, but very cold. Battalion very much regret the great loss of our C.O. who died in hospital today. He had been with the Battalion since its arrival in France over 2 years ago, and the loss is felt greatly by all ranks.	
	28.4.18.		Battalion in line. Weather very changeable. Day and night very quiet.	
	29.4.18.		Do. Do. Battalion relieved by 19th D.L.I. (104th Brigade.) and marched to tents and shelters between FORCEVILLE and HEDAUVILLE.	
HEDAUVILLE	30.4.18.		Battalion in Divisional Reserve. Weather very wet. Day quiet except for usual artillery work.	

Mahone Buford for, Major,

Comdg. 18th (G.Y.) BN. HIGHLAND LIGHT INFANTRY.

SECRET.   OPERATION ORDER. No.123.   11.4.18.
             HIGHLAND LIGHT INFANTRY.   Copy No. 1.

Map Reference 57D.S.E.
              1/20,000.

1. The 106th Infantry Brigade will be relieved in the left Sector by the 104th Infantry Brigade on the night 11/12th April 1918. The Battalion will be relieved by the 19th D.L.I.

2. Companies will be relieved as follows:-
      Y Coy. D.L.I. relieves Z Coy. H.L.I.
      W "   "   "   W "   "
      X "   "   "   Y "   "
      Z "   "   "   X "   "

3. Guides for incoming Battalion will report to Battalion Headquarters at 7.p.m. as follows:-
      W Coy. 1 guide per platoon and Coy. Headquarters.
      X, Y, and Z Coys. 1 guide per Coy.

4. O.C., Z Coy will be responsible that the relieving Coy. are put in touch with Units on the flanks.
   O.C., Y Coy. will turn over Wire Dump to relieving Coy.

5. All Coys. will turn over Dispositions and information known of the enemy. On completion of relief Coys. will march to Billets at HEDAUVILLE.
   Route. CROSS Roads W.1.D. BOUZINCOURT/HEDAUVILLE.

6. Guides will meet Coys. at CROSS ROADS P.34.c. to guide Coys. into billets.

7. All empty petrol tins will be carried out on relief.
   Trench stores, including tools, extra bandoliers S.A.A. will be collected at Coy. Dumps and carefully handed over, receipts obtained, and forwarded to Bn. Headquarters by 12 noon 12.4.18.

8. Relief complete will be reported by runner to Bn. Headquarters. This runner will bring a D.L.I. runner with him to show him the route to Headquarters. Code word "SLICK".

                        (Sgd.) J.W. BOW. Lieut. & A/Adjt.
                               HIGHLAND LIGHT INFANTRY.

SECRET.   OPERATION ORDER. No.124.   14.4.18.
                       HIGHLAND LIGHT INFANTRY.

1. The 106th Infantry Brigade will relieve the 105th Infantry Brigade
   in the right Sector. The Battalion will relieve the SHERWOOD
   FORESTERS in the left sub Sector.

2. DISPOSITIONS.
      Front line Coys;   Left Coy.   W Coy.
                         Right Coy. X Coy.
         Support Coy.   Z Coy.
         Reserve Coy.   Y Coy.

3. GUIDES. Two Guides per Coy. as under will be at X Roads W.13.a.5.9.
   BOUZINCOURT at 9 p.m.
      W Coy. 2 Guides from Lt. Morgan's Coy.
      X Coy. 2 Guides from Capt. Morell's Coy.
      Z Coy. Right half Coy.   One Guide from Capt. Morell's Coy.
             Left half Coy.   One Guide from Lt. Morgan's Coy.
      Y Coy. Right half Coy.   One Guide from Capt. Morell's Coy.
             Left half Coy.   One Guide from Lt. Morgan's Coy.

4. MARCH. Coys. will move off in the following order:- W. X. Z. Y. H.Q.
   100 yards interval will be observed between Coys.
   ROUTE. HEDAUVILLE - BOUZINCOURT.
   TIME. 7.45 p.m.

5. Limbers to carry Lewis Guns and Water will move with Companies
   under arrangements notified later. These limbers will be off loaded
   at X Roads W.13.a.5.9.
   A limber conveying S.A.A. and L.G. ammunition will be off loaded
   at road junction W.8.a.4.3. O.C. Y Coy. will be responsible that
   ammunition dump for Battalion is formed at this point.

6. PATROLS. Companies in the front line will actively patrol their
   fronts during the hours of darkness.

7. All trench stores, S.A.A., Bombs, tools, etc. will be taken over
   on relief and lists forwarded to Battn. Headquarters at DAWN.15.4.18.
   Tactical progress and Patrol reports to reach Battn. Headquarters
   at DAWN daily.

8. REPORTS. Battn. Headquarters at W.7.d.6.7.
            Brigade Headquarters at SENLIS V.10.d.8.2.

9. Completion of relief will be reported by wire and runner to Battn.
   Headquarters. Code Word "WHISKEY".

        Issued at 12 noon.   (Sgd.) W.F.M. MACARA. Capt. & Adjt.
                                            HIGHLAND LIGHT INFANTRY.

   Copy No. 1 War Diary.
           2 O.O. File.
           3. Do.
           4 O.C. W Coy.
           5 O.C. X "
           6 O.C. Y "
           7 O.C. Z "
           8 2nd in Command.
           9 Transport Officer.
          10. Quartermaster.

SECRET. OPERATION ORDER. No.125.   23.4.18.
HIGHLAND LIGHT INFANTRY.   Copy No.1

I. The 106th Inf. Brigade will relieve the 105th Inf. Brigade in the Left Brigade front on the night of the 23/24th. Battalion will be disposed as follows as right Battalion:-
W Coy. will relieve 1 Coy. D.L.I. in Front Line.
X   "   "   "   1 " North Staffs. in Valley.
Y   "   "   "   In Support.
Z   "   "   "   In Corps Line.

II. Guides, for Coys. except Z Coy. will be at X roads W.1.d.8.6. Z Coy's guides will be at X roads V.6.d.4.0.

III. Coys. will move off at 8.30 p.m. in the following order:-
W, X, Y, Z, 200 yards between Coys. Route:- HEDAUVILLE - BOUZINCOURT road to point V.11.b.1.4. thence cross country to W.1.d.8.7.

IV. All Trench Stores, Spare Ammunition, Air photos, S.O.S. Signals, Schemes of Work to be taken over, receipts taken and forwarded to the Adjutant by dawn next day. Separate receipt will be taken for tools taken over, care being taken that Numbers are checked before signing receipts, as a similar number have to be handed over to 105th Inf. Brigade from Battalion reserve.

V. Coys. will send down 1 runner after taking over line, for duty with Battalion Headquarters. He will be rationed and stay at Headquarters.

VI. Completion of relief will be sent to Battalion Headquarters by wire. Code word "AGAIN".

23.4.18.
(Signed.) W.F.M. MACARA.
Capt. & Adjt.
HIGHLAND LIGHT INFANTRY.

Copy No.1. War Diary.
2. O.O. File.
3.   Do.
4. O.C. W Coy.
5. O.C. X "
6. O.C. Y "
7. O.C. Z "
8. 2nd in Command.

35

Army Form C. 2118.

Instructions regarding War Diaries and Intelligence Summaries are contained in F.S. Regs., Part II. and the Staff Manual respectively. Title pages will be prepared in manuscript.

WAR DIARY From 1st to 31st May 1918 inclusive.
INTELLIGENCE SUMMARY 18th (G.Y.) Bn. HIGHLAND LIGHT INFANTRY.
Index No.28.

(Erase heading not required.)

28 P
6 sheets

Vol 28

Place	Date	Hour	Summary of Events and Information	Remarks and references to Appendices
RUBEMPRE.	1.5.18		Battalion on the move. Battalion moved to RUBEMPRE from HEDAUVILLE arriving about 6 p.m. (10 miles) Weather very warm.	
	2.5.18.		Battalion in rest at RUBEMPRE under canvas. Weather very warm.	
	3.5.18.		Battalion cleaning up and training for shooting and other competitions. Weather still good.	
	4.5.18.		Battalion in training. A good deal of specialist training was carried out, chiefly Lewis Gun and Bombing, this being in accordance with instructions received that each man in the Unit ought to be able to handle a Lewis Gun or throw a Bomb with good effect.	
	5.5.18.		Battalion in training. Inter-platoon and Pool shooting Competitions practised. Some good scoring Specialist training as before.	
	6.5.18.		Battalion in training as before. Usual practices fired at range. Bayonet Fighting and Physical training classes carried on under Instructor. Weather continues to be very good.	
	7.5.18.		Battalion in training as before. Weather still very good.	
	8.5.18.		Battalion still in training. Weather dull, with some rain. Clear in afternoon.	
	9.5.18.		Battalion in training. 2 Companies carried out a practice attack under inspection of Army Commander General Byng. In afternoon semi-final of Divisional Football Competition was played, the Battalion team beating 19th Northumberland Fus. by 3 goals to 2. Weather very good.	
	10.5.18.		Battalion in training as before. Specialist training also carried out. Weather very good. Corps Commander presented Ribbons of Honours won by various officers and other ranks in the Battalion.	
	11.5.18.		Battalion in training. Weather good. Final of Divisional Football Competition was played and Battalion team won it by scoring 6 goals against 15th CHESHIRE REGT.	
	12.5.18.		Battalion in training as before. Weather very good.	
	13.5.18.		Battalion carried out usual training, shooting being carried on well into the afternoon. Weather very good.	
	14.5.18.		Battalion still in training. While one company was on the range shooting, a long range enemy shell landed in the vicinity severely wounding one man.	
	15.5.18.		Battalion in training as beofre. Weather very warm.	
	16.5.18.		Do. Several officers reconnoitred the section of the line which the Battalion has to take over about two days hence.	

T2134. Wt. W708—776. 500000. 4/15. Sir J.C.&S.

Army Form C. 2118.

WAR DIARY
INTELLIGENCE-SUMMARY
(Erase heading not required.)

Instructions regarding War Diaries and Intelligence Summaries are contained in F. S. Regs., Part II. and the Staff Manual respectively. Title pages will be prepared in manuscript.

Place	Date	Hour	Summary of Events and Information	Remarks and references to Appendices
RUBEMPRE.	17.5.18.		Battalion training as before in forenoon. Weather still extremely warm. Afternoon spent in pre-paring for move next day. Weather very warm.	
	18.5.18.		Battalion on the move to VARENNES, arriving about 10.30 p.m. going into bivouacs and tents for the night. Operation Order attached.	127
VARENNES.	19.5.18.		Battalion moved to the line relieving 16th ROYAL WELSH FUSILIERS on Left Battalion Front of AVELUY WOOD near ALBERT. Casualties:- 1 Officer and 2 other ranks killed and 8 Other Ranks wounded. Operation Order attached.	128
AVELUY WOOD.	20.5.18.		Battalion in the Line. Enemy artillery was very active in the earlier part of night 19/20 and our artillery replied with very harassing fire practically all night. Patrols out during night, but saw no signs of enemy.	
	21.5.18.		Battalion in the line. Weather very good. A direct hit by an enemy shell on one of our M.G. Posts killed the whole crew of 7 without in any way damaging the gun. Usual harassing fire carried out by our artillery. Enemy artillery normal. Owing to the continuous patrolling of the front by our aeroplanes the enemy artillery and machine guns have been very inactive and very little movement observed behind the lines. 2 Observers wounded. Battalion relieved by 18th LANC. FUS. No Casualties during relief. O.O attached	129
HEDAUVILLE.	22.5.18.		Battalion in reserve, bivouacked near HEDAUVILLE. This camp, being in the vicinity of several batteries of guns, was shelled on several occasions but no casualties occurred. Weather dull. Some rain.	
	23.5.18.		Battalion in reserve. Usual artillery activity in back areas. Situation normal.	
	24.5.18.		Do.	
AVELUY WOOD.	25.5.18.		Battalion moved into the line, relieving 18th LANC. FUSILIERS. 4 O.R.s wounded. About 9.30 p.m. when Battalion was paraded ready to move to the line an enemy aeroplane came down to within about 300 yards and opened machine gun fire on the camp. Five of our planes immediately swooped down and forced the enemy to descend and the occupants were made prisoners. Operation Order attached.	~~129~~
	26.5.18.		Battalion in the line. Situation very quiet. Practically no action from either side. Weather exceptionally warm. 1 O.R. wounded	
	27.5.18.		Battalion in the line. About 4 p.m. enemy opened up a heavy barrage using shells of all calibres and also some gas shells. Our artillery replied effectively. No machine guns took part in the action. A good deal of movement was observed behind the enemy lines and was dispersed by artillery.	

Army Form C. 2118.

WAR DIARY
INTELLIGENCE SUMMARY

3.

(Erase heading not required.)

Instructions regarding War Diaries and Intelligence Summaries are contained in F.S. Regs., Part II. and the Staff Manual respectively. Title pages will be prepared in manuscript.

Place	Date	Hour	Summary of Events and Information	Remarks and references to Appendices
AVELUY WOOD.	28.5.18.		Battalion in the line. In reply to S.O.S. about 3.30 a.m. our artillery put down a very heavy barrage and apparently did considerable damage to enemy positions. Enemy's barrage was very heavy, especially in MARTINSART VALLEY. The rest of the day was ususually quiet 1 Officer wounded.	
	29.5.18.		Battalion in the line. Enemy artillery was very active, firing about 250 - 300 rounds H.E. all calibres in Support Area. Otherwise the front was quiet and nothing of interest happened. Work was carried on repairing and improving the front and communication trenches. Weather very warm. Battalion relieved about 10 p.m. Casualties:- 1 officer killed and 4 O.R. wounded.	
HEDAUVILLE.	30.5.18.		Battalion in reserve at HEDAUVILLE. Weather very warm. Day spent in cleaning up and resting. Enemy shelled somewhat near the camp but no casualties occurred.	
	31.5.18.		Battalion in reserve. Weather very fine. Situation normal. Day very quiet.	

[signature]
A/Comdg. 18th (G.Y.) Bn. HIGHLAND LIGHT INFANTRY.

SECRET.   OPERATION (MOVE) ORDER. No.127   Copy No.
              'B' HIGHLAND LIGHT INFANTRY.   17.5.18.

Ref. Sheet 1/40,000. 57D.
     57D. S.E. 1/20,000.

1. The 106 Infantry Brigade will march to Forward Area on the 18th May 1918.

2. The Battalion, less Battalion Details, Quartermaster's and Trans--port personnel will march to billets at VARENNES.
   Starting point. Road junction T.14.a.4.3.
   Time.   2.15 p.m.
   Order of march. H.Q., W., X., Y., Z Coys.
   Route.   HERISSART - TOUTENCOURT - HARPONVILLE - VARENNES.
   Distance.   West of TOUTENCOURT-100 yards between Coys.
                                        300 yards between Battalions.
               In and East of TOUTENCOURT- 200 yards between Coys.
                                           500 yards between Battalions.
   Dress: Fighting Order.

3. TRANSPORT. Cookers (filled with water) and Lewis Gun Limbers will march with Companies. Water carts, filled, will march with Bn. H.Q.
   BAGGAGE. All Officers' valises, men's packs, mess stores, etc. will be dumped at Q.M. Stores by 9.30 a.m.

4. Battn. Details, Transport and Q.M. personnel will move to HARPON--VILLE UNDER ORDERS TO BE ISSUED LATER.

5. REPORTS. On the march, to the head of Column.
            In VARENNES, to Battn. H.Q.(position to be notified later)
   Present Brigade H.Q. will close at 6 p.m. on the 19th May and re-open at V.4.central at same hour.

                          (Signed.) W.F.M. MACARA. Capt. & Adjt.
                                    'B' HIGHLAND LIGHT INFANTRY.

Issued at 8 p.m.

Copy No. 1. War Diary.
         2. O.O. File.
         3.   Do.
         4. O.C. W Coy.
         5. O.C. X "
         6. O.C. Y "
         7. O.C. Z "
         8. 2nd In Command.
         9. Medical Officer.
        10. Transport Officer.
        11. Quartermaster.

SECRET. OPERATION (RELIEF) ORDER No.128. Copy No.
'B' HIGHLAND LIGHT INFANTRY. 17.5.18.

Ref. Sheet 57D. S.E. 1/20,000.

1. The 106 Infantry Brigade will relieve the 113 Infantry Brigade in the AVELUY CENTRE SECTOR on the night 19/20th May as follows:
ROYAL SCOTS will relieve 14th R.W.F. (Right Battalion.)
B. HIGH.L.I.   "   "   16th R.W.F. (Left Battalion.)
A. HIGH.L.I.   "   "   13th R.W.F. (In reserve.)

2. DISPOSITION OF BATTALION as follows:-
Right front Coy.   Y Coy. H.L.I. will relieve A Coy. 16th R.W.F.
Left front Coy.   Z "   "   "   "   D "   "
Right Reserve Coy. X "   "   "   "   B "   "
Left Reserve Coy.   W "   "   "   "   C "   "

3. MARCH.
Starting Point. Cross Roads P.26.c.1.4.
Time.   8 p.m. Leading Coy. will not pass N - S grid between V.5 and V.6. before 9.15 p.m.
Order of March. Y, Z, X, W Coys. H.Q.
Route.   P.26.c.1.4. - Cross Roads P.32.central - P.33.c & d. - HEDAUVILLE - ARTILLERY HOUSE - TRACK to V.12.b.
Distance.   100 yards between platoons. 200 yards between Coys.
Guides.   Guides, 4 per Coys, and 2 for Battn. H.Q. will be at track junction V.12.b. ay 9.15 p.m.

4. Spare ammunition, air photos, S.O.S. signals, trench stores, tools Defence Schemes, and Schemes of Work will be taken over on relief. Receipts will be forwarded to Adjutant with R.P.R. next morning.

5. REPORTS.
Completion of Relief will be reported to Battn. H.Q. Code word "STICK IT".
Battn. H.Q. at W.7.b.1.5.
Brigade H.Q. V.4.central.

Issued at 8 p.m.   (Signed.) W.F.M. MACARA. Capt. & Adjt.
                                        'B' HIGHLAND LIGHT INFANTRY.

Copy No.1. War Diary.
     2. O.O. File.
     3.   Do.
     4. O.C. W Coy.
     5. O.C. X "
     6. O.C. Y "
     7. O.C. Z "
     8. 2nd in Command.
     9. Medical Officer.
    10. Transport Officer.
    11. Quartermaster.
    12. 16th R.W.F.

SECRET.

ADMINISTRATIVE INSTRUCTIONS
issued with
OPERATION ORDERS No.127 and No.128.
'B' HIGHLAND LIGHT INFANTRY.

Copy No.
17.5.'18.

1. The Battn. will march to VARENNES tomorrow as per Operation (Move) Order No.127.
Lieut. Hutchison, with 1 N.C.O. per Coy. will meet Staff Captain at Town Major's Office VARENNES at 10 a.m. on morning of the 18th inst. when billets will be allotted. These N.C.O.s will report to Lieut. Hutchison at 9.30 a.m. and must be able to ride a bicycle.

2. Camp will be left standing in present position and all tents, in--cluding those at Transport Lines, will be handed over to Town Major. Receipts will be obtained and forwarded to Brigade H.Q.

3. BATTLE SURPLUS. The following officers and O.R. will be left behind as Battle Surplus:-
    2nd in Command.
    2nd Lieut. Smith.
    2nd Lieut. Bryce.
    2nd Lieut. Johnstone.
    2nd Lieut. Orr.
    Adjutant.
    Assist/Adjutant.
    Coy. S.M.s of W and Z Coys.
    33% of Signallers of H.Q. and all Coys.
    33% Runners of H.Q. and all Coys.
    1 Sgt. 1 Cpl. and 1 L/Cpl. per Coy.
    1 Rifle Bomber, 1 Scout, 2 Lewis Gunners per Platoon.

4. Transport. Q.M. Stores and all Details (including Battle Surplus) will be accommodated at HARPONVILLE. Transport and Q.M. Stores will move on the 19th inst. and take over lines and accommodation of the Battalion whom they relieve in the line.
Details will move to HARPONVILLE on the 20th inst.

5. The Adjutant will detail an Advance party of 1 Officer and 4 N.C.O.s to meet Staff Captain at the Town Major's Office, HARPONVILLE at 10 a.m. 19th inst. to take over billets. Adjutant will also de--tail 1 Officer to hand over present Camp to Town Major. This Officer will remain behind at RUBEMPRE for 3 hours after Details have moved out. He will receive and investigate any Claims which may be lodged, and obtain Certificate from Town Major that all billets and Camp have been left clean.

6. One lorry for the Battalion will report at Church RUBEMPRE AS follows:-
May 18th. 9 a.m. To move Battalion to VARENNES.
  19th. 9 a.m. To move Q.M. Stores to HARPONVILLE.
Adjutant will detail 1 guide to meet lorry each day.

7. Transport Officer will arrange to move Officers' baggage, Coy. Cookers, and Water carts from VARENNES on the 19th May, when Battn. moves forward to front line.

Issued at 8 p.m.
            (Signed.)W.F.M. MACARA.Capt. & Adjt.
              'B' HIGHLAND LIGHT INFANTRY.

Copies as per Operation Order 127.

SECRET.   OPERATION (RELIEF) ORDER No.129.   Copy No.
          'B' HIGHLAND LIGHT INFANTRY.   21.5.18.

1. The 106 Inf. Brigade will be relieved on the night 21/22nd May by the 104 and 105 Inf. Brigades extending their front inwards.

2. The Battalion will be relieved by 2 Coys. of the 18th L.F. (Less one platoon) as follows:-
   X Coy. L.F. will take over SAUCHIEHALL front and support lines
       from Z and Y Coys. H.L.I. through W.9.a.7.5.
   Z Coy. L.F. less 1 platoon will take over SAUCHIEHALL RESERVE
       line from W and X Coy. H.L.I.

3. GUIDES.
   O.C. Coys. will furnish the following guides to bring in their Relief:-
   Number. Front Line. 1 Guide per post.
           Support & Reserve Line. 1 Guide per platoon.
   Place. Road Junction W.2.b.4.1.
   Time.   10 p.m.

4. All other details of Relief to be arranged by O.C. Coys. concerned Garrisons and posts not taken over by relieving Units will remain in position until remainder of Company has been relieved.

5. On completion of Relief Companies will move to following loaction.
   W Coy.   P.29.c.
   X Coy.   Will be accommodated in support line of PURPLE SYSTEM with Lewis Guns in front line of PURPLE SYSTEM from E and W grid between W.7. and W1. to E and W grid between W.1. and Q.31.
   Y Coy.   P.29.c.
   Z Coy.   P.29.c.
   Batt. H.Q. P.29.c.

6. Advance Party. On receipt of these orders O.C. X Coy. will send 1 Officer and 4 O.R. to reconnoitre accommodation allotted in PURPLE SYSTEM and to act as guides for his Coy. after Relief.

7. Trench Stores, tools, Defence Schemes, S.O.SSignals, and S.A.A. will be handed over on relief.
   The two extra bandoliers of S.A.A. per man will be taken out on relief.
   Receipts for Trench Stores, etc. will be forwarded to Adjutant by NOON 22.5.18.

8. Completion of Relief will be reported to Battn. H.Q. Code Word "CHEER".

21.5.18.   (Signed.) W.F.M. MACARA. Capt. & Adjt
                                      'B' HIGHLAND LIGHT INFANTRY.

WAR DIARY from 1st to 30th June inclusive.

Army Form C. 2118.

INTELLIGENCE=SUMMARY 18th (G.Y.) Bn. HIGHLAND LIGHT INFANTRY.

Index No. 29.

(Erase heading not required.)

Place	Date	Hour	Summary of Events and Information	Remarks and references to Appendices
MARTINSART.	1.6.18.		Battalion in Purple Defence System in Support to 17th LANCS.FUSILIERS. Weather very good. Heavy Artillery activity.	
	2.6.18.		Battalion in line. Situation normal. Battalion moved into line at night taking over position to right of AVELUY WOOD.	
	3.6.18.		Do. Some artillery and aircraft activity. Weather very good. Several concentrations fired by Artillery into enemy positions evidently did considerable damage. Weather very good.	
	4.6.18.		Do. Weather very good. Situation normal.	
	5.6.18.		Do. Aircraft generally active; our planes doing good work and keeping the lines clear. Inter-Company relief carried out.	
	6.6.18.		Battalion in line. Working and wiring carried out. Weather very good. Situation normal.	
	7.6.18.		Do. Work as usual carried out improving the line. Do. Do.	
	8.6.18.		Do. Do. Do. We heavily gassed the enemy's defences in the rear of his lines, sending over some 1200 gas shells and doing considerable damage.	
	9.6.18.		Battalion in line. Weather continues to be very good, only occasional sharp showers of rain have fallen. Work as usual. Inter-Company relief carried out. The enemy lines were again gassed successfully. Do. Do. Another successful bombard-	
	10.6.18.		Battalion in line. Weather still very good. Work as usual. Situation normal.	
	11.6.18.		Do. -ment of gas shells was carried out.	
	12.6.18.		Battalion in line. Weather very good. Work as usual. Situation normal.	
	13.6.18.		Do. Do.	
	14.6.18.		Do. Do.	
	15.6.18.		Do. Do.	
	16.6.18.		Battalion in line. Weather very good. Battalion relieved by 6th ROYAL WEST KENT REGT., 37th Inf. Brigade. During the tour in the line the Battalion had about 70 casualties, this being heavy in comparison to the somewhat normal conditions. Battalion marched to WARLOY. Operation Order attached.	130
WARLOY-BAILLON.	17.6.18.		Battalion in billets. Weather very good. Battalion marched to billets at ARQUEVES where the Brigade is in G.H.Q. Reserve, and under 9 hours' notice. Operation Order attached.	131

Army Form C. 2118.

WAR DIARY

INTELLIGENCE SUMMARY
2.

(Erase heading not required.)

Instructions regarding War Diaries and Intelligence Summaries are contained in F. S. Regs., Part II. and the Staff Manual respectively. Title pages will be prepared in manuscript.

Place	Date	Hour	Summary of Events and Information	Remarks and references to Appendices
ARQUEVES.	18.6.18.		Battalion in billets. Men resting and cleaning up. Weather very good.	
	19.6.18.		Do. Do.	
	20.6.18.		Do. Battalion commence training, special attention being paid to Musketry and Lewis Guns.	
	21.6.18.		Do. Weather changeable: some rain. Training carried out as usual.	
	22.6.18.		Do. Weather good. Do.	
	23.6.18.		Do. A Presentation Parade was carried out during which the Divnl. Commander presented ribbons.	
	24.6.18.		Do. Weather good. Training carried out as usual.	
	25.6.18.		Do. Do.	
	26.6.18.		Do. Do.	
	27.6.18.		Do. The major portion of the Battalion marched to ACHEUX in the afternoon to relieve a composite Battalion of the 104th Infantry Brigade which was doing working parties. Battle Surplus and Details remained at ARQUEVES. Operation Order attached.	132
	28.6.18.		Battalion at ACHEUX carried out Working Parties; remainder at ARQUEVES carried on with Training.	
	29.6.18.		Major proportion of Battalion, which had been at ACHEUX returned to ARQUEVES in the morning under Orders received from Brigade. The Battle Surplus left for the Divisional Reception Camp in the afternoon. Weather very good. Operation Order attached.	133
	30.6.18.		Orders having been received to prepare for Move, the Battalion spent the day in preparation and marched off at 8.45 p.m. entraining at DOULLENS after a march of 10 miles. Weather very fine.	

Mure
Capt. & Adjt,
for Lt.-Col.
Comdg. 18th(H.Y.) Bn. Highland Light Infantry.

SECRET.   OPERATION ORDER No. 130.   Copy No. 12
                       'B' HIGHLAND LIGHT INFANTRY.   21.6.18.

Ref. Sheet 57D. 1/40,000.

1. The 35th Division is at present the left supporting Division
   of the V Corps, and will be prepared to :-
   a.   Occupy all or part of the Purple, Brown, or Red Systems
        within the Divisional Boundaries.
   b.   Counter attack to regain any part of the Purple System
        which may have been lost.
   c.   Support either the centre or left Divisions in the line.

2. The Divisional Boundaries are as follows :-
   Northern boundary. Line passing through P.1. P.2. P.3. P.4. P.5.
   central. P.5.a.& b.central. Q.1. Q.2. Q.3. Q.4. Q.5. Q.6.a.& b.
   central.
   Southern Boundary. Line passing through O.29. O.30.central.
   P.25. P.26. P.27. P.28. P.29. P.30.central. Q.25. Q.26. Q.27.
   Q.28. Q.29.central.

3. In the event of the Division being ordered to occupy the Brown
   System, the probable disposition will be as follows:-
   Right Sector.   105 Inf. Brigade.
   Left Sector.   106 Inf. Brigade.
   Div. Reserve.   104 Inf. Brigade.
   The dividing line between right and left Sector is the grid
   line P.14.central - P.15.central.

4. On receiving the order "Occupy Brown System, Left Sector",
   106 Inf. Brigade will take up position as follows:-
   Right Battalion.   12 H.L.I.   P.16.c.central - P.10.d.5.2.
   Left Battalion.   B H.L.I.   P.10.b.5.2. - Division Northern
                                                Boundary.
   Reserve Battalion. R.SCOTS.   ACHEUX WOOD.

5. Disposition in Brown System.
   The Battalion will be disposed as follows:-
   Right Coy.   X Coy.   P.10.b.5.2. - P.11.b.6.5.
   Left Coy.   Z "   P.11.b.6.5. - P.5.central.
   Right Support Coy.W "   P.10.b.5.2. - Grid between P.11 - P.5.
   Left Support Coy. Y "   Grid between P.11 - P.5. to P.5.central.
   Battalion H.Q.   P.10.b.5.
   Flanks.   X Coy. is responsible for touch with 12th H.L.I. on right,
             Z " is responsible for touch with troops of --- Corps
                   on left. X

6. MARCH.
   Starting Point. Road Junction O.14.c.8.8.
   Time.   ZERO plus 5 min.
   Route.   Track A at O.20.c. - O.24.c.central - Track running
                    N.E. to O.24.b.6.9. - Track junction O.12.c.8.3.
                    thence track running E. to P.10.c. & d.
   Order of march. Z, X, W, Y Coys. H.Q., 1st line Transport.
   Formation and Advanced Guard. Column of route 200 yards between
                    Coys. Z Coy. will throw out an Advanced Guard of
                    one platoon.
   Dress.   Fighting Order.

7. TRANSPORT.
   1st Line Transport will accompany the Battalion under T.O. and
   will park in ACHEUX WOOD.
   2nd line Transport, Q.M. Stores, Battle surplus will remain in
   present location. Battle Surplus will proceed to TALMAS.

2.

8. **Brigade Ammunition Reserve.** T.O. will send two S.A.A. limbers to report to the Brigade H.Q. Adjutant will detail two cycle orderlies to accompany S.A.A. limbers to Brigade H.Q.; these orderlies will act as runners for Brigade Ammunition Reserve.

9. **Dump.** S.A.A. in Brown System is dumped as follows:-
50 boxes for each 1000 yards of defensive line.

10. **Medical.** Aid Post at Batt. H.Q. until further orders.

11. **REPORTS.**
Brigade H.Q. at ~~No.72 Billet MEALVILLERS~~. P & L S.O. ACHEUX WOOD
Report Centre. ACHEUX CHATEAU. R.13.b.7.8.

Battalion H.Q. at R.10.b.0.5.

12. ACKNOWLEDGE.

Issued at 2.30 p.m.
(Signed.) W.F.M. MACARA.
Capt. & Adjt.
'B' HIGHLAND LIGHT INFANTRY.

Copy No. 1. War Diary.
2 O.C. File.
3 Do.
4 O.C. W Coy.
5 O.C. X "
6 O.C. Y "
7 O.C. Z "
8 2nd in Command.
9 Medical Officer.
10 Transport Officer.
11 Quartermaster.
12 106 Inf. Brigade.

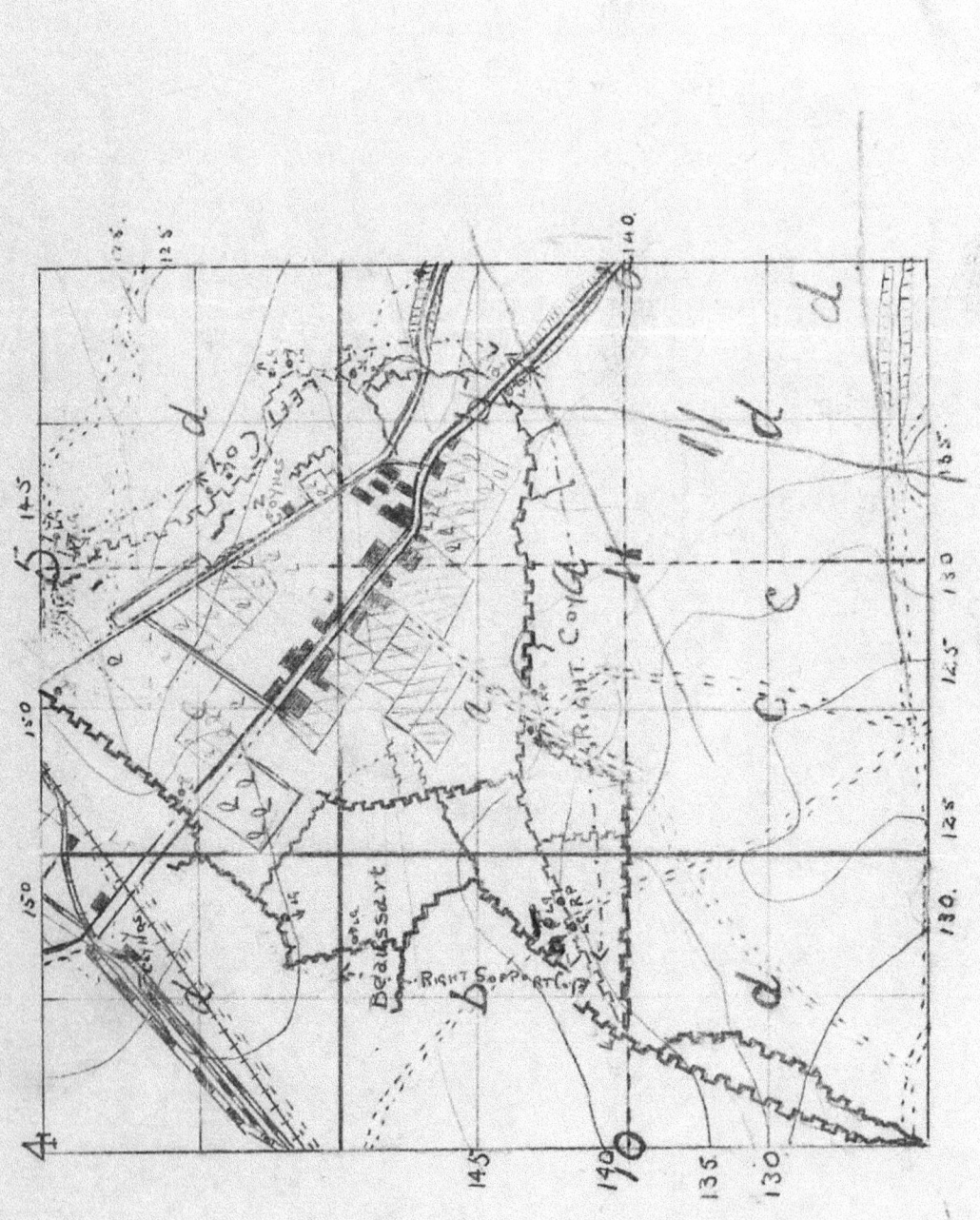

ADDENDUM to OPERATION ORDERS No.   Copy No.
'B' HIGHLAND LIGHT INFANTRY.

Reference Operation Order No.   dated 26.6.18.

Paras. 4 & 5.
1. The dispositions given in this order will be known as A disposi-
   -tion and will come into force on receipt of order 'Occupy
   "Brown System, Left Sector."

2. On receipt of order "Occupy Brown System" the disposition (which
   will be known as B disposition) will be as follows:-
   Right Coy.   X Coy. P.16.central. - P.10.d.9.3. 3.9
   Centre Coy.   W Coy. P.10.d.9.3. - P.11.b.4.3.
   Left Coy.   Z Coy. P.11.b.4.3. - to Corps Northern Boundary.
   Support Coy.   Y Coy. in Support line W. of BEAUSSART.

SECRET.　　　　　　OPERATION ORDERS. No.130.　　　　Copy No.
　　　　　　　　　　'B' HIGHLAND LIGHT INFANTRY.　　　　16.6.18.

1.　The 106th Infantry Brigade will be relieved by the 37th Inf. Brigade
　　on the night of the 16/17th June 1918.

2.　The Battalion will be relieved by the 6th Battalion R.W. KENTS as
　　follows:-
　　W Coy. H.L.I. will be relieved by A Coy. R.W.K.
　　X　"　　"　　　"　　"　　"　　 B　"　 R.W.K.
　　Y　"　　"　　　"　　"　　"　　 C　"　 R.W.K.
　　Z　"　　"　　　"　　"　　"　　 D　"　 R.W.K.

3.　Companies, on relief, will march to WARLOY.
　　Route. Cross Country Track to HEDAUVILLE - WARLOY ROAD and thence
　　by main road to WARLOY.
　　Billet Guides. will meet Companies outside WARLOY.
　　On 17th inst. Battalion will march to ARQUEVES under orders to be
　　issued later.

4.　GUIDES. 4 Guides per Coy. and 2 for Bn. H.Q. will report to Adjutant
　　at 8.30 p.m.

5.　All trench stores, tools, trench covers, etc., will be handed over
　　on relief and receipts obtained.
　　These receipts will be handed to Adjutant at WARLOY at Noon 17th inst.

6.　The two Bandoliers S.A.A. extra per man will be carried out.
　　Empty Petrol Tins, Lewis Guns, and Magazines will be carried out
　　on relief and loaded on Limber at '8 trees'.

7.　Completion of Relief will be notified to Battalion H.Q. by Code
　　Word "CLICK".

8.　Acknowledge.

　　Issued at noon.　　　　　　　　　(Signed) W.F.MACARA. Capt. & Adjt.
　　　　　　　　　　　　　　　　　　　　　　　 'B' HIGHLAND LIGHT INFANTRY.

Copy No.1. War Diary.
　　　 2. O.O. File.
　　　 3.　 Do.
　　　 4. O.C. W Coy.
　　　 5. O.C. X　"
　　　 6. O.C. Y　"
　　　 7. O.C. Z　"
　　　 8. 2nd in Command.
　　　 9. Medical Officer.
　　　10. Transport Officer.
　　　11. Quartermaster.

SECRET.   OPERATION ORDERS. No.131.   Copy No.
            'B' HIGHLAND LIGHT INFANTRY.
                                                17.6.18

1. Battalion will march into Billets at ARQUEVES.
    MARCH.
            Starting Point. Road Junction at U.23.d.7.6.
            Time.   4.30 p.m.
            Dress.   Fighting Order.
            Distance.   100 yards between Coys.
                             300   "   "   Battalions.
                             100   "   "   every 10 Vehicles.
            Order of March. Hdqrs., W, X, Y, Z.

2. Transport.
    First line Transport, less two cookers will march to Transport
    Lines at ARQUEVES, as 1 p.m.

3. Reports.
            On march.   To head of Column.
            At ARQUEVES. Battalion H.Q. will be notified later.

4. Acknowledge.

    Issued at noon.   (Signed.) W.F.M. MACARA. Capt. & Adjt
                                           'B' HIGHLAND LIGHT INFANTRY.

    Copy No.1. War Diary.
         2. O.O. File.
         3.   Do
         4. O.C. W Coy.
         5. O.C. X "
         6. O.C. Y "
         7. O.C. Z "
         8. 2nd in Command.
         9. Medical Officer.
        10. Transport Officer.
        11. Quartermaster.

SECRET.   OPERATION ORDERS. No.132.   Copy No.
                       'B' HIGHLAND LIGHT INFANTRY.   26.6.18.

Ref. Map 57D.

1. The Battalion will relieve a Composite Battalion of the 104th
    Infantry Brigade, now working under C.E. V Corps, and billeted
    in ACHEUX, after work on the afternoon of the 27th inst.

2. STRENGTH. Companies will detail 3 Officers and 90 men per Company
    with N.C.O.s, cooks, servants, and stretcher bearers in addition.
    They will proceed to ACHEUX tomorrow afternoon. When detailing
    these men, Companies will leave out the following:-
    a. The newest Lewis Gunners, to form a Class.
    b. Men requiring further instruction in Musketry.
    c. Observers.
    d. Signallers.

3. MARCH. The Battⁿ. will pass Starting point O.8.a.3.4. at 3.30 p.m
    in the following order:- Z, Y, X, W.
    Route. Track running alongside the north side of the main ARQUEVES
    -LEALVILLERS Road, then by cross-country Track to ACHEUX.

4. DRESS:- Fighting order : steel helmets: box respirators.
            2 extra bandoliers of Ammunition.

5. VALISES. All valises of officers going forward will be dumped at
    the Q.M. Stores at 2 p.m. tomorrow.

6. TRANSPORT. The Transport Officer will make arrangements to send
    forward 3 Cookers (W, X, and Y) 1 Watercart, Messcart. These
    will move in rear of the Battalion.

7. LEWIS GUNS. Companies will take forward 6 Lewis Guns per Coy.
    These will be packed in Coy. limbers and move with the Bn. Coys.
    will make arrangements to load their own Lewis Guns, Magazines,
    spare parts, etc., also Coy. Mess Stores on Coy. limbers.

8. HEADQUARTERS. The following men of Headquarters will proceed
    forward under Sgt. Campbell and will move in rear of the last Coy.
        2 Runners, with bicycles.   4 Pioneers.
        4 Officers' servants.

9. ADVANCE PARTY. Lieut. D.G. Hutchison, 4 QMS.s, and 1 N.C.O. for
    Headquarters will leave Bn. Headquarters at 2 p.m. tomorrow to
    take over Billets etc.

10. MEDICAL. The Medical Officer and staff will proceed forward.

    Issued at 11 p.m.   (Signed.) W.F.M. MACARA. Capt. & Adjt.

SECRET.   OPERATION ORDERS. No. 133.   Copy No.
                  'B' HIGHLAND LIGHT INFANTRY.   28.6.18.

1. The Battalion will move into billets at ARQUEVES on the 29th
   June 1918.

2. March.
   Starting Point.   P.7.c.5.3.
   Time.   8 a.m.
   Order of March.   X, Z, Y, W Coy. H.Q.
   Route.   Track to ARQUEVES.
   Distance.   200 yards between Coys.

3. Transport. Coy. limbers, teams for Cookers, etc. will report to
   Coys. at 7.15 a.m.

4. Baggage. Officers' Valises, Mess Stores, etc., will be at W Coy.
   billet at 7.15 a.m.
   W Coy. will provide a loading party of 1 N.C.O. and 12 men.

5. Marching out States and billeting Certificates will be rendered
   to Adjutant by 7.45 a.m.

6. Reports to head of column.

   Issued at 10.45. p.m.   (Signed.) W.F.M. MACARA. Capt. & Adjt.
                                         'B' HIGHLAND LIGHT INFANTRY.

SECRET.   OPERATION ORDERS. 134.   Copy No.
          'B' HIGHLAND LIGHT INFANTRY.   30.6.18.

Ref. Map. 1/40,000.
     HAZEBROUCK 1/100,000.

1. The Division will move by rail, the 106th Inf. Brigade entraining at DOULLENS (South Yard.) detraining at ARQUES.

2. The Battalion, less X Coy. will entrain No.8. train leaving 2.22 a.m. 1.7.18. X Coy. with L.G. limber, cooker and teams will entrain No.14 train leaving 8.22 a.m. 1.7.18.
All troops will arrive at entraining station one hour before departure of train.
Transport will arrive at entraining station 2 hours before departure of train.

3. MARCH.
   Starting Point.   O.14.b.3.9.
   Time.   Battalion, less X Coy. 8.45 p.m. 30.6.18.
                     X Coy. 2.45 a.m. 1.7.18.
   Route.   Road junction O.8.c.1.9. - road junction
                     H.36.d.3.1. - MARIEUX - SARTON - DOULLENS.
   Order of March.   Z, Y, W Coys., H.Q.
   Distance.   100 yards between Coys.
   Dress.   Full marching order: Balmorals: 1 day's ration.

4. TRANSPORT. Will move under separate orders issued to T.O.

5. BAGGAGE. Officers' Valises, baggage etc. to be at Q.M. Stores ready for loading at 4 p.m. All vehicles to be packed ready for moving at 7 p.m.

6. BILLETING PARTY. Lt. Bryce, 1 N.C.O. per Coy. and H.Q. will report to Battalion H.Q. at 8 p.m.

7. Strict March and Train Discipline will be observed as per special Memo attached.

8. REPORTS on March to head of Column.

9. ACKNOWLEDGE.

Issued at 11.30 a.m.   (Signed.) .WF.M. MACARA.Capt. & Adj
                                  'B' HIGHLAND LIGHT INFANTRY.

Copy No.1. War Diary.
     2. O.OL File.
     3.   Do.
     4. O.C. W Coy.
     5. O.C. X "
     6. O.C. Y "
     7. O.C. Z "
     8. 2nd in Command.
     9. Transport Officer and Quartermaster.
    10. Medical Officer.

SECRET.   OPERATION ORDERS No.   Copy No.
                 'B' HIGHLAND LIGHT INFANTRY (Situation No.5)

Ref. Map 57D. 1/40,000.   26.6.18.
         57D. S.E. 1/20,000.

1. a. The enemy has attacked on line ALBERT - ARRAS. The right supporting
      Division has restored the situation on the right.
      106 Inf. Brigade has occupied the Brown system from FORCEVILLE to
      BEAUSSART. The remaining Brigades, Pioneer Bn, and Field Companies
      have moved forward to assembly positions near LEALVILLERS.
      Definite news is received from IV Corps that their front has been
      driven back and the enemy has occupied SAILLY AU BOIS and BAYENCOURT.
      At the same time reports are received that the enemy are in COLIN-
      CAMPS and COURCELLES and are apparently moving on to BOIS-LES-ARTOIS
      which is held by the French.
      The Battalion is in touch with the left Division holding the line at
      MAILLY MAILLET.
   b. The 106 Inf. Brigade will form to its left and hold the line
      BEAUSSART - BERTRANCOURT as follows:-
      Right Battalion   18th H.L.I. from P.5.a.6.0. - P.4.a.8.7.
      Left Battalion.   17th R. Scots " P.4.a.8.7. - J.34.c.2.8.
      Reserve Battalion.   12th H.L.I. at P.9.b.

2. a. The 35th Division will form up WEST of MAILLY-MAILLET - ENGLEBELMER
      WOODS, attack northwards, retake COLINCAMPS and COURCELLES with all
      Three Inf. Brigades and attack enemy's left flank between HEBUTERNE
      and SAILLY-AU-BOIS.
   b. 105th Inf. Brigade will attack on right.
      104th   "   "   "   "   in the Centre.
      106th   "   "   "   "   on the left.
   c. Boundaries of 106th Inf. Brigade.
      Right boundary P.5.a.5.0. - J.30.a.8.0. - K.13.a.6.6.
      Left boundary J.34.c.0.8. - J.29.a.4.9. - J.12.c.7.0.

3. General plan of attack. The attack of the 106th Brigade will be
   carried out by the 18th H.L.I. on the right, 17th Royal Scots on
   the left. The 12th H.L.I. and T.M.Batt. will be in reserve.
   The attack will be carried out in two bounds; each bound will be
   timed by lift of the Artillery.
   1st Objective.- COURCELLES-AU-BOIS.
   2nd Objective.- SAILLY-AU-BOIS.
   Details of Attack.- Battalion boundaries.
        RIGHT BOUNDARY. P.5.a.5.0. - J.30.a.8.0. - K.13.a.6.6.
        LEFT BOUNDARY. J.34.d.7.7. - J.35.a.7.7. - J.24.c.6.2. - J.12.d.8.4

4. DISPOSITIONS. The Battalion will attack on a 2 Coy. front.
   The boundary between right and left Companies will be P.4.b.7.4. -
   J.30.c.0.3. - J.18.d.8.0. - K.13.a.5.9.
   Each Coy. will attack on a two platoon front.
   The left Coy. will be Coy. of direction and will maintain touch
   with Royal Scots on the left.

5. 1st OBJECTIVE. COURCELLES-AU-BOIS will be taken by an enveloping
   movement. The Battalion will take the Eastern edge, the Royal Scots
   the western edge.
   As soon as COURCELLES is taken the Battalion will push on and
   occupy the high ground in J.24.C. and D. within Battalion boundaries
   and will reform for attacking next objective as follows:-
                     Right Coy.   W Coy.
                     Left Coy.   X Coy.
                     Support Coy. Y Coy.
                     Reserve Coy. Z Coy.
   2nd OBJECTIVE. High ground in J.18 d. and b. - J.13.c.

6. a. ARTILLERY. A heavy artillery bombardment previous to ZERO on APPLE
      TREE HILL, COLINCAMPS, COURCELLES-AU-BOIS has been arranged.
      From ZERO onwards the V Corps Heavy Artillery will bombard APPLE
      TREE HILL, the SUGAR FACTORY, COLINCAMPS, and COURCELLES.
      From/

From ZERO plus 70 it will protect the East Flank of the Attack from BEAUMONT HAMEL VALLEY to OBSERVATION WOOD (K.28.b.)

The IV Corps Heavy Artillery will bombard HEBUTERNE, the spur in K.21. and SAILLY-AU-BOIS until ZERO plus 145, at which time it will concentrate on HEBUTERNE and protect the Flank of the Division between HEBUTERNE and OBSERVATION WOOD.(K.28.b.)

Artillery Barrage: 1st Attack. Along the line APPLE TREE HILL - OLD CHALKPIT - CEMETRY south of COLINCAMPS - Southern edge of COURCELLES-AU-BOIS.

At ZERO plus 75 this barrage will lift and creep back to a line 200 yards beyond the first objective when it will remain as a protective barrage creeping backwards and forwards for 500 yards till ZERO plus 115 minutes.

Second Attack. At ZERO plus 130 minutes a barrage will be formed on the general line LA SIGNY FARM (K.27.d.) to the Cross Roads in J.23.a. At ZERO plus 135 minutes the barrage will creep forward at 100 yards in 2 minutes to a general line beyond the final objective K.15.d.8.8. - K.8.Central.- J.12. Central.

One battery will be affiliated to 106th Inf. Brigade to deal with special targets under the orders of the Brigadier General 106th Inf. Brigade.

b. 106th T.M.Battery will take up position on high ground in J.23.d. - J.24.c. and d. and will be prepared to advance and support the attack on the final objective.

c. Machine Guns. During the two Attacks 35th Battalion M.G. Corps will take up positions on a line P.6.central - Q.8.central, and cover the right flank of the right Brigade (105th).

As soon as the final objective has been captured two Coys. 35th M.G. Corps will be moved forward to cover the captured positions from North and North East. The remaining two Coys. will remain in positions already occupied on line P.6.central - Q.28.central, to cover the enemy approaches SERRE and BEAUMONT HAMEL.

7. TANKS. During the attack Tanks will operate on the left flanks of 106th Infantry Brigade, securing connection with the troops on our left. As soon as the final objective has been reached, Tanks will move along the captured positions north of SAILLY-AU-BOIS and eastwards to the spur in K.21.central and assist Infantry to join hands all along the line.

8. Action after final Objective has been taken.
  a. Consolidation will be commenced at once.
  b. Companies will at once establish touch with neighbouring units. O.C. W Coy. will be responsible that a mixed post is established with 104th Brigade on his right about K.13.a.8.7. X Coy. will be responsible that a mixed post is established with 17th Royal Scots about J.18.b.6.2.
  c. O.C. W & X Coy. will each send out two strong fighting patrols into the low part of the village SAILLY-AU-BOIS.
  d. Prisoners will be collected and sent back in charge of small escorts to Battalion H.Q. No N.C.O. or man will accompany prisoners to the rear without direct orders from an officer.

9. Communication.
  a. Signalling Officer will arrange for opening of Visual communication after each Objective is gained.
  b. Each Company will have 8 runners available at Coy. H.Q. and will detail 2 more to accompany Battalion H.Q.
  c. A contact aeroplane will report situation of attacking troops between ZERO plus 2 hours and dark. Its signal will be one green light. Front troops will light flares at ZERO plus 2 hours, ZERO plus 3 hours ZERO plus 4 hours, and when called for by contact aeroplane.

10. Dress and Equipment.
  Dress:- Fighting Order - Iron Ration.- Filled Water Bottle.
  Platoons will be equipped according to Special Battn. Memo. dated 23.6.18.
  Each amn will carry 2 aeroplane flares.
  Each Coy. H.Q. will carry 3 packets Very Lights - S.O.S. rockets.
  Reserve Coy. will bring forward 100 shovels and 50 picks.

3.

11. TRANSPORT.
Transport will remain parked in present position in ACHEUX WOOD under Transport Officer.
Pack mules will assemble 200 yards S. of Cross Roads in P.4.d. and come under orders of R.S.M.

12. Watches will be synchronised at approximately ZERO - 3 hours, and again on re-forming for attack on 2nd Objective.

13. ZERO will be the hour at which Battalion will proceed from BEAUSSART - BERTRANCOURT and will be notified later.

14. Battalion H.Q. will be 100 yards W. of Cross Roads in P.4.d. and will move forward with Reserve Coy.
After 1st Objective has been taken Battalion H.Q. will move to about J.24.d.4.4.
Brigade H.Q. will be at P.9.b. till ZERO plus 120 and from that hour onwards in COURCELLES-AU-BOIS.

Issued at 3.30 p.m.   (Signed.) W.F.M. MACARA. Capt. & Adjt.
                                    'B' HIGHLAND LIGHT INFANTRY.

Copy No. 1. War Diary.
        2. O.O. File.
        3.   Do.
        4. O.C. W Coy.
        5. O.C. X "
        6. O.C. Y "
        7. O.C. Z "
        8. 2nd in Command.
        9. Medical Officer.
       10. Transport Officer & QrMr.
       11. Medical Officer.
       12. 106th Inf. Brigade.

WAR DIARY
or
INTELLIGENCE SUMMARY. 18th (S.) Bn. HIGHLAND LIGHT INFANTRY.

Army Form C. 2118.

From 1st to 31st July 1918 inclusive.

Index No.30.

Instructions regarding War Diaries and Intelligence Summaries are contained in F. S. Regs., Part II. and the Staff Manual respectively. Title pages will be prepared in manuscript.

(Erase heading not required.)

Place	Date	Hour	Summary of Events and Information	Remarks and references to Appendices
ARQUES.	1.7.18.		Battalion detrained at ARQUES at 8.45 a.m. and marched to billets in EBBLINGHEM. Weather very warm.	
EBBLINGHEM.	2.7.18.		Battalion marched to RENESCURE and embussed for ZERMEZEELE at 8 p.m. arriving in billets at 11.30 p.m. Weather very good. Operation Order attached.	135
ZERMEZEELE.	3.7.18.		Battalion left ZERMEZEELE at 3 p.m. and marched to tents near WINNEZEELE. Advance parties left to take over Section of line from French. Weather very good. Operation Order attached.	136
WINNEZEELE.	4.7.18.		Battalion left WINNEZEELE at 11.30 a.m., had dinner on main STEENVOORDE - GODEWAERSVELDE ROAD and moved off for line at 8 p.m. Battalion relieved 5th Bn. of the 221stC Regt. of French in the LOCRE Sector. Relief complete at 2.30 a.m. Situation quiet. Weather good.	
LOCRE Sector.	5.7.18.		Battalion in Line. Situation quiet. Weather good. 1 O.R. killed and 1 wounded.	
	6.7.18.		Do. Do. 1 O.R. wounded.	
	7.7.18.		Do. Do.	
	8.7.18.		Battalion in line. Weather bad; severe thunderstorm during early part of night. Situation quiet.	
	9.7.18.		Weather dull. Situation quiet.	
	10.7.18.		Weather changeable. Situation quiet. Battalion relieved by 17th R.SCOTS. Relief complete 2 a.m. 11.7.18. Operation Order attached.	137.
GODERS-VELDE	11.7.18		Battalion in Reserve Billets. Resting and cleaning up. Weather changeable.	
	12.7.18.		Do. "Stand to" ordered at 3 a.m.: nothing happened. Weather changeable.	
	13.7.18.		Do. Weather good.	
	14.7.18.		Battalion moved from GODEWAERSVELDE to Billets West of BOESCHEPE. Arrived in billets 5 p.m. Weather dull. Operation Order attached.	137A.
	15.7.18.		Battalion in Reserve Billets. Weather dull.	
	16.7.18.		Do. W end Y Coys. left to relieve 12th H.L.I. in Support positions to LOCRE Sector, i.e. Mt. VIDAGNE. Relief complete 11.30 p.m. Weather good. Operation Order attached.	138
Mt.VIDAGNE	17.7.18.		Battalion in Support. X and Z Coys. carry out relief. Work on defensive position of Mt. VIDAGNE Weather good.	
	18.7.18.		Do. Weather good. Situation quiet	
	19.7.18.		Battalion in Support. Do. Work on defensive positions.	
	20.7.18.		Do. Do.	
	21.7.18.		Do. Do.	
	22.7.18.		Do. Do. Weather dull and thundery. Moved into Front line Relieved 12th H.L.I. in LOCRE SECTOR.	

Army Form C. 2118.

WAR DIARY
INTELLIGENCE-SUMMARY
(Erase heading not required.)

Instructions regarding War Diaries and Intelligence Summaries are contained in F.S. Regs., Part II. and the Staff Manual respectively. Title pages will be prepared in manuscript.

Place	Date	Hour	Summary of Events and Information	Remarks and references to Appendices
LOGRE Sector.	23.7.18.		Battalion in front line. Situation active. Weather good.	
	24.7.18.		Do. Situation very active. Do.	
	25.7.18.		Do. Situation quiet. Do.	
	26.7.18.		Battalion relieved by 2/15th LONDON REGT. (90th Brigade.) Relief complete 12.30 a.m. Operation Order attached.	139
BOESCHEPE.	27.7.18.		Battalion arrived in billets West of BOESCHEPE at 4 a.m. Weather changeable. Wet nearly all day. Battalion left BOESCHEPE for ECKE.	
ECKE.	28.7.18.		Battalion reorganising and training. Weather good.	
	29.7.18.		Do.	
	30.7.18.		Do.	
	30.7.18.		Do. Night operations from 7.30 p.m. to 3 a.m. 31.7.18	

signature
Lieut.
Intelligence Officer,
for Major,
Comdg. 18th (S) Bn. HIGHLAND LIGHT INFANTRY.

SECRET.   OPERATION ORDERS. No. 135.   Copy No.
                       'B' HIGHLAND LIGHT INFANTRY.   2.7.18.

Ref. Map HAZEBROOCK 5A. 1/10,000.

1. The 106th Inf. Brigade Group will move to ZERMEZEELE today.

2. The Battalion will embus at RENESCURE CHATEAU at 2.45 p.m.

3. March to RENESCURE.
   Starting Point.   EBBLINGHEM CHATEAU 4E.90.79.
   Time.   1.30 p.m.
   Distance.   100 yards between Coys.
   Dress.   Full marching order.

4. Transport will move under separate orders of T.O. and will pass CHURCH LE NIEPPE 12 noon.

5. Baggage. All officers' valises, baggage etc. will be collected by T.O. at 9 a.m.

6. Billeting Party. Lt. Johnstone, 1 N.C.O. per Coy. and H.Q. will meet Staff Captain at Area Commandant's Office, ZERMEZEELE 11.30 a.m. Lt. Hutchison will remain behind at EBBLINGHEM till 4.30 p.m. to s settle any claims.

7. Acknowledge.

   Issued at 9.30 a.m.   (Signed.) W.F.M. MACARA. Capt. & Adjt.
                                              'B' HIGHLAND LIGHT INFANTRY.

   Copy No. 1. War Diary.
           2. O.O. File.
           3.   Do.
           4. O.C. W Coy.
           5. O.C. X "
           6. O.C. Y "
           7. O.C. Z "
           8. 2nd in Command.
           9. Transport Officer.
          10. Quartermaster.
          11. Medical Officer.

SECRET.   OPERATION ORDERS. No.136.   Copy No.
                   'B' HIGHLAND LIGHT INFANTRY.   3.7.18.

Ref. Map. HAZEBROUCK 5A 1/100,000.

1. The 106th Inf. Brigade will march today to WINNEZEELE area.

2. The Battalion will march to WINNEZEELE as follows:-
   Starting Point.   X roads 350 yards east of D in RIETVELD.
   Time.   3 p.m.
   Order of March.   Hdqrs. W. X. Y. Z.
   Distance.   100 yards between Coys.
   Route.   OUDEZEELE thence by track going East to WINNEZEELE
   Dress.   Full marching order.

3. Transport will move under separate orders of T.O. and will pass the above mentioned starting point at 12 noon.

4. Baggage. All Officers' Valises, baggage, etc. will be collected by T.O. at 10.30 a.m.

5. Billeting Party. Lt. Bryce, 1 N.C.O. per Coy. and 1 from Hdqrs. will meet Staff Captain at Church WINNEZEELE at 12 noon.

6. Lt. Hutchison will remain behind at ZERMEZEELE till 6 p.m. to settle any Claims.

7. March Discipline. Companies will take necessary steps to see that strict march discipline is maintained on the march :- No man being allowed to fall out without a 'chit' to that effect signed by his Company Commander and that only when the man is really unable to continue the march.
   A small rear-guard will be detailed by O.C. Z Coy. to collect stragg--lers. An officer will be in charge.

Issued at 10 a.m.   (Signed.) W.F.M. MACARA. Capt. & Adjt.
                                              'B' HIGHLAND LIGHT INFANTRY.

Copy No.1. War Diary.
       2. O.O. File.
       3.   Do.
       4. O.C. W Coy.
       5. O.C. X "
       6. O.C. Y "
       7. O.C. Z "
       8. 2nd in Command.
       9. Transport Officer.
      10. Quartermaster.
      11. Medical Officer.

SECRET.   OPERATION ORDERS. No.137.   Copy No.
          'B' HIGHLAND LIGHT INFANTRY.   9.7.18.

1. The Battalion will be relieved by the - ROYAL SCOTS in the Right
   Sub Sector of the LOCRE Sector on the night of 10/11th July 1918
   as follows:-
   Z Coy. R.S. will relieve W Coy. on the right.
   Y "   "   "   "   "   X " in the Centre.
   W "   "   "   "   "   Z " on the left.
   X "   "   "   "   "   Y " in Support.

2. <u>Guides</u> as follows will be supplied.
   Y Coy. will supply 2 guides per Coy. for W, X, and Y Coys. to guide
   Z, Y, and X Coys. R.S. from Ration Dump to Hdqrs. of Y Coy.
   Guides will report to Lt. Bryant at Ration Dump at 10 p.m.
   W and X Coys. will supply 1 guide per Platoon to guide the Coys.
   to Front Line from Y Coy. Hdqrs.   These guides will report to
   an officer of Y Coy. by 10.30 p.m.
   Z Coy. will supply 1 guide per platoon to report at Bn. Hdqrs
   at 10.30 p.m.

3. All trench stores (both French and English) Aeroplane photos,
   Defence Schemes, Maps, Programme of Work in hand and proposed
   will be handed over, receipts taken and forwarded to the Adjutant
   on Monday after relief.

4. Completion of relief will be sent to Battalion Hdqrs. by Runner,
   the code word "WET" being used.   The Runner bringing this message
   should be accompanied by 2 Royal Scots Runners so as to instruct
   the latter in the road to Batt. Hdqrs.

5. Companies on relief will march back to Reserve Billets near
   GEDEWAERSVELDE about Q.11 central. Guides to guide Companies to
   Billets will meed them at Railway Crossing Q.12.d.7.7.

6. Limbers, 1 per Company and 1 for Hdqrs. will be at Ration Dump
   to await arrival of Coys. Limber Drivers, will, if necessary,
   lead Coys. to rendezvous where guides are to be met.

7. All Lewis Guns, Magazines, all Petrol tins, gas rattles, and all
   other Coy. Stores will be carried out and <u>not</u> handed over.

8. Coys. will notify the Adjutant tonight if they have not any one
   who can guide Coy. to Ration Dump.

9. Acknowledge.

Issued at 12 midnight.   (Signed.) W.F.M. MACARA. Capt. & Adjt
                                      'B' HIGHLAND LIGHT INFANTRY.

Copy No. 1. War Diary.
         2. O.O. File.
         3.   Do.
         4. O.C. W Coy.
         5. O.C. X "
         6. O.C. Y "
         7. O.C. Z "
         8. 2nd in Command.
         9. Transport Officer.
        10. Quartermaster.
        11. Medical Officer.

SECRET.   OPERATION ORDERS. No.137A   Copy No.
           'B' HIGHLAND LIGHT INFANTRY.   14.7.18.

Ref. May. Sheet 27. 1/40,000.

1. Battalion will move this afternoon to Billets in Area R.8. and 9.

2. **Order of March.**   Z, X, Y, W, H.Q.
   Starting Point.   Cross Roads R.1.c.9.0.
   Route.   Starting Point – By Route through R.7.a.,
   8.c. and d. and to Billets.
   Dress.   Fighting Order (200 rounds S.A.A. per man.)
   Time.   Leading Company to pass Starting Point by
                         3 p.m.
   Interval.   10 minutes interval between Companies.
   Guides.   Guides will meet Companies at house on
                         road R.8.c.8.5.

3. Transport Officer will make necessary arrangements for each Company's Cooker and Limber to march with its Company.

4. Officers' Valises, surplus Mess Stores, etc. to be left behind will be dumped by 1 p.m. outside the various Coy. H.Q. Billets. Transport Officer will arrange to collect and convey these to Q.M. Stores before Companies move off.

5. Companies will take with them the bombs presently in Company limbers.

6. Transport Officer will arrange to collect and convey back to Q.M. Stores the S.A.A. previously dumped with Companies.

Issued at 11.15 a.m.   (Signed.) W.F.M. MACARA. Capt. & Adjt.
                                  'B' HIGHLAND LIGHT INFANTRY.

Copy No. 1. War Diary.
      2. O.O. File.
      3.   Do.
      4. O.C. W Coy.
      5. O.C. X "
      6. O.C. Y "
      7. O.C. Z "
      8. 2nd in Command.
      9. Transport Officer.
     10. Quartermaster.
     11. Medical Officer.

SECRET. OPERATION ORDERS. No.138. Copy No.
'B' HIGHLAND LIGHT INFANTRY. 15.7.18.

Reference Sheets 27 and 28 1/40,000.

1. The Battalion will relieve the 'A' H.L.I. in the Support System in the right Sub-Sector of the LOCRE Sector on the night of July 16/17th.

2. The Companies will be disposed as follows:-
   W Coy. along road running through M.21.a. from M.21.a.2.0. N.E.
   X "   Area around Bde. Hdqrs. M.20.d.3.3.
   Y "   "   "   Hill 130 in M.21.a.
   Z "   "   "   Hill 120 in M.21.c.

3. Advance Parties. One Officer per Coy. and 1 N.C.O. per platoon to report at 'A' H.L.I. Hdqrs. (M.21.a.5.4.) at 11 p.m. tonight. This Party will remain in Support System during July 16th.

4. Guides. 1 Guide per platoon from Advance Party and 1 N.C.O. for Hdqrs. will be at Ration Dump M.20.d.4.6.at 10.30 p.m. tomorrow night to guide Companies and Hdqrs to positions.

5. Coys. will leave present billets in time to pass starting point Cross Roads R.9.b.8.3. as follows:-
   W Coy. 9.15 p.m.   X Coy. 9.25 p.m.   Y Coy. 9.35 p.m.
   Z Coy. 9.45 p.m. Hdqrs. 9.50 p.m.
   Coys. will move by half Coys. at 100 yards intervals.

6. All trench stores, aeroplane photographs, maps, tools, programme of work in hand and proposed, Defence Schemes, etc. will be taken over and receipts forwarded to the Adjt. by 12 noon, 17th July.

7. Completion of relief will be sent to Bn. Hdqrs. by quickest method. Code word 'AWAKE'.

Issued at midnight.   (Signed.) W.E.M.MACARA. Capt.& Adjt.
                                    'B' HIGHLAND LIGHT INFANTRY.

Copies to
   1. War Diary.
   2. O.O. File.
   3.   Do.
   4. O.C. W Coy.
   5. O.C. X "
   6. O.C. Y "
   7. O.C. Z "
   8. 2nd in Command.
   9. Transport Officer.
   10. Quartermaster.
   11. Medical Officer.

SECRET. OPERATION ORDERS. No.139. Copy No.
'B' HIGHLAND LIGHT INFANTRY. 25.7.18.

Reference Maps. Sheets 27 and 28 1/40,000.

1. The Battalion will be relieved by the 2/15th LONDON REGT. in the Right Sub-sector of the LOCRE Sector on the night 26/27th July, as follows:-
   W Coy. H.L.I. will be relieved by A Coy. L.R. on the right.
   Y "   "   "   "   "   " C "   "   "   " Centre.
   X "   "   "   "   "   " B "   "   "   " left "
   Z "   "   "   "   "   " D "   "   "   "   "

2. <u>Advance parties</u> as under will report tonight 25/26th, for the purpose of seeing the line and will remain in the line during 26th July:-
   1 Offr. Hdqrs.
   1   "   per Coy.
   1 N.C.O. " Platoon.

3. <u>Guides.</u> 2 per Company and 1 for Hdqrs will report tonight to the Adjutant immediately they have rations for tomorrow. These guides will be sent to the Hdqrs 2/15th LONDON REGT. tonight and will remain there to guide in Companies tomorrow night to where platoon guides will be met.
   1 guide per platoon and 1 guide for Coy. Hdqrs. will be sent from Left and Left Centre Companies to Battalion Hdqrs at 10.30 p.m. tomorrow night.
   1 guide per platoon and 1 for Coy. Hdqrs. from Right and Right Centre companies will be sent to Right Coy. Hdqrs at 10.30 p.m. tomorrow night.

4. On relief, Companies will march to Reserve Area in R.8. and R.9 and must be west of a north and south line through R.11.central and R.23.central by 3.15 a.m. Lt. Peat will arrange to have guides to guide Companies to billets at X Roads (R.9.b.8.3.) He will detail 1 limber per Coy. and 1 for Hdqrs. to be at Ration Dump at 12.30 a.m.

5. The undermentioned will be left in Front Line system for a period of 24 hours with incoming Unit:-
   1 Officer Battn. Hdqrs.
   1 Officer per Coy.
   1 N.C.O. per platoon.

6. All trench stores, air photos, Defence Schemes, etc. will be handed over, receipts obtained and forwarded to the Adjutant by 12 noon 27th. Tools will be handed over and <u>separate</u> receipts obtained for same.

7. During forenoon 27th July, Battalion will march to billets in Q.20.c.8.8. Further orders will be issued later.

8. Completion of relief will be sent by runner, the code word 'BERT' being used. These runners will bring back runners of LONDON REGT. to acquaint them with the road to Battn. Hdqrs.

(Signed.) W.F.M.MACARA. Capt. & Adjt
'B' HIGHLAND LIGHT INFANTRY.

<u>Issued at 12 noon.</u>

Copy No.1. File.
     2. Do.
     3. War Diary.
     4. O.C. W Coy.
     5. O.C. X "
     6. O.C. Y "
     7. O.C. Z "
     8. 2/15th LONDON REGT.

SECRET.   18th (G.Y.) Bn. HIGHLAND LIGHT INFANTRY.

DEFENCE SCHEME while in reserve in QUEVE de VACHE Area.

Reference Map. Sheets 27 and 28 1/40,000.

1. The Battalion, while in present area is in Corps Reserve, and tactically will act directly under orders of Corps H.Qrs.

2. There are three probable contingencies in case of attack.
   a. To counter attack on any part of the front, according to the situation.
   b. To man and hold the Corps System on the line EEKE - KRUESTRAETE, both inclusive.
   c. To man and hold the Corps System N. of Mt. KOKERELLE and N.W. of WESTOUTRE, known as VRENVIEKHORE and WEST MOLEN Sector.

3. For contingency a orders to move will be issued from Battalion Headquarters, on receipt of orders from Brigade.
   In this contingency Battalion will be moved forward to selected assembly positions close up to the crest line of the hills. It may be employed for counter attack to maintain or regain any lost portion of the MAIN LINE of the INTERMEDIATE SYSTEM. (This is the line on the front crest of the hills on the Brigade front.)
   It will not be employed for counter attack into the front System unless by permission of Divisional Headquarters or the Senior Brigadier. Possible lines of attack and counter attack will be issued later.

4. Contingency b.   Battalion Front will extend from North and South Grid Line between Q.19 and 20 and 25 and 26 on the right, to Cross roads R.19.a.5.3. on the Left.
   Right Front:- Z Coy. plus 1 platoon W Coy.
   Centre Front:- X Coy. plus 1 platoon W Coy.
   Left Front:- Y Coy.
   Reserve:- W Coy. less 2 platoons.
   Company Frontages have already been allotted to Companies.
   Battalion H.Q.:-   Railway cutting about Q.22.d.7.6.
   Battalion Ammunition Refilling Point:- About Q.16.central.

5. Contingency c. Battalion Frontage will extend from line drawn from R.10.d.5.5. to R.17.central on the right, and the road passing through M.1.d. - M.2.c. - and M.8.a. on the left.
   Right Front:-   X Coy.
   Left Front:-   Y Coy.
   Right Reserve:-   Z Coy.
   Left Reserve:-   W Coy.
   Company Frontages have been allotted to Company Commanders.
   Battalion H.Q.:-   R.11.c.95.60.
   Battalion Ammunition Refilling Point:- About R.4.d.6.8.

6. In Contingencies b and c troops will proceed to allotted positions in accordance with attached Tables B and C respectively.

7. For contingencies b and c the Battalion will be prepared to act as laid down herein and the positions once occupied will be held at all costs, arrangements being made by Companies for the collecting and reforming of all stragglers passing back through the lines and the employing of these to strengthen the position, the general principles of defence in all cases being that troops will hold on to their allotted positions to the last, whether their flanks are in the air or not, and troops in supporting positions, if the front is penetrated at any point will bear in mind that it is better to remain in the good defensive position they are in than to counter attack, unless, from the nature of the breach, it appears there is a fair chance of restoring the situation by an immediate counter attack. No such opportunity of restoring the line will be missed.
   In moving up to positions to be occupied, Companies will be prepared for/

2.

for anything, even to the enemy being already in possession of their allotted zones, in which case energetic action will be taken to drive him out and carry on with the occupation.

If it is impossible to reach the allotted areas owing to its occupation by the enemy in too great strength, Companies will report the fact to Battalion Headquarters and will take up a position as near as possible to the point reached, and prepare to hold on where they are at all costs, pending the receipt of further orders.

8. When orders are received from Corps, if contingency (a) has arisen preliminary orders will be issued, and, if possible, a conference of Company Commanders will be called to explain the situation.
If contingency (b) or (c) arises, orders will be issued :-
"Contingency (b) or (c) move, zero — a.m. or p.m." when Companies will act as laid down herein.
In any case Companies will move to the position of deployment by platoons at 100 yards distance. The Lewis Gun limber will follow the 2nd platoon and pack ponies the rear platoon of each Company.
Cookers and Water Carts will rejoin the Transport at Transport Lines at once.
The R.S.M. will be prepared to move with the Battalion Ammunition Reserve to the point selected as Battn. Amm. refilling point. A cycle orderly will be attached for duty to the R.S.M.

12.7.18.
(Signed.) W.A. MURRAY. Major,
Comdg. 18th (G.Y.) Bn. Highland Light Infantry.

SECRET.   OPERATION ORDERS   Copy No.____
          15th. High. L. Inf.

Reference sheets 27 & 28 1/40,000
----

1. The battalion will be relieved by the 2/15th. LONDON REGT. in the Right Sub-sector of the LOCRE Sector on the night of the 26/27th. inst as follows:-

   W Coy. H.L.I. will be relieved by A Coy. L.R. in Right.
   Y "   "   "   "   "   " C "   "   " Centre.
   X "   "   "   "   "   " B "   "   " Left "
   Z "   "   "   "   "   " D "   "   "

2. **Advance parties.** as under will report to-night 25th/26th. for the purpose of seeing the line and will remain in the line during 26th. July:-

   1 Offr. Bn. HdQrs.
   1 "   per Company
   1 N.C.O. " Platoon.

3. **Guides. 2 per company.** and 1 guide for HdQrs. will report to-night to the Adjutant immediately they have rations for to-morrow. These guides will be sent to the HdQrs 2/15th. LONDON REGT to-night and will remain there and guide in companies to-morrow night to where platoon guides will be met.
   1 Guide per platoon and 1 guide for Coy. HdQrs. will be sent from Left and Left Centre companies to Battalion Headquarters at 10.30 p.m to-morrow night.
   1 guide per platoon and 1 for coy. HdQrs. from Right and Right Centre companies will be sent to Right Coy. HdQrs at 10.30 p.m. to-morrow night.

4. On relief companies will march back to Reserve Area in R.8 & R.9 and must be West of a North & South line through R.11.central and R.23.central by 3.15 a.m. Lt. PEAT will arrange to have guides to guides companies to billets at X Roads R.9.b.8.3. He will detail 1 limber per coy. and 1 for HdQrs. to be at Ration Dump at 12.30 a.m.

5. The undermentioned will be left in Front Line System for a period of 24 hours with incoming Unit:-

   1 Officer Battn. HdQrs.
   1   "   Coy.   HdQrs.
   1 N.C.O. per platoon.

6. All trench stores, air photos, defence schemes. etc. will be handed over, receipts obtained and forwarded to the Adjutant by 12 noon 27th. Tools will be handed over and separate receipts obtained.

7. During forenoon 27th. JULY Battalion will march to billets in Q.20.c.8.3. Further orders will be issued later.

8. Completion of relief will be sent by runner, the code word 'BERT' being used. These runners will bring back 2 runners of L.REGT. to acquaint them with the road to Battn. Hdqrs.

                          (Sd.) W.F.M.MACARA. Capt. & Adjt.
                          15th. (G.Y.) Bn. High. Light Inf.
Issued at:- 12 noon.
Copies to:- 4 companies.
            2 File.
            1 2/15th. LONDON REGT.

WAR DIARY

From 1st to 31st August 1918 inclusive

Army Form C. 2118.

INTELLIGENCE SUMMARY (Erase heading not required.)

18th (S.) Bn. HIGHLAND LIGHT INFANTRY.

Index No. 30.

Vol 31

Instructions regarding War Diaries and Intelligence Summaries are contained in F.S. Regs., Part II. and the Staff Manual respectively. Title pages will be prepared in manuscript.

Place	Date	Hour	Summary of Events and Information	Remarks and references to Appendices
MT. ROUGE.	1.8.18.		Battalion left Billets in EECKE at 10.30 p.m. 31.7.18 and marched to MT. ROUGE, arriving 1.45 a.m. Weather good. Situation quiet.	
	2.8.18.		Weather dull and wet. Operations on DRANOUTRE RIDGE cancelled owing to conditions of ground. Situation quiet.	
	3.8.18.		Weather dull with showers. Situation quiet. Battalion relieved by 15th SHERWOOD FORESTERS. Relief completed 1.30 a.m. 4.8.18. Operation Orders attached	141
West of BOESCHEPE.	4.8.18.		Battalion arrived in Camp West of BOESCHEPE at 3 a.m. Weather good.	
	5.8.18.		Wet all day. Left Camp at 9.30 p.m. for MT. ROUGE, with intent to carry out operation on DRANOUTRE RIDGE on 7th inst. Arrived MT. ROUGE 1 a.m. 6.8.18. Very Wet. Operation Order attached.	142
	6.8.18.		Weather very wet. Situation quiet. Operation on DRANOUTRE RIDGE again cancelled owing to condition of ground.	
	7.8.18.		Weather dull. Situation quiet. Battalion relieved by 1/6th CHESHIRES, 21st Brigade, 30th Division. Relief complete 2.15 a.m. Moved to MT. VIDAGNE.	
MT. VIDAGNE.	8.8.18.		Weather good. Situation normal. Battalion relieved by 1/2nd SOUTH LANCS. 89th Brigade, 30th Division. Relief complete 1.30 a.m. 9.8.18.	
EECKE.	9.8.18.		Battalion marched to camp N.W. EECKE for Divisional Rest. Arrived in Camp at 6 a.m. Weather good.	
	10.8.18.		Battalion in Camp N.W. EECKE. Weather good. Bn. Parade 9 a.m. Bn. cleaning up and reorganising Lt.-Col. Gooderson returned from 1 month's Leave.	
	11.8.18.		Do. Weather good. 1 Officer and 12 other ranks went to special Church Service at TERDEGHEM at which the King was present. After Service, party marched past the King. Bn. Church Parade on Bn. Parade Ground at 10 a.m. Afternoon: Sports, Football etc.	
	12.8.18.		Do. Weather good. Bn. carried out Training in Musketry, P.T. & B.F. Major Murray M.C. left on 2 days' Course at MERKEGHEM (Xth Corps School.)	
	13.8.18.		Do. Weather good. Bn. carried out Training in Musketry P.T. & B.F. and Platoon Schemes.	
	14.8.18.		Do. Do. Major Murray returned from Course at MERKEGHEM.	
	15.8.18.		Do. Weather good. Bn. Parade 9 a.m. Bn. training. Lt.-Col. Gooderson took over command of 106th Infantry Brigade.	
	16.8.18.		Do. Weather good. C.O.s Parade 9 a.m. Bn. training. Z Coy's Sports day.	

Army Form C. 2118.

WAR DIARY
or
INTELLIGENCE—SUMMARY.
(Erase heading not required.)

Instructions regarding War Diaries and Intelligence Summaries are contained in F.S. Regs., Part II. and the Staff Manual respectively. Title pages will be prepared in manuscript.

Place	Date	Hour	Summary of Events and Information	Remarks and references to Appendices
EECKE.	17.8.18.		Battalion in Camp N.W. of EECKE. Training in Musketry, Platoon Schemes etc. carried out. Weather good.	
	18.8.18.		Do.	
	19.8.18.		Do.	
	20.8.18.		Battalion Sports held very successfully. Weather dull but dry.	
	21.8.18.		Training in Musketry, Platoon Schemes etc. Do.	
	22.8.18.		Do. Weather good.	
	23.8.18.		Do. Bathing carried out. Do.	
	24.8.18.		Battalion moved from Camp to LE WAST, marching to CASSEL, entraining there at 2 p.m. and de--training at DESVRES at 9.30 p.m., thence by march to LE WAST, arriving there at 12.30 a.m. on the 25.8.18. Operation Order attached.	143
LE WAST.	25.8.18.		Battalion in Billets at LE WAST. Weather good. Firing of complete Musketry Course commenced by Battalion in the morning. Two Companies completed first practises.	
	26.8.18.		Do. Weather showery. Two Companies completed several of the practises, but rain interfered with firing.	
	27.8.18.		Do. First two companies finished their Course.	
	28.8.18.		Do. Owing to the heavy rain two companies were not able to complete their firing.	
	29.8.18.		Battalion left LE WAST, two companies marching to DESVRES, entraining there and detraining at CASSEL, thence by march to Camp near EECKE, and two companies travelling by motor lorry to Camp near EECKE, both parties arriving at Camp about 4 p.m.	
EECKE.	30.8.18.		Battalion in Camp near EECKE. Day spent in preparations for move into the line. Battalion marched off at 2.45 p.m. but all orders were cancelled, and Battalion returned to Camp an hour afterwards.	
	31.8.18.		Battalion in Camp at EECKE. Training carried on, special attention being paid to Tactical Schemes practising employment of weapons as for open fighting.	

Rodgers Capt
Intelligence Officer,
for Major,
Comdg. 18th Bn. Highland Light Infantry.

SECRET.   COPY NO.

15th.(S)Bn.The Sherwood Foresters.
OPERATION ORDER NO.54.   1/8/18.

Ref : Map Sheet 27.1/40,000.

1. **INTENTION.** The Battalion will move into SUPPORT POSITION to-morrow night Aug.2nd/3rd. in relief of the 18th H.L.I. and on completion of relief will be at disposal of B.G.C. 106th Inf.Bde. in case of emergency or to assist in carrying.

2. **DETAIL.**
   (a) DRESS. Fighting Order.
   (b) ORDER OF MARCH. "Z", "Y", H.Q., "W", "X" Coys. by platoons at 100 yards Interval.
   (c) STARTING POINT. Coy. Billets.
   (d) TIME.   "Z"Coy. 9.30 pm.   "Y"Coy. 9.45 pm.
        Bn.H.Q. 9.55 pm.   "W" 10 pm.   "X"Coy. 10.15pm
   (e) ROUTE. BOESCHEPE, Water Tower, thence by Track to MONT ROUGE.

3. **DISPOSITIONS.** Coys. will occupy same positions as during previous Tour in Support.

4. **ADVANCE PARTIES.** Advance Parties consisting of 1 Officer, 1 N.C.O. & 1 man per Coy. will proceed at 5 pm Aug.2nd. to take over Shelters and Trench Stores.

5. **STORES.** All Packs, Officers Valises & other Stores will be stacked at Bn.H.Q. by 9 pm.
   Lieut.N.G.Smith,M.C. will be in charge of this Dump until handed over to Quarter-Master.

6. **TRANSPORT.** 2 L.G.Limbers per Coy. and 1 for Bn.H.Q. will report at Bn.H.Q. as early as possible after 8.30 pm. These Limbers will convey Lewis Guns, Ammunition, & 2 days Rations & Water. On arrival at Bn.H.Q. Limbers will be sent direct to O.C.Coys. and will proceed to Support Positions under the Orders of O.C.Coys.

7. **RUNNERS.** 1 Runner per Coy., who will be temporary attached Bgde H.Q. will report to the Adjutant on arrival at Support Position. Runner from "W" & "Y" Coys. must know the right of Line, and Runner from "X" & "Z" Coys. the Left of the Line.

8. **TRENCH STORES.** Trench Stores must be carefully handed & taken over. Lists shewing (a) Stores handed over to 15th Cheshires in Reserve, & (b) Stores taken over from 18th H.L.I. in Support must be forwarded to the Adjutant by 2 am Aug.3rd.

9. **A.A.POSITIONS.** 1.A.A.Position per Coy. will be mounted.

10. **CODE.** Arrival in Support will be notified to Bn.H.Q. by phone or runner. Code word "H O T".

ACKNOWLEDGE.

Issued at 9 pm.

Copies to :- NO.1. C.O.   NO.11. 18th H.L.I.
              2. "W" Coy.   12. File.
              3. "X" "   13. War Diary.
              4. "Y" "
              5. "Z" "
              6. H.Q.
              7. Bde.   (Sd) Graham Callow. Capt. & Adjt.,
              S.R.S.M.   15th.(S)Bn.The Sherwood Foresters.
              9. T.O.
              10. Quarter-Master

SECRET.   OPERATION ORDERS. No.141.   Copy No.
            'B' HIGHLAND LIGHT INFANTRY.   3.8.18.

Reference Sheets 27 and 28. 1/40,000.

1. a. The Battalion will move from present location at 10.30 p.m. into Reserve Area with Hdqrs. about R.9.a.4.5., taking over available accommodation from 15th SHERWOOD FORESTERS.
   b. While in this Area the Battalion with the remainder of 106 Brigade will be in divisional Reserve.

2. Companies will take over from 15th SHERWOODS as follows:-
   W Coy. from W Coy. S.F.   X Coy. from X Coy. S.F.
   Y "   " Y "   "   Z "   " Z "   "

3. Advance parties consisting of one Officer per Coy. and one N.C.O. per platoon will be sent to take over and arrange advanced accommodation. They will report at Bn. Hdqrs. at 5.30 p.m. Lt. Hutchison and one N.C.O. will report for Hdqrs.

4. Guides from Advanced parties will meet Companies at MIDNIGHT at Cross Roads R.9.b.8.3. (W. end of BOESCHEPE.)

5. All S.A.A., bombs, picks and shovels, flares, S.O.S. rockets, petrol tins, and all other equipment brought in by Bn. will be taken out. O.C. Coys. will ensure that no material is lost, as it will be required in the near future.

6. One limber per Coy, and one for Hdqrs. will report at Ration Dump near Brigade Hdqrs.
   Companies will arrange to dump LEWIS Guns and magazines, camp kettles petrol tins and bombs and mess stores at above dump at 10 p.m. Nos.1 of gun teams will remain at dump as a loading party and will accompany limbers, which should be met at W. end of BOESCHEPE by guides.

7. Order of march.   W, X, Y, Z, Hdqrs.
   Starting Point.   Brigade Hdqrs.
   TIME.   10.30 p.m.
                      Platoons at 100 yards distance.
   ROUTE.   WESTOUTRE - road through M.8.c.d. - M.7.d. -
                      R.18.a.5.7. - track to R.11.d.0.6. - BOESCHEPE.

8. Companies will render to Bn. Hdqrs. by 6 p.m., list of trench stores to be handed over. These will be forwarded to 12th H.L.I. who are handing over present billets to 15th CHESHIRES.
   Battalion Bombs will NOT be included in these lists.
   O.C. Companies will render Certificates by 9 p.m. that all billets are left clean.

9. Companies will report departure to Bn. Hdqrs. and their arrival in new billets to Bn. Hdqrs. in reserve, giving location of Coy. Hdqrs. by runners.

10. ACKNOWLEDGE.

    Issued at 4 p.m.   For O.C. 18th H.L.I.
                                        (Signed.) ROB. DAGGER. Capt.

    Copy No.1. War Diary.
         2. O.O. File.
         3. O.C. W Coy.
         4. O.C. X "
         5. O.C. Y "
         6. O.C. Z "

SECRET.   OPERATION ORDERS. No.142.   Copy No.
                    'B' HIGHLAND LIGHT INFANTRY.   4.8.18.

1. Battalion will move to Forward Area (Mont Rouge) and occupy loca-
   -tions occupied by it until night of 3/4th inst.
   Companies will occupy bivouacs they were in before.

2. Battalion will leave Camp at 9 p.m. in order to reach starting
   point Road Junction at R.17.central at 10.30 p.m.
   Order of march.   W, X, Y, Z, Hdqrs. 100 yards distance between
                                              platoons.

3. One limber per Coy. will report to Companies to load Lewis Guns,
   Bombs, and Mess Stores.
   Nos.1 of Gun teams will act as loading party.
   In the event of limbers not being loaded in time to move off with
   Company, above loading party will stand by guns etc., load, and
   accompany limbers forward to Ration Dump. O.C. Coys. will in this
   event arrange for carrying parties to remove their Stores from the
   dump on arrival of limbers.

   Issued at 2 p.m.   For O.C. 18th H.L.I.
                                                 (Sgd.) ROB. DAGGER. Capt.

   Copy No.1. War Diary.
        2. O.O. File.
        3.   Do.
        4. O.C. W Coy.
        5. O.C. X "
        6. O.C. Y "
        7. O.C. Z "

SPECIAL BATTALION ORDER No. 16.

Ref: Combined Sheet 27 S.E. & 28 S.W. 1/20,000.
St SYLVESTRE & BORRE 1/20,000.

8.8.1918.

1. The Battalion, less "B" Team, will relieve the front line from S.4.b.2.2. to M.28.d.4.3. in two stages. First stage to commence to-morrow night 8/9th August in accordance with attached march table, first company to move off at 6 p.m. Detailed order for 2nd stage will be issued later.

2. GUIDES. One guide for Battalion Headquarters and One guide per Platoon will meet battalion near LADGET FARM, R.11.c.80.90. at 10 p.m. Coy. H.Qrs. will march with the leading platoon.

3. OFFICERS' VALISES. Will be ready for loading at Quartermaster store at 4 p.m. Officers of "B" Team will stack their valises separately.

4. OFFICERS' MESS KIT. Will be packed on their Lewis Gun Limber under Coy. Commander's arrangement. Any kit not taken up the line will be stacked at Q.M. Stores at 4 p.m. for storeage.

5. LEWIS GUNS. Companies Lewis Guns will be taken on one Lewis Gun limber with 20 magazines per gun in buckets. These limbers will proceed with transport to BENGAL COTTAGES R.18.a.6.8. from where guns will be manhandled.

6. TRANSPORT.
(a). Will proceed under arrangement of Transport Officer and will meet battalion at R.7.a.70.90. at 8.30 p.m.
(b). One limber will report to Battn. H.Qrs at 5 p.m. for Officers' mess kit etc., and will proceed with Transport.
(c). Signal Limber. Half the signal limber will proceed with Transport to BENGAL COTTAGES from where equipment required must be manhandled.
(d). Maltese Cart. will not be required.

7. RATIONS & WATER. Will be delivered to Companies at their new Headquarters tomorrow night, 8/9th inst., under arrangements of Transport Officer. Time to be notified later. No water must be drawn from wells in vicinity of SUPPORT Battalion Headqrs.

8. "B" TEAMS. As already detailed, will parade under Major Stather at a time and place to be notified later.

9. ADVANCE PARTY. 2/Lt.WREN for Headquarters and One Officer per Coy. and One NCO. per Platoon will go direct to the front line to-~~morrow~~ Day, 8th inst, and will be at 106th Infantry Brigade H.Qrs at M.20.d.3.3. at 8 p.m. where guide will meet them. This party will report to Orderly Room at 4 p.m., 8th inst.

10. COMPLETION OF RELIEF. Will be reported by runner to Battalion H.Qrs

11. BATTALION HEADQUARTERS. Will close at present camp at 5 p.m. and re-open at M.21.a.50.30. at 11 p.m.

12. REG: AID POST. Will be established at Battalion Headquarters.

13. ACKNOWLEDGE.

Captain & Adjutant.
2nd Bn. South Lancs Regiment.

Issued at 10 a.m.
Copies to :-
O.C.ALL Coys.
  " H.Qrs.
Q.M. T.O. M.O.
18th H.L.I.
Major Mott.
War Diary.
C.O. FILE.

SECRET.   OPERATION ORDERS. No.143.   Copy No:
                           'B' HIGHLAND LIGHT INFANTRY.   23.8.18.

Reference Maps. HAZEBROUCKE 5A 1/100,000.
                CALAIS 13.

1. The Battalion will move tomorrow, 24th inst. by train and march route
   to COLEMBERT Area for Musketry Training, relieving the 17th Royal
   Scots in that Area.
   Battalion will march to CASSEL station and entrain there for
   DESVRES, from which point they will march to billets in LE WAST.

2. The following Details will remain behind:-
        Transport, and certain personnel of the Q.M. Stores.
        O.C. Coys. will detail 2 men per Coy. to remain as guards on
        Coy. Lines: 1 cook per Coy: All men detailed for Leave and
        men detailed for medical treatment.
   Nominal Roll of all personnel being left behind will be rendered
   to Bn. Orderly Room by 8 p.m. tonight.
   All prisoners under-going F.P. will rejoin their Companies on Bn.
   Parade tomorrow morning.
   Capt. Eekhout will remain behind in charge of Details and will be
   responsible for the safe custody of all tentage and stores.

3. All surplus Coy. and Mess Stores, Officers' spare kit, etc. to be
   in Q.M. Stores by 8 p.m. tonight. Officers' valises and Mess stores
   accompanying Battalion will be dumped outside H.Q. Mess by 8 a.m.
   tomorrow morning.

4. All Lewis Guns, packed, spare parts and 16 magazines per gun to be
   taken with Companies. Coy. Lewis Gun Limbers will be loaded tonight
   and a report to this effect rendered to the Adjutant by 8 p.m. tonight.

5. ORDER OF MARCH.   H.Q., W, X, Y, Z.
                          Coy. Limbers with Companies.
                          Baggage wagons, plus any other wheeled vehicles
                          under Transport Officer.
                          Usual intervals: 100 yards between Coys.
   Time.   9.30 a.m.

Issued at 5 p.m.   (Signed.) R. DAGGER. Capt. & A/Adjt
                                                'B' HIGHLAND LIGHT INFANTRY.

Copy No.1. War Diary.
      2. O.O. File.
      3.   Do.
      4. O.C. W Coy.
      5. O.C. X "
      6. O.C. Y "
      7. O.C. Z "
      8. 2nd in Command.
      9. T.O. & QrMr.
     10. Medical Officer.
     11. R.S.M.

Map Sheet 27.

SECRET

OPERATION ORDER NO: 176.

29/8/18.

1. The 35th British Division will relieve the 36th British Division between 29th and 31st August 1918.

2. The 104th Infty Brigade will relieve the 106th Infty Brigade in area S. of STEENVOORDE on Aug 30th, and will be in Divisional Reserve.

3. The 18th Lancashire Fusiliers will relieve the 18th H.L.I. in camp about Q 19 b 6.8 on the afternoon of Aug 30th.
Route: LE GRAND BRUXELLES - road junction P 30 a 5.1 - road junction Q 20 c 3.9.
Order of march: Band and Headquarters
                  "W" Company
                  "X"   "
                  "Y"   "
                  "Z"   ".
100x between companies will be maintained on the march.
Dress. Full marching order.
The head of the column will rest at LE GRAND BRUXELLES ready to move at 5 pm.

4. Advance parties, consisting of six O.R's per company and H.Q., will report to Lieut. Lingeman at Battn.H.Q. at 8 am.

5. Lewis gun limbers and cookers will accompany companies.

6. The camp will be left scrupulously clean.

7. Officers' valises, company stores, etc. will be dumped at Coy.HQ by 2 pm. (H.Q. at gate on the road).

8. All tents and trench covers will be handed over to the incoming Battalion in situ.

9. Guides (found by advance party) will be met at road junction Q 20 c 3.9.

10. The remainder of the Transport and Q.M.Stores will move independently during the day.

11. Acknowledge.

Lieutenant & A/Adjutant,
18th Service Battalion Lancashire Fusiliers.

Hour of issue ......
Copies to:- 1. Comdg Officer
             2. 2nd in Command
             3. O.C. "W" Company
             4. "   "X"   "
             5. "   "Y"   "
             6. "   "Z"   "
             7. Officer i/c Headquarters
             8. Quartermaster
             9. Transport Officer
            10. Medical Officer
            11. R.S.M.
            12. War Diary
            13. File.
            14. O.C. 18th H.L.I.

WAR DIARY
INTELLIGENCE SUMMARY.

From 1st to 30th September 1918 inclusive
Army Form C. 2118.

16th (G.Y.) Bn. HIGHLAND LIGHT INFANTRY.

(Erase heading not required.)

Index No. 21.

Place	Date	Hour	Summary of Events and Information	Remarks and references to Appendices
BECKM.	1.9.18.		Battalion in Camp near BECKM in Divisional Reserve. Preparations for move next day proceeded with. Weather fool.	
ROAD CAMP.	2.9.18.		Battalion marched to ROAD CAMP in ST. JAN-TER-BIEZEN area, arriving there about 2 p.m. Weather good.	
	3.9.18.		Battalion in billets. During the earlier part of the day the Battalion completed preparations for the line, and at 8.25 p.m. entrained at ELSENDAM STATION, to relieve the 119th Regiment of the 30th American Division in the CANAL SECTOR of II Corps Front. Relief carried out without incident.	144 Operation Order attached.
CANAL SECTOR.	4.9.18.		Battalion in the Line. Enemy artillery very active during the day, to which our own artillery replied effectively. Patrolling done by Front Companies. Casualties:- 1 Officer and 5 men wounded.	145 Operation Order attached.
	5.9.18.		Battalion in the Line. Enemy artillery continued its activity sending over a large number of gas shells. Patrolling in daylight carried out with important results. Casualties:- 1 man killed; 6 men wounded; 2 men gassed.	
	6.9.18.		Battalion in the Line. Considerable enemy activity. Inter Company relief carried out. Casualties 4 men wounded.	
	7.9.18.		Battalion in the Line. Enemy artillery active. Casualties: 2 men killed. Weather unsettled.	
	8.9.18.		Do. Day passed without incident. Weather showery.	
	9.9.18.		Battalion in the Line. Weather unsettled. On the night 9/10th the Battalion was relieved in the front line by the 18th H.L.I. and took over dispositions in support Battalion Area. Relief completed and Support positions occupied without incident. O.O. attached.	146
	10.9.18.		Battalion in Support. Weather fair. Enemy aircraft active.	
	11.9.18.		Do.	
	12.9.18.		Do. On the night 12/13th the Battalion was relieved by the 15th CHESHIRE REGT. (105th Inf. Brigade.) and marched to Reserve billets near V.M.SAMILLIE. Relief completed without incident. Operation order attached.	147
VLAMER- TINGHE.	13.9.18.		Battalion in reserve. Bathing carried out. Weather showery.	
	14.9.18.		Do. Weather wet.	
	15.9.18.		Do. Weather broken.	
	16.9.18.		Do. During the night 16/17th the Battalion relieved the 18th LANC. FUSILIERS in the left sub-sector of the CANAL SECTOR. Relief completed without incident. O.O. attached.	148

WAR DIARY
or
INTELLIGENCE SUMMARY

(Erase heading not required.)

Army Form C. 2118.

Place	Date	Hour	Summary of Events and Information	Remarks and references to Appendices
CALAIS SECTOR.	17.9.18.		Battalion in the line. Enemy shelling active. Casualties: 1 man killed and 10 men wounded.	
	18.9.18.		Do. A good deal of shelling from both sides during the day. Casualties:- 6 men wounded.	
	19.9.18.		Battalion in the line. Enemy active.	
	20.9.18.		Do. Inter Company relief carried out without incident.	
	21.9.18.		Do. Casualties: 2 men wounded.	
	22.9.18.		Do. Do. 3 do. The Battalion was relieved by units from the 104th and 106th Inf. Brigades, and proceed to billets in BRAEMBOEK Area. Operation order attached.	149.
BRAEMBOEK.	23.9.18.		Battalion in billets. Day spent in resting and cleaning. At 7.15 p.m. the Battalion embussed for School Camp, ST. JAN-TER-BIEZEN Area, arriving there later and taking up good billets. Relief completed without incident.	
SCHOOL CAMP.	24.9.18.		Battalion in billets. Weather dull but dry. Parades were held under O.C. Companies for completing Battle Equipment.	
	25.9.18.		Battalion in billets. Weather wet during forenoon. Parades under O.C. Companies as before.	
	26.9.18.		Do. Refitting of Battle Equipment completed. At 8 p.m. the Battalion marched to ABEELE where they embussed, and debussed at VLAMERTINGHE and occupied the billets which they had vacated on the 23rd inst. arriving there about midnight. O.O. attached.	150.
	27.9.18.		Battalion in billets. In the evening the Battalion marched out to take up their assembly positions in view of the attack to commence on the following morning. O.O. attached.	151.
	28.9.18.		Battalion attacked under orders of Brigade and took all objectives. Attack still in progress. Operation Order attached.	152.
	29.9.18.		Attack still in progress.	
	30.9.18.		Do.	

[signature]
Capt.
For Lt.-Col.
Comdg. 18th (G.Y.) Bn. Highland Light Infantry.

SECRET.   OPERATION ORDERS. No.144.   Copy No.
                 'B' HIGHLAND LIGHT INFANTRY.

Reference Map. Sheet 27. 1/40,000.

1. The 106th Infantry Brigade Group will move to St.JAN-TER-BIEZEN, tomorrow 2nd September 1918.

2. The Battalion will march tomorrow, 2nd September to St.JAN-TER-BIEZEN (Road Camp L.2.a.)

3. The Battalion will march from Battalion Parade Ground in the fol-
    -lowing order:-
                    Hdqrs. W, X, Y, Z.
    Starting time. 9 a.m.
    Coy. Cookers and Limbers and 1st Line Transport will be in rear of Battalion under Transport Officer.
    Route.   Road Junction R.32.d.4.0.- RATHCOT K.16.b.8.8.-
                    WATOU CHURCH E.4.b.5.7.- CROSS ROADS E.30.c.4.6.-
                    St.JAN-TER-BIEZEN.
    100 yards between Companies.
    500 yards between Battalions.
    25 yards between every six vehicles.
    Strict march discipline must be maintained.

4. O.C. Y Coy. will detail a rear guard of 1 Officer and 1 platoon to collect stragglers.

5. Reports to Head of Column.

    Issued at 9.15 p.m.
                                              Rob Scygged
                                              Capt. & A/Adjt.
                                           'B' HIGHLAND LIGHT INFANTRY.

    Copy No.1. War Diary.
         2. O.O. File.
         3.   Do.
         4. O.C. W Coy.
         5. O.C. X "
         6. O.C. Y "
         7. O.C. Z "
         8. 2nd in Command.
         9. Quartermaster.
        10. Transport Officer.
        11. Medical Officer.

1/9/18

SECRET.   OPERATION (MARCH) ORDERS. No.145.   Copy No.
                           'B' HIGHLAND LIGHT INFANTRY.   3.9.18.

1. The Battalion will move into the Forward Area CANAL Sector on night
   3/4th Septr. by march and rail.

2. Battalion will entrain at BLUEGRASS Station F.28.a.2.0. and detrain
   at YALE Station H.15.d.0.6.

3. MARCH. Starting Point.   ROAD CAMP.
           Time.   5 p.m.
           Order.   H.Q., X, W, Y, Z Coys.
           Dress;   Fighting Order.

4. ENTRAINING. Battn. H.Q. and X Coy. will entrain at 6.40 p.m.
                W, Y, Z Coys. will entrain at 6.50 p.m.

5. TRANSPORT. Limbers for carriage of L.G. and water will proceed
   with H.Q. and Companies to entraining station.

   Issued at 12 noon.
                                               [signature]
                                               Capt. & A/Adjt.
                                        'B' HIGHLAND LIGHT INFANTRY.

   Copy No.1. War Diary.   Copy No.7. O.C. Z Coy.
        2. O.C. File.   8. 2nd in Command.
        3.   Do.   9. Transport Officer.
        4. O.C. W Coy.   10. Quartermaster.
        5. O.C. X "   11. Medical Officer.
        6. O.C. Y "   12. 106th Infantry Brigade.

SECRET.   File   OPERATION ORDERS No.   Copy No.
                              18th. HIGHLAND LIGHT INFANTRY.
                                                    4th. September. 1918.
Reference sheets YPRES & WYTSCHAETE. 1/10.000
----

1. The 41st. Division on our right attacked at 5.30 a.m. to-day and report situation as follows:-
   <u>Left Battn. Right Brigade.</u> Dug in 600 Yds. East of railway running North & South through N.19. Central and in touch with Battalion on the left. One company 100 Yds. East of Craters in N.18.b.
   <u>Right Battn. Right Brigade.</u> Echeloned in rear to the Right.
   <u>Left Brigade.</u> Objectives reached at RIFLE BRIDGE and touch established with Right Company 18th. High. L. Inf.
   F.O.O., 160th. Inf. Brigade reports at 6.55 a.m. Craters at N.24.c. 8.4. and OAK TRENCH (N.24.a.) held by enemy.

2. In the event of the 41st. Division moving forward towards MESSINES- St. ELOI ROAD, 106th. Inf. Brigade will advance and hold St. ELOI - LOCK 8 Road.

3. The Battalion will attack on a two company front as follows:-

              RIGHT COY.   Y COY.
              LEFT   "   X "
              SUPPORT "   Z "
              RESERVE "   W "

4. BOUNDARIES.
   Battalion Boundaries. Right. MOATED GRANGE (O.1.a.) - O.4. Central
                         Left I.31.d.25.40 - I.32.d.0.3.
   <u>Company Boundaries.</u>
   Right Coy. Right Boundary. MOATED GRANGE (O.1.a.) - O.4.Central.
              Left Boundary. O.1.b.2.8. - O.2.b.05.70.
   Left Coy. Right Boundary. O.1.b.2.8. - O.2.b.05.70.
              Left Boundary. I.31.d.25.40 - I.32.d.0.3.

5. <u>OBJECTIVES.</u> St. ELOI - LOCK 8 ROAD between Battalion Headquarters.

6. LIAISON. O.C. Y Coy. will maintain touch with 10th. Bn. QUEENS, 124th. Inf. Brigade on his Right.
            O.C. X Coy. will maintain touch with Y Coy. on his Right and also with 12th. H.L.I. on his left.

7. ACTION DURING ASSAULT. At ZERO the assaulting companies will leave their trenches and attack on a two platoon frontage.
            Support company will leave G.H.Q. line and take up position in VOORMEZEELE SWITCH.
            Reserve company will receive special orders.

8. ACTION AFTER ASSAULT. On the objectives being gained the assaulting companies will consolidate in depth within their respective boundaries as far back and including FRENCH TRENCH.
            Support company will occupy and strengthen VOORMEZEELE SWITCH
            Mixed posts will be established with Units on the flanks of the assaulting companies.
            Reserve company will be disposed about VOORMEZEELE and MIDDLE-SEX LANE, but will not take up it's position until the receipt of special orders.

9. ARTILLERY. Second Corps Heavy Artillery will not fire West of the Line O.3.a.0.0. - I.33.c.0.7. - MIDDLESEX ROAD - LA CHAPELLE - MANOR FARM until further notice.

~~13.~~ A contact aeroplane, marking 2 black flaps (one on each wing) will fly over the front as the situation demands.

10. **TRENCH MORTARS.** Officer of 106th. T.M.B. attached to 18th.H.L.I will report to O.C. 18th. H.L.I. for special orders.

11. **DRESS.** Battle Order. Each man will carry 200 Rounds of S.A.A. and 2 bombs per man as far as possible with the usual exceptions A proportion of ground flares and aeroplane discs will be carried by Front Line Companies.

12. **MEDICAL.** Aid Post will be established at I.31.c.3.7.

13. **REPORTS.** Os.C. Companies will constantly keep Battn. H.Q. Informed of the situation.
   Battle Battn. H.Q. will be established at I.31.c.3.7.

14. ZERO Hour will be notified later.

15. Contact Aeroplanes, Markings 2 Black Flaps, (one on each Wing) will fly over the front as the situation demands.

16. ACKNOWLEDGE.

George Reid
Lieut. & A/Adjt.,

Issued at 7 p.m. by runner.   18th. Highland Light Infantry.

Copies to O.C. W Coy.
      " X "
      " Y "
      " Z "
Medical Officer.
O.C. 12th. H.L.I.
" 10th. QUEENS.
" 106th. T.M.Battery.
H.Q. 106th. Inf. Brigade.
War Diary & File.

SECRET.   OPERATION (RELIEF) ORDERS. No.145   Copy No.
                           'B' HIGHLAND LIGHT INFANTRY.

Reference Map. 1/40,000 Sheet 27 and 28.
               1/20,000 Sheet 23 N.W.

1. The 55th British Division will relieve the 30th American Division in the CANAL Sector of IIad Corps Front commencing night 3/4th September.

2. 106th Inf. Brigade will relieve 119th American Regiment, less one Batt. on night Sept. 3/4th as follows:-
   (a) 18th H.L.I. will relieve H.Q. and 2 Front Coys. 3rd Batt. 119th Regt. on Right Front.
   (b) 15th H.L.I. will relieve H.Q. and 2 front Coys. 1st Batt. 119th Regt. on Left Front.
   (c) 17th R.SCOTS will relieve 2 Coys. 3rd Batt. 119th Regt. and 2 Coys. 1st Batt. 119th Regt. in Support.

3. Disposition of Battalion.
   Right Front Coy. Y Coy. 18th H.L.I. will relieve G. Coy. 119th Regt.
   Left Front Coy.   X "   "   "   "   E. "   "
   Support Coy.   Z "   "   "   "   Parts of K and M
                                                     Coy. 119th Regt.
   Reserve Coy.   W "   "   "   "   "   "   "

4. GUIDES. Guides, 6 per Coy. and 1 for Batt. H.Q. will be at Road Junction H.32.a.3.9. at 8.30 p.m.

5. LIAISON. O.C. Y Coy. will be responsible that liaison is established with 3rd Batt. 105th American Regt. on right.
   O.C. X Coy. will be responsible that liaison is established with 18th H.L.I. on left.

6. Air photos, Defence Schemes, Work, S.O.S. Signals, S.A.A. Trench Stores etc., will be taken over on relief.
   Receipts for stores taken over will be forwarded to Batt. H.Q. with T.P.R. on the morning 4th Sept.

7. MEDICAL. Aid Post at H.24.c.30.10.

8. REPORTS. Battalion H.Q. at H.36.a.65.80.
   Brigade H.Q. at H.22.a.4.0.
   On completion of relief 2 runners per Company will accompany runners reporting Relief and will remain at Battn. H.Q. for Duty during the period of the tour.

9. Completion of relief will be reported to Batt. H.Q. by Runner. Code word "GOOD".

10. ACKNOWLEDGE.

    Issued at 12 noon.
                                              Capt. & A/Adjt.
                                              'B' HIGHLAND LIGHT INFANTRY.

Copy No.1. War Diary.
        2. O.C. Wlc.
        3.   Do.
        4. O.C. W Coy.
        5. O.C. X "
        6. O.C. Y "
        7. O.C. Z "
        8. 2nd in Command.
        9. Transport Officer.
       10. Quartermaster.
       11. Medical Officer.
       12. 106th Infantry Brigade.

2/9/18

SECRET.

OPERATION ORDERS No. 146. Copy No. _____
18th. HIGHLAND LIGHT INF.

8th., September, 1918.

Reference sheets. YPRES & WYTSCHAETE. 1/10,000
----

1. The battalion will be relieved ~~by B High. L.~~ I. in the Right Sub-Sector CANAL SECTOR on the night 9th/10th. Sept. 1918. by the A Bn. High. L.Inf. as follows:-
   B Coy. A H.L.I. will relieve Z Coy. B. H.L.I. Right Front Coy.
   C "   "   "   "   "   W "   "   "   Left   "   "
   D "   "   "   "   "   Y "   "   "   Support.   "
   A "   "   "   "   "   X "   "   "   Reserve   "

2. ADVANCE PARTIES. Parties of 1 Officer per Coy. and 1 N.C.O. per platoon from A H.L.I. will proceed into the line 24 hours in advance
   Parties of 1 Officer and 2 O.Rs. per coy. of B. H.L.I. will leave Bn. H.Q. at 10.30 a.m. 9th. Sept. 1918. to take over dispositions in Support Battalion Area.

3. GUIDES. 5 guides per company will report at Bn. H.Q. at 8 p.m. 9th. Sept. 1918. to guide in relieving companies.

4. TRENCH STORES. All aeroplane photographs, defence schemes, maps, programmes of work, patrols etc., will be handed over on relief.
   Companies will carry out on relief, aeroplane flares, discs, two bombs and 200 Rounds S.A.A. per man and all petrol tins.

5. SUPPORT BATTALION AREA. On relief companies will take over dispositions in Support Battalion Area of relieving companies, i.e.,
   W Coy. B. H.L.I. take over from C Coy. A H.L.I.
   X "   "   "   "   "   "   A "   "   "
   Y "   "   "   "   "   "   D "   "   "
   Z "   "   "   "   "   "   B "   "   "

6. Rations and water for H Q., W, X, & Y coys. will be at PIONEER JUNCTION to-morrow night.
   Z Coy's. rations and water will be at WHITEHOUSE STATION.
   Companies will draw their own rations and water on arrival in new Area.

7. Completion of relief in forward area will be notified to Bn.H.Q. by wire using code word 'WEDDING'.
   Arrival in Reserve Area will be notified to Bn. H.Q by wire using code word 'BELLS'.

8. ACKNOWLEDGE.

Lieut. & A/Adjt.,

Issued at _____ p.m. by runner.   18th. HIGHLAND LIGHT INFANTRY.

Copies to O.C. W Coy.
          "   X "
          "   Y "
          "   Z "
          W.D. & File.

SECRET.
OPERATION ORDERS No. 147.   Copy No. _____
18th. Highland Light Inf.
11th., September, 1918.

Ref. map. Sheet 28. 1/40,000

1. The 106th. Inf. Brigade will be relieved by the 105th. Inf. Bde. in the Right Sub-Sector of the CANAL SECTOR on the night 12th./13th., September, 1918.

2. The battalion will be relieved in the Support Area by the 15th. Bn. CHESHIRE REGT. as follows:-

   W Coy. 15th. Cheshires will relieve X Coy. 18th. H.L.I.
   X   "   "   "   "   W   "   "   "
   Y   "   "   "   "   Y   "   "   "
   Z   "   "   "   "   Z   "   "   "

3. **GUIDES.** 4 Guides per coy. and one guide from Bn. HdQrs. will meet incoming Unit at Roads Junction H.21.b.9.9. These guides will report to Battn. HdQrs at 6.45 p.m. 12th. Sept., 1918.

4. **TRENCH STORES.** Companies will hand over on relief all aeroplane photographs, defence and 'Advanced Guard' schemes, trench stores, and dumps of S.A.A. Etc. Receipts for stores handed over to reach Adjutant by noon 13th. inst.
   Companies will carry out on relief, aeroplane flares, discs, 2 bombs and 200 rounds S.A.A. perman, and all petrol tins.

5. On relief, the battalion will march to Reserve billets evacuated by 15th. Bn. CHESHIRE REGT., in G.11.c. and d and G.12.a.

6. **ROUTE.** Road Junction (H.22.a.35.90). - Road Junction (H.14.b.45.75 - Road Junction (H.8.d.70.30.) - H.8.a.50.25. - G.12.a.50.90.

7. **Advance Parties.** A party of 1 Officer and 1 N.C.O. per Coy and Lieut. J. BRYCE M.C. and 1 O.R. for HdQrs. will leave present Bn. H.Q at 2.30 p.m. 12th. inst. to take over billets in Reserve Area.
   Guides from this party will be at Road Junction G.12.a.50.90 at 8.30 p.m. to meet battalion and guide companies to coy. billets.

8. Completion of relief will be notified by wire to Battn. HdQrs. using the code word 'VALISE'.
   Companies will report arrival in billets to Battn. HdQrs. (G.11.d.8.1.). by runner.

9. ACKNOWLEDGE.

                                        Lieut. & A/Adjt.,
Issued at 2.30 p.m. by runner.   18th. Highland Light Infantry.

   Copies Nos. 1 To O.C. W Coy.
              2 "   "   X "
              3 "   "   Y "
              4 "   "   Z "
              5 "   2nd. in Command.
              6 "   15th. Bn. CHESHIRE REGT.
              7-9 " W.D. & O.C. FILE.

SECRET. OPERATION ORDERS. No.148.   Copy No.
         'B' HIGHLAND LIGHT INFANTRY.   16.9.18.

Reference Map 28 N.W. 1/20,000.

1. The 106th Inf. Brigade will relieve the 104th Inf. Brigade in the Left Sub-sector of the CANAL SECTOR on the night 16/17th inst.

2. The Battalion will relieve the 18th Lancs. Fus. on the Right Front of the Left Sub-sector as follows:-
   W Coy. 18th H.L.I.   Front Line Coy.
   X   "   "   Support   "
   Y   "   "   Right Reserve "
   Z   "   "   Left   "   "
   The Battalion will move off by Companies, leaving present billets in the following order:- H.Q., W Coy., X Coy., Y Coy., Z Coy.
   Starting Point. Head of Column will pass Road Junction G.18.a.50.86. at 6.10 p.m. 100 yards interval will be maintained between Companies to Cross Roads H.8.d.6.3., where the Battalion will halt until light allows of moving forward. Thereafter, Companies will move by platoons a distance of 50 yds. between each platoon being maintained.

3. GUIDES. 5 guides per Company will be met at Battalion Headquarters, BELGIAN BATTERY CORNER (H.24.a.50.85. Guides to posts as required by W and X Coys. will be picked up at CANAL BANK at I.26.c.20.70.

4. TRENCH STORES. All aeroplane photographs, defence schemes, programme of work on hand and contemplated, S.A.A., bombs, tools etc., will be taken over and lists sent to Adjutant at Bn. H.Q. before 12 noon 17th inst.

5. Completion of relief will be notified to Battalion Headquarters by the quickest method, the Code Word 'APPLE' being used.

6. Battalion Headquarters will be at H.24.a.50.85.

                                   (Sgd.) ROB. DAGGER.
                                         Capt. & A/Adjt.,
Issued at   by runner.   'B' HIGHLAND LIGHT INFANTRY.

Copies to O.C. W Coy.
          "   X "
          "   Y "
          "   Z "
          2nd in Command.
          W.D. & O.O. FILE.
          O.C. 18th L.F.

SECRET.   Operation Orders No. 149.   Copy No. 8
                 'B' HIGHLAND LIGHT INFANTRY.
                              22nd., September, 1918.

Ref. map. YPRES 1/10,000.

1. On the night 22/23rd. September, 1918, 'B' Bn. Highland Light Inf.
will be relieved by Units of the 104th. & 105th. Ind. Brigades as
follows;-

H.L.I. Units.	AREA.	Relieving Units.
Right Front Coy.	Front Line Area.	4th. N. STAFFS R.
Y Coy.	About LA CHAPELLE	O Coy.
	Two Supporting platoons.	P " Do.
	Platoon Area around	
	IRON BRIDGE.	Q " Do.
Left Front Coy.	Southern Area.	N Coy. 15th. SHERWOOD FORR.
Z Coy.	Northern Area.	M " DO. Do.
	Coy. H.Q. at	
	BEDFORD HOUSE.	Bn. H.Q. Do. Do.
Right Support Coy.	G.H.Q. 1st.Line)	
X Coy.	& Area behind.)	-S Coy. 4th. N. STAFFS R.
	H.30.d.8.0. -)	
	H.25.a.2.5.)	
	G.H.Q. 1st.Line)	
	and area behind)	-R Coy. 15th. SHERWOOD FORR.
	H.25.a.2.5. -)	
	H.19.c.5.1.)	
	X Coy. H.Q. and)	-W Coy. H.Q. & 1 Platoon
	area about H.24.d)	17th. LANCS. FUS.
	7.7.)	
Left Support Coy.	Rear platoon about)	-12th. Platoon Y Coy. 17th. LANCS.F.
W Coy.	H.19.a.4.2.)	
	G.H.Q. 1st.Line)-)	3 Platoons of W Coy.
	Right & Centre Pltn.)	17th. LANCS. FUS.
	G.H.Q. 1st.Line.)-	11th. Platoon Y Coy.
	Left Platoon.)	17th. LANCS. FUS.
	W Coy. H.Q. at)	Battn. H.Q. 17th. LANCS. F.
	SWAN CHATEAU)	

The relief will be an area relief, i.e. the incoming Units
will not necessarily take over exact dispositions as held by the
'B' Bn. Highland Light Infantry.

2. GUIDES for advanced parties (Y & Z Coys. only) will be in readiness
at Coy.H.Q. at 7 p.m. as per attached table. Guides for relieving
Units will be at Bn. HdQrs. as per attached table.

3. TRENCH STORES. All trench stores, maps, etc., will be handed over
on relief and receipts obtained for same. All petrol tins, ground
flares, extra bandoliers of S.A.A. etc. will be taken out.

4. TRANSPORT. Limbers for conveyance of Lewis Guns, Petrol tins,
Stores. etc. will be at A.D.S. BELGIAN BATTERY CORNER.

5. After relief, companies will proceed to billets in BRANDHOEK AREA.
ROUTE:- BELGIAN BATTERY CORNER,-H.16.d.1.1.-LEICESTER FARM,- INN
Corner- H.14.b.45.75 - Road Junction(H.8.d.7.3.) - Road
Junction (H.8.a.50.25.)
Guides to conduct companies to billets will be at Road Junction
H.8.a.50.25.

6. Completion of relief will be notified to B.H.Q. by code word 'CLICK'
7. ACKNOWLEDGE.

                                   R Dagger
                                   Capt. & A/Adjt.,
Issued at   a.m. by runner.   'B' Bn. Highland Light Infantry.
Copies to:- 1. W Coy., 2. X Coy., 3 Y Coy., 4 Z Coy.,
          5,6. O.O.File. 7 Medical Officer, 8 Transport Off.& Q.M.

SECRET.   OPERATION (MOVE) ORDER. No.150.   Copy No.
                       'B' HIGHLAND LIGHT INFANTRY.   26.9.18.

Reference Map. Sheets 27 and 28.

1.   Battalion will move by LORRY Route from present Billets to Billets
     vacated by Battn. on 23rd inst. in Vicinity of H.7.central,
     VLAMERTINGHE.

2.   Time. Coys. will be in readiness to move at 8 p.m. All Battle Equip-
     -ment, Lewis Guns, Petrol Tins (Full), Bombs etc. will be carried.
     Dress: Battle Equipment: Steel Helmets will be worn.
     Lorries will be provided for transport of troops and will pick up
     at L.3.b.5.9. Parties of 25 to each bus.
     Order of Moving: Hd.Qrs. W, X, Y, Z.

3.   All Camp stores will be returned to Large NISSEN Hut in centre of
     Camp by 7 p.m.

4.   All Lines and latrines must be left thoroughly clean. Certificates
     certifying that this has been done to be sent to Orderly Room by 7 p.m.

5.   Officers' Valises and Coy. H.Q. stores will be dumped on road adjoin-
     -ing Officers' Quarters by 5.30 p.m. ready for removal.

Issued at 3.30 p.m.
                                                    Capt. & A/Adjt.
                                              'B' HIGHLAND LIGHT INFANTRY.

Copy No.1. War Diary.   Copy No.5. O.C. X Coy.
       2. O.O. File.   6. O.C. Y "
       3.   Do.   7. O.C. Z "
       4. O.C. W Coy.   8. 2nd in Command.

SECRET.   OPERATION ORDER. No.151.   Copy No.
           'B' HIGHLAND LIGHT INFANTRY.   27.9.18.

Reference Maps. Sheet 28.
               YPRES 1/10,000.

1. On the evening of J minus 1 day the battalion will move forward
    to Assembly position as follows:-
    W Coy. to RAILWAY EMBANKMENT, Eastern portion as reconnoitred.
    X "   to RAILWAY EMBANKMENT, Western portion as reconnoitred.
    Y "   H.H.Q. 1st line, Northern portion as reconnoitred.
    Z "   G.H.Q. 1st line, Southern portion as reconnoitred.
    Batt. H.Q.   I.20.d.9.9.

2. MARCH.
    Order of March.   H.Q., W, X, Y, Z Coy.
    Starting Point.   Road Junction H.8.a.5.3.
    Time.   9.15 p.m.
    Route.   Cross Roads.H.8.d.7.3.-H.8.d.9.6.-Road Junction
                       H.9.a.75.55.-H.9.b.4.2.-H.16.central.-H.16.d.
                       15.80.-Light Railway Track.H.17.c.25.85.-
                       H.17.d.0.7.-H.18.c.0.7.-H.18.c.85.20.-BRISBANE
                       DUMP.-CARTRIDGE.-I.19.b.25.25.-DERBY ROAD.
                       No troops are to pass railway junction H.17.c.
                       25.85. on light railway before 10.30 p.m.
    Interval.   Usual intervals between Coys. and platoons will
                       be observed.
    O.C. will report their Coys. ready to move off at 8.50 p.m.

3. Strict silence must be maintained until ZERO hour.

4. Coys. will report by runner to Batt. H.Q. I.20.d.9.9. when their
    assembly is complete.

5. ACKNOWLEDGE.

    Issued at 2 p.m.
                                            Capt. & A/Adjt.
                                        'B' HIGHLAND LIGHT INFANTRY.

    Copy No.1. War Diary.
         2. O.O. File.
         3.   Do.
         4. O.C. W Coy.
         5. O.C. X "
         6. O.C. Y "
         7. O.C. Z "

SECRET.   OPERATION ORDER No.152.   Copy No. 2.
                    'B' HIGHLAND LIGHT INFANTRY.   25.9.18.

Reference Maps. Sheets 27 and 28.
                YPRES 1/10,000.
                GHELEVELT 1/10,000.

INFORMATION.
  1. The enemy division opposite is the 40th (Saxon) Division. Their
     morale is considered poor.

INTENTION.
  1. The 35th Division will attack and capture ALASKA HOUSES and ZANDE-
     -VOORDE. The order of battle NORTH to SOUTH is 106 Inf. Brigade,
     104 Inf. Brigade, 105 Inf. Brigade. The Divisions on the NORTH and
     SOUTH are co-operating.

  2. (a) The 104 and 105 Inf. Brigades will advance under barrage and
     capture high ground I.30.b.4.3. - I.34.d.3.4. They will then push
     on and capture high ground CANADA TUNNELS - KLEIN ZILLEBEKE.
     The 106 Inf. Brigade will advance under barrage and capture high
     ground J.19.b.- CANADA TUNNELS (exclusive)
     (b) After the capture of the above objectives the 106 and 104 Inf.
     Brigades will continue the attack to ALASKA HOUSES and ZANDEVOORDE.

PLAN OF ATTACK for 106 Inf. Brigade.
     At ZERO the 12th H.L.I. will advance to the attack and capture 1st
     objective J.19.b.- CANADA TUNNELS. The 18th H.L.I. will be ready
     to support the 12th H.L.I. at ZERO if necessary.
     At ZERO plus 1.20 the 18th H.L.I. will advance and take up position
     on first objective ready to continue the advance.
     At ZERO plus 4.20 the battalion will advance and capture ALASKA
     HOUSES.
     O.C. Y Coy. will establish a mixed post (strength 1 platoon) with
     a unit of 104 Inf. Brigade in vicinity of J.25.central.

INSTRUCTIONS.
  1. ASSEMBLY. On the night (to be notified later) the Brigade will
     assemble as follows :-
     12th H.L.I. in area I.21. I.22 between ZILLEBEKE LAKE and RAILWAY
                 EMBANKMENT.
     18th H.L.I. will assemble, W and X Coys. on RAILWAY EMBANKMENT,
                 Z and Y Coys. on G.H.Q. I first line.
     17th ROYAL SCOTS in reserve.

  2. ADVANCE. The advance to the 1st objective (ZERO plus 1.20) will be
     carried out according to the amount of shelling, W and Z Coys.
     moving the SOUTH SIDE of PLUMERS DRIVE, X and Y Coys. moving the
     NORTH SIDE of PLUMERS DRIVE. Companies will move at least 100 yards
     between platoons and 300 yards between Companies. H.Q. will move
     in front of Z Coy.
     It may be necessary to deploy into artillery formation, but taking
     shelling into account all possible use must be made of roads, avoid-
     -ing bad ground so as to lessen fatigue. Companies will maintain
     touch by means of liaison patrol.
     The advance to the 2nd objective (ZERO plus 4.20) will be in diamond
     formation as follows:-

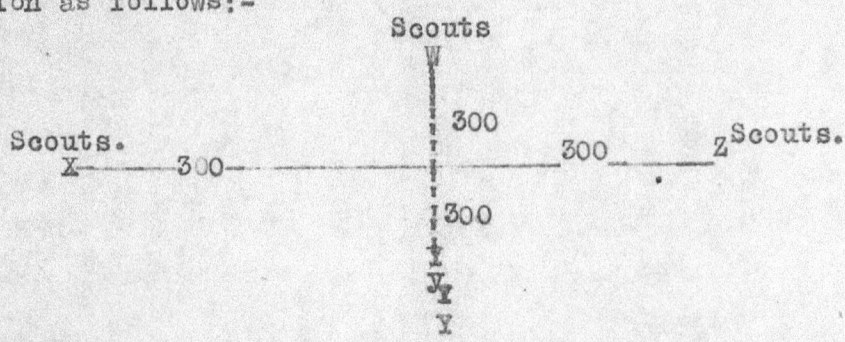

     W Coy. will be the Coy. of direction and will move along line
     FOREST ROAD.

3. **Action during the Assault to 2nd objective.** Companies will press forward with vigour in order to prevent the enemy reorganising. Scouts will be sent forward and on flanks in order to keep Coy. Commanders continually informed of the situation in front. Prisoners will be sent to Batt. H.Q. No N.C.O. or man is to escort prisoners to the rear without a direct order from an officer.

4. **Action after objective has been gained.**
   a. White Very Lights will be sent up when 2nd objective has been gained.
   b. Consolidation in depth will be commenced at once.
   c. Companies will establish touch with neighbouring units.
   d. Strong patrols will be sent forward to exploit success.

5. **ARTILLERY.** The attack will be well supported by Artillery. From ZERO plus 2.35 no artillery except observed fire or from guns under orders of Brigade will fire west of a line P.2.c.0.8. - O.4.c.0.8., consequently the Battalion can exploit up to these limits. During the halt on 1st objective the limit of H.A. will move EAST to a line J.21.a.0.0. - P.3.c.0.8. At ZERO plus 3.30 the limit of H.A. will move to a line K.22.a.0.0. - P.4.c.0.0.

6. **COMMUNICATIONS.**
   a. Contact aeroplanes (markings 1 black flap on each lower plane) will fly over at ZERO plus 1 and at every clock hour afterwards. Section Commanders in the forward line will be responsible that 3 flares close together are lit, and that discs are shewn when called for by aeroplane.
   Call from aeroplanes is a succession of As or (and) a single white light.
   b. Counter-attack aeroplanes will patrol at ZERO plus 40. Signal from aeroplanes will be a red parachute flare.
   c. Visual communication to Brigade H.Q. will be established on the high ground at the 1st objective.
   d. A telephone wire will be run from Brigade H.Q. to HEDGE ST TUNNELS where Brigade Report Centre will be established.
   e. Signal Officer will establish telephonic communication to Brigade Report Centre as soon as situation permits.
   f. Popham panels will be shewn to indicate Batt. H.Q.
   g. V strips calling for ammunition supply from aeroplanes will only be shewn NORTH of ALASKA HOUSES. These strips will only be shewn by order of O.C. Coys. in case of emergency.
   h. WHITE VERY LIGHTS WILL BE SENT UP WHEN 2nd Objective has been gained.

7. **DRESS and EQUIPMENT.**
   Dress: Fighting Order. 1 day's rations. 1 Iron ration. 2 filled Water bottles.
   Each man will carry :-
       175 rounds S.A.A.
       2 Bombs.
       2 Aeroplane Flares.
   Runners, Signallers, Lewis Gunners (except Nos. 1 and 2) will carry 100 rounds S.A.A.
   Each rifle bomber will carry 8 rifle grenades.
   Each Coy. H.Q. and Batt. H.Q. will carry :-
       5 packets Verys Lights.
       S.O.S. rockets.
       4 rolls of white tape.

8. **MEDICAL.**
   Aid Post I.20.d.60.95.
   After advance from 1st Objective, Regtl. Aid Post will be established at HEDGE ST. TUNNELS; any forward move of Aid Post from this point will be notified later.
   During/

3.

During the advance wounded will be collected in groups under cover as far as possible; these groups will be indicated by reversed rifle in the ground. NO combatant is to leave his section to carry wounded during the advance.

9. ZERO will be notified later.
   Watches will be synchronised. Time to be notified later.

10. <u>REPORTS.</u>
    Situation Reports will be sent to Batt. H.Q. by runner every ½ hour.
    Special Reports on the situation are to be sent in addition.
    Brigade H.Q.   I.20.d.8.9.
    Brigade Report Centre. HEDGE ST. TUNNELS.
    Batt. H.Q.   I.20.d.75.95.
    During the advance Batt. H.Q. will be near Reserve Coy. (Y Coy.)
    Position of Batt. H.Q. after capture of 2nd Objective will be noti-
    -fied later.

Robsagged

25.9.18.
Issued at
                                         Capt. & A/Adjt.
                       'B' HIGHLAND LIGHT INFANTRY.

Copy No. 1. War Diary.
     2. O.O. File.
     3.   Do.
     4. O.C. W Coy.
     5. O.C. X "
     6. O.C. Y "
     7. O.C. Z "
     8. Signal Officer.
     9. Medical Officer.
   10. Transport Officer and Q.M.
   11. 2nd in Command.
   12. 106 Inf. Brigade. (for information.)
   13. 17th LANC. FUSILIERS.
   14. 2nd Bn. HAMPSHIRE REGT.

18th (G.Y.) Bn. HIGHLAND LIGHT INFANTRY.

Narrative of Operations from night 27/28th September to night 1/2nd October 1918.

Reference Maps. YPRES. 1/10,000.)
GHELUVELT. 1/10,000.) Belgium and France Sheet 28.
WERVICQ. 1/10,000.)

27.9.18. At 1800 hours on the night 27th September, I addressed the Battalion under my command on the forthcoming operations generally and what was expected of them in particular. There was a decided spirit of confidence amongst all ranks.

Starting Point. At 21.15 the Battalion moved off from the BRANDHOEK Area situated in G.7, and proceeded by march route to the Assembly positions in G.H.Q. 1st line and Railway Embankment in H.20.a. and 20.b. The enemy persistently shelled the latter part of the route with 5.9s, mixing H.E. with gas, but, happily, no casualties were sustained.

28.9.18. About 0215 the Battalion was reported to Brigade to be in Assembly Positions.

General Idea. The 35th Division was to form part of a general attack along the Army Front.

Special Idea. The 106th Brigade (12th and 18th Bns. H.L.I. and 17th R.Scots) was given as its first objective the high ground extending from CANADA TUNNELS-I.30.a.80.25.- JAM LANE-I.24.b.90.60.-, and its second objective ALASKA HOUSES in J.33.b.

Plan of attack. The 12th Bn. H.L.I. was to assault and capture the first objective. The 18th Bn. H.L.I. was to be held in readiness to support the former if required, and, at ZERO plus 1.20 to advance from Assembly position to the first objective, the 17th R. SCOTS being in support.

ZERO. At ZERO hour minus 5 minutes, i.e. 0525 on 28th September the barrage came down and lasted for 5 minutes. At 0530 the 12th Bn. H.L.I. advanced to the capture of the 1st objective, behind the artillery barrage, which proceeded by successive lifts till it rested on the ridge. At ZERO plus 1.20, i.e. 0650 the 18th Bn. H.L.I. moved out from Assembly positions on the 1st objective in support of the leading Battalion.

Dispositions. The Disposition adopted was diamond artillery formation.

The attack. Rain was now falling heavily and the going was extremely bad; furthermore, visibility was poor, rendering maintenance of direction difficult. The shelling from enemy artillery for the first 1000 yards or so from Assembly positions was fairly heavy (5.9 Hows.) and later some slight machine gun opposition was met with from the flanks. At this point the Battalion suffered several casualties, including Lieuts. Hurll, McDonald, Mason, and J.C. Stewart. About 400 yards from the 1st objective, a low flying enemy plane passed over our heads. This was heavily engaged by machine gun and rifle fire and finally brought down. The first objective was reached at 0815 where the Battalion waited till 0950, preparatory to jumping off for the capture of ALASKA HOUSES.

Second Objective. At 0950, in accordance with Operation Orders, the Battalion moved down the forward slope of the ridge in diamond formation, taking advantage of ground, but pushing forward with vigour and determination. There was considerable difficulty from the moment of attack, owing to heavy machine gun and sniping fire from Shrewsbury Wood: Lieuts. A.F.M'Cubbin and C.E.Missen were wounded; notwithstanding this, however, the leading Company pushed boldly forward; I ordered the right Company to move up and if possible neutralise the fire coming from my right. I could see no signs of the Brigade on my right moving forward, nor would there appear to be any troops on my left. Proceeding up the slope towards ALASKA HOUSES, my left Company was fired upon from enemy light field pieces, at point blank range, inflicting many casualties and causing a temporary halt in the advance. I ordered the leading Company to send round/

SECRET.   18th (G.Y.) Bn. HIGHLAND LIGHT INFANTRY.

Narrative of events from night 27/28th September to 1/2nd October 1918.

Reference Maps. YPRES 1/10,000.   )
              GHELEVELT 1/10,000.) Belgium and France Sheet 28.
              WERNICQ. 1/10,000.   )

27.9.18. At 1800 on the night 27th September I addressed the Battalion under my command on the forthcoming operations generally and what was expected of them in particular. There was a decided spirit of confidence amongst all ranks.

STARTING POINT. At 2115 the Battalion moved off from the ERANDHOEK Area situated in G.7. and proceeded by march route to the Assembly positions in G.H.Q. 1st Line and RAILWAY EMBANKMENT in H.20.a. and H.20.b. The enemy persistently shelled the latter part of the route with 5.9s, mixing H.E. with Gas, but happily no casualties were sustained.

28.9.18. About 0215 the Battalion was reported to Brigade to be in Assembly positions.

GENERAL IDEA. The 35th Division was to form part of a general attack along the Army Front.

SPECIAL IDEA. The 106th Inf. Brigade (12th H.L.I., 18th H.L.I. and 17th ROYAL SCOTS) was given as its first objective the High Ground extending from CANADA TUNNELS I.30.a.80.25.-JAM LANE I.24.b.90.60., and its second Objective ALASKA HOUSES in J.33.b.

PLAN OF ATTACK. The 12th Bn. H.L.I. was to assault and capture the 1st Objective. The 18th H.L.I. was to be held in readiness to support the former if required, and at ZERO plus 1.20 to advance from Assembly positions to the 1st Objective, the 17th ROYAL SCOTS being in support.

ZERO. At ZERO hour minus 5 minutes, i.e. 0525 on 28th September the Barrage came down and lasted 5 minutes. At 0530 the 12th H.L.I. advanced to the capture of the 1st Objective behind the Artillery Barrage, which proceeded by successive lifts till it rested on the ridge. At ZERO plus 1.20, i.e. 0650, the 18th Bn. H.L.I. moved out from Assembly Positions on the 1st Objective in support of the leading Battalion.

DISPOSITIONS. The Disposition adopted was diamond artillery formation.

THE ATTACK. Rain was now falling heavily, and the going was extremely bad. furthermore, visibility was poor, rendering maintenance of direction difficult. The shelling from enemy artillery for the first 1000 yards or so from Assembly Positions was fairly heavy (5.9 Hows.) and later some slight machine gun opposition was met with from the flanks. At this point the Battalion suffered several casualties, including Lieuts. J.McG. Huxall, J. McDonald, G.B.Mason, and J.C. Stewart. About 400 yards from the 1st Objective a low flying enemy plane passed over our heads. This was heavily engaged by machine gun and rifle fire and finally brought down. The first Objective was reached at 0815, where the Battalion waited till 0950 preparatory to jumping off for the capture of ALASKA HOUSES.

SECOND OBJECTIVE. At 0950, in accordance with Operation Orders the Battalion moved down the forward slope of the ridge in diamond formation, taking advantage of ground but pushing forward with vigour and determination. There was considerable difficulty from the moment of attack owing to heavy machine gun and sniping fire from SHREWSBURY WOOD. Lieuts. A.F.M'Cubbin and C.E. Missen were wounded. Notwithstanding this, however, the leading Company pushed boldly forward; I ordered the right Company to move up, if possible, to neutralise the fire coming from my right. I could see no signs of the Brigade on my right moving forward, nor would there appear to be any troops on my left. Proceeding up the slope towards ALASKA HOUSES my left Company was fired upon from enemy light field pieces at point blank range, inflicting many casualties and causing a temporary halt in the advance. I ordered the leading Company to send round/

round a force to the right to endeavour to capture these pieces. A few minutes afterwards the advance was continued and the objective was gained to find that the field pieces had moved off. It was evident that they had been limbered up ready to move. The Objective was taken by 1230 on 28.9.18 and consolidation proceeded with. 18 prisoners were taken, 3 machine guns 1 5.9 how. and 1 77 millimetre gun.
I immediately ordered patrols to push forward and exploit as far as HAY HOUSES in J.34.d. The Patrols proceeded as far as UGLY WOOD, where they came under heavy machine gun fire. Throughout, considerable difficulty was experienced in maintaining touch with the 29th Division; endeavouring to do this, 2 platoons of my left Company became detached. About 1330 the 17th ROYAL SCOTS took up a system of posts on my left, thereby establishing Liaison with the 29th Division and the 2 platoons above referred to rejoined their Companies. The B.H.Q. was established at FUNNY FARM J.32.d.0.4. The night 28/29th September was spent in consolidating the position and exploiting the success.

29.9.18. At 11.25 I received a message from O.C. 17th LANCS.FUSILIERS that the 105th Inf. Brigade were ordered to attack ZANDVOORDE at 12.15. At 1400 I received orders to advance in support (in conjunction with 17th ROYAL SCOTS) of that Brigade in their attack on ZANDVOORDE. At 1500 I was informed that the 17th ROYAL SCOTS would push on, on the left of the 105th Inf.Brigade and that the 12th and 18th Bns. H.L.I. would halt and await further orders. At 1700 I was informed that ZANDVOORDE had been taken, and that I was to push on at once in support and make good the line TENBREILEN-BLEGNAERT FARM. The Battalion was immediately assembled in area J.33.a. facing south-east. The Assembly and immediate advance was extremely difficult owing to a concentration of gas and H.Es. The area in rear was also shelled heavily with 5.9 Hows. I ordered the Battalion to move forward quickly in order to get out of the gas area. At this period 2/Lt. A.Hose was wounded by shell fire and 2/Lt. I.F.G. Kinnear slightly gassed. The going was very difficult both on account of ground, wired shell holes etc., and on account of men having to wear gas masks. Beyond this we met with no opposition at all until we finally got close to the Support Company of the ROYAL SCOTS. On reaching line J.10.a.4.3. - J.4.d.3.3. It was now dark and I was informed the Objective was reached, so I gave orders for the Battalion to dig in. At 1925 orders were received for the 106th Inf. Brigade to take WERVICQ; 12th H.L.I. on right: 18th H.L.I. on the left, passing through the line of the ROYAL SCOTS, they being in Support. In company with the O.C. of the 12th H.L.I. I reconnoitred the Assembly Positions along the KRUISECK-TENBREILEN Road and made arrangements for forming up the Battalion.

30.9.18. By 0545 the Companies were on their Assembly Positions from P.11.c.0.7. to P.11.a.6.4. The 12th H.L.I. were on my right and the ROYAL SCOTS were about 800 yards in rear. My Battalion was disposed as follows:- 2 Companies in Front Line, 1 Company in Support, and 1 in Reserve. At 0615 both Battalions, i.e. 12th and 18th H.L.I. moved forward to the attack on WERVICQ. The 12th H.L.I. - the Battalion of direction, with their right on the ZANDVOORDE-TENBREILEN Road to LES CASERNES, P.29.b.5.1. The advance met with little opposition until they reached the line P.24.c.0.0.-P.24.b.9.9. when they were held up by machine gun fire from the front and both flanks, and especially from houses situated at P.24.a.5.6. At this point my left front Company met with great opposition. The left supporting Company, under the initiative of the Coy.Commander, immediately pushed up on the left and the guns situated in the aforesaid houses were silenced. Meanwhile the Battalion on my right was pushing boldly forward. About 0930 the opposition on my left increased and I called for assistance from the Support/

Support Battalion, when 2 Companies were sent forward on my left, the remaining 2 Companies being echeloned in rear to form a defensive flank. Shortly afterwards my right Company was forced from the Railway about P.30.b.2.4. owing to very heavy machine gun fire, and finally took up a position at P.24.d.3.2. Here Lieut. H. Fleming was killed and Lieuts. R.J. Hutchison and R.D. Orr were wounded. The Battalion was finally disposed in posts and farmhouses from P.24.d.2.3. to P.19.c.1.7. the ROYAL SCOTS on left, the 12th H.L.I. on right; Touch was maintained with 12th H.L.I. on right; There was a gap of about 200 yards between my left flank and the unit on my left; 2 Vickers guns were ordered to take up positions to cover this flank; the remaining 2 guns of the section under my orders were placed temporarily in the front line to neutralise any machine gun fire. These were withdrawn later. From 0920 complete liaison was established between the 3 Battalions of the Brigade and remained so onwards throughout the operations.

About 1645 our heavies and the 18 pounders bombarded the village; from this time onwards things considerably quietened down. About 1845 I ordered Patrols to push forward and get in touch with the enemy. Patrols got out to about 300 yards in front of my line and came under machine gun fire; patrols withdrew, but no special information was gained beyond the fact that the enemy was still holding machine gun posts. At 2015 orders were received from the Brigade that the 7th Bn. IRISH RIFLES would relieve the 106th Inf. Brigade. Beyond heavy shelling on the TENBREILEN Road the relief was carried out without incident, and was complete at 2215. The Battalion proceeded by march route to battle bivouacs in KRUISECK.

GENERAL REMARKS. I cannot speak too highly of the conduct of all officers, non-commissioned officers and men of the Battalion throughout the operations. With no hot meals for the whole period, bad inclement weather, tired with long advances over difficult ground, there was not a single grumble. There was never any hesitation when ordered to advance and their action was vigorous on all occasions, deserving of the highest praise. They have come out of the battle with the spirit imbued in them that they are better than the enemy, and there is a complete feeling of confidence throughout all ranks in the Battalion. The Casualties have been heavy - 12 officers and   other ranks, with a large proportion of N.C.Os. Every Officer, Non-Commissioned Officer and Man has done well, but I should specially like to bring to the notice of the Brigadier General commanding the following:-

See list attached.

V.E. Anderson
Lt. Col.
Comd 18th H.L.I.

1st Oct. 1918.

RECOMMENDATIONS IN ORDER OF MERIT.

Officers.

A/Capt. Henry George Smith, M.C.
2/Lieut. James Buchanan.
Lieut. David Gerald Hutchison.
Lieut. John Vassie Lindsay.
2/Lieut. William Grant Stewart.
T/Capt. Robert Russell Brown.

Other Ranks.

4483	Sig.Sgt.	Thomas Gibson.
32160	Pte.	Duncan McMinn.
4804	CSM.	James McQuillan.
4333	Pte.	Charles Henderson.
55394	"	George Ross.
15015	Cpl.	Andrew McIndoe.
5509	L/C.	Andrew Adair.
A/7937	Sgt.	Samuel Orr.
202616	L/C.	Samuel Davies.
350475	Pte.	James McMullen.
30053	"	James Muir.
350527	L/C.	John Hamilton.
51608	Pte.	George Petrie.
55314	"	James Flannagan.
41497	"	Clarence William Holmes.
43464	"	William Prentice.
37808	Sgt.	William Balnaves.
350433	Cpl.	John Prew.

18th (G.Y.) Bn. HIGHLAND LIGHT INFANTRY.

Narrative of Operations from night 27/28th September to night 1/2nd October 1918.

Reference Maps. YPRES. 1/10,000.   )
                GHELEVELT. 1/10,000.) Belgium and France Sheet 28.
                WERVICQ. 1/10,000.   )

27.9.18. At 1800 hours on the night 27th September, I addressed the Battalion under my command on the forthcoming operations generally and what was expected of them in particular. There was a decided spirit of confidence amongst all ranks.

Starting Point. At 21.15 the Battalion moved off from the BRANDHOEK Area situated in G.7, and proceeded by march route to the Assembly positions in G.H.Q. 1st line and Railway Embankment in H.20.a. and 20.b. The enemy persistently shelled the latter part of the route with 5.9s, mixing H.E. with gas, but, happily, no casualties were sustained.

28.9.18. About 0215 the Battalion was reported to Brigade to be in Assembly Positions.

General Idea. the 35th Division was to form part of a general attack along the Army Front.

Special Idea. The 106th Brigade (12th and 18th Bns. H.L.I. and 17th R.Scots) was given as its first objective the high ground extending from CANADA TUNNELS-I.30.a.80.25.-JAM LANE-I.24.b.90.60.-, and its second objective ALASKA HOUSES in J.33.b.

Plan of attack. The 12th Bn. H.L.I. was to assault and capture the first objective. The 18th Bn. H.L.I. was to be held in readiness to support the former if required, and, at ZERO plus 1.20 to advance from Assembly position to the first objective, the 17th R. SCOTS being in support.

ZERO. At ZERO hour minus 5 minutes, i.e. 0525 on 28th September the barrage came down and lasted for 5 minutes. At 0530 the 12th Bn. H.L.I. advanced to the capture of the 1st objective, behind the artillery barrage, which proceeded by successive lifts till it rested on the ridge. At ZERO plus 1.20, i.e. 0650 the 18th Bn. H.L.I. moved out from Assembly positions on the 1st objective in support of the leading Battalion.

Dispositions. The Disposition adopted was diamond artillery formation.

The attack. Rain was now falling heavily and the going was extremely bad; furthermore, visibility was poor, rendering maintainence of direction difficult. The shelling from enemy artillery for the first 1000 yards or so from Assembly positions was fairly heavy (5.9 Hows.) and later some slight machine gun opposition was met with from the flanks. At this point the Battalion suffered several casualties, including Lieuts. Hurll, McDonald, Mason, and J.C. Stewart. About 400 yards from the 1st objective, a low flying enemy plane passed over our heads. This was heavily engaged by machine gun and rifle fire and finally brought down. The first objective was reached at 0815 where the Battalion waited till 0950, preparatory to jumping off for the capture of ALASKA HOUSES.

Second Objective. At 0950, in accordance with Operation Orders, the Battalion moved down the forward slope of the ridge in diamond formation, taking advantage of ground, but pushing forward with vigour and determination. There was considerable difficulty from the moment of attack, owing to heavy machine gun and sniping fire from Shrewsbury Wood: Lieuts. A.F.M'Cubbin and C.E.Missen were wounded; notwithstanding this, however, the leading Company pushed boldly forward; I ordered the right Company to move up and if possible neutralise the fire coming from my right. I could see no signs of the Brigade on my right moving forward, nor would there appear to be any troops on my left. Proceeding up the slope towards ALASKA HOUSES, my left Company was fired upon from enemy light field pieces, at point blank range, inflicting many casualties and causing a temporary halt in the advance.   I ordered the leading Company to send round/

round a force to the right to endeavour to capture these pieces. A few minutes afterwards the advance was continued and the objective was gained to find that the field pieces had moved off. It was evident that they had been limbered up ready to move. The Objective was taken by 1230 on 28.9.18 and consolidation proceeded with. 18 prisoners were taken, 3 machine guns 1 5.9 how. and 1 77 millimetre gun.

I immediately ordered patrols to push forward and exploit as far as HAY HOUSES in J.34.d. The Patrols proceeded as far as UGLY WOOD, where they came under heavy machine gun fire. Throughout, considerable difficulty was experienced in maintaining touch with the 29th Division; endeavouring to do this, 2 platoons of my left Company became detached. About 1330 the 17th ROYAL SCOTS took up a system of posts on my left, thereby establishing Liaison with the 29th Division and the 2 platoons above referred to rejoined their Companies. The B.H.Q. was established at FUNNY FARM J.32.d.0.4. The night 28/29th September was spent in consolidating the position and exploiting the success.

29.9.18. At 11.25 I received a message from O.C. 17th LANCS.FUSILIERS that the 105th Inf. Brigade were ordered to attack ZANDVOORDE at 12.15. At 1400 I received orders to advance in support (in conjunction with 17th ROYAL SCOTS) of that Brigade in their attack on ZANDVOORDE. At 1500 I was informed that the 17th ROYAL SCOTS would push on, on the left of the 105th Inf.Brigade and that the 12th and 18th Bns. H.L.I. would halt and await further orders. At 1700 I was informed that ZANDVOORDE had been taken, and that I was to push on at once in support and make good the line TENBREILEN-BLEGNAERT FARM. The Battalion was immediately assembled in area J.33.a. facing south-east. The Assembly and immediate advance was extremely difficult owing to a concentration of gas and H.Es. The area in rear was also shelled heavily with 5.9 Hows. I ordered the Battalion to move forward quickly in order to get out of the gas area. At this period 2/Lt. A.Hose was wounded by shell fire and 2/Lt. I.F.G. Kinnear slightly gassed. The going was very difficult both on account of ground, wired shell holes etc., and on account of men having to wear gas masks. Beyond this we met with no opposition at all until we finally got close to the Support Company of the ROYAL SCOTS. On reaching line J.10.a.4.3. - J.4.d.3.3. It was now dark and I was informed the Objective was reached, so I gave orders for the Battalion to dig in. At 1925 orders were received for the 106th Inf. Brigade to take WERVICQ; 12th H.L.I. on right: 18th H.L.I. on the left, passing through the line of the ROYAL SCOTS, they being in Support. In company with the O.C. of the 12th H.L.I. I reconnoitred the Assembly Positions along the KRUISECK-TENBREILEN Road and made arrangements for forming up the Battalion.

30.9.18. By 0545 the Companies were on their Assembly Positions from P.11.c.0.7. to P.11.a.6.4. The 12th H.L.I. were on my right and the ROYAL SCOTS were about 800 yards in rear. My Battalion was disposed as follows:- 2 Companies in Front Line, 1 Company in Support, and 1 in Reserve. At 0615 both Battalions, i.e. 12th and 18th H.L.I. moved forward to the attack on WERVICQ. The 12th H.L.I. - the Battalion of direction, with their right on the ZANDVOORDE-TENBREILEN Road to LES CASERNES, P.29.b.5.1. The advance met with little opposition until they reached the line P.24.c.0.0.-P.24.b.9.9. when they were held up by machine gun fire from the front and both flanks, and especially from houses situated at P.24.a.5.6. At this point my left front Company met with great opposition. The left supporting Company, under the initiative of the Coy.Commander, immediately pushed up on the left and the guns situated in the aforesaid houses were silenced. Meanwhile the Battalion on my right was pushing boldly forward. About 0930 the opposition on my left increased and I called for assistance from the Support/

Support Battalion, when 2 Companies were sent forward on my left, the remaining 2 Companies being echeloned in rear to form a defensive flank. Shortly afterwards my right Company was forced from the Railway about P.30.b.2.4. owing to very heavy machine gun fire, and finally took up a position at P.24.d.3.2. Here Lieut. H. Fleming was killed and Lieuts. R.J. Hutchison and R.D. Orr were wounded. The Battalion was finally disposed in posts and farmhouses from P.24.d.2.3. to P.19.c.1.7. the ROYAL SCOTS on left, the 12th H.L.I. on right; Touch was maintained with 12th H.L.I. on right; There was a gap of about 200 yards between my left flank and the unit on my left; 2 Vickers guns were ordered to take up positions to cover this flank; the remaining 2 guns of the section under my orders were placed temporarily in the front line to neutralise any machine gun fire. These were withdrawn later. From 0920 complete liaison was established between the 3 Battalions of the Brigade and remained so onwards throughout the operations.

About 1645 our heavies and the 18 pounders bombarded the village; from this time onwards things considerably quietened down. About 1845 I ordered Patrols to push forward and get in touch with the enemy. Patrols got out to about 300 yards in front of my line and came under machine gun fire; patrols withdrew, but no special information was gained beyond the fact that the enemy was still holding machine gun posts. At 2015 orders were received from the Brigade that the 7th Bn. IRISH RIFLES would relieve the 106th Inf. Brigade. Beyond heavy shelling on the TENBREILEN Road the relief was carried out without incident, and was complete at 2215. The Battalion proceeded by march route to battle bivouacs in KRUISECK.

GENERAL REMARKS. I cannot speak too highly of the conduct of all officers, non-commissioned officers and men of the Battalion throughout the operations. With no hot meals for the whole period, bad inclement weather, tired with long advances over difficult ground, there was not a single grumble. There was never any hesitation when ordered to advance and their action was vigorous on all occasions, deserving of the highest praise. They have come out of the battle with the spirit imbued in them that they are better than the enemy, and there is a complete feeling of confidence throughout all ranks in the Battalion. The Casualties have been heavy - 12 officers and other ranks, with a large proportion of N.C.Os. Every Officer, Non-Commissioned Officer and Man has done well, but I should specially like to bring to the notice of the Brigadier General commanding the following:-

See list attached.

1st Oct 1918.

RECOMMENDATIONS IN ORDER OF MERIT.

Officers.

A/Capt. Henry George Smith, M.C.
2/Lieut. James Buchanan.
Lieut. David Gerald Hutchison.
Lieut. John Vassie Lindsay.
2/Lieut. William Grant Stewart.
T/Capt. Robert Russell Brown.

Other Ranks.

4483	Sig.Sgt.	Thomas Gibson.
32160	Pte.	Duncan McMinn.
4804	CSM.	James McQuillan.
4333	Pte.	Charles Henderson.
55394	"	George Ross.
15015	Cpl.	Andrew McIndoe,
5509	L/C.	Andrew Adair.
A/7937	Sgt.	Samuel Orr.
202616	L/C.	Samuel Davies.
350475	Pte.	James McMullen.
30053	"	James Muir.
350527	L/C.	John Hamilton.
31608	Pte.	George Petrie.
55314	"	James Flannagan.
41497	"	Clarence William Holmes.
43464	"	William Prentice.
37808	Sgt.	William Balnaves.
350433	Cpl.	John Frew.

SECRET   OPERATION ORDER NO.153
                18th HIGHLAND LIGHT INFANTRY.   Copy No.

                                               7th October, 1918.

Map Reference:- Belgium and France, Sheet 28.
----

1.   106th Infantry Brigade will relieve 104 and 105th Infantry Brigades on the night 7/8th October as follows:-
             18th H.L.I.   Front Line
             12th H.L.I   Support Line
             17th R.S.   Reserve Line.

2.   The Battalion will relieve part of the 17th Lanc. Fus. and part of 15th Sherwoods, as follows:-
             "W" Coy.   Right Company.
             "X" "   Centre Company.
             "Y" "   Left Company.
             "Z" "   In Support.

3.   One Officer per Company will proceed in advance to 105th Infantry Brigade H.Q. at K.15.d.3.4. and obtain necessary details re relief.

4.   GUIDES. One Guide per platoon will meet Companies at TERHAND Cross Roads at 18 hours.

5.   TRENCH STORES. All aeroplane photographs, maps, Defence Schemes, Ground Flares, S.O.S. Signals, Dumps of S.A.A. and Bombs, Tools etc., will be taken over on relief. List shewing stores taken over will be forwarded to Battalion H.Q. with T.P.R.

6.   Completion of relief will be communicated to Battalion H.Q. by runner by code word "CLICK".

7.   REPORTS.   Battalion H.Q.   K.29.b.2.8.
                 Bde. H.Q.   K.15.d.1.4.

8.   ACKNOWLEDGE.

                                             Rob Sagger
                                          Capt. & A/Adjt.
                                18th HIGHLAND LIGHT INFANTRY.

Copies to War Diary
         O.C. File
         2nd in Command
         O.C. W Coy.
         O.C. X Coy.
         O.C. Y Coy.
         O.C. Z Coy.
         T.O. & QrMr.
         Medical Officer.
         17th Lanc. Fus.
         15th Sherwoods.

SECRET.

MOVE ORDERS
Accompanying Operation Orders No.153

1. The Battalion will relieve parts of the 17th Lanc. Fus., and of 15th Sherwoods on the night 7/8th Octr. 1918.

2. MARCH. Starting Point:- Belgian Battery Corner - 13 hours.
   Route:- YPRES - ZONNEBEKE - BROODSEINDE - BECEALLRE and TERHAND.
   Distance:- 100 Yards between heads of platoons.
   200 Yards between heads of Companies.
   Dress:- Fighting Order.
   Order of March:- Headquarters - W, X, Y, Z.

3. TRANSPORT. Cookers and Lewis Gun Limbers will march in rear of Companies.

4. HALT. A Halt will be made for Tea at J.6.c.0.3 for 3/4 hour.

5. PARADE Companies will parade in Camp ready to march off 12.30.

6. RATIONS. Rations for consumption on 8th inst. will be issued individually before marching off.

                                    Capt. & A/Adjt.
7th Octr. 1918   18th HIGHLAND LIGHT INFANTRY.

Copies to War Diary
         O.C. File
         2nd in Command
         O.C. W. Coy
         O.C. X "
         O.C. Y "
         O.C. Z "
         T.O. & QRMR.
         Medical Officer.

SECRET.   OPERATION ORDER. No. 154.   Copy. No.
         'B' HIGHLAND LIGHT INFANTRY.   10.10.18.

Reference Map. DADIZEELE. 1/10,000.

1. The 9th Bn. R.I.F. on our left will attack and hold GOLDFLAKE FARM (L.19.c.1.9.) The attack will commence at 1010 tomorrow 11.10.18.

2. During the night 10/11th October GOLDFLAKE FARM and adjoining structures will be bombarded intermittently by Heavy Artillery till 0500. From 0515 till 0530 4.5 Hows. and 18 pounders will open a heavy fire on GOLDFLAKE and MARTELL FARM. From 0530 till 1000 there will be no artillery bombardment.

3. From 1000 to 1010 Trench Mortars and 4.5 Howitzers will bombard GOLDFLAKE FARM. A smoke Screen will also be put down lasting from 1000 till 1040 - limits E. and S. of GOLDFLAKE FARM on the general line L.19.a.9.- L.19.a.8.5.- L.19.a.7.0. - L.19.c.6.6.- L.19.c.0.5. - K.24.d.6.5. to screen the movements of the Infantry. From 1000 to 1010 artillery will also fire on houses in K.24.b.79.15.

4. At 1000 2 platoons of 9th R.I.F. assembled at TWIG FARM. K.24.b.95.55. will move under cover of smoke and bombardment and at 1010 will rush and occupy the Farm.

5. The Battalion will co-operate as follows:-
(a) O.C. X Coy. will arrange L.G. fire from post at K.24.d.00.45- fire to be directed between DIBSLAND FARM and PILL BOX K.14.d.90.70.
(b) O.C. Y Coy. will withdraw post at MONKS FARM to post at K.23.b.00.20. forthwith. Post at MONKS FARM will be re-established as soon as possible after the operation (suggested that this be done before smoke screen lifts).
(c) O.C. Z Coy. will hold 2 platoons in readiness for emergency.
(d) O.C. Companies will ensure that a sufficient quantity of S.A.A. L.G. ammunition and Bombs is held in readiness.
(e) O.C. X and Y Coys. will keep B.H.Q. informed of the progress of the operations as far as possible.
(f) Re-occupation of original Dispositions and liaison with 9th R.I.F. will be reported to B.H.Q. by runner.

6. Reports to be sent to B.H.Q. K.29.b.8.2.

10.10.18.
                                                    Lt.-Col.
                    Comdg. 18th (G.Y.) Bn. Highland Light Infantry.

Copy No. 1. War Diary.
        2. O.O. File.
        3.   Do.
        4. O.C. W Coy.
        5. O.C. X "
        6. O.C. Y "
        7. O.C. Z "

SECRET.   OPERATION ORDER. No.135.   Copy No.
               'B' HIGHLAND LIGHT INFANTRY.   11.10.18.

Reference Maps. Sheet 29. 1/40,000.
                DADIZEELE 1/10,000.

1. The 106th Inf. Brigade will be relieved by the 104th and 105th Inf. Brigades in the line on the night 11/12th October 1918.

2. **Details of Relief.**
   X and Y Coys. H.L.I. will be relieved by the 17th LANCS. FUSILIERS.
   Z Coy. will be relieved by Units of the 104th Inf. Brigade.
   W Coy. will be relieved by the 15th CHESHIRE REGT.
   GUIDES.
   W Coy.   1 Guide per platoon.
             1   "   for Coy. H.Q.
   X Coy.   1   "   per platoon.
             1   "   for Coy. H.Q.
   Y Coy.   1   "   per platoon.
             1   "   Coy. H.Q.
             1   "   for left liaison post.
   Z Coy. will not send any guides.
   All guides will report at B.H.Q. at 1900. Care should be taken to send intelligent men as guides.

3. On relief Companies and H.Q. will move to J.21.
   Route. MOLENHOEK (K.27)-Track (K.26.c.0.5.)-GHELUVELT-MENIN ROAD.-GHELUVELT.
   Guides to meet Companies en route to billets will be on main road at K.20.b.7.9.

4. TRANSPORT.
   Limbers for conveyance of Petrol Tins, Lewis Guns, Salvage, etc. will be at K.28.b.7.9. Care should be taken that troops and transport do not march through Corps areas other than XIX Corps.

5. All Dispositions, day and night liaison, hostile intelligence, S.O.S. etc. will be handed over on relief. Aeroplane photos and maps will will not be handed over.
   All empty Petrol tins will be taken out and packed in Coy. Limbers.

6. Completion of Relief will be notified to Bn. H.Q. by wire and runner -Code word: JIMMY.

11.10.18.
                                    V.E. Gooderson
                                                      Lt.-Col.
                   Comdg. 18th (G.Y.) Bn. Highland Light Infantry.

Copy No.1. War Diary.
     2. O.O. File.
     3.   Do.
     4. O.C. W Coy.
     5. O.C. X "
     6. O.C. Y "
     7. O.C. Z "
     8. Transport Officer.

SECRET.   OPERATION ORDER. NO.156.   Copy No.
           'B' HIGHLAND LIGHT INFANTRY.   12.10.18.

Ref. Maps 28 and 29. 1/40,000.
     DADEZEELE 1/10,000.

1. **INTENTION.** The 35th Division with 105th Infantry Brigade on Right and 104th Infantry Brigade on Left is attacking on "J" Day at "H" Hour. 106th Infantry Brigade will be in Divisional Reserve. ("J" day is the day of attack and "H" is ZERO hour.)

2. **MODE OF ATTACK.** (of 105th and 104th Infantry Brigades) The two attacking Brigades (105th and 104th) are attacking on one Battalion front. At H - 2 minutes, the hour at which the barrage falls, all three Battalions of both Brigades will move forward. The leading Battalions go straight through to the second pause line on a line L.22 and L.27 and consolidate. The two remaining Battalions of each Brigade go through second pause line on to final objective. The line to be consolidated will depend on the ground but will be such that the enemy is pushed down into the low ground and is not allowed to retain any foothold on the Ridges surrounding the LYS. KLOEFHOEK and KAPPELHOEK, and the spur about SCHOONWATER will be fully occupied.

3. **MOVE OF 106th INFANTRY BRIGADE.** On night J - 1//J the 106th Infantry Brigade will move to positions of readiness about K.20 clear of the Artillery.
    H.Q.12th High.L.I.   will be K.20.a.3.8.
    H.Q.17th R. Scots   "   " K.20.a.5.8.
    H.Q.18th High.L.I.   "   " K.14.c.5.3.
    "A" Coy. 35th Bn.M.G.C.   "   " J.19.b.4.8.
    H.Q. 106th Inf. Bde.   "   " J.24.b.8.4.
   Move Orders will be issued separately.

4. **ROLE OF 106th INFANTRY BRIGADE.** The Brigade will not be used without reference to 35th Division H.Q. except that in case of urgent necessity B.G.C. Brigade may order up 12th High.L.I. to support the Left of the 104th Infantry Brigade.

5. **PRISONERS OF WAR.** 35th Division P.O.W. Cage will be at K.25.a.2.7.

6. **INFORMATION.** The following information is given which might afford Commanders assistance during operations.
   (1) The road and railway through K.23.d. to K.24.c. & a receive a good deal of shell fire.
   (2) A good track runs across the front K.23.b.15.20. to K.23.d.45.45.
   (3) Suitable as H.Q. Pillbox K.23.a.45.75. DEBENHAM HOUSE K.23.d.65.15. Pillbox LEDHALL COPSE K.24.a.00.25.

7. **SYNCHRONIZATION OF WATCHES.** One Officer from the Battalion will visit Brigade Signal Officer 106th Inf. Brigade H.Q. J.24.b.8.4. at 5 p.m. October 13th to synchronise watches.

8. **ZERO HOUR "H" AND ZERO DAY "J"** will be notified later.

9. Situation Reports and Progress Reports will be sent 10 minutes after ZERO and at every half hour afterwards in addition to special reports.

10. **ACKNOWLEDGE.**

Issued at 1800.
                                        Lieut. & A/djt.
                                'B' HIGHLAND LIGHT INFANTRY.

SECRET.   MOVE ORDER ISSUED IN CONJUNCTION WITH OPERATION ORDER 156.

'B' HIGHLAND LIGHT INFANTRY.

12th October 1918.

Reference Map. Sheet 28.

1. The Battalion will move on the afternoon of 13th October 1918 into area K.14 with Battalion Headquarters at K.14.c.5.3.

   Starting Point:-   Road Junction J.21.b.3.2.
   Time:-   1600 hours.
   Order of March:-   H.Q., W, X, Y, Z.
   Intervals:-   100 yards between platoons - 200 yards between Coys
   Dress:-   Fighting Order. Water bottles full.
   Parade:-   The Battalion will parade on the MENIN ROAD
                      (J.20.b.6.9.) at 1515 hours.

2. RECONNAISSANCE. 2/Lieut. Stewart from Headquarters, and one officer and one N.C.O. from each Company will reconnoitre new area and means of approach.
   This party will parade at Battalion Headquarters at 0915 hours.

3. BLANKETS, CAMP KETTLES, etc.
   All Camp Kit will be dumped on Main Road as follows:-

   Blankets (rolled in bundles of 10)   1000 hours.
   Valises   1300   "
   Tents, Shelters, Camp Kettles.   1300   "

4. Lewis Guns, Magazines, etc., will be carried forward to new area by Companies. Transport Officer will arrange to carry water forward as far as possible on pack mules.

5. Arrival on new area will be notified to Battalion Headquarters by runner.

6. ACKNOWLEDGE.

Issued at 1830 hours.

                                        Lieut. & A/Adjt.
                                        'B' HIGHLAND LIGHT INFANTRY.

WAR DIARY
— INTELLIGENCE SUMMARY —

Instructions regarding War Diaries and Intelligence Summaries are contained in F.S. Regs., Part II. and the Staff Manual respectively. Title pages will be prepared in manuscript.

18th (G.V.) Bn. HIGHLAND LIGHT INFANTRY.

Index No.32.

Army Form C. 2118.

From 1st to 31st October 1918 inclusive.

(Erase heading not required.)

Place	Date	Hour	Summary of Events and Information	Remarks and references to Appendices
WARVICQ.	1.10.18.		Holding Objectives gained after the attack on the 28th September (See narrative of Operations attached) Battalion was relieved on the night 1/2nd and moved into battle bivouacs at KRUSECK CORNER. Weather very wet.	
KRUSECK.	2.10.18.		In battle bivouacs. Battalion moved on the night 2/3rd to billets near YPRES. Weather fine.	
YPRES.	3.10.18.		Battalion resting and refitting in billets near YPRES. Weather dull and misty with rain.	
	4.10.18.		Do. Do.	
	5.10.18.		Do. Do.	
	6.10.18.		Do. Do.	
	7.10.18.		Battalion relieved 104th and 105th Inf. Brigades in the line. Weather dry and clear. Operation Order attached.	153.
	8.10.18) to 11.10.18)		Holding Line taken over. Co-operated with Unit on left in Attack on GOLDFLAKE FARM. Weather bright and warm. Operation Order attached.	154. 155
	12.10.18.		Relieved in the Line by 104th and 105th Infantry Brigades on night 11/12th. Battalion moved into battle bivouacs near GHELUVELT. Weather very wet. Operation Order attached.	156.
GHELUVELT.	13.10.18. to 21.10.18.		Battalion moved into Assembly Position in reserve to 104th and 105th Infantry Brigades for continuation of attack. Weather very wet. See Narrative of Operations attached.	
COURTRAI.	22.10.18.) to 24.10.18.)		Battalion in Billets in COURTRAI- resting, refitting and training. Moved forward on night 24/25th to Area near SWEVEGHEM. Operation Order attached.	157.
	25.10.18.		Battalion at call of 41st Division in Billets near SWEVEGHEM.	
	26.10.18.		Do. Do.	
SCHELDT.	27.10.18.) to 31.10.18.)		Relieved 122nd Infantry Brigade, (41st Division) in the line on night 25/27th. Held Dispositions taken over. Battalion did not attack during period. Carried out vigorous Patrolling on the SCHELDT CANAL. On the night 31st October/1st November Battalion was relieved by 122nd Infantry Brigade. Operation Order attached.	158 & 159

W.R. Stewart,
Intelligence Officer,
for Lt.-Col.
Comdg. 18thB n. Highland Light Infantry.

1/11/18

SECRET   OPERATION ORDER NO.153
                   18th HIGHLAND LIGHT INFANTRY   Copy No.

                                                    7th October, 1918.

Map Reference:- Belgium and France, Sheet 28.
----

1. 106th Infantry Brigade will relieve 104 and 105th Infantry
   Brigades on the night 7/8th October as follows:-
            18th H.L.I.   Front Line
            12th H.L.I   Support Line
            17th R.S.   Reserve Line.

2. The Battalion will relieve part of the 17th Lanc. Fus. and part
   of 15th Sherwoods, as follows:-
            "W" Coy.   Right Company.
            "X" "   Centre Company.
            "Y" "   Left Company.
            "Z" "   In Support.

3. One Officer per Company will proceed in advance to 105th Infantry
   Brigade H.Q. at K.15.d.5.4. and obtain necessary details
   re relief.

4. GUIDES. One Guide per platoon will meet Companies at TERHAND
   Cross Roads at 18 hours.

5. TRENCH STORES. All aeroplane photographs, maps, Defence Schemes,
   Ground Flares, S.O.S. Signals, Dumps of S.A.A. and Bombs, Tools
   etc., will be taken over on relief. List showing stores taken
   over will be forwarded to Battalion H.Q. with T.F.R.

6. Completion of relief will be communicated to Battalion H.Q. by
   runner by code word "CLICK".

7. REPORTS.   Battalion H.Q.   K.29.b.2.8.
               Bde. H.Q.   K.15.d.1.4.

8. ACKNOWLEDGE.

                                           Rob Sagger
                                       Capt. & A/Adjt.
                                    18th HIGHLAND LIGHT INFANTRY.

Copies to War Diary
         O.C. File
         2nd in Command
         O.C. W Coy.
         O.C. X Coy.
         O.C. Y Coy.
         O.C. Z Coy.
         T.O. & MrMr.
         Medical Officer.
         17th Lanc. Fus.
         15th Sherwoods.

SECRET.

MOVE ORDERS
Accompanying Operation Orders No. 123

1. The Battalion will relieve parts of the 17th Lanc. Fus., and of 15th Sherwoods on the night 7/8th Octr. 1918.

2. MARCH.   Starting Point:- Belgian Battery Corner - 12 hours.
   Route:- YPRES - ZONNEBEKE - BROODSEINDE - BECELAERE and TERHAND.
   Distance:- 100 Yards between heads of platoons.
   200 Yards between heads of Companies.
   Dress:- Fighting Order.
   Order of March:- Headquarters - W, X, Y, Z.

3. TRANSPORT. Cookers and Lewis Gun Limbers will march in rear of Companies.

4. HALT. A Halt will be made for Tea at J.6.c.0.3 for ½ hour.

5. PARADE. Companies will parade in Camp ready to march off 12.30.

6. RATIONS. Rations for consumption on 8th inst. will be issued individually before marching off.

R. Dagge
Capt. & A/Adjt.
18th HIGHLAND LIGHT INFANTRY.

7th Octr. 1918

Copies to War Diary
O.C. File
2nd in Command
O.C. W. Coy
O.C. X "
O.C. Y "
O.C. Z "
T.O. & QMR.
Medical Officer.

SECRET.   OPERATION ORDER. No. 154.   Copy No.
          'B' HIGHLAND LIGHT INFANTRY.   10.10.18.

Reference Map. D.DIXMUDE. 1/10,000.

1. The 9th Bn. R.I.F. on our left will attack and hold GOLDFLAKE
   FARM (L.19.c.1.9.) The attack will commence at 1010 tomorrow 11.10.18.

2. During the night 10/11th October GOLDFLAKE FARM and adjoining
   structures will be bombarded intermittently by Heavy Artillery till
   0500. From 0515 till 0530 4.5 Hows. and 18 pounders will open a
   heavy fire on GOLDFLAKE and MARTELL FARM. From 0530 till 1000
   there will be no artillery bombardment.

3. From 1000 to 1010 Trench Mortars and 4.5 Howitzers will bom-
   -bard GOLDFLAKE FARM. A smoke screen will also be put down lasting
   from 1000 till 1040 - limits E.and S. of GOLDFLAKE FARM on the
   general line L.19.a.9.- L.19.a.8.5.- L.19.a.7.0. - L.19.c.6.6.-
   L.19.c.0.5. - K.24.d.6.5. to screen the movements of the Infantry.
   From 1000 to 1010 artillery will also fire on houses in K.24.b.79.15.

4. At 1000 2 platoons of 9th R.I.F. assembled at TWIG FARM.K.24.b.95.55.
   will move under cover of smoke and bombardment and at 1010 will rush
   and occupy the Farm.

5. The Battalion will co-operate as follows:-
   (a) O.C. X Coy. will arrange L.G. Fire from post at K.24.d.00.45-
   fire to be directed between DIBSLAND FARM and PILL BOX K.14.d.90.70.
   (b) O.C. Y Coy. will withdraw post at MONKS FARM to post at
   K.23.b.00.20. forthwith. Post at MONKS FARM will be re-established
   as soon as possible after the operation (suggested that this be done
   before smoke screen lifts).
   (c) O.C. Z Coy. will hold 2 platoons in readiness for emergency.
   (d) O.C. Companies will ensure that a sufficient quantity of S.A.A.
   L.G. ammunition and Bombs is held in readiness.
   (e) O.C. X and Y Coys. will keep B.H.Q. informed of the progress
   of the operations as far as possible.
   (f) Re-occupation of original Dispositions and liaison with 9th
   R.I.F. will be reported to B.H.Q. by runner.

6. Reports to be sent to B.H.Q. K.29.b.8.2.

                                              Lt.-Col.
10.10.18.
          Comdg. 18th (G.Y.) Bn. Highland Light Infantry.

Copy No. 1. War Diary.
       2. O.O. File.
       3.   Do.
       4. O.C. W Coy.
       5. O.C. X "
       6. O.C. Y "
       7. O.C. Z "

SECRET. OPERATION ORDER. No. 155.   Copy No.
'B' HIGHLAND LIGHT INFANTRY.   11.10.18.

Reference Maps. Sheet 29. 1/40,000.
    DADIZEELE 1/10,000.

1. The 106th Inf. Brigade will be relieved by the 104th and 105th Inf. Brigades in the line on the night 11/12th October 1918.

2. Details of Relief.
   X and Y Coys. H.L.I. will be relieved by the 17th LANCS. FUSILIERS.
   Z Coy. will be relieved by Units of the 104th Inf. Brigade.
   W Coy. will be relieved by the 15th CHESHIRE REGT.
   GUIDES.
   W Coy.   1 Guide per platoon.
            1   "   for Coy. H.Q.
   X Coy.   1   "   per platoon.
            1   "   for Coy. H.Q.
   Y Coy.   1   "   per platoon.
            1   "   Coy. H.Q.
            1   "   for left liaison post.
   Z Coy. will not send any guides.
   All guides will report at B.H.Q. at 1900. Care should be taken to send intelligent men as guides.

3. On relief Companies and H.Q. will move to J.21.
   Route.   MOLENHOEK (K.27)-Track (K.26.c.0.5.)-GHELUVELT-MENIN ROAD.-GHELUVELT.
   Guides to meet Companies en route to billets will be on main road at K.20.b.7.9.

4. TRANSPORT.
   Limbers for conveyance of Petrol Tins, Lewis Guns, Salvage, etc. will be at K.28.b.7.9. Care should be taken that troops and transport do not march through Corps areas other than XIX Corps.

5. All Dispositions, day and night liaison, hostile intelligence, S.O.S. etc. will be handed over on relief. Aeroplane photos and maps will will not be handed over.
   All empty Petrol tins will be taken out and packed in Coy. Limbers.

6. Completion of Relief will be notified to Bn. H.Q. by wire and runner -Code word: JIMMY.

11.10.18.
                                                    Lt.-Col.
                    Comdg. 18th (G.Y.) Bn. Highland Light Infantry.

Copy No. 1. War Diary.
        2. O.O. File.
        3.   Do.
        4. O.C. W Coy.
        5. O.C. X "
        6. O.C. Y "
        7. O.C. Z "
        8. Transport Officer.

SECRET.　　　　OPERATION ORDER. No.15a　　　　Copy No.
　　　　　　　'B' HIGHLAND LIGHT INFANTRY.　　　12.10.18.

Ref. Maps 28 and 29. 1/40,000.
　　　DADIZEELE 1/10,000.

1. INTENTION. The 35th Division with 105th Infantry Brigade on Right and 104th Infantry Brigade on Left is attacking on "J" Day at "H" Hour. 106th Infantry Brigade will be in Divisional Reserve. ("J" day is the day of attack and "H" is ZERO hour.)

2. MODE OF ATTACK. (of 105th and 104th Infantry Brigades)
The two attacking Brigades (105th and 104th) are attacking on one Battalion front. At H - 2 minutes, the hour at which the barrage falls, all three Battalions of both Brigades will move forward. The leading Battalions go straight through to the second pause line on a line L.22 and L.27 and consolidate. The two remaining Battalions of each Brigade go through second pause line on to final objective. The line to be consolidated will depend on the ground but will be such that the enemy is pushed down into the low ground and is not allowed to retain any foothold on the Ridges surrounding the LYS. KIDEFHOEK and KAPPELHOEK, and the spur about SCHOONWATER will be fully occupied.

3. MOVE OF 106th INFANTRY BRIGADE. On night J - 1//J the 106th Infantry Brigade will move to positions of readiness about K.20 clear of the artillery.
　　H.Q. 12th High.L.I.　　　will be K.20.a.5.8.
　　H.Q. 17th R. Scots　　　 "　 " K.20.a.5.8.
　　H.Q. 18th High.L.I.　　　"　 " K.14.c.5.3.
　　"A" Coy. 35th Bn.M.G.C.　 "　 " J.19.b.4.8.
　　H.Q. 106th Inf. Bde.　　 "　 " J.24.b.8.4.
Move Orders will be issued separately.

4. ROLE OF 106th INFANTRY BRIGADE. The Brigade will not be used without reference to 35th Division H.Q. except that in case of urgent necessity B.G.C. Brigade may order up 12th High.L.I. to support the Left of the 104th Infantry Brigade.

5. PRISONERS OF WAR. 35th Division P.O.W. Cage will be at K.25.a.2.7.

6. INFORMATION. The following information is given which might afford Commanders assistance during operations.
(1) The road and railway through K.23.d. to K.24.c. & a receive a good deal of shell fire.
(2) A good track runs across the front K.23.b.15.20. to K.23.d.45.45.
(3) Suitable as H.Q. Pillbox K.23.a.45.75. DEBENHAM HOUSE K.23.d.65.15. Pillbox IMHALL COPSE K.24.a.00.25.

7. SYNCHRONIZATION OF WATCHES. One Officer from the Battalion will visit Brigade Signal Officer 106th Inf. Brigade H.Q. J.24.b.8.4. at 5 p.m. October 13th to synchronise watches.

8. ZERO HOUR "H" AND ZERO DAY "J" will be notified later.

9. Situation Reports and Progress Reports will be sent 10 minutes after ZERO and at every half hour afterwards in addition to special reports.

10. ACKNOWLEDGE.

　　　　　　　　　　　　　　　　　　　　Lieut. & A/Adjt.
Issued at 1800.　　　　　　　　　　　'B' HIGHLAND LIGHT INFANTRY.

SECRET.   MOVE ORDER ISSUED IN CONJUNCTION WITH OPERATION ORDER 156.

'B' HIGHLAND LIGHT INFANTRY.

12th October 1918.

Reference Map. Sheet 28.

1. The Battalion will move on the afternoon of 13th October 1918 into area K.14 with Battalion Headquarters at K.14.c.5.3.

   Starting Point:-   Road Junction J.21.b.3.2.
   Time:-   1600 hours.
   Order of March:-   H.Q., W. X. Y. Z.
   Intervals:-   100 yards between platoons - 200 yards between Coy.
   Dress:-   Fighting Order. Water bottles full.
   Parade:-   The Battalion will parade on the MENIN ROAD
                      (J.20.b.6.9.) at 1515 hours.

2. RECONNAISSANCE. 2/Lieut. Stewart from Headquarters, and one officer and one N.C.O. from each Company will reconnoitre new area and means of approach.
   This party will parade at Battalion Headquarters at 0915 hours.

3. BLANKETS, CAMP KETTLES, etc.
   All Camp Kit will be dumped on Main Road as follows:-
        Blankets (rolled in bundles of 10)   1000 hours.
        Valises   1300 "
        Tents, Shelters, Camp Kettles.   1300 "

4. Lewis Guns, Magazines, etc., will be carried forward to new area by Companies. Transport Officer will arrange to carry water forward as far as possible on pack mules.

5. Arrival on new area will be notified to Battalion Headquarters by runner.

6. ACKNOWLEDGE.

Issued at 1830 hours.   Lieut. & A/Adjt.
                                           'B' HIGHLAND LIGHT INFANTRY.

SECRET.   OPERATION (MOVE) ORDERS. No. 157.   Copy No.
          'B' HIGHLAND LIGHT INFANTRY.   24.10.18.

Reference Map. Sheet 29. 1/40,000.

1. The 106th Infantry Brigade will march into Billets in the
   SWEVEGHEM Area; the Brigade is temporarily attached to the 41st
   Division, which is at present holding the line P.1.c. - O.12.b.-
   O.17.b. - O.23.a. - O.22.d. - O.22.central, to HOOGSTRAATJE.

2. The Battalion will parade in column of route facing East, with
   head of Column at H.33.d.4.5.
   Order of March.   Z. Y. X. W. Hdqrs.
   Time.   15.30 hours.
   Dress.   Fighting Order.

3. Transport. Cookers and Limbers will move in rear of Companies;
   Water Carts in rear of Bn. Headquarters.

4. Route.
   Starting Point. H.33.d.4.5.-Road Junction H.33.d.4.7.-Road
   Junction H.33.d.6.9.-Road Junction H.33.a.7.0.-Main COURTRAI-
   SWEVEGHEM Road.
   Distances.   50 yards between Platoons.
                 100 yards between Companies.

5. Reports to head of Column.

   Issued at 14.45 hours.

                                         Lieut. & A/Adjt.
                                         'B' Highland Light Infantry.

Copy No.1. War Diary.
     2. O.O. File.
     3.   Do.
     4. O.C? W Coy.
     5. O.C. X "
     6. O.C. Y "
     7. O.C. Z "
     8. Transport Officer.
     9. 2nd in Command.

SECRET.   OPERATION ORDER. No.158.   Copy No.
          'B' HIGHLAND LIGHT INFANTRY.   26.10.18.

1. Reference Map Sheet 29. 1/40,000.

2. The 106th Inf. Brigade will relieve the 122nd Inf. Brigade (41st Division) in the line on the night of 26/27th October 1918.

3. The 18th H.L.I. will relieve the 15th Bn. HANTS REGT. on the right: 17th ROYAL SCOTS will relieve the 12th EAST SURREYS on the left, 12th H.L.I. will be in reserve.

4. The Battalion will be disposed as follows:-
    Right Front Coy.   Z Coy.
    Left   "   "   Y "
    Support Coy. (X Coy.) will be located at WOFFELSTRAAT if situation permits.
    W Coy. will be in reserve at OKKERDRIESCH.

5. GUIDES. Four Guides each for front line Coys. and two each for Support, Reserve, and Bn. H.Q. will be furnished by 15th HANTS, an will meet Battalion at South of Windmill at O.36.a.3.3. at 2200 hours.

6. Brigade H.Q. will be established at KAPPELLE MILAENE (O.14.a.central.) Battalion H.Q. at V.2.a.3.3.

7. FLANKS. O.C. Front line Companies will establish liaison with units on their respective flanks and report same to B.H.Q. together with their dispositions. The latter should be carefully verified.

8. 1½ sections A Coy. M.G. Bn. and 2 Stoked Guns will be attached to the Battalion during the Operation.

9. Relief will be notified by runner to B.H.Q., the code word "COMPLETE" being used.

10. MEDICAL. R.A.P. will be situated at Bn. H.Q.

11. ACKNOWLEDGE.

    Issued at 1745.
        26.10.18.
                                            Lieut. & A/Adjt.
                                        'B' HIGHLAND LIGHT INFANTRY.

Copy No.1. War Diary.
     2. O.O. File.
     3.   Do.
     4. O.C. W Coy.
     5. O.C. X "
     6. O.C. Y "
     7. O.C. Z "
     8. Medical Officer.

SECRET.   OPERATION ORDER No.159.   Copy No.
          'B' HIGHLAND LIGHT INFANTRY.   31.10.18.

REFERENCE MAP. 1/40,000.

1. The 106th Infantry Brigade, (35th Division) will be relieved by 122nd Infantry Brigade (41st Division) in the line on night 31st October 1918.

2. The Battalion will be relieved by 15TH HANTS REGT. as follows:-
Y and Z Coys. H.L.I. in front line will be relieved by A Coy. 15th HANTS REGT.
X Coy. H.L.I. in Support will be relieved by C. Coy 15th HANTS.
W " will not be relieved by incoming Unit, but will move off from present location on receipt of orders from Bn. H.Q.

3. GUIDES. O.C. Y Coy. will detail 2 Platoon Guides and 1 for Coy. H.Q.
    "   " Z "   "   "   2   "   "   1   "   "
    "   " X "   "   "   3   "   "   1 for Coy. H.Q.
Lt. Stewart will detail 2 Guides for Bn. H.Q. and 1 for R.M.O.
O.C. Coys. will detail 1 N.C.O. who will be in charge of guides.
Guides will be at Road Junction P.31.d.5.1. at 18.30 hours to guide in incoming Unit.

4. Trench Stores. All battle stores, including S.O.S. Signals will be taken out on relief.

5. Billets. The Battalion will take over the billets at present occupied by 15th HANTS REGT. in N.24.a.
Route will be as follows:-
To Windmill at 0.36.a.3.6. (same route as coming in) - thence through HOSKE - KETBERG to Road Junction 0.23.c. - Road Junction 0.28.a. - Track to 0.27.b.6.1. - Road 0.27.b.6.2. - Cross Roads 0.31.b.8.9. - thence to 0.25.d. and c. - N.24.d. and c. - to N.24.a.
Companies will be met by guides before arriving in N.24.a.

6. Relief. Completion of relief will be notified to Bn. H.Q. by Runner: Code Word: "PLINK".
On arrival in new area, O.C. Companies will forward locations of their Coy. H.Q. by runners to Bn. H.Q.

7. ACKNOWLEDGE.

Issued at 1600 hours.
                                    Lieut. & A/Adjt.
                              'B' HIGHLAND LIGHT INFANTRY.

Copy No. 1. War Diary.
        2. O.O. File.
        3.   Do.
        4. O.C. W Coy.
        5. O.C. X "
        6. O.C. Y "
        6. O.C. Z "

SECRET.   OPERATION (MOVE) ORDERS. No. 157.   Copy No.
            'B' HIGHLAND LIGHT INFANTRY.   24.10.18.

Reference Map. Sheet 29. 1/40,000.

1. The 106th Infantry Brigade will march into Billets in the SWEVEGHEM Area; the Brigade is temporarily attached to the 41st Division, which is at present holding the line P.1.c. - O.12.b.- O.17.b. - O.23.a. - O.22.d. - O.22.central, to HOOGSTRAATJE.

2. The Battalion will parade in column of route facing East, with head of Column at H.33.d.4.5.
   Order of March.   Z. Y. X. W. Hdqrs.
   Time.   15.30 hours.
   Dress.   Fighting Order.

3. Transport. Cookers and Limbers will move in rear of Companies; Water Carts in rear of Bn. Headquarters.

4. Route.
   Starting Point. H.33.d.4.5.-Road Junction H.33.a.4.7.-Road Junction H.33.a.6.9.-Road Junction H.33.a.7.0.-Main COURTRAI-SWEVEGHEM Road.
   Distances.   50 yards between Platoons.
                 100 yards between Companies.

5. Reports to head of Column.

Issued at 14.45 hours.   [signature]
                                        Lieut. & A/Adjt.
                                        'B' Highland Light Infantry.

Copy No. 1. War Diary.
         2. O.O. File.
         3.   Do.
         4. O.C. W Coy.
         5. O.C. X "
         6. O.C. Y "
         7. O.C. Z "
         8. Transport Officer.
         9. 2nd in Command.

SECRET.   OPERATION ORDER. No. 158.   Copy No.
          'B' HIGHLAND LIGHT INFANTRY.   26.10.18.

1. Reference Map Sheet 29. 1/40,000.

2. The 106th Inf. Brigade will relieve the 122nd Inf. Brigade (41st Division) in the line on the night of 26/27th October 1918.

3. The 18th H.L.I. will relieve the 15th Bn. HANTS REGT. on the right: 17th ROYAL SCOTS will relieve the 12th EAST SURREYS on the left, 12th H.L.I. will be in reserve.

4. The Battalion will be disposed as follows:-
   Right Front Coy.   Z Coy.
   Left   "   "   Y "
   Support Coy. (X Coy.) will be located at WOFFELSTRAAT if situation permits.
   W Coy. will be in reserve at OKKERDRIESCH.

5. GUIDES. Four Guides each for front line Coys. and two each for Support, Reserve, and Bn. H.Q. will be furnished by 15th HANTS, and will meet Battalion at South of Windmill at O.35.a.3.3. at 2200 hours.

6. Brigade H.Q. will be established at KAPPEILE MILAENE (O.14.a.central.) Battalion H.Q. at V.2.a.3.3.

7. FLANKS. O.C. Front line Companies will establish liaison with units on their respective flanks and report same to B.H.Q. together with their dispositions. The latter should be carefully verified.

8. 1½ sections A Coy. M.G. Bn. and 2 Stoked Guns will be attached to the Battalion during the Operation.

9. Relief will be notified by runner to B.H.Q., the code word "COMPLETE" being used.

10. MEDICAL. R.A.P. will be situated at Bn. H.Q.

11. ACKNOWLEDGE.

Issued at 1745.
26.10.18.
                                            Lieut. & A/Adjt.
                                       'B' HIGHLAND LIGHT INFANTRY.

Copy No. 1. War Diary.
      2. O.O. File.
      3.   Do.
      4. O.C. W Coy.
      5. O.C. X "
      6. O.C. Y "
      7. O.C. Z "
      8. Medical Officer.

SECRET.   OPERATION ORDER No.159.   Copy No.
         'B' HIGHLAND LIGHT INFANTRY.   31.10.18.

REFERENCE MAP. 1/40,000.

1. The 106th Infantry Brigade, (35th Division) will be relieved by 122nd Infantry Brigade (41st Division) in the line on night 31st October 1918.

2. The Battalion will be relieved by 15th HANTS REGT. as follows:-
   Y and Z Coys. H.L.I. in front line will be relieved by A Coy. 15th HANTS REGT.
   X Coy. H.L.I. in Support will be relieved by C. Coy 15th HANTS.
   W " will not be relieved by incoming Unit, but will move off from present location on receipt of orders from Bn. H.Q.

3. GUIDES. O.C. Y Coy. will detail 2 Platoon Guides and 1 for Coy. H.Q.
   "   Z "   "   "   2   "   "   "   "   "   "
   "   X "   "   "   3   "   "   & 1 for Coy. H.Q.
   Lt. Stewart will detail 2 Guides for Bn. H.Q. and 1 for R.M.O.
   O.C. Coys. will detail 1 N.C.O. who will be in charge of guides.
   Guides will be at Road Junction P.31.d.5.1. at 18.30 hours to guide in incoming Unit.

4. Trench Stores. All battle stores, including S.O.S. Signals will be taken out on relief.

5. Billets. The Battalion will take over the billets at present occupied by 15th HANTS REGT. in N.24.a.
   Route will be as follows:-
   To Windmill at O.36.a.3.6. (same route as coming in) - thence through HOSKE - AMTBERG to Road Junction O.23.c. - Road Junction O.23.a. - Track to O.27.b.6.1. - Road O.27.b.6.2. - Cross Roads O.31.b.8.9. - thence to O.25.d. and c. - N.24.d. and c. - to N.24.a.
   Companies will be met by guides before arriving in N.24.a.

6. Relief. Completion of relief will be notified to Bn. H.Q. by Runner: Code Word: "PLINK".
   On arrival in new area, O.C. Companies will forward locations of their Coy. H.Q. by runners to Bn. H.Q.

7. ACKNOWLEDGE.

   Issued at 1600 hours.   Lieut. & A/Adjt.
                                        'B' HIGHLAND LIGHT INFANTRY.

Copy No.1. War Diary.
     2. O.C. File.
     3.   Do.
     4. O.C. W Coy.
     5. O.C. X "
     6. O.C. Y "
     6. O.C. Z "

SECRET.   18th (G.Y.) Bn. Highland Light Infantry.

Narrative of Operations for period 13.10.18 to 19.10.18.

13.10.18. The Battalion on this date occupied bivouacs at J.203 near GHELUVELT, having been relieved in the line two days previously by units of the 104th and 105th Brigades.
   In view of the forth-coming operations the question of re-fitting and re-organising was expedited by every possible means. At 1600, vide Brigade Operation Orders, the Battalion 350 strong, left starting point at ROAD JUNCTION J.21.b.3.2. for first Assembly Position in Area K.14.c. Rain had fallen heavily during the previous night and continued intermittently throughout the day, with the result that the ground was sodden and the going extremely heavy. There was some desultory shelling en route, but the Battalion reached Assembly Position at 1815 without casualty. Battalion Headquarters was established at K.14.c.2.2. and liaison effected with 12th H.L.I. and 17th Royal Scots.

14.10.18. Barrage came down 0535 prompt. 18th H.L.I. being reserve Battalion of reserve Brigade remained at first Assembly Position vide instructions received. The morning proved dull and misty and visibility for any distance was impossible. At 0905 I received a message from Brigade H.Q. (BR.56) giving second Assembly Position, and instructions not to move my Battalion without further orders. After the initial barrage had ceased, enemy artillery fire became more or less desultory, but at 1150 six H.V. shells burst on the area occupied by the Battalion, killing 5 other ranks and wounding three. At 1203 I received orders to move, and by 1430 had reached second Assembly position in L.20.c. in support to the 12th H.L.I., 17th Royal Scots being in reserve. Throughout the afternoon and evening we were persistently shelled by long range howitzers. Battalion Headquarters was here established at L.20.c.8.4.

15.10.18. About 1400 I received warning instructions verbally regarding relief of 104th and 105th Infantry Brigades in the line by the 106th Infantry Brigade on the night 15/16th October. As the relief was likely to be somewhat complicated, I thereupon made tentative arrangements in communication with the C.Os. concerned, and at the same time reconnoitred the ground. Later, however, I learned that the proposed relief was cancelled, and at 2030 received orders to attend a conference at Brigade Headquarters near ELBOW CORNER at 2230, it having been decided to attack and hold the high ground commanding the bridgehead crossing the LYS opposite the village of MARCKE with an unlimited objective should the situation so warrant.

16.10.18.   The conference adjourned at 0015, and ZERO hour having been fixed for 0530, it will be appreciated how narrow was the margin in which to get my Battalion on to its Assembly Position nearly five miles distant, and on a front, and by a route which had not been previously reconnoitred. Furthermore while feeling out way along, five belts of concertina wire drawn across the road were encountered between BAILIFF Cross Roads in L.36.a. and the WEMELGHEM-GULLEGHEM Road, and it was only by the greatest effort and co-operation on the part of all ranks that I succeeded in getting the Battalion on its Assembly Position at 0515 - 15 minutes before ZERO. In order to facilitate/

2.

facilitate communication to Brigade Headquarters I established an intermediate B.H.Q. at CABIN COPSE in L.35.b. while during the opening phase of the attack I remained at Farm at G.26.d.4.5. At 0530 I despatched a runner to the former reporting Battalion in position for transmission by wire from there to Brigade H.Q. About 0700 I succeeded in getting into telephonic communication with Brigade Intelligence Officer and reported the situation verbally to him.

The barrage came down prompt at 0530 well in front of Assembly Position and my Battalion moved forward on a two Company front, one Company being in Support and one in Reserve, the latter remaining under my immediate orders.

During the night a continuous drizzle had fallen which lasted more or less throughout the entire day. Visibility was poor, and the going, over cultivated ground in parts, was extremely heavy. The enemy response to our artillery fire was not very heavy, and little machine gun opposition was met with. Four machine guns were, however, found near the railway in G.34 having been recently abandoned. On reaching the WEVELGHEM-BISSENGHEM Road, determined machine gun opposition was encountered from the tile works, and from farm houses in the vicinity of the high ground commanding the approaches to the river and which evidently had been withdrawn across the LYS under pressure of our artillery barrage followed by our advance. My two leading Companies, however, worked gradually forward by short rushes and succeeded in making good the high ground overlooking the LYS. At this point the machine gun fire became intense, and being in full view of the enemy from the opposite bank, and at the same time subjected to a considerable amount of sniping, it was impossible to make further ground without suffering heavy casualties. At 1030 therefore my dispositions were as reported in my R.B.72 of 16th October, my front line running roughly M.4.c.0.1. to M.5.a.8.4. Touch was effected with 12th H.L.I. on left, but no troops could be observed on my right during the attack. I immediately ordered a patrol to get in touch with Division on right, and this was effected at 1730. Patrols were also sent forward to ascertain condition of bridges, and depth and width of river, but owing to the vigilance of the enemy, these could not be carried out till after dusk. Battalion Headquarters was established in pill-box at G.34.c.4.5.

17.10.18.   Machine gun fire persistent throughout the day, also light artillery active. Notwithstanding a very valuable daylight reconnaissance was carried out by the O.C. my left Company on the condition of the bridge opposite his front. I ordered my left Company, as a safeguard, to establish a post at bridge over LYS at M.5.c.2.2., also my right Company at footbridge at M.10.a.60.25 and at the same time to occupy the high ground at M.10.d.5.3. thus denying it to the enemy. This latter post I arranged to have strengthened by two Vickers. In view of the operation carried out same night by Royal Scots and 12th H.L.I. under artillery preparation these posts were of considerable tactical value.

18.10.18.   As the attack of the preceding night was not successful in clearing the village of the enemy, a further operation was decided upon, and at a conference held at 12th H.L.I. H.Q. I received instructions to place my right Company for the purpose of the operation at the disposal of the 17th Royal Scots. In agreement with the latter I arranged to strengthen the posts already held by this Company on enemy side of river, the same to form an assembly position for Royal Scots, the company of 18th H.L.I. to be in reserve.

ZERO hour was 2200. At ZERO plus 3 my right Company advanced behind Royal Scots, two platoons supporting their right along KNOCKE-MARCKE Road, and two supporting their left along the railway. On reaching the village of MARCKE the work of mopping/

mopping up was proceeded with, and in a pill-box in the tile works they were successful in capturing a machine gun and team which had previously given considerable trouble. Meantime the Royal Engineers assisted by a platoon of my left Company were busy repairing the bridge over the LYS at M.5.c.2.2. and which was ready for the passage of troops by 0030 October 19th.

GENERAL REMARKS.

    Throughout the entire operations there has been a decided spirit of confidence amongst all ranks. Casualties have been light in consideration of the results achieved. Certain operations had necessarily to be carried out at extremely short notice, but officers and men alike displayed a spirit of cheerfulness and adaptability to conditions dependant on a war of movement, and it was only through their whole-hearted endeavour and helpful co-operation that I was enabled successfully to carry out the operations entrusted to the Battalion under my command.

    Supply and Transport arrangements worked exceedingly well. My Transport Officer, Lieut. Walker, especially was indefatigueable in getting his limbers up to the Battalion over entirely new country, roads conjested with traffic, and often under enemy shell fire. Great credit is due to this officer for the spirited manner in which he overcame these difficulties.

    While bringing to your notice the splendid fighting spirit displayed by all ranks throughout the operations, ending in the successful crossing of the LYS, I should like to bring the following Officer and Warrant Officer to your notice:-

      Captain Wm. DEVEREUX BRYAN, M.C.
4804 C.S.M. JAMES McQUILLAN, D.C.M. & BAR, M.M.

20.10.18.

Lieut.-Colonel.
Comdg. 18th (G.Y.) Bn. Highland Light Infantry.

SECRET.   18th (G.Y.) Bn. HIGHLAND LIGHT INFANTRY.

Narrative of Operations subsequent to crossing of
the LYS on night 18/19th October to 21st October 1918.

Reference Map. 29.S.W. 1/20,000.

19.10.18. After the crossing of the LYS and the village of MARCKE had been successfully cleared of the enemy, my right Company in support to the 17th ROYAL SCOTS remained on enemy side of stream. On the afternoon of October 19th, I received orders for the remainder of the Battalion to cross over and take up billets in the village preparatory to a further advance the following morning.

20.10.18. In accordance with Operation Orders received, the Battalion paraded in column of route ready to move forward in conjunction with 17th ROYAL SCOTS and 12th H.L.I. from Brigade starting point M.12.c.3.6. at 0700. Position of Assembly was roughly square N.18, dependent of course on the situation in front and progress made by the two Brigades in the line.

It is here worthy of mention that this is the first instance of the Battalion having marched off as part of the Brigade to take up a position for attack, in column of route, complete with first line Transport.

The morning was damp and misty and visibility was low. Nothing of incident occurred until we were near the village of HOOGHE in N.9. At this point the situation became obscure in front; an attack beyond the village was in progress, and the village and main COURTRAI Road was then being shelled by the enemy. The Brigade was halted on the low ground west of west of the village while the situation was being ascertained. About 0900 I received instructions to put my Battalion under cover in an adjoining farm and await orders. This done, I established my B.H.Q. in Chateau N.2.d.9.5. At 1430 I attended a conference at Brigade H.Q. and there received orders to work in conjunction with the 12th H.L.I. in holding the high ground in N.36.c.31.26. and 27., and later to leap-frog through them.

At 1635 the Battalion moved off in column of route in a S.E. direction along the main COURTRAI Road towards N.35. central, while I rode ahead to ascertain the situation. On getting in touch with the LANCS. FUSILIERS H.Q. I learned that the enemy resistance along the high ground which was to have been our objective, had given way and a new situation now presented.

Under instructions from Brigade H.Q. and in conjunction with O.C. 12th H.L.I.,with whom I was collaborating, I gave orders for a line to be taken up running roughly N.36.d. - O.31.a. - O.31.b. - and O.26.d. with 2 Companies holding positions along the road N.36.a. - N.36.b. - O.25.c.- O.25.d. and O.25.b. The 12th H.L.I. meantime were to make good DRIE-LINDEN in O.20.c. and extend their line northwards.

I thereafter established my H.Q. at N.35.a.9.3. and went forward to ascertain the situation. On arriving at a point about O.25.c.5.2. I found that B Coy. 12th H.L.I. were held up by enemy M.G.fire coming from the direction of O.25.d.3.6. I then went forward to reconnoitre LAATSTE-OORTJE farm to see whether it was held by the enemy. On investigation I discovered that the place had just been vacated and was informed by the civilian occupants that the enemy was holding a post about 2 minutes' walk along the road. I immediately ordered my Y Coy. to occupy the farm and put it in a state of defence. Whilst this was being done I met the O.C. 12th H.L.I., who informed me that he had also met with strong M.G. opposition from the direction of the Cross roads at O.31.b.8.9., and in conjunction with him, agreed to hold the line of posts up to the farm with my W and X Coys. whilst I utilised my remaining two Companies to hold the line of posts from road junction at N.35.d.7.3. to O.31.b.2.5. Meanwhile the 12th H.L.I. were to push forward and extend the line northwards. The posts were duly established about 2300 and my final dispositions wired to Brigade H.Q. together with situation report.

21.10.18. About 0200 the situation became quiet. Intimation having been received that the Battalion was to be relieved early on the morning of the 21st, rations were not sent forward, but a hot meal prepared for the men on coming out. This was modified subsequently and the cookers actually met the Companies en route to billets.

General remarks. Throughout the period the weather was most inclement and the officers and men alike were seldom dry. Nothwithstanding cases of sickness were almost negligible and I cannot speak too highly of the cheerfulness and endurance of all ranks.

Lieut.-Colonel,
Comdg. 18th (G.Y.) Bn. Highland Light Infantry.

SECRET.   18th (G.Y.) Bn. Highland Light Infantry.

Narrative of Operations for period 13.10.18 to 19.10.18.

13.10.18. The Battalion on this date occupied bivouacs at J.20.3 near GHELUVELT, having been relieved in the line two days previously by units of the 104th and 105th Brigades.

In view of the forth-coming operations the question of re-fitting and re-organising was expedited by every possible means. At 1600, vide Brigade Operation Orders, the Battalion 350 strong, left starting point at ROAD JUNCTION J.21.b.3.2. for first Assembly Position in Area K.14.c. Rain had fallen heavily during the previous night and continued intermittently throughout the day, with the result that the ground was sodden and the going extremely heavy. There was some desultory shelling en route, but the Battalion reached Assembly Position at 1815 without casualty. Battalion Headquarters was established at K.14.c.2.2. and liaison effected with 12th H.L.I. and 17th Royal Scots.

14.10.18. Barrage came down 0535 prompt. 18th H.L.I. being reserve Battalion of reserve Brigade remained at first Assembly Position vide instructions received. The morning proved dull and misty and visibility for any distance was impossible. At 0905 I received a message from Brigade H.q. (BR.56) giving second Assembly Position, and instructions not to move my Battalion without further orders. After the initial barrage had ceased, enemy artillery fire became more or less desultory, but at 1150 s six H.V. shells burst on the area occupied by the Battalion, killing 5 other ranks and wounding three. At 1203 I received orders to move, and by 1430 had reached second Assembly position in L.20.c. in support to the 12th H.L.I., 17th Royal Scots being in reserve. Throughout the afternoon and evening we were persistently shelled by long range howitzers. Battalion Headquarters was here established at L.20.c.8.4.

15.10.18. About 1400 I received warning instructions verbally regarding relief of 104th and 105th Infantry Brigades in the line by the 106th Infantry Brigade on the night 15/16th October. As the relief was likely to be somewhat complicated, I thereupon made tentative arrangements in communication with the C.Os. concerned, and at the same time reconnoitred the ground. Later, however, I learned that the proposed relief was cancelled, and at 2030 received orders to attend a conference at Brigade Headquarters near ELBOW CORNER at 2230, it having been decided to attack and hold the high ground commanding the bridgehead crossing the LYS opposite the village of MARCKE with an unlimited objective should the situation so warrant.

16.10.18. The conference adjourned at 0015, and ZERO hour having been fixed for 0530, it will be appreciated how narrow was the margin in which to get my Battalion on to its Assembly position nearly five miles distant, and on a front, and by a route which had not been previously reconnoitred. Furthermore while feeling out way along, five belts of concertina wire drawn across the road were encountered between CALLIFF Cross Roads in L.36.a. and the WAMBEEGHEM-GULLEGHEM Road, and it was only by the greatest effort and co-operation on the part of all ranks that I succeeded in getting the Battalion on its Assembly Position at 0515 - 15 minutes before ZERO. In order to facilitate/

2.

facilitate communication to Brigade Headquarters I established an intermediate R.H.Q. at CABLE HOUSE in L.33.b. While during the opening phase of the attack I remained at Farm at G.29.d.4.5. At 0530 I despatched a runner to the former reporting battalion in position for transmission by wire from there to Brigade H.Q. About 0700 I succeeded in getting into telephonic communication with Brigade Intelligence Officer and reported the situation verbally to him.

The barrage came down prompt at 0535 well in front of assembly position and my Battalion moved forward on a two Company front, one Company being in support and one in Reserve, the latter remaining under my immediate orders.

During the night a continuous drizzle had fallen which lasted more or less throughout the entire day. Visibility was poor, and the going over cultivated ground in parts, was extremely heavy. The enemy response to our artillery fire was not very heavy, and little machine gun opposition was met with. Four machine guns were, however, found near the railway in G.34 having been recently abandoned. On reaching the WEVELGHEM-BISSENGHEM Road, determined machine gun opposition was encountered from the tile works, and from farm houses in the vicinity of the high ground commanding the approaches to the river and which evidently had been withdrawn across the LYS under pressure of our artillery barrage followed by our advance. My two leading Companies, however, worked gradually forward by short rushes and succeeded in making good the high ground overlooking the LYS. At this point the machine gun fire became intense, and being in full view of the enemy from the opposite bank, and at the same time subjected to a considerable amount of sniping, it was impossible to make further ground without suffering heavy casualties. At 1030 therefore my dispositions were as reported in my R.B.72 of 16th October, my front line running roughly M.4.c.9.1. to M.5.a.6.4. Touch was effected with 12th H.L.I. on left, but no troops could be observed on my right during the attack. I immediately ordered a patrol to get in touch with Division on right, and this was effected at 1730. Patrols were also sent forward to ascertain condition of bridges, and depth and width of river, but owing to the vigilance of the enemy, these could not be carried out till after dusk. Battalion Head--quarters was established in pill-box at G.34.c.4.5.

17.10.18.   Machine gun fire persistent throughout the day, also light artillery active. Notwithstanding a very valuable daylight reconnaissance was carried out by the O.C. my left Company on the condition of the bridge opposite his front. I ordered my left Company, as a safeguard, to establish a post at bridge over LYS at M.5.c.2.2., also my right Company at footbridge at M.10.a.60.25 and at the same time to occupy the high ground at M.10.d.5.3. thus denying it to the enemy. This latter post I arranged to have strengthened by two Vickers. In view of the operation carried out same night by Royal Scots and 12th H.L.I. under artillery preparation these posts were of considerable tactical value.

18.10.18.   As the attack of the preceding night was not successful in clearing the village of the enemy, a further operation was decided upon, and at a conference held at 12th H.L.I. H.Q. I received instructions to place my right Company for the purpose of the operation at the disposal of the 17th Royal Scots. In agreement with the latter I arranged to strengthen the posts already held by this Company on enemy side of river, the same to form an assembly position for Royal Scots, the company of 18th H.L.I. to be in reserve.

ZERO hour was 2200. At ZERO plus 3 my right Company advanced behind Royal Scots, two platoons supporting their right along KNOCKE-MARCKE Road, and two supporting their left along the railway. On reaching the village of MARCKE the work of mopping/

3.

mopping up was proceeded with, and in a pill-box in the tile works they were successful in capturing a machine gun and team which had previously given considerable trouble. Meantime the Royal Engineers assisted by a platoon of my left Company were busy repairing the bridge over the LYS at M.5.c.2.2. and which was ready for the passage of troops by 0030 October 19th.

GENERAL REMARKS.

Throughout the entire operations there has been a decided spirit of confidence amongst all ranks. Casualties have been light in consideration of the results achieved. Certain operations had necessarily to be carried out at extremely short notice, but officers and men alike displayed a spirit of cheerfulness and adaptability to conditions dependant on a war of movement, and it was only through their whole-hearted endeavour and helpful co-operation that I was enabled successfully to carry out the operations entrusted to the Battalion under my command.

Supply and Transport arrangements worked exceedingly well. My Transport Officer, Lieut. Walker, especially was indefatigueable in getting his limbers up to the Battalion over entirely new country, roads conjested with traffic, and often under enemy shell fire. Great credit is due to this officer for the spirited manner in which he overcame these difficulties.

While bringing to your notice the splendid fighting spirit displayed by all ranks throughout the operations, ending in the successful crossing of the LYS, I should like to bring the following Officer and Warrant Officer to your notice:-

    Captain Wm. DEVEREUX BRYAN, M.C.
4804 C.S.M. JAMES McQUILLAN, D.C.M. & BAR, M.M.

20.10.18.

Lieut.-Colonel.
Comdg. 18th (G.Y.) Bn. Highland Light Infantry.

SECRET.   18th (G.Y.) Bn. HIGHLAND LIGHT INFANTRY.

Narrative of Operations subsequent to crossing of
the LYS on night 18/19th October to 21st October 1918.

Reference Map. 29.S.W. 1/20,000.

19.10.18. After the crossing of the LYS and the village of HARCKE had
been successfully cleared of the enemy, my right Company
in support to the 17th ROYAL SCOTS remained on enemy side of
stream. On the afternoon of October 19th, I received orders
for the remainder of the Battalion to cross over and take up
billets in the village preparatory to a further advance the
following morning.

20.10.18. In accordance with Operation Orders received, the Battalion
paraded in column of route ready to move forward in conjunction
with 17th ROYAL SCOTS and 12th H.L.I. from Brigade starting
point N.12.c.3.6. at 0700. Position of Assembly was roughly
square N.18, dependent of course on the situation in front and
progress made by the two Brigades in the line.
    It is here worthy of mention that this is the first
instance of the Battalion having marched off as part of the
Brigade to take up a position for attack, in column of route,
complete with first line Transport.
    The morning was damp and misty and visibility was low.
Nothing of incident occurred until we were near the village of
HOOGHE in N.9. At this point the situation became obscure
in front; an attack beyond the village was in progress, and
the village and main COURTRAI Road was then being shelled by
the enemy. The Brigade was halted on the low ground west of
west of the village while the situation was being ascertained.
About 0900 I received instructions to put my Battalion under
cover in an adjoining farm and await orders. This done, I
established my B.H.Q. in Chateau N.2.d.9.5. At 1430 I attended
a conference at Brigade H.Q. and there received orders to work
in conjunction with the 12th H.L.I. in holding the high ground
in N.36.c.31.26. and 27., and later to leap-frog through them.
    At 1635 the Battalion moved off in column of route in a
S.E. direction along the main COURTRAI Road towards N.35.
central, while I rode ahead to ascertain the situation. On
getting in touch with the LANCS. FUSILIERS H.Q. I learned that
the enemy resistance along the high ground which was to have
been our objective, had given way and a new situation now
presented.
    Under instructions from Brigade H.Q. and in conjunction
with O.C. 12th H.L.I., with whom I was collaborating, I gave
orders for a line to be taken up running roughly N.36.d. -
O.31.a. - O.31.b. - and O.25.d. with 2 Companies holding posi-
-tions along the road N.36.a. - N.36.b. - O.25.c.- O.25.d. and
O.25.b. The 12th H.L.I. meantime were to make good DRIE-
-LINDEN in O.20.c. and extend their line northwards.
    I thereafter established my H.Q. at N.35.a.9.3. and went
forward to ascertain the situation. On arriving at a point
about O.25.c.5.2. I found that B Coy. 12th H.L.I. were held
up by enemy M.G.fire coming from the direction of O.25.d.3.6.
I then went forward to reconnoitre MAATSEN-OORTJE farm to see
whether it was held by the enemy. On investigation I dis-
-covered that the place had just been vacated and was informed
by the civilian occupants that the enemy was holding a post
about 2 minutes' walk along the road. I immediately ordered
my Y Coy. to occupy the farm and put it in a state of defence.
Whilst this was being done I met the O.C. 12th H.L.I., who
informed me that he had also met with strong M.G. opposition
from the direction of the Cross roads at O.31.b.8.9., and in

2.

conjunction with him, agreed to hold the line of posts up to the farm with my W and X Coys. whilst I utilised my remaining two Companies to hold the line of posts from road junction at R.35.d.7.3. to O.31.b.2.5. Meanwhile the 12th H.L.I. were to push forward and extend the line northwards. The posts were duly established about 2300 and my final dispositions wired to Brigade H.Q. together with situation report.

21.10.18. About 0200 the situation became quiet. Intimation having been received that the Battalion was to be relieved early on the morning of the 21st, rations were not sent forward, but a hot meal prepared for the men on coming out. This was modified subsequently and the cookers actually met the Companies en route to billets.

<u>General remarks.</u> Throughout the period the weather was most inclement and the officers and men alike were seldom dry. Notwithstanding cases of sickness were almost negligible and I cannot speak too highly of the cheerfulness and endurance of all ranks.

V.E.Woodersen
Lieut.-Colonel,
Comdg. 18th (G.Y.) Bn. Highland Light Infantry.

WAR DIARY From 1st to 30th November 1918 inclusive. Army Form C. 2118.

INTELLIGENCE-SUMMARY. 18th (G.Y.) Bn. HIGHLAND LIGHT INFANTRY.

(Erase heading not required.)

Index 33.

Instructions regarding War Diaries and Intelligence Summaries are contained in F.S. Regs., Part II. and the Staff Manual respectively. Title pages will be prepared in manuscript.

Place	Date	Hour	Summary of Events and Information	Remarks and references to Appendices
	1.11.18.		Battalion in Billets 4 miles S.E. of COURTRAI, having been relieved in the line on the night 31st Octr./1st Novr.; weather wet and dull.	
	2.11.18.		Battalion in Billets. Day spent in refitting and re-organising; Medal Ribbons were presented to the N.C.Os and men who had gained medals in the recent operations.	
	3.11.18.		Battalion in Billets; Company Inspections and parades carried out. Weather wet.	
	4.11.18.		Orders were received to move to HOOGE area, but were subsequently cancelled. Battalion proceeded to the line to relieve HANTS REGT. 41st Division. Weather dry and clear. O.O.attached.	160
BERCHEM.	5.11.18.		Battalion holding line of SCHELDT in front of BERCHEM; enemy artillery active: weather extremely wet.	
	6.11.18.		Do.	
	7.11.18.		Do.	
	8.11.18.		Do. Inter Coy. Relief carried out.	
	9.11.18.		Crossing of the SCHELDT and general advance to the line of the RENAIX-NUKERKE Road - see narrative attached.	
	10.11.18.			
BOSCHSTRAAT.	11.11.18.		Battalion moved for ward and billeted in BOSCHSTRAAT area; weather wet. O.O. attached.	160a
	12.11.18.		Battalion in Billets; day spent in cleaning and resting.	
DONDERY.	13.11.18.		Battalion moved to BOYENBURG and billeted there; weather dry. Operation Order attached.	161
	14.11.18.		Battalion in billets in NUKERKE area. Battalion Parade held and programme of training carried out. Weather dry.	
	15.11.18.		Do.	
	16.11.18.		Do.	
	17.11.18.		Church Parades were held for all denominations. Weather dry but cold.	
	18.11.18.		Battalion marched to INGOYGHEM en route for COURTRAI and billeted there overnight; weather cold; slight fall of snow. Operation Order attached.	162
	19.11.18.		Battalion marched from INGOYGHEM to COURTRAI and billeted there; weather fine; rest of day spent in resting and cleaning. Operation Order attached.	163.
COURTRAI.	20.11.18.		Battalion in billets; Battalion parade and full programme of training carried out, along with arrangements for completing equipment of men.	
	21.11.18.		Do. Training programme carried out. Weather dull. Recreational training started.	
	22.11.18.		Do. Weather dry but cold.	
	23.11.18.		Do. Inter-company Football com-petitions commenced.	

WAR DIARY
INTELLIGENCE SUMMARY

(Erase heading not required.)

Army Form C. 2118.

Place	Date	Hour	Summary of Events and Information	Remarks and references to Appendices
COURTRAI	24.11.18.		Battalion in billets; Training Programme carried out. Weather fine.	164.
	25.11.18.		Do. Do.	
	26.11.18.		Do. Preparations for move completed.	
	27.11.18.		Battalion commenced march to the ST.OMER - EPERLECQUES - WATTON Area. Started from COURTRAI and staged first night in MENIN. Weather dry. Operation Order attached. Stage 1.	
	28.11.18.		Battalion continued its march, and staged second night in VLAMERTINGHE. Weather wet. Stage 2.	
	29.11.18.		Do. staged third night in ST. ELOI Area. Do. Stage 3.	
	30.11.18.		Do. staged fourth night in LEDERZEELE. Weather good. Stage 4.	

W.F. Stewart 2/Lt. Intelligence Officer
For Lieut.-Colonel.
Comdg. 18th (G.Y.) Bn. Highland Light Infantry.

SECRET.   OPERATION (WARNING) ORDER. No.160.   Copy No.
             'B' HIGHLAND LIGHT INFANTRY.   4.11.18.

Reference Map 29. 1/40,000.

1. The Battalion will move into the Line tonight, and will be dis-
    -posed as follows:-
        W Coy.   Right Front Company.
        Y "   Left   "   "
        X and Z Coys. in Support.

2. Brigade Headquarters will be at P.13.c.5.7.
    Other Locations will be notified later.

3. Companies will be prepared to move at 15 minutes Notice from 17.00
    hours.

4. <u>Dress</u>:   Battle Order.
    <u>Rations</u>: Rations for tomorrow will be issued individually.

5. <u>Transport</u>. 1 Limber for W and Y Coys. and 1 Limber for X and Z
    Coys. will report to Companies at 16.00 hours, to carry forward
    Lewis Guns and Magazines and Trench Gear.
    A G.S. Wagon will report at all Company Hdqrs between 15.30 and
    16.00 hours to collect Officers' Valises and Surplus Mess Stores
    of Companies to dump at Q.M. Stores.

6. Packs of men going forward with Companies will be carried by
    Companies to Q.M. Stores at once and dumped there.
    Blankets will be rolled in bundles of 10 and dumped at Q.M.Stores
    by 15.30 hours.

7. Companies will render Strength Return for Line, and Nominal Roll
    of Details, and will report to Bn. Orderly Room before 17 hours
    that all surplus kit has been returned to Q.M.Stores, and that
    their Companies are complete with Battle Equipment.

8. ACKNOWLEDGE.

Issued at 14.30 hours.
                                            Lieut. & A/Adjt.
                                  18th (G.Y.) Bn. Highland Light Infantry.

Copy No.1. War Diary.
        2. O.O. File.
        3.   Do.
        4. O.C. W Coy.
        5. O.C. X "
        6. O.C. Y "
        7. O.C. Z "
        8. 2nd in Command.
        9. Transport Officer.

SECRET.   18th (G.Y.) Bn. HIGHLAND LIGHT INFANTRY.

Headquarters,
    105th Infantry Brigade.

    Narrative of Operations from 8.11.18 to 10.11.18,
    during period 18th (G.Y.) Bn. Highland Light Infantry
    was under command of 105th Infantry Brigade.

Reference Map. BELGIUM. Sheet 29. 1/40,000.

8.11.18. On this date the Battalion held the line of the SCHELDT from P.19.d.8.3. to P.21.a.8.6., on a one Company front with the 15th Bn. SHERWOOD FORESTERS on the right and the 16th OAMS on the left. The Areas in the vicinity of the SCHELDT were heavily shelled throughout the morning including a considerable amount of gas. As, through information received, it was thought that the enemy intended to retire on this front, vigorous patrolling was carried out in order to keep in touch with him.

9.11.18. On receipt of your BM.743, ordering a strong fighting patrol to be pushed across the river, immediate action was taken, but in view of the fact that the BERCHEM was impassable and there were no other bridges extant, some difficulty was anticipated in effecting a speedy crossing. Fortunately, however, the bridging material arranged for in 35th Divisional Order No. G.127/4 of November 8th had, by this time, been brought forward and dumped, and my O.C. Front Line Company, with the assistance of this material, was enabled, by 0530 to get one Platoon across and through BERCHEM as far as line of the railway. Meantime, a second platoon was being got over as rapidly as possible. On being informed verbally that a joint advance was intended the same morning, Operation Orders were at once issued for the whole Battalion to effect the crossing of the SCHELDT by bridges, which were then in course of erection, and by any means available and to establish the line of the railway beyond BERCHEM within the Battalion boundary. This was successfully carried out, the line being held on a two Company Front, one Company being in Support and one in Reserve. No opposition was encountered. At ZERO (Noon) vide your Bm.495, the Battalion moved forward, (Companies in Diamond formation) to its objective - roughly, the line KRAAI (W.5.d.9.4.) - KLEINHOOGVELD - LAMONT (Q.26.b.) all inclusive to Q.30.d.5.0. This Line was successfully reached by 1400 and readjusted in accordance with your BM.500, the line running roughly due North and South on Grid Line through Q.36.central. No opposition was encountered, nor contact with the enemy obtained.

    Instructions having been received to make good the line of the RENAIX - NUKERKE road within Battalion Boundary - i.e. R.21.c.4.0. due east - R.32.b.0.0. due east, I utilised my Reserve Company for this purpose, and, having in view the considerable distance this position was ahead of my Front Line, I considered it advisable to support it by a second Company, which I located in the vicinity of SULSIQUE (R.25.b. and d.) Touch was established on right flank with 15th SHERWOOD F FORESTERS and on left with the 41st Division.

10.11.18. About 1000 approximately, the advanced Guard of the 104th Infantry Brigade passed through our front towards its Objective N.2.d.7.0.-N.27.c.4.0.-BOSCHSTRAAT village inclusive-T.3.a.4.0 and at 1200 the Battalion again came under the orders of the B.G.C. 105th Infantry Brigade

11.11.18.   Capt. & A/Adjt.
                A/Comdg. 18th (G.Y.) Bn. HIGHLAND LIGHT IN

SECRET.   OPERATION ORDER. No.160a.   Copy No.
           'B' HIGHLAND LIGHT INFANTRY.   11.11.18.

Reference Maps. Sheets 29 and 30. 1/40,000.

1. The Brigade will move today, 11th Novr. to area N.27., N.33.
   and N.34.
   The Battalion will move into billets in BOSCHSTRAAT in N.33.c.

2. <u>Starting Points.</u> Hdqrs, W, and Y Coys. will parade in column
   of route, facing south in that order, with head of Column at
   B.H.Q. (R.25.d.65.85)   Time 08.30.
   X and Z Coys. will parade in column of route facing South,
   with head of column at road junction R.33.a.6.9. at 08.45 hours
   and will move under orders of Lieut. Dare to join column in rear
   of Y Coy. at cross roads at X.3.c.1.2. (Rear of Y Coy. should
   pass this cross roads at about 09.30 hours.)

3. <u>Route.</u> Cross roads R.25.d.5.2. - HOOGBERG - T Road X.2.d.5.0. -
            Cross Roads X.3.c.1.2. - thence road running through X.
   3. - 4. - 5. - 6.- S.1. - 2. - 3. - cross roads M.33.d.9.9.-
   road junction S.5.c.3.3. - S.11.b.0.7. - cross roads N.31.d.0.4.
   - BOSCHSTRAAT.

4. <u>Distances.</u>   As per F. S.R.

5. <u>Transport.</u> 1 Limber will report at Hdqrs, W, and Y Coys. by 07.00
   hours, to carry L.Gs. Magazines etc. This limber will be loaded
   by 08.00 hours and will report to O.C. Y Coy. at that hour ready
   to move off in rear of that Company.
   1 Limber will report to X and Z Coys. at 07.00 hours and will,
   when loaded report to O.C. Z Coy. and move in rear of that Coy.

6. <u>Discipline.</u> All Companies will ensure that water bottles are
   filled before marching off and that strict march discipline is
   observed in line of march.

7. Reports en route to head of column.
   B.H.Q. in BOSCHSTRAAT will be notified later.

8. <u>Medical.</u> 1 Pack Mule will be at the disposal of M.O. for conveyance
   of Medical Stores.
   Medical personnel will move in rear of Y Coy. from starting point
   to Cross roads X.3.c.1.2. (where X and Z Coys join column) thence
   in rear of Z Coy.

9. ACKNOWLEDGE.

   Issued at 0330 hours.   Capt.
                                    Comdg. 'B' HIGHLAND LIGHT INFANTRY.

   Copy No.1. War Diary.
        2. O.O. File.
        3.   Do.
        4. O.C. W Coy.
        5. O.C. X "
        6. O.C. Y "
        7. O.C. Z "
        8. Medical Officer.
        9. Transport Officer.

SECRET.　　　　　OPERATION (MOVE) ORDERS. No.161.　　　Copy No.
　　　　　　　　　'B' HIGHLAND LIGHT INFANTRY.　　　　　13.11.18.

　　　　　　　　　29 and
Reference Map. Sheets 30. 1/40,000.

1. The 41st Division is taking over the Outpost Line on the Corps
   Front today, 13.11.18.   The 35th Division will concentrate
   East of the ESCAUT.

2. The 106th Infantry Brigade will march with 1st Line Transport
   and Q.M. Stores to BOIMBERE Area, Sheet 29. R17.
   Starting Point:　　　N.27.a.3.9.
   Time:　　　　　　　　1000 hours.

3. The Battalion will parade in Column of Route facing North East
   on road running through N.32.d.8.0. - N.33.c.3.0. - N.33.c.2.5.
   with Head of Column at N.33.c.2.5. in the following order:-
   　　Hdqrs., X, Y, Z, W.

4. ROUTE.　N.33.c.2.5. - Road Junction N.27.d.1.1. - Cross Roads
   　　　　　N.27.a.3.9. - Cross Roads S.11.b.0.7. - Cross Roads
   　　　　　N.33.d.9.9. thence by road which will be reconnoitred
   　　　　　under Brigade arrangements to BOIMBERE.
   Time.　　Battalion will parade at 0915 hours.
   Dress.　 Fighting Order.

5. TRANSPORT. Transport Officer will detail one half-limber per Com-
   -pany and Battalion Headquarters, and one limber for Orderly
   Room and Canteen to report to respective Companies at 0800 hours
   for conveyance of Lewis Guns, Magazines, etc.; these vehicles
   must be loaded by 0830 hours and will be collected by Transport
   Officer into his Convoy, which will move in rear of Battalion
   Column.

6. Officers' Valises, Mess Stores, etc. will be returned to Q.M.
   Stores by 0800 hours.

7. ACKNOWLEDGE.

Issued at 0400 hours.　　Alexander Moffatt　　　Lieut. & A/Adjt.
　　　　　　　　　　　　　　　　　　　　　　　　　'B' HIGHLAND LIGHT INFANTRY.

Copy No.1. War Diary.
　　　　2. O.O. File.
　　　　3.　Do.
　　　　4. O.C. W Coy.
　　　　5. O.C. X "
　　　　6. O.C. Y "
　　　　7. O.C. Z "
　　　　8. Transport Officer.
　　　　9. Quartermaster.
　　　10. 2nd in Command.
　　　11. R.S.M.
　　　12. M.O. & Padre.

To Recipients of OPERATION (MOVE) ORDER. No.162, and
Battalion Routine Orders, dated 17.11.18.

OPERATION ORDERS. No.162.

Reference paras. 1, 2, and 4, all times should read one hour later than originally ordered.

Battalion Routine Orders.

Reference R.Os.Nos.2986 and 2988, all times should read one hour later than originally ordered.

17.11.18.

Capt. & A/Adjt.
'B' HIGHLAND LIGHT INFANTRY.

SECRET.   OPERATION (MOVE) ORDERS. No.162.   Copy No.
                 'B' HIGHLAND LIGHT INFANTRY.   17.11.18.

Reference Map. Sheet 29. 1/40,000.

1. Yje 106th Infantry Brigade will move by march route to the COURTRAI
   - STACEGHEM - HAARLEBEKE Area, commencing on the 18th November 1918
   staging night 18/19th November in the INGOYGHEM Area.
        Starting Point. Nukerke Church, R.15.d.
        Time.   12th Bn. H.L.I.   09.50 hours.
                     18th Bn. H.L.I.   10.05   "
                     17th Royal Scots. 10.20   "

2. The Battalion will parade on Bn. Parade Ground at 09.15 hours.
   Markers. 09.10 hours.
   Dress.   FIGHTING ORDER.

3. Route. Road Junction R.22.d.7.5. - NUKERKE CHURCH, R.15.d.4.1. -
          Cross Roads, R.21.a.6.8. - R.15.c.8.2. - R.14.b.3.6. -
          R.19.d.3.7. - BOOMGAANDRIES - BERCHEM - Eastern Pontoon
          Bridge - Q.7.b.8.6. - TIEGHEM - INGOYGHEM.

4. Transport. Transport will move in rear of the Battalion, and will
   parade at 09.15 hours on road running through R.23.a., facing west
   with head of Column at R.23.a.8.2.
   Distances.   500 yards between Battalions.
                 100 yards between Companies.
                 100 yards between Battalion and Transport.
                  50 yards between each section of 12 vehicles.

5. Advance Parites. Orders re Advance Parties will be issued later.

6. Reports on the line of march to Head of Column.

7. Location of Battalion Headquarters in INGOYGHEM will be notified
   later.

8. Orders for march from INGOYGHEM to COURTRAI area will be issued at
   INGOYGHEM.
   Locations of Companies will be notified to Battalion Headquarters
   as soon as possible after arrival in INGOYGHEM.

9. ACKNOWLEDGE.

   Issued at 16.00 hours.   Capt. & A/Adjt.
                                             'B' HIGHLAND LIGHT INFANTRY.

   Copy No.1. War Diary.
          2. O.O. File.
          3.   Do.
          4. O.C. W Coy.
          5. O.C. X "
          6. O.C. Y "
          7. O.C. Z "
          8. 2nd in Command.
          9. Transport Officer.
         10. Quartermaster.

SECRET.   To the Recipients of OPERATION (MOVE) ORDERS. No.163, dated 18.11.18 and Battalion Routine Orders, dated 18.11.18.

OPERATION (MOVE) ORDERS.

Ref. paras. 1, 2, and 3, Read times 1 hour EARLIER than originally stated.

Battalion Routine Orders.

Ref. paras. 2994, 2995. Read times 1 hour EARLIER than originally stated.

18.11.18.

[signature]

Capt. & A/Adjt.
'B' HIGHLAND LIGHT INFANTRY.

SECRET.   OPERATION (MOVE) ORDERS. No.163.   Copy No.
           'B' HIGHLAND LIGHT INFANTRY.   18.11.18.

Reference Map. Sheet 29. 1/40,000.

1. The 106th Infantry Brigade will continue the march to the COURTRAI Area tomorrow, 19th November 1918.
   Starting Point.   P.2.b.7.9.
   Time.   12th H.L.I.   09.25 hours.
                      18th H.L.I.   09.40   "
                      17th Royal Scots. 09.55 hours.

2. The Battalion will parade at 09.15 hours in Column of Route facing south-west on the road running from P.3.a.7.4. to P.3.b.2.8. with head of Column at P.3.a.7.4., in the following order:-
       Z, Y, X, W, Headquarters.
   Distances.   250 yards between half Battalions.
                150 yards between Battalion and Transport.
                50 yards between each section of 12 vehicles.
   Route.   P.3.a.7.4. - P.2.b.7.9. - VICHTE - Cross Roads,
                I.24.d.9.3. - Road Junction I.28½d.6.5. - I.25.central
                - STACEGHEM - COURTRAI.

3. Transport will parade on Main Road running through P.3.d. and a. with head of Column at INGOYGHEM Church, P.3.a.7.3.

4. <u>Advance Parties.</u> Orders re Advance Parties will be issued later.

5. Battalion Headquarters in COURTRAI will be notified later. Companies will render locations in COURTRAI to Bn. Headquarters as soon after arrival as possible.

6. ACKNOWLEDGE.

Issued at 18.30 hours   George Rees
                                         Capt. & A/Adjt.
                                         'B' HIGHLAND LIGHT INFANTRY.

Copy No.1. War Diary.
       2. O.O. File.
       3. Do.
       4. O.C. W Coy.
       5. O.C. X "
       6. O.C. Y "
       7. O.C. Z "
       8. 2nd in Command.
       9. Transport Officer.
      10. Quartermaster.

SECRET.   OPERATION (MOVE) ORDERS. No.164.   Copy No.
             'B' HIGHLAND LIGHT INFANTRY.   27.11.18.

Reference Map. Sheets 28 and 29. 1/40,000.

1. The 106th Infantry Brigade Group will move by march route to the ST. OMER – EPERLECQUES – WATTON Area, commencing tomorrow, 27th November 1918.
   The Brigade will stage in areas around the following places:-
   Stage 1. Night of the 27/28th November 1918.   MENIN.
   "   2.   "   "   28/29th   "   VLAMERTINGHE.
   "   3.   "   "   29/30th   "   STEENVOORDE.
   "   4.   "   "   30th Novr/1st Decr. 1918.   LEDEZEELE.
   "   5. Arriving at final destination, which will be notified later, on 1st December 1918.

2. STAGE 1.
   The Battalion will move by march route to MENIN tomorrow, 27th inst.
   Starting Point.   Cross-roads, a quarter mile north-east of the COURTRAI-INGELMUNSTER Railway (H.25.b.0.3.)
   Time.   10.00 hours.
   Route.   Main Road COURTRAI – BISSEGHEM – WEVELGHEM – MENIN.
   Distances.   100 yards between Companies.
                     100 "   "   Battalion and Transport.
                      50 "   "   every 12 vehicles.
   Dress.   Full marching-order, less blankets.

3. The Battalion will parade in Column of Route facing north-east in the following order :-
        Headquarters, X, Y, Z, W.
   along road running from H.25.d.4.5. to H.31.b.65.65. with head of Column at H.25.d.4.5. at 09.50 hours.
   Transport will parade in read of Column.

4. Advance Parties of 1 Officer, 1 N.C.O and 3 Other Ranks per Coy. and 1 N.C.O. and 2 Other Ranks from Hdqrs. will report to 2/Lt. Arneil at Cross-roads No.14.c.4.9. (MENIN) at 11.00 hours.

5. Battalion Hdqrs in MENIN will be notified later.

6. Companies will report locations to Bn. Hdqrs as soon after arrival in MENIN as possible.

7. Orders for Stages 2, 3, 4, and 5 will be issued later.

8. ACKNOWLEDGE.

                                                    Capt. & A/Adjt.
Issued at 20.00 hours.   'B' HIGHLAND LIGHT INFANTRY.

Copy No. 1. War Diary.
         2. O.O. File.
         3.   Do.
         4. O.C. W Coy.
         5. O.C. X "
         6. O.C. Y "
         7. O.C. Z "
         8. 2nd in Command.
         9. Transport Officer.
        10. Quartermaster.

SECRET.   OPERATION (MOVE) ORDERS. No.164.   Copy No.
              'B' HIGHLAND LIGHT INFANTRY.

Reference Maps. TOURNAI 5 and HAZEBROUCK 5a. 1/100,000

   STAGE 2.

1. The 106th Infantry Brigade will continue its march to the ST. OMER - EPERLECQUES - WATTON Area tomorrow, 28th November 1918, and stage night 28/29th November 1918 at VLAMERTINGHE.
   Starting Point.   Junction of MENIN - YPRES Road.
   Times.   18th H.L.I.   08.25 hours.
                         17th R. Scots.   08.40 hours.
   Route.   Main MENIN - YPRES Road - VLAMERTINGHE.

2. The Battalion will parade in Column of route, facing north, in Rue de LILLE, with head of Column at Southern entrance to Square, (3. B. 45,55.) in the following order :-
         Z,   W,   Hdqrs,   Y,   X.
   at 08.10 hours.

3. **Transport.** Transport, less Cookers, will parade in rear of Column. Cookers of W and Z Coys. will parade in rear of right half Battalion. Cookers of X and Y Coys. will parade in rear of left half Battalion.
   Distances. 250 yards between right and left half Battalions.
                   100 yards between Battalion and Transport.

4. The Battalion will halt for dinner at 11.30 hours, and will resume march at 13.00 hours.
   Transport Officer will ensure that horses are watered and fed. (Waterpoint at GHELUVELT.)

5. Advance Parties, as per Clause 4 of Operation (Move) Order, dated 27.11.18, will hold themselves in readiness to proceed in advance to VLAMERTINGHE at an early hour tomorrow. Orders will be issued later.

6. Battalion Hdqrs at VLAMERTINGHE will be notified later.

7. Companies will report locations to Bn. Hdqrs. as soon after arrival in VLAMERTINGHE as possible.

8. Orders for Stages 3, 4, and 5 will be issued later.

9. ACKNOWLEDGE.

Issued at 16.00 hours.
                                              Capt. & A/Adjt.
                                         'B' HIGHLAND LIGHT INFANTRY.

Copy No. 1. War Diary.
         2. O.O. File.
         3.   Do.
         4. O.C. W Coy.
         5. O.C. X "
         6. O.C. Y "
         7. O.C. Z "
         8. 2nd in Command.
         9. Transport Officer.
        10. Quartermaster.

SECRET.   OPERATION (MOVE) ORDERS. No.164.   Copy No.
                      'B' HIGHLAND LIGHT INFANTRY.   28.11.18.

Reference Map. HAZEBROOKE 5a. 1/100,000.

STAGE 2.

1. The 106th Infantry Brigade will continue its march to the ST. OMER-
   EPERLECQUES-WATTON Area tomorrow, 29th November 1918, and stage night
   29/30th November 1918 in the STEENVOORDE area.
   Route. Main VLAMERTINGHE-POPERINGHE Road to POPERINGHE, thence
   POPERINGHE-ABEELE-STEENVOORDE Road to STEENVOORDE.

2. The Battalion will parade in column of route in the under-noted order,
   facing west, on the main VLAMERTINGHE-POPERINGHE Road, with head of
   Column ar road junction 2. J. 7.0. at 08.15 hours.
          Y,   X,   Hdqrs.   W,   Z.

3. Transport, less Cookers will parade in rear of Column.
   Cookers of X and Y Coys. will parade in rear of right half Battalion.
   Cookers of W and Z Coys. will parade in rear of left half Battalion.
   Distances. 250 yards between right and left half Battalions.
               100 yards between Battalion and Transport.

4. The Battalion will halt for dinner at 12.35 hours and will resume
   march at 13.35 hours.

5. Advance Parties as per Operation (Move) Orders No.164, dated 27.11.18
   will report to 2/Lt. Arneil in the Square, STEENVOORDE at 11.00 hours.
   Guides from these parties will be sent back to meet Battalion on main
   ABEELE-STEENVOORDE Road, one mile east of STEENVOORDE. Battalion should
   reach this point about 14.00 hours.

6. Battalion Hdqrs. in the STEENVOORDE Area will be notified later.

7. Companies will report locations to Bn. Hdqrs. as soon after arrival
   in the STEENVOORDE as possible.

8. Orders for Stages 4 and 5 will be issued later.

9. ACKNOWLEDGE.

Issued at 20.40 hours.   Capt. & A/Adjt.
                                          'B' HIGHLAND LIGHT INFANTRY.

Copy No. 1. War Diary.
         2. O.O. File.
         3.   Do.
         4. O.C. W Coy.
         5. O.C. X "
         6. O.C. YY "
         7. O.C. Z "
         8. 2nd in Command.
         9. Transport Officer.
        10. Quartermaster.

SECRET.   OPERATION (MOVE) ORDERS. No.164.   Copy No.
                       'B' HIGHLAND LIGHT INFANTRY.   29.11.18.

Reference Map. Sheet 27. 1/40,000.

STAGE 4.

1. The Battalion will continue its march to the ST. OMER- EPERLECQUES- WATTON Area tomorrow, 30th November 1918, and will stage the night 30th Novr./1st Decr.1918 in CROMESTRAATE.
   Route.   STEENVOORDE - CASSEL - LEDERZEELE - CROMESTRAATE.

2. The Battalion will parade in Column of Route in the under-noted order on the main ABEELE - STEENVOORDE Road, facing west, with head of Column at road junction K.32.d.4.0.
          Hdqrs.,   X,   W,   Z,   Y.

3. Transport as per Stages 2 and 3.

4. The Battalion will halt for dinner at 14.45 hours, and will resume march at 15.30 hours.

5. Advance Parties, as per Stages 2 and 3 will report to 2/Lt. Arneil at CROMESTRAATE by 11.30 hours.
   Guides from these parties will be sent back to meet Battalion at LEDERZEELE Cross Roads G.28.b.0.3.
   Battalion should reach this point about 15.30 hours.

6. Battalion Hdqrs. in the CROMESTRAATE Area will be notified later.

7. Companies will report locations to Bn. Hdqrs. as soon after arrival in the CROMESTRAATE Area as possible.

8. Orders for Stage 5 will be issued later.

9. ACKNOWLEDGE.

Issued at 22.00 hours.
                                                    Capt. & A/Adjt.
                                                'B' HIGHLAND LIGHT INFANTRY.

Copy No.1. War Diary.
       2. O.O. File.
       3.   Do.
       4. O.C. W Coy.
       5. O.C. X "
       6. O.C. Y "
       7. O.C. Z "
       8. 2nd in Command.
       9. Transport Officer.
      10. Quartermaster.

WAR DIARY

INTELLIGENCE SUMMARY.

From 1st. to 31st. December, 1918. 18th. (G.V.) Bn. Highland Light Infantry.

Index No. 34.

Army Form C. 2118.

(Erase heading not required.)

Instructions regarding War Diaries and Intelligence Summaries are contained in F. S. Regs., Part II and the Staff Manual respectively. Title pages will be prepared in manuscript.

Place	Date	Hour	Summary of Events and Information	Remarks and references to Appendices
SERQUES.	1.12.18.		Battalion in billets. Training and cleaning up. Weather very dull.	
	2.12.18.		" " " Do. Do. Do.	
	3.12.18.		" " " Billets re-allotted. Weather dull & wet.	
	4.12.18.		" " " Training & recreation. Weather very dull & wet.	
	5.12.18.		" " " Battalion cleaning & preparing for move to new area to-morrow. Weather wet.	
MILLAM.	6.12.18.		Battalion on the move to MILLAM Area. Weather dull & wet. Operation Orders attached. No.165.	
	7.12.18. to 14.12.18.		Battalion in camp. Training, recreation, and Educational classes. Weather during this period, very changeable, generally wet & dull.	
	15.12.18.		" " " Brigade Ceremonial parade & presentation of ribbons.	
	16.12.18. & 17.12.18.		" " " Training, recreation and Educational classes carried on. Weather still wet.	
	18.12.18.- 21.12.18.		Battalion engaged in filling in trenches in area around MILLAM, and collecting wiring material	
	22.12.18.		Battalion in camp. Church parades, & recreation in afternoon. Weather bright.	
	23 & 24.12.18.)		" " " Filling in trenches in area around MILLAM.	
	25.12.18.		Battalion in camp. Church parades in forenoon. Battalion Xmas Dinner.	
	26.12.18.		" " " Battalion on route march in forenoon, with recreation in afternoon.	
	27.12.18.		" " " Trench filling and collecting of wiring material. Weather very wet.	
	28.12.18.		" " " Inspection of camp & billets by C.O. Training, & Educational classes.	
	29.12.18.		" " " Church parades. Weather dull.	
	30.12.18.		" " " Training and education in huts. Weather very wet.	
	31.12.18.		" " " Trench filling by two companies. one coy. on Musketry. one on Coy. training. Educational classes. Weather very dull.	
	1.1.19.			

W.G.Stewart
2/Lieut.
Bn. Intelligence Officer.
for Lieut.-Colonel,
Commanding, 18th. Bn. Highland Light Infantry.

SECRET.   OPERATION (MOVE) ORDERS. No.165.   Copy No.
                  'B' HIGHLAND LIGHT INFANTRY.   5.12.18.

Reference Map. ST. OMER. 1/40,000.

1. The Battalion will move by march route tomorrow 6.12.18, to billets in MILLAM.

   Starting Point.   Crossing of Road and Railway (L.32.d.7.5.)

   Time.   13.05. hours.

   Order of March.   Hdqrs. X, Z, Y, W, Transport.

   Route.   L.32.d.7.5. - Main Road along Western bank of Canal to WATTON - WATTON DAM - LES. CLITRES - MILLAM.

   Distances.   100 yards between Companies.
                     100 yards between Battalion and Transport.
                      50 yards between each section of 12 vehicles.

   Dress.   Full marching order, less blanket.

2. Coy. Blankets, Officers' Valises, Mess Stores etc. Officers' Valises, Mess Stores, and Balnkets rolled in bundles of 10, securely tied and labelled, will be stacked outside Coy. Hdqrs. Billets by 10.00 hours tomorrow.
   One motor lorry will convey Stores and Baggage of W and Y Coys. and will report to W Coy. at 10.00 hours.
   One motor lorry will convey Stores and Baggage of Z and X Coys. and will report to Z Coy. at 10.00 hours.
   Guides have been arranged for these lorries; Companies will arrange their own loading parties.

3. TRANSPORT. 2 Limbers for Bn. Hdqrs' blankets, etc., 1 limber for Hdqrs' Officers' Valises, Mess Cart for Hdqrs' Mess, 1 limber for Orderly Room and Canteen, and 6 limbers for Q.M. Stores will report to their respective places by 11.00 hours tomorrow. These willbe loaded by 12.00 hours, and will report to Transport Officer at collecting Station to be selected by him.

4. Companies will arrange early dinners at times most suitable to them. Teas will be on arrival in billets in MILLAM.

5. Advance Parties. Advance Parties of 1 Officer, 1 N.C.O. and 4 O.R? per Coy. and 2/Lt. W.G.Stewart and 2 O.R. for Hdqrs., 1 N.C.O. from Transport and 1 O.R. from Q.M. Stores will report to 2/Lt. Arneil at MILLAM CHURCH (F.29.c.2.1.) at 11.00 hours tomorrow.
   Guides from these parties will be sent back to meet Battalion at LES CLITRES Cross-roads (L.4.a.8.8.) Battalion should reach this point by 14.30 hours.

6. Battalion Hdqrs. in MILLAM will be notified later.

7. Companies will report location as soon after arrival in MILLAM as possible.

8. ACKNOWLEDGE.

   Issued at 23.59 hours.   Capt. & Adjt.
                                                   'B' HIGHLAND LIGHT INFANTRY.

   Copy No.1. War Diary.   Copy No.6. O.C. Y Coy.
           2. O.O. File.   7. O.C. Z "
           3.   Do.   8. 2nd in Command.
           4. O.C. W Coy.   9. Transport Officer.
           5. O.C. X "   10. Quartermaster.

WAR DIARY

INTELLIGENCE SUMMARY From 1st., to 31st., January, 1919 Army Form C. 2118.
13th. Bn., Highland Light Infantry.
Index No. 55.

(Erase heading not required.)

Place	Date	Hour	Summary of Events and Information	Remarks and references to Appendices
MILLAM.	1.1.19.	Battalion in camp.	Divine services. Recreation in afternoon. Weather very cold, but dry.	
Do.	2.1.19.	"	Bn. engaged on filling in MILLAM-MERCKEGHEM Trench system. Also bathing.	
	3.1.19.	"	Do. Do. Do. Do. Do.	
	4.1.19.	"	Divine services. Weather changeable. Some snow.	
	5.1.19.	"	Companies on general training and educational classes. Also recreation.	
	6.1.19.	"	Do. Do. Do. Do. Do.	
	7.1.19.	"	Do. Do. Do. and bathing.	
	8.1.19.	"	Battalion inspected by Corps Commander. Recreation in afternoon.	
	9.1.19.	"	General training & educational work carried out. Weather dry & cold.	
	10.1.19.	"	Do. Do. Do. Do. Do.	
	11.1.19.	"	Do. Do. Do. Do. Do.	
	12.1.19.	Divine Services.	Lieut-Col. V.E. Gooderson, D.S.O., & 3 men awarded BELGIAN Croix de Guerre.	
	13.1.19.	Battalion in Camp.	General training, educational & musketry, carried out. Weather changeable.	
	14.1.19.	"	Do. Do. Do. Do. Weather very cold.	
	15.1.19.	"	Do. Do. & bathing Do. Do. Do.	
	16.1.19.	"	Do. Do. Do. Do. Do.	
	17.1.19.	"	Do. Do. Do. Do. wet.	
	18.1.19.	"	Battalion route marche. Educational classes carried on. Weather dry & cold.	
	19.1.19.	"	Divine Services. Recreation in afternoon. Weather very cold.	
	20.1.19.	"	General company training carried on. Lectures during educational hours(11 - 12hrs)	
	21.1.19.	"	Do. Do. Do. Do.	
	22.1.19.	"	Battalion engaged on filling in trenches in MILLAM-MERCKEGHEM System.	
	23.1.19.	"	Brigade Route March. Do Educational work. Weather very sharp.	
	24.1.19.	"	General company training & education. Bathing parades during the day.	
	25.1.19.	"	Battalion inspection by Commanding Officer. Weather very cold.	
26 - 28.1.19.		"	Divine Services. Recreation in afternoon. Several football matches, etc.	
CALAIS.	29.1.19.	Battalion on move.	General company training, education, lectures, recreation etc.	
			Owing to unrest at CALAIS, Battalion was ordered there as garrison. The	
	30.1.19.	Battalion under canvas.	disturbance was soon quelled, & offenders dealt with. Battalion under canvas.	
			Very cold. A good of snow has fallen during the last two days. No further	
			trouble was experienced here, but town picquets were supplied and kept	
			town cleared.	
	31.1.19.	"	Battalion still on garrison. preparations were made for returning to MILLAM	

37. ℈
Vol 34

WAR DIARY
or
INTELLIGENCE SUMMARY.

From 1st., to 28th February 1919. Army Form C. 2118.
18th Batt. Highland Light Infantry.
Index No. 37.

(Erase heading not required.)

Instructions regarding War Diaries and Intelligence Summaries are contained in F.S. Regs., Part II. and the Staff Manual respectively. Title pages will be prepared in manuscript.

Place	Date	Hour	Summary of Events and Information	Remarks and references to Appendices
CALAIS.	1.2.19.		As part of division, quartered in CALAIS, on duty during disturbance in town.	
No.6 L.Camp.	2.2.19.		Entrained CALAIS (Doune Station) 0930. ---- Arrived WATTEN, Station 1515. --- Camp MILLAM 1630.	
MILLAM.	3.2.19.		Educational and recreational training carried out during process of demobilization.	
Do.	5.2.19. 6.2.19.		Draft of 65 other ranks arrived from Base and were posted to companies.	
Do.	7.2.19.		Party of 5 officers and 141 other ranks proceeded to ST.OMER on detachment for duty as train guard on supply trains between ST. OMER, HAZEBROUCK and POPERINGHE.	
Do.	8 – 28.2.19.		Modified training carried out during process of demobilization, and re-engagement for Army of Occupation.	
	28.2.19.		Demobilized to date.----- 12 officers and 401 other ranks.	

W.G. Stewart
2/Lieut. Intelligence Officer,
18th Batt. Highland Light Infantry.

www.ingramcontent.com/pod-product-compliance
Lightning Source LLC
Chambersburg PA
CBHW081434300426
44108CB00016BA/2367